THE RELIGIOUS IMAGINATION
AND THE SENSE OF GOD

THE RELIGIOUS IMAGINATION AND THE SENSE OF GOD

BY

JOHN BOWKER

PROFESSOR IN THE
DEPARTMENT OF RELIGIOUS STUDIES
UNIVERSITY OF LANCASTER

CLARENDON PRESS · OXFORD
1978

Oxford University Press, Walton Street, Oxford OX2 6DP

OXFORD LONDON GLASGOW NEW YORK
TORONTO MELBOURNE WELLINGTON CAPE TOWN
IBADAN NAIROBI DAR ES SALAAM LUSAKA ADDIS ABABA
KUALA LUMPUR SINGAPORE JAKARTA HONG KONG TOKYO
DELHI BOMBAY CALCUTTA MADRAS KARACHI

British Library Cataloguing in Publication Data

Bowker, John
The religious imagination and the sense of God.
1. God
I. Title
291.2'11   BL205   77-30459
ISBN 0-19-826646-4

Printed in Great Britain by
Butler & Tanner Ltd, Frome and London

FOR MARGARET
Multum in amore fides,
multum constantia prodest

PREFACE

'HUGE volumes, like the Oxe roasted whole at Bartholomew Fair, may proclaim plenty of labour and invention, but afford less of what is delicate, savoury and well concocted, than smaller pieces.'[1] So Francis Osborn advised his son, in the seventeenth century. Three centuries later I have made an attempt to respect his implied criticism, though the length of this book may not suggest it. However, an adequate treatment of the theme proposed for the Wilde Lectures[2] would actually require a great deal more than has been attempted in this and the previous volume (*The Sense of God*).

In that book (which was based on the first year of the lectures) I tried to report some of the characteristic features in the behavioural study of religion and of theistic belief at the present time, and in particular of the accounts given in such study of the ways in which a sense of God originates in human consciousness. That exploration suggested two further areas of inquiry in the remaining lectures: first, I wished to see whether the account which theistic traditions give of the way in which a sense of God originates and develops in human consciousness correlates with the behavioural account, or not; and second, I wished to take much further the very tentative remarks made in *The Sense of God* about the possible importance of the study of information process and systems analysis in understanding religious belief and its transmission in religious communities. Where those areas of research are concerned, it is becoming increasingly obvious that they are of the very greatest importance indeed. A *limited* application has been made in this book in, for example, the examination of Israel's transformation of the religious symbols and characterizations of God in her environment, and (as another example) in an attempt to restate the insights of traditional Christology; but a detailed exploration was not possible, in view of the already designated subject of the lectures.

Nevertheless, it is obvious that the account of religious continuity and change offered in this book can be applied with profit

[1] Osborn, p. 6.
[2] For the intention of Wilde in founding the Wilde Lectures, see Bowker, *The Sense of God*, p. 8.

to almost any of the problems which the existence and coexistence of religions pose. It has, for example, highly important implications for the ways in which religious belief-systems are translated into political expression. Events in Northern Ireland, in the Middle East and in the Indian sub-continent are obvious examples of the intransigence of religious systems in political expression. To grasp the constitutive importance of information process in the continuity of religious traditions is to understand why they are so often intransigent in their defence of what is fundamentally resourceful (since if they become casual in that respect the system will predictably collapse, as is pointed out in the opening chapter, pp. 21 f.).

But at the same time, a decisively important insight opens up from this analysis into the way in which the intransigence can be dissolved *without* a dissolution of the system in question: the point of focus must be to discern and specify within the systems at issue the means which all systems actually contain (though they may not actually practise) of tolerating the coexistence of alternatives to themselves. Despite the violence of cries for holy wars and inquisitions, all systems also contain the conceptualization of coexistence in some form. Whether one can then release the expression of the *rapprochement* which is legitimate—legitimate that is *within the resources* of the systems in question—is another matter. But certainly the underlying and prior political initiative must be based on an analysis of the terms of boundary-acceptance which lie within the resources of the systems at issue with each other—the terms, so to speak, which the systems in question can identify within their own authoritative resources, which in turn allow and legitimize coexistence or even 'peace with honour'. Peace, sadly, does not automatically follow, since many other rivalries (no doubt principally economic) are involved. But such a procedure is a highly important precondition of reconciliation and may be a powerful reinforcement of it. It hardly needs to be said that such analysis rarely if ever takes place, principally because far too few politicians have read Religious Studies at a university, and therefore literally do not know what they are talking about when they try to solve issues involving rival religious systems.

The account offered here also has extensive implications for tackling the problem of rival truth-claims between religions, since one can bring into the same frame of analysis the different information systems in question, and on the basis of an analysis of resource and appropriation in each case one can indicate exactly what is at issue; and in a preliminary way, some of the discussion in this book attempts to exemplify that procedure. It leads to the culturally and religiously intriguing prospect that provided one is clear-headed (and uncompromising) about the resourcefulness of a particular life-way, it may be possible to live with a deliberately multiple resourcefulness which does not betray the conditions of continuity and appropriateness in the systems in question, and which does not lapse into a casual syncreticism. But although that is a conceptually obvious possibility, exemplification of it in detail would require another set of lectures as long as the Wildes; and the Wildes were intended to explore, not those topics, but the sense of God as it occurs in theistic traditions.

But how to proceed? The obvious course to follow, in books or lectures about religion, is to make a survey of a large number of different religions. But that procedure necessarily makes detailed discussion impossible. For that reason, I decided to concentrate on four religious traditions only, in order to pick up the question raised at the end of *The Sense of God*. At the end of that volume, I drew attention to the curious paradox that those who work in the so-called behavioural sciences usually adopt an attitude of methodological atheism (i.e., in order to arrive at natural explanations of religious belief and behaviour, they excise, so far as possible, specifically *religious* determinants of religious behaviour—meaning by that, they excise the possible contribution to human life of what are supposed to be other-than-natural realities, such as gods or devils, without commenting on whether such putative realities exist or not); nevertheless, the fact remains that repeatedly within those disciplines, the possibility of a differentiating effect being derived in some lives from reality external to those lives, characterized theistically, seems to be demanded by their own evidence.

But that conclusion, although it was very far removed from what I had expected when I set out to write the lectures, nevertheless remained vague unless it could be tied to evidence arising within theistic traditions themselves that the human sense of God does occur in consciousness as the behavioural sciences seem to be suggesting that it sometimes does. If so, then theologians have every right (on the basis of evidence arising both within their own traditions and within the behavioural sciences) to insist that externality is a necessary characteristic of claimed theistic reality. It may even be reasonable to conclude that it is no longer so impossible or absurd as it has seemed in recent years to infer that a reality exists, external to ourselves, which creates differentiating effects in the construction of human lives, and which is (or has been, up to the present) characterized theistically.

But how does that vague inference connect with the realities and practice of theistic belief? It is obvious that characterizations of putative theistic reality are neither stable nor simple: they have changed dramatically through the course of time, and they have frequently been multiple and diverse—gods many and lords many, of whom the majority, as Mencken observed (the quotation opens the Introduction), are evidently dead. A main purpose of this book is to ask why, since so many characterizations of theistic reality have gone to extinction, do some, not simply survive, but undergo considerable recharacterization, when they have come under the strain of implausibility. One feature seems to be recurrent and of importance, the extent to which those who transact major transformations in existing characterizations of God are themselves dislodged by a sense of theistic reality external to themselves insisting on its own nature and presence, often in contrast to the existing ideas about God which they have held up to that time. The initial sense of God for most people is almost invariably a consequence of the culture and the circumstances in which they are born. What, then, moves some people beyond their point of departure into new discoveries and new landmarks in their exploration of relationship with God?

To explore these themes, I have chosen four traditions in which dramatic transformations occurred, Judaism, Christianity, Islam, and Buddhism. In the opening chapter, I have tried to pick up some of the threads from *The Sense of God*, and in particular I have tried to summarize why the study of information process and systems behaviour yields highly important insight into the way in which religious traditions perpetuate themselves through time, and (at the individual level) into the way in which human beings become religiously, and theistically, informed. I have then turned to the four traditions mentioned above and I have tried to give as detailed a consideration as space allows of the evidence about some formative moments in the sense of God in those traditions.

Space, needless to say, does not allow enough. Nevertheless, in

one respect I have become, like Toad, a reformed character. Some
critics complained about the extremely lengthy footnotes in *The
Sense of God*. In fact, I would defend them by saying that an
attempt was made in that book to allow the practitioners of the
various disciplines involved to speak for themselves, so that consequently substantial quotations were indispensable. However, in
this volume, I have gone back to the primary evidence and I have
eliminated the secondary discussion so far as that was feasible.
In this, I am encouraged by the engaging note of de Saint-Pierre,
attached to his 'Preamble to the Arcadia':

The Ancients, who wrote much better than we do, never subjoined
Notes to their text; but they stepped aside from it, to the right and to
the left, according as occasion required. In this manner wrote the most
celebrated Philosophers and Historians of Antiquity, such as *Herodotus*,
Plato, Zenophon [*sic*], *Tacitus*, the good *Plutarch*. Their digressions, if
I may be permitted to judge, diffuse a very pleasing variety over their
Works. They shew you a great deal of the country in a little time; and
conduct you by the lakes, over the mountains, through the forests; but
never fail to lead you to the mark, and that is no easy matter. This mode
of travelling however does not suit the Authors, nor the Readers, of our
times, who are disposed to find their way only through the plains. To
save others, and especially myself, some part of the intricacies of the
road, I have composed Notes, and separated them from the Text. This
arrangement presents a farther accommodation to the Reader; he will
be spared the trouble of perusing the Notes if he grows tired of the
Text.[3]

I owe a great debt of thanks to those who have commented on,
and criticized, both the original lectures and these. In particular,
I would like to thank Peter and Brigitte Berger, Ralph Burhoe,
John Carmody, David Edwards, Freda Jackson, Patrick Master-
son, Hugo Meynell, Betty Scharf, and John Sturdy (who corrected
mistakes in the transcription of Andrew Lang's letter).[4] I have
tried to profit from their suggestions and criticisms. To Mrs. Irene
Stewart and Mrs. Geraldine Towers I owe not only gratitude but
admiration: they typed what I would have thought was an impossible manuscript, and remained cheerful throughout. I would like
to thank again the electors to the Wilde Lectureship, who gave me

---

[3] de Saint-Pierre, pp. 3 f.
[4] *The Sense of God*, p. 188: for Martez read Master; for Reeves, sleeves; for
officer, officio. We are both defeated by the word left as a blank in the
transcription.

the opportunity to undertake this work. Finally, to Margaret, my wife, a particular thank you: in the midst of writing new courses of lectures after our move to Lancaster, she encouraged me to persist with this book. Without her, it would not have been written.

CONTENTS

INTRODUCTION:
THE DEATH AND THE LIFE OF
GOD

IT is now a little over fifty years since H. L. Mencken held his memorial service for the gods, who, as he put it, have 'gone down the chute':

What has become of Sutekh, once the high god of the whole Nile Valley? What has become of

Reseph	Isis
Anath	Ptah
Ashtoreth	Anubis
Baal	Addu
Astarte	Shalem
Hadad	Dagon
El	Sharrab
Nergal	Yau
Nebo	Amon-Re
Ninib	Osiris
Melek	Sebek
Ahijah	Molech?

All these were once gods of the highest eminence. Many of them are mentioned with fear and treambling in the Old Testament. They ranked, five or six thousand years ago, with Jahveh himself; the worst of them stood far higher than Thor. Yet they have all gone down the chute, and with them the following:

Bile	Iuno Lucina
Ler	Saturn
Arianrod	Furrina
Morrigu	Vediovis
Govannon	Consus
Pwyll	Cronos
Ogyrvan	Enki
Dea Dia	Engurra

Gwydion	Belus
Manawyddan	Dimmer
Nuada Argetlam	Mu-ul-lil
Tagd	Ubargisi
Goibniu	Ubilulu
Odin	Gasan-lil
Llaw Gyffes	U-dimmer-an-kia
Lleu	Enurestu
Ogma	U-sab-sib
Mider	U-Mersi
Rigantona	Tammuz
Marzin	Venus
Mars	Bau
Ceros	Mulu-hursang
Vaticanus	Anu
Edulia	Beitis
Adeona	Nusku[1]

This list continues for another page. Then Mencken asks:

Where is the grave-yard of dead gods? What lingering mourner waters their mounds? . . . Men laboured for generations to build vast temples to them—temples with stones as large as hay-wagons. The business of interpreting their whims occupied thousands of priests, wizards, arch-deacons, evangelists, haruspices, bishops, archbishops. To doubt them was to die, usually at the stake. Armies took to the field to defend them against infidels: villages were burned, women and children were butchered, cattle were driven off . . . They were gods of the highest standing and dignity—gods of civilized peoples—worshipped and be-lieved in by millions. All were theoretically omnipotent, omniscient and immortal. And all are dead.

In point of fact, Mencken's question, 'Where are the graves of the gods?' had already been answered. It had been answered by Nietzsche's lunatic—

that madman who in the early morning brightness, lit a lantern, ran to the market square and cried out without ceasing, 'I seek God! I seek God!' A number of those who have no faith were standing around, so great laughter erupted. 'Is he lost, then?' said one, 'Has he lost his way, like a child?' said another, 'Or has he gone into hiding? Is he afraid of us? Has he gone on a journey? Taken up residence elsewhere?' So they shouted and laughed. *Der tolle Mensch* sprang into their midst, and cut through them with the look he gave them. 'Where has God gone to?' he cried, 'I will tell you: we have killed him—you and I' . . . It is said also that *der tolle Mensch* on the same day went into a number of churches and sang there his *Requiem aeternam deo*. His reply, when he was brought out to account for himself, is said to have been, 'What are these churches, if they are not the tombs and graves of God?'[2]

Nietzsche proclaimed that the death of God was 'a recent event' (*neuere Ereignis*). Those are the exact words with which he opened the Fifth Book of *Die fröhliche Wissenschaft*, which was added to the second edition in 1887, so that the word 'recent' is relative to that date. So what he clearly meant by God was the Christian God; and the continuation of the passage makes precisely that point: it is faith in the Christian God which has become untenable. It is that creed, to use his own words, which has become incredible (*unglaubwürdig*). But the Christian sense of God is not the only sense of God available to the human condition: and this means that Mencken's Protestant memorial service and Nietzsche's Catholic requiem are lamentations, not for the death of God, but for the death of those particular characterizations of the sense of God.

In the strictest construction of the words, it is not the ability to believe which has ceased, nor has the sense of God always died along with the death of its particular characterizations. Sometimes, certainly, it does, but not always. Frequently, in these crises of plausibility, some other renewed characterization of God is reconstructed beyond the ruins of a particular disintegration; and one of the purposes of this book is to explore, through a number of examples, how and why this happens.

Since the time of Nietzsche and Mencken, the celebrations of theistic mortality have become increasingly familiar; so too have the corresponding attempts to detach truths, wisdoms, values, mental states, and visions from the institutional forms of religious expression, and to arrive at religionless religions—at, for example, religionless Christianity, or at transcendent forms of meditation. The protest against the dead (or perhaps even the corrupting) hand of institutional religion was very graphically expressed a few years ago by Geddes MacGregor:

That the spiritually lame and myopic are attracted to the Body of Christ is no more remarkable than that tubercular people are attracted to sanitaria . . . The world has no right to belittle the Church for the presence in her of ignorance, neurosis, or even vice. The world's complaint would be justified, however, if it could be shown that, over a fairly extensive period of time, ignorance or neurosis or vice triumphed in the Church, in the sense that they were actively encouraged by the very structure of the church or by forces within her that seemed to be inextricably tied to her institutional nature . . . Few people are now so simplicist in their objections to the Church as to be troubled by turpitude rising to the top in the person of an occasional bad bishop or moderator or Salvation Army general. The objection now is that in the Church one can almost depend upon the triumph of ignorance, neurosis and vice. It is the exceptions that are noteworthy . . . Worst of all, the Church, not content with persecuting her scholars, belittling the voices of sanity and humanity in her ranks, and crucifying her saints, is increasingly showing herself willing to use, perhaps as never before in her history, the learning of her scholars, the sanity and humanity of her counsellors, and the spiritual vitality of her saints, to advance her ugliest and most perverse ends. If Christian values are to be upheld at all, then such antics must be accounted prostitution in its worst possible form. Church historians will remember that this charge is, moreover, precisely what the 16th century Reformers levelled at the late medieval Latin Church they called Scarlet Woman, Devil's Harlot, Satan's Whore. The language is 16th century in its robustness. The phenomenon is 20th century, at least equally and perhaps even *par excellence*.[3]

It is beside the point to debate whether that protest is well founded or not. It is quoted simply as an example of a feeling which has been widespread in recent years, that the institutions and structures of organized religion are a barrier and a hindrance to belief and vision. There must be, to quote a phrase, a 'stripping of the altars' if a new freedom of spirit is to be set loose in the world.

But the forms which the protest have taken in recent years have often been confused and naïve, because they have failed to take sufficiently seriously the fact that truths, wisdoms, values, and the rest do not pervade the universe like the disembodied spirits or the immaterial essences of Lewis Carroll's *Sylvie and Bruno Concluded*:[4] they are mediated to us through the social process which supplies the cues and signals of information and which alone can feed our imagination and enable us to be human.

The point is obvious when you ask yourself, how did you become you? An answer would obviously make reference to the basic genetic inheritance which creates the fundamental parameters or boundaries of possibility. On this planet (*pace* Dr. Who) we do not have blue eyes one day and brown the next. But then, as Michael

Astor put it in trying to answer his own self-posed question, 'Who am I?', 'I am not primarily concerned with my family tree.'[5] How has each one of us become a unique individual, possessed of our own thoughts and memories, and with our own picture and understanding of the universe in which we live? We have done so by becoming *informed subjects*. And we have done *that* by becoming staging-posts in the transformation of energy. We have become part of the restless, unimaginably vast and complicated flow of energy which constitutes this planet and the universe—taking in energy and setting it forth in a whole range of physical and verbal utterance. By no means all of this expression of energy is externally audible and visible. Much of it is internal, occurring within the boundary of the body. Included within this sea-change of energy is the flow of information—of signals, not necessarily in verbal form at all—which our peculiar constitution of atoms and molecules is able to scan, identify, interpret, store, and retrieve. It is also able (and this is essential for our peace of mind) to select, extinguish, or ignore particular signals. The process of information —the cues of information which arrive at our receptor centres or sites, and the signals which run within the boundary of a body—is a very specialized part of the general flow of energy in the universe, but that is what it is: a part of the energy flow of the universe.

It is important to stress at the outset that information process does not necessarily occur in verbal forms, and to that extent, the word 'information' is probably misleading, because it does seem to suggest verbal communication. But in the technical sense it refers simply to the cues and signals of information which occur in the body, or which arrive at our receptor sites, and which can be assimilated (or not) into our on-going behaviour. It follows that information flow may be entirely non-verbal:

> The floating clouds their state shall lend
> To her; for her the willow bend;
> Nor shall she fail to see
> Even in the motions of the storm
> Grace that shall mould the maiden's form
> By silent sympathy.
>
> The stars of midnight shall be dear
> To her; And she shall lean her ear
> In many a secret place

>   Where rivulets dance their wayward round,
>   And beauty born of murmuring sound
>   Shall pass into her face.[6]

That familiar poem by Wordsworth has a title which is very appropriate: 'Three Years She Grew'. For that *is* how we grow, how I become I and you you, on the the genetic base which initiates us. We receive, not only from the universe at large, but from family, from school, from media, from people we encounter, cues of information which our brains are selectively able to store and retrieve until we build up our own identities and our own means of identifying new occurrences, as well as our general situation in space and time.

It hardly needs to be said that very little is known about the way in which the brain is able to do this. At present, detailed understanding of the brain is very elementary. On the other hand, it has become much clearer in recent years what theoretically must be taking place in terms of information process, even though the mechanism has not been penetrated in detail. Such a statement does not in the least deny or qualify the richness of mental and personal life which occurs. In fact, it reinforces it, because it emphasizes the rewards which have accrued to human beings as a consequence of the human capacity to verbalize information. Although information flow *may* be non-verbal, the fact that it can be verbalized leads not only to an almost limitless personal imagination, but also to a shareable understanding of life and the universe:

>   The mind can make
>   Substance, and people planets of its own
>   With beings brighter than have been, and give
>   A breath to forms, which can outlive all flesh.[7]

That is by Byron, though it might equally have been by Keats or Shelley; and the title is again appropriate, 'The Dream'. It is the capacity to verbalize information which creates the all-precious idiosyncrasy of human form. It creates, indeed, the *idiotes*, the private, the individual, the unique. It was no mean discovery of the Greeks to see that man is supremely man by virtue of the fact that he is capable of being (to extend the word into its English sense) idiotic.

It is the capacity to verbalize information which enables the con-

text figures of infancy, who teach us to talk, to be the Prospero to
the Caliban which we must otherwise be:

> I pitied thee,
> Took pains to make thee speak, taught thee each hour
> One thing or other: when thou didst not, savage,
> Know thine own meaning, but wouldst gabble like
> A thing most brutish, I endowed thy purposes
> With words that made them known.[8]

Again, it is the capacity to verbalize information which paradoxically
enables us to rebel against the very process through which (and
through which alone) we became human—we became, that is, informed consciousness. Bound, like Prometheus, to the social process of information, we yet transcend, or feel that we can transcend,
the in principle explicable conditions of our circumstance, as in the
famous passage which stands at the head of chapter xvi in George
Eliot's *Daniel Deronda*:

Men, like planets, have both a visible and an invisible history. The
astronomer threads the darkness with strict deduction, accounting so for
every visible arc in the wanderer's orbit; and the narrator of human
actions, if he did his work with the same completeness, would have to
thread the hidden pathways of feeling and thought which lead up to
every moment of action, and to those moments of intense suffering
which take the quality of action—like the cry of Prometheus, whose
chained anguish seems a greater energy than the sea and sky he invokes
and the deity he defies.[9]

The deity he defies: it is the repeated paradox of human autonomy that its consummate expression occurs when it turns on the
very *nomos*—on the very law and custom—which first and fundamentally made its own occurrence possible. Without that paradox,
there could be very little development and very little novelty in
any field of human enterprise. One might even say that the saving
grace of humanity is boredom. Yet even so we have to recognize
that perhaps the greatest consequence of our capacity to verbalize
information is that we can share it with each other, and that we
can share it systematically, particularly when networks of information are devised or simply come into being. A school or university
is a particularly simple example of systematically public information. We are able—systematically—to identify and make available

to others what are designated as worthwhile cues of information: we are able, for example, to design a curriculum of physics, or of English, or of mathematics, and we try to monitor the ways in which we transmit the cues of worthwhile information. For this reason, the designated cues of worthwhile information do not remain static: the curriculum changes as the designated cues come under the strain of truth or plausibility or relevance, or when the modes of transmission from teacher to pupil are changed. But the general consequence of the systematic transmission of what are designated as worthwhile cues of information in, for example, music, or chemistry, or history, is that the recipient becomes, or has the chance to become, a musically informed subject, or a chemically informed subject, or a historically informed subject. This does *not* mean that the subject 'knows everything about music' or simply files 'bits of information'. That is not the educational or the informational point, which is equally concerned with the creation and sharing of value and experience. In *that* sense, Matthew Arnold's final words as an Elementary Schools' Inspector are correct, that 'of education information is the least part'.[10] Nor does it mean that to make worthwhile cues available automatically leads to an informed subject—any teacher knows that the process is not automatic. Signals of information are all too easily extinguished.

But the general point is clear. Information flow in the human community is not random, nor is it virginal. It is socialized, and it is frequently systematic: mechanisms of transmission, and information networks of varying degrees of formality, are developed which enable the process of information from one individual to another, or from one group to another, or from one generation to another. Schools are an obvious example. But so also are the complexities of behaviour, institution, and belief which are referred to as 'religions'. Religions exhibit exactly the same characteristics of information process. They are systematic ways in which what are claimed to be worthwhile cues of information are transmitted and made available in community, and they result (or they aim to result) in religiously informed subjects: they result in individuals whose brain-behaviour is informed with particular cues of information and pictures of reality which are retrieved for the construction of life.

The question of what makes a religious system of information process specifically 'religious' is an important one which will be taken up below. At the moment, the point being made is the slightly simpler one, that religions exhibit the characteristic features of bounded systems of information process, in which human beings are offered fundamental resources for the construction of their lives. From the point of view of the external observer, religions can be analysed within the general theory and analysis of systems behaviour. In the case of any particular religion, there can be identified in its institutions, its ritual, its texts, its worship, its personnel, and its career structures, a means of continuity and a consensus in fundamental items of information which are transmitted from life to life. Once again, it must be emphasized that transmission does not necessarily occur in verbal forms alone. Often, in the religious case, it is least of all in these. Consider the Bishop, in Chekov's story of that name: his emotions are evoked in the opening pages through a whole succession of informational inputs which do not occur in discernible words at all, although the background murmur of prayer is one of them. In some forms of Zen Buddhism much emphasis is given to 'transmission outside the scriptures', in the silent relation between teacher and disciple; but it is not denied that transmission is taking place.

Looked at from this point of view, it is clear that religions are open systems (which does not mean, incidentally, 'open-ended'; it simply refers to a system which interacts with its environment); at the same time, they are bounded systems. Religious boundaries are certainly permeable, in the sense that few religious systems have succeeded in excluding information flow from outside the religious environment, even though some have tried. But short of that, regions often exemplify concern about the control and definition of those boundaries, not least in their relation with each other, where the words 'assimilation' and 'syncretism' summarize two different attitudes to information flow across the boundaries;[11] similarly, religious systems are often concerned with orthodoxy and dissent, dogma and heresy, allegiance and schism.

So where individual lives are concerned, there may be much that is informationally resourceful in the construction of those lives in addition to inputs from a religious context of information. But so far as the religious system is concerned, the information flow is primarily from its own designated resources, which thus establish constraints over the possible outcomes in human and social behaviour. The individual can be analysed as a continuity of information processing—which is actually the title of a recent textbook of psychology: *Human Information Processing; An Introduction to Psychology*;[12] and the system can be analysed in terms of self-maintenance, entropy, sub-systems, purpose, feedback, prolepsis, conceptual space, actual space, and all the other characterizing features of systems behaviour.

Put these two together (the individual appropriating information through and within the environment of a particular system), and the result is that when human beings are born in these bounded contexts (or when, as some religious traditions would put it, they are converted and born again), there is made available to them the means with which to identify who and what they are, what they are for, where they are going, what sort of place the universe is, what sort of goals are worth aspiring to, what counts as appropriate behaviour. As a result, they are given the means through which to construct a route from birth to death—and in the case of most religious contexts, a way through death as well. They are given also the means to relate to externality which may in some of its aspects be characterized theistically, or in personified terms.

But what, then, makes them specifically *religious* contexts of information process? It is not possible to evade the question of content by insisting first on the process of information, since that may be theoretically indifferent to the content of what is being transmitted. In *The Sense of God* it was argued that there is no reason in principle which makes it necessary to suppose that there must have been some separable, definable reality, 'religion', *ab initio*: that from the moment, so to speak, when emerging man swung down from the trees into the savannah (or as Hockett and Ascher put it, were thrown out of the trees),[13] 'religion' must always have been a separable, definable 'thing'. On the contrary, the emergence of what later comes to be referred to as 'religion' is much better understood as part of human evolutionary development. Obviously, as language and the consequent beginnings of culture developed, the sophistication and the variety of the ways in which men sought (and still seek) to maintain and continue their life-way became very diverse—and it is not necessarily their *own* life-way; it may equally be that of a group, or of their family. However, as men scan the compounds of limitation which circumscribe a projected life-way (whether in detail or in general), they either find a way through, or they do not; and if they fail in the face of major limitations, they go to extinction.

It is in this context that the emergence of what later comes to be described as religion can be set. And although we cannot seriously hope to recover any certain knowledge about the origins of religion—not least, because, as J. Z. Young put it, 'rituals and dances like fears of devils or aspirations towards gods, leave few or no remains'[14]—and therefore, although we cannot finally falsify the current speculation that spacemen arrived in flying saucers and were misidentified in a way which led to religious beliefs about super-human realities, the emergence of religion is wholly intelligible in the same evolutionary context as that in which other human enterprises and achievements also emerged. There is no reason to suppose that what is now referred to as 'religious' was not in origin an undifferentiated part of this exploration of environment and of the limitations which circumscribe projected action.

A brief example of this was given in *The Sense of God* (p. 65) of the attempt to get a mammoth up a hillside into a cave: one can use prayer and sacrifice, one can use pulleys and levers; and the route of pulleys and levers leads eventually to Archimedes saying that if only he had somewhere to stand he could move the earth. But the mistake which Tylor and Frazer made (and many others after them) was to deduce from this a before-and-after relationship between religion and science, regarding magic as technology in its primitive form and religion as primitive science. That was an understanding of the relationship between them which inevitably relegated religion to the infancy and immaturity of the human race, and it involved the equal mistake of taking evolution in a naïvely chronological sense and not in its invariably necessary sense of the continuity and defence of life.

Those deductions, in the first enthusiasm of evolution, *were* mistaken, because what is obvious is that religion and technology, despite all that has been said in the last 250 years about the warfare between science and religion, have not come apart in any clear or easily correlated way. They may indeed be divided in *practice*; in the way, for example, that the main road to Agra divided the spiritual from the material in the Suddar Bazaar in the period before the First World War: 'It was possible on a Sunday evening to stand in the road outside the Church and hear, on one side, the parson with his monotonous clerical voice preaching about the spiritual joys of life, and on the other side the shrill and equally monotonous cries of the girls in the brothel advertising its material joys'.[15] Or as William Blake put it, 'Prayers plough not, praises reap not.'[16] But it is still the case, particularly in Italy and the north of England, that one can be driven in cars with a St. Christopher on the dashboard. The driver is undoubtedly committed to technology in maintaining the continuity of his life-way in a situation where the limitations circumscribing it are considerable—brick walls, errant buses, other drivers, volatile fuel not far from his feet. But he combines with it something which is derived from a religious context of interpretation.

This at once raises the question of superstition; but the general point to be made is that the religious and the scientific, prayer and technology, are still very frequently combined in the construction of human lives or in the construction of particular actions or words. And the reason why this is so is *not*, as Tylor supposed, because religious practices are a survival from the infancy of the human race (or, as it has been put more recently and looking at it from the other end, because Man has come of age but some individual men have not); that is to make the mistake of supposing that religion and science are *only* linked chronologically with religion preceding science and yielding reluctantly to it. Certainly it is possible to exemplify that relationship between them. But they are also linked by their both being means through which human beings scan their environment, interpret it, and seek to find a way through the limitations which circumscribe their projected life-way. Then the issues between them, if issues there are, become pragmatic—whether, to put it crudely, one is willing to allow that there *are* religious determinants of behaviour, and whether, therefore, one is willing to incorporate the resources available in a religious context of interpretation in the construction of one's own life-way. And that in turn depends eventually on plausibility. The world might be a more rational (and duller) place if one could say that it depended on truth: ultimately, questions of truth are very much at issue, as much in the religious as in the scientific area, and certainly nothing is gained by reassigning religious utterances to the category of poetry *if* that reassignment involves ignoring the fact that a very large number of religious utterances are propositional in appearance and are apparently, even though expressed poetically, about putative matters of fact—a point, incidentally, very well made by Webb when commenting on earlier forms of pragmatism at the Oxford Congress in 1908:

The association of pragmatism with a fruitful line of theological thought is not sufficient to enable it to give a satisfactory form to religious conviction. The reason why religious dogma naturally assumes a form of expression more like that appropriate to a scientific assertion than that which we use in our moral and aesthetic judgements still demands an answer. The strength of scholasticism . . . always lay and still lies in its stress upon the independent nature of the object of knowledge.[17]

But in fact the majority of us *live* on a less exalted level, where we depend on the plausibility and general attractiveness of what is offered, both internally in our brain behaviour, and externally from our environment, for the construction of our lives. Plausibility may be eroded by truth established in other ways, or it may be reinforced by truth, or be coincident with it. But it is certainly not synonymous with truth. And since the verification of many religious propositions is not simple (and some would argue, is often not possible here and now), the distinction between plausibility and truth becomes highly important in understanding the relation between faith and reason—between the present intention and the ultimate confirmation (supposing it occurs). Thus the direct intuition of God (which phenomenologically is widely attested) is not based on an immediate (unmediated) vision of God, but the grounds for it and the claimed experience of it are sufficiently persuasive (plausible) for many to devote their lives to its further realization.

The proposal, then, is that religions belong to the general human enterprise of evolutionary continuity and survival. They become sociologically recognizable as they develop the means of the informational transmission of the resources from which human lives can appropriately (appropriate in terms of the system itself) be constructed in relation to the compounds of limitation which threaten the continuity of that construction. But it still has to be asked, why *religious*? How and why do we arrive at those particular complexes of belief, behaviour, ritual, institution, worship, to which we want to give some such word as 'religious'?

To answer this, attention has to be paid to the kinds of limitation in relation to which religious systems of information process offer a resolution or way through, and to the kinds of resources which they offer. Where the latter are concerned, religious systems characteristically offer resources external to the individual which may help—or hinder—the construction of his life-way. These are resources which have been described traditionally as gods, devils, angels, spirits, *jinn*, *devas*, and the like. Putting the point a little more austerely, religions are characterized by a belief that there are resources other than the immediately observable which are—or can be—of effect in the construction of life, history, and the universe. Such practices as prayer and sacrifice are linked to these as being both resourceful in their own right and also a means of relation to those other resources.

Where limitation is concerned, although religions offer resources for a life-construction day by day, in quite undramatic circumstances—saints at the kitchen sink—they are also characterized by the fact that they offer ways through (or resolutions of) particularly intransigent limitations which circumscribe human life-ways. This was the point seized by Marx and Freud, but seized in too limited and too distorting a way, when they concentrated on death, compensation, and projection in their analyses of religion. Nevertheless, one can accept that those complexes of belief and behaviour which we feel the need to identify by some such word as 'religious' *have* come apart and become identifiable because they have remained attentive to even the most intransigent of the limitations which circumscribe our projected actions: the cessation of conscious life in this body is certainly one:

'Let the wild bee sing,
And the blue bird hum!
For the end of your lives has certainly come!'
    And Mrs. Discobbolos said
    Oh! W! X! Y! Z!
    We shall presently all be dead,
On this ancient runcible wall
    Terrible Mr. Discobbolos.'[18]

Perhaps Mrs. Discobbolos might evade that particular circumstance of death by getting off the runcible wall, but not *a* circumstance of death at some point. But there are many other examples of comparable intransigence: one is the gap established by constraints in the universe or in the immediate environment between what we can dream and desire, and what we can realize:

Here we are all by day; by night w'are hurled
By dreams, each one into a sev'rall world.

We can dream, like the contemporaries of Bacon, of what life on the moon might be like, but there are constraints in the universe which prevent the realization of the dream until the constraints are themselves sufficiently understood for appropriate action to be taken in relation to them. But dreaming, as Charles Fisher put it, 'permits each and every one of us to be quietly and safely insane every night of our lives'.[19] Religions have undoubtedly exploited that gap—some would say, they have exploited that lunacy.

Or again, to take another example, religions have been and remain attentive to the limitation implicit in the apparent irreversibility of time. No one knows what is going to happen in the future, and it is not difficult to find examples, of great variety, in religions of the means through which some kind of insight into the future can be gained. It may be of a limited nature: 'Shall I go up to attack Ramoth-gilead or not?'[20] Or it may be of a distant, even of an eschatological, future, so that apocalyptic becomes, as Austin Farrer once put it, a kind of Cook's Tour of heaven. Equally to the point, no one can recover the time which has gone by. It is not possible to undo what has been done: 'We have left undone those things which we ought to have done, and we have done those things which we ought not to have done, and there is no health in us';[21] and religions exemplify, again in prolific variety, the means through which people can be healed in relation to the irreversibility of time, through procedures of penitence, confession, expiation, forgiveness, absolution.

It is not difficult to think of other examples: they can be seen in the intransigence of moral evil, not least in one's own case—'The good that I would I do not, and the evil that I would not, that I do';[22] or in the indifference and independence of the environment—the fact, for example, that natural disasters cannot always be predicted or controlled. In origin there is no need to suppose that these intransigent limitations, implicit in death or imagination or the irreversibility of time, were differentiated from *other* limitations, which *eventually* proved to be more amenable to technology. This is simply another way of stating the same argument, that there is no reason why religion must have been a separable entity *ab initio*. What comes to be referred to as religion appears as a part and consequence of the general attempts of men to scan their environment, to discern the limitations which circumscribe a projected action (or the continuity of their life-way as such), and to engage whatever resources they accept (whether consciously or not) as appropriate to the penetration or understanding of any particular compound of limitation.

For this reason, reductionist critics were wrong to suppose that religions can be essentially characterized by their attention to only isolated limitations, like suffering, or death and the way through death. Religions offer resources for the *total* construction of a lifeway which may indeed be attentive to the limitation of death, but which is attentive to all other limitations as well. Furthermore, those resources have yielded inspiration, creativity, and culture of profound worth and value *in their own right*, and therefore yield their own justification in experience, where adherents are concerned. Nevertheless, it is possible that one reason why the religious has come apart from the scientific to the extent that it has, lies in the fact that religions have *remained* attentive to those intransigent limitations, and have projected ways through them which are sufficiently plausible to their adherents for them to continue to adhere—since otherwise presumably there would be no religions left. Plausibility may undoubtedly collapse and alienation may occur; but this has not happened universally yet. But if a scientist is attentive to the reality of ageing and dying he is very unlikely to be attentive to it in his professional work in a religious way.

This summarizes the distinction between the religious and the scientific contexts of information—or to put it another way, it summarizes an important reason why religion and science have come apart, so far as they have: it is because the route of the levers and pulleys has yielded its own rewards and has therefore established its own constraints for the achievement of appropriate (or some might say, successful) utterance: it is not possible to split the atom by sacrificing a goat. In addition, the route of levers and pulleys has, at various points, falsified particular religious propositions, and it has established distinct informational resources (though they are not yet *entirely* separate, since natural theology is not yet an extinct animal). So it is not the case that the relation between 'science' and 'religion' suddenly becomes easier as a result of this analysis. But what does become easier is to see that both belong to the same evolutionary exploration by men of their ecological niche, and that what they are trying to explicate is what counts as legitimately resourceful in the construction of human life-ways and as legitimate in the goals which are described as attainable.

Religions thus emerge as bounded systems of information process and transmission, built up through a long accumulation of tradition in which plausibility may very frequently have been threatened or even destroyed; but in which the general description of man in his environment and of the possibilities which are available to him and of what counts as appropriate action, if he is to live a life with an ultimately successful outcome, remains sufficiently plausible for individuals to continue to *incorporate* it—or in other words, to allow it to become informative in the construction of their lives. If not, then those gods and those religions go without further ceremony, as Mencken put it, straight down the chute.

Religions, therefore, as bounded systems of information process and transmission, establish constraints over the possible outcomes in human thought and behaviour. The word 'constraints' sounds very negative but it can in fact have an extremely positive consequence, in Ashby's cybernetic sense, that where a constraint exists advantage can usually be taken of it.[23] If a person knows where he is, where he has come from, and where he is going to (those bits of information acting, therefore, as constraints), he no longer has to waste time reading a map and trying to use a compass. If, of course, his information is factually incorrect, he may well find himself up some remote river without a paddle; and that remains the empirical challenge to religion; but it does not affect the observation of what is actually happening, in informational terms, in human brain behaviour.

On this basis, religions can be analysed in terms of systems behaviour in a completely straightforward manner, particularly in terms of the procedures and mechanisms they exhibit, through which input, storage, scan, retrieval, and output occur in the construction of religious life. It is in this way that religions are able to offer resources—usually fundamental and pervasive resources—for the human enterprise of life-construction; and in the religious case, although there may be much that is legitimately resourceful, there are frequently basic constitutive resources, such as scripture, the words of the Buddha, the utterance of an oracle, and so on. Even within a particular religious continuity there may be very great disagreement about what counts as resourceful in that sense: is it scripture alone, or scripture plus the Pope *ex cathedra*? Is it Quran and *hadith*, or Quran and *hadith* plus the inspired *imam*? Does God speak to us directly or must it be mediated through some institution or person? There is unending scope for variation. But what makes a Christian recognizable as somewhere within the Christian universe—as opposed, say, to the Muslim; or what makes a Muslim recognizable as somewhere within the Muslim universe (even though, as with the Woking mosque, other Muslims may regard him as heretical), is that in each case there is an intended relation of assent to whatever is fundamentally designated or accepted as resourceful—and as necessarily so, as a matter of obligation. This means that William Blake was perfectly correct to draw attention to discrepancy within the Christian universe of meaning:

> The vision of Christ that thou dost see
> Is my vision's greatest enemy.
> Both read the Bible day and night,
> But thou read'st black where I read white.[24]

But there is sufficient consensus in what is to count as resourceful for disagreement to take place—and indeed, for those in dispute to know what they are disagreeing about.

It follows that within a particular religious universe there may be divergent, even polemically inimical, appropriations of the resources; and it is certainly the case that individuals or groups may well draw on resources for life-construction from outside the boundaries which up to that point have constituted the discernible outline of that particular religion. The result may well take on the appearance of a new sect or a new religion. When, for example, the Manichaeans assimilated information from Christian resources, were they identifiably Christians or not?[25] They sang hymns to Jesus, and perhaps some of them regarded themselves as the only authentic Christians. Were they Christians or not? There are only two ways in which an answer can be obtained: one is to turn up on the Day of Judgement, supposing there is going to be one, and get an answer beyond which, presumably, there is no further appeal. The other is to go, not forwards but backwards, and test what is proposed or projected in the Manichaean case against what is, or has been up to that point, accepted as resourceful in the construction of appropriate Christian utterance. Such judgements are necessarily relative: they are relative to what *is* regarded as resourceful, and to the way in which those resources function exegetically at any moment in time. This means that even when religions *do* arrive at, for example, a canon of scripture—itself a significant word in this context, the Greek *kanon* meaning 'rod' or 'rule'—the way in which the canon is applied to the formation of judgement may change enormously. But the basic procedure remains uniform: testing the degree of match or mismatch between a projected utterance and what is at any particular point regarded as indispensably resourceful for the construction of appropriate utterance.

Religions, then, are contexts of information process, from which individuals acquire material for life-construction and from which they derive procedures and goals, all of which act as constraints over the otherwise near-infinite possibilities of outcome in any human life. It is important to emphasize that the process of information in any particular human life may not be consciously intellectual or deliberated to any great extent. Input, storage, retrieval, output may simply occur as a consequence of the particular religious context in which an individual happens to be born or to live. Although the colloquial sense of 'information' suggests an intellectual or perhaps verbal activity, the more basic sense employed here is concerned with the much wider range of experiences through which the human being becomes an informed subject and then expresses his life; in operation, much of this may be subconscious. It perhaps also needs to be added (since it is not uncommon for religions to have moments when they rely on theologies, not of hope, but of fear, and indeed of terrorization) that religions are by no means simply abstract or neutral contexts in which materials are made available. Personnel, rituals, institutions can occur within religions by means of which materials for life-construction are imposed on others. It is not for nothing that when Winwood Reade published in 1872 his famous universal history (the Secularist Bible, as it came to be known), which included, of course, 'the melancholy history of religion', he published it under the title *The Martyrdom of Man*:

The gospel or good tidings which the Christians announced was this. There was one God, the Creator of the World. He had long been angry with men because they were what he had made them. But he sent his only-begotten son into a corner of Syria, and because his son had been murdered his wrath had been partly appeased. He would not torture to eternity all the souls that he had made; he would spare at least one in every million that were born. Peace unto earth and goodwill unto men if they would act in a certain manner; if not, fire and brimstone and the noisome pit . . . Those who joined the army of the cross might entertain some hopes of being saved; those who followed the faith of their fathers would follow their fathers to hell-fire. This creed with the early Christians was not a matter of half-belief and metaphysical debate, as it is at the present day, when Catholics and Protestants discuss hell-fire with courtesy and comfort over filberts and port wine. To those credulous and imaginative minds God was a live king, hell a place in which real bodies were burnt with real flames, which was filled with the sickening stench of roasted flesh, which resounded with agonizing shrieks. They saw their fathers and mothers, their sisters and their dearest friends, hurrying onward to that fearful pit unconscious of danger, laughing and singing, lured on by the fiends whom they called the gods . . . The Christians of that period felt more and did more than those of the present day, not because they were better men but because they believed more; and they believed more because they knew less. Doubt is the offspring of knowledge: the savage never doubts at all.[26]

The style and the epigrams are typical of the Tylor/Frazer mode of argument, which at least makes them enduringly readable. Yet within the epigrams, Reade has obviously caught a highly important point about religion, not simply that religions (in this case Christianity, though the same would be true of Buddhism[27] or of most other religious systems) do so often rely on theologies of fear, but the reason why they do so. In terms of surface meaning, it is because the subject matter of religion might be ultimately important, in the sense that its anthropology (its account of human nature) is *teleological*, or perhaps better, teleonomic:[28] it has to do with man's final end and goal. Religions, in other words, project ways through even the limitation of death. Many of those projections have broken down; they have become implausible and have gone to extinction. Perhaps in the end they all will, as Reade supposed. The final sentences of his book make exactly that point: 'A season of mental anguish is at hand . . . The soul must be sacrificed; the hope in immortality must die. A sweet and charming illusion must be taken from the human race, as youth and beauty vanish never to return.'[29]

But while plausibility remains (not truth, which in this case could only be verified eschatologically); and while projected ways in particular religions remain plausible for some people, as they clearly do; then those religions confer ultimate dignity on anthropology. But religions cannot do *that*, or indeed do anything, without being what they are—without being what has just been summarized: social and systematic contexts of information in which particular resources for life-construction are made available and kept in being from one generation to another.

This at once explains why religions are inevitably conservative; it is incumbent on them to be so, depressing though it is when one sees the consequences in synodical government or in many of the pronouncements of the Vatican. The reason is both obvious and necessary: it is that religious universes are structurally derivative from precisely those resources which are in turn offered as materials for life-construction; they could not offer those resources unless they defended them and ensured their continuity into an undetermined future.

If that jargonistic phrase is unpacked and expressed in terms derived from one particular religious tradition, it can then be said that religions are defending whatever in the past has been established in their own estimate as 'necessary for salvation'. It is this which gives, not only the appearance, but the reality of conservative reaction in religious continuity. A religion is unlikely to have survived to any moment in time, x, unless up to that moment it has been plausibly and in fact life-enabling to some, probably to the majority, of its adherents; and if that is so, then it is surely irresponsible at $x + 1$ to disintegrate, or change radically, whatever has been life-enabling. It is irresponsible until, of course, crises of plausibility begin to become extensive, or until sufficient individuals in the information net in question develop, perhaps for entirely *positive* reasons (out of the inspiration of the system in question), new forms of life-giving, life-enabling, life-enhancing symbolism.

That last point should not be underestimated. It is all too easy to fall into the dismal trap of thinking only negatively about religious change, and of seeing it as a defensive manœuvre in crises of plausibility which are evidenced in declining numbers and reduced cultural importance. That caricature comes close to being a habit of mind in some modern commentators. In fact, much religious change occurs because of the value of a particular system which inspires new forms of expression. Nevertheless, the informational point remains, that once fundamental resources are designated within a religious system as offering a legitimate constraint over the outcomes of any human behaviour or utterance which is to count as appropriate (or which is to come to an ultimately successful outcome, such as salvation or nirvana), that system will develop mechanisms of transmission and control which will ensure continuity from life to life and from generation to generation. In theoretical terms, even this must not be evaluated negatively, even though in practice the consequence has all too often been oppression and intolerance, and even though the consequence (particularly in ritual) is often an obsessional concern for detail if attention to the boundary markers of successful or appropriate utterance becomes virtually an end in itself. Then the question frequently arises in religious systems whether attentive behaviour of that sort is itself appropriate, or whether 'the letter killeth, but the Spirit giveth life'(2 Cor. 3:6), a familiar tension in religious history, and an inevitable one, once religions are understood as systems of information process and transmission. But these are not the only implications, and Ashby's point can yet again be emphasized, that where a constraint exists, advantage can usually be taken of it. Thus even in the most conservative and authoritarian system, individuals can be set free to explore experience within the boundaries. The way in which religious systems have supplied and reinforced the building of diverse cultures is an example of the confidence which is derived from the acceptance of boundaries and resources.

The resources on which religions draw can attain a high degree of formality; indeed, in some instances, they come very close to establishing isomorphic maps of behaviour. This can be seen, for example, in the development of the Pali Canon, in which the utterances of the Buddha were related with increasing formality to the life-construction of the *bhikkhus,* or again in the emergence of Judaism, where Torah became increasingly formalized as the resource from which one can distinguish appropriate from inappropriate utterance; it can be seen equally in a monastic rule, or in Quran and *hadith*, or in the Vedas and priestly ritual. Perhaps the word 'isomorphic' is too strong, because no religious resources map every detail of behaviour to such an extent that correspondent actions at a later time are nothing but a formal reproduction, though some devotional exercises come close to proposing this. On a more modest level, the present Archbishop of Canterbury exemplified the point, when on 22 January 1975 he encouraged those who were listening to him on 'Thought for the Day' to recover 'the authentic form of Christianity, that is to say, loyalty to the New Testament'. But a literal reproduction would be impossible. And in fact, to go back to one of the examples just given, it was because Torah could *not* function isomorphically in any exact sense that there was set up among Jews a pressure towards exegesis, until eventually the traditional interpretations of rabbinic Judaism acquired a status comparable to that of Torah—but they became Torah *shebeal peh*, Torah transmitted by word of mouth. So undoubtedly isomorphic is too strong a word; but it is a useful word, because it draws attention to the informational significance of what is happening. For what is certainly the case is that when individuals, who are attempting to construct a life-way within a particular religious universe, seek to inform their behaviour from those resources in the past, it is possible for them to be using those resources as an isomorphic map of what their behaviour should be, imprecise though that map actually is.

> He has shown you, O man, what is required of you
>> to act justly,
>> to love mercy,
>> and to walk humbly with your God.[30]

Torah maximizes information about what counts as justice, what counts as mercy, what counts as walking *en akribeia* (precisely, exactly), as the Greek Ecclesiasticus translates the phrase, with God.

This then is an outline of a general theory of religion, which sets religion in the context of human evolutionary development and history, and which takes as fundamental the importance in individual lives and in societies of the processing of information and its transmission. There are undoubtedly immense dangers in using information-language in attempting to analyse, or understand better, human behaviour. This is partly because some of the jargon has come to be used so loosely that it has almost become meaningless—information theory is a notorious example. Information theory as such is of virtually no applicability whatsoever; and it would be a great help if the phrase were never used except in its technical reference within the theory of semantic information, where mathematically it is a somewhat sophisticated aspect of the theory of inductive probability. In any case, the actual transmission of information, fundamental though it may be in the nervous system, leaves us a very long way from understanding complex animal behaviour.

But information process, in the cybernetic sense of establishing a control system, is very different indeed. The limitations here are of a different sort: they are not so much theoretical, in the sense that the theory itself has a limited scope, as practical. Therefore, it is common to find statements of what is in principle possible in the cybernetic simulation of behaviour, but is in practice not yet feasible. An example would be the relation of computers to biology, as in this passage:

There are, of course, technical difficulties. We do not as yet know sufficient of colloidal chemistry to construct systems of the same colloidal materials of which humans are built; but though we cannot at present construct the analog of human behaviour in hardware, these purely technical difficulties are irrelevant to matters *in principle*.[31]

So to talk of systems of information process is to talk necessarily in crude, premature language. Yet I would still insist that no matter how crude our understanding is at present, no matter how little we may ever be able, for the sake of argument, to understand the detailed mechanism of brain behaviour, this *is* the correct and central question to ask: how *does* the human organism become an informed subject? To recognize this as the central question at once brings into alignment, not into competition, the poetic as much as the behavioural endeavour to understand how and what we are. For the first time almost since the eclipse of Latin we have a common language of concepts. No matter who we are, priest or poet, psychiatrist, social welfare worker, or behavioural engineer, all can equally contribute to this single central question: how does the human organism, moving from conception to birth to maturity, become an informed subject? And it is salutary to bear in mind that we who reflect on that question became what we are through that very process. In this context, it is then possible to ask the more particular questions, how does the human organism become a religiously informed subject, and how does it become a theistically informed subject? How *does* a sense of God originate in human consciousness?

If what has been argued so far as a general theory of religion is correct, then it is not difficult to derive from it a special theory of theistic belief. It would probably be fairly easy to establish a correlation between the 'ways through' a particular limitation projected in a religious universe and the conceptual supports required for the plausibility of that projection. If a way through death is projected as a literal reconstruction of the bones of the dead, it may be that one will require for the reinforcement of plausibility a figure on the other side of the grave who is capable of that work of reconstruction. However, this brings us face to face with the issue which Freud (constrained, or indeed paralysed, by his own experience) failed, and probably refused, to face. Let it be granted, for the purpose of the argument, that projective and compensatory views of theistic belief are entirely correct, and that theistic belief is constructed initially from within the needs of the psyche—the need to deny the oblivion of death, the need to have a father or a mother figure, the need to secure one's own status by finding and imposing a justification for the alienation of labour. Let it be granted, in other words, that our reasons or motives for theistic belief are always, in Freud's sense, abject. How can we be sure that the projection does not in fact identify, or coincide with, something which is as a matter of fact both real and correct? And how can we be sure that there is never any response from the object (supposing there is one) of belief (no matter how 'projectively' constructed from the human end) which might challenge our abject motives and characterization and move us, so to speak, from those points of departure?

Freud made exactly that move in the case of sex: we are drawn, he argued, to another person through appetite and libido; but in relation to the other, because of the nature of the other in response, it is possible to experience feelings which transcend our point of departure and which we label appropriately as love. How can we be so sure that this cannot happen in worship and prayer; that in relation to the other, because of the nature of the other in response, we can experience feelings which we label appropriately as theistically derived, as god-relatedness?[32] Because, comes the obvious reply, even if it were possible to specify what counts as 'a response of the other' in the theistic case, is one saying anything more than that characterizations of 'the other' theistically conceived—God, Zeus, Theos, Allah, Vishnu—are culturally transmitted and inherited? We are not entailed in any ontological commitment.

That argument is certainly correct, so far as it goes: characterizations of God *are* culturally transmitted and acquired. But putting the argument the other way round, that observation cannot *of itself* eliminate the possibility that the characterizations, however approximate they may be as descriptions, are characterizations of an existent but unseen reality. From that point of view, the people who are of particular interest are those who have inherited cultural characterizations of God, but for whom the worth of those characterizations of God has broken down, not because of a scepticism or a doubt, but because of their sense of 'that which has inadequately been characterized as God' insisting on its own nature and presence in their experience. Up to this very point, the theoretical account which has been offered is entirely and unequivocally anthropocentric: it accepts that religion is generated from within the mental processes of the human organism: the theory can dispense with the possibility of God's independent reality.

But now the question has to be faced whether that account is adequate to the evidence, or at least testimony, of human beings, that the externality which they characterize theistically contributes to the construction of their beliefs and behaviour. It is important to note that, even if the testimony is correct in its description of that experience, the process of religious continuity will remain the same, unless one wants to locate God in the gaps of the process. *However* theistic reality becomes apparent to human consciousness (supposing it does), it will not presumably dispense with the process of that consciousness. But equally, the analysis of the process cannot of itself eliminate the possibility that God is an informational resource, however mediated, and that he can consequently be genuinely resourceful in the construction of life.

The issue here can be seen very clearly in the way in which Ernest Jones (with his enthusiasm for Freud and the psychoanalytic revolution) excised God from Christianity:

As to the beliefs of Christianity, psycho-analytic investigation of the unconscious mental life reveals that they correspond closely with the phantasies of infantile life, mainly unconscious ones, concerning the sexual life of one's parents and the conflicts this gives rise to. The Christian story, an elaborate attempt to deal on a cosmic plane with these universal conflicts, can be fully accounted for on human grounds alone without the necessity of invoking supernatural intervention.[33]

But Jones then went on: 'Whether, nevertheless, such intervention took place as well must remain a matter of opinion, but the story itself is no proof of it.' But that is far too naïve. 'Supernatural intervention,' if one wants to call it that (i.e. inputs into consciousness from a resource external to the subject), does not have to be in addition to experienced consciousness, but apprehended through it. Neither Freud nor Jones were so solipsistic that they rejected *all* external reality in the analysis of the psyche. Consequently, if there *is* an informational resource external to ourselves which human beings have characterized theistically (i.e., as God) then that externality, in order to be informatively resourceful in the construction of human life, would have no need to dispense with whatever is psycho-analytically true in any particular case, because that would be to dispense with consciousness. No one, in order to be a theist, needs to deny the process of information flow: what he needs to know is the ground or the resource of what is flowing informatively through the process. The issue *then* becomes whether Jones's (or anybody else's) absolute reduction is descriptively correct, or whether the inference of input from externality is necessary and correct, in order to account for the evidence.

The development of this theory, therefore, does not in any way eliminate or make unnecessary ontological question and comment. Indeed, when one surveys the constantly recurring death of gods and yet surveys also the continuity of the sense of God beyond the ruin of particular characterizations, such comment seems to be demanded, at least in the phenomenological sense of asking what would have to be the case for such appearances in consciousness to occur as do occur, particularly in the widely reported human experience of responsive transcendence—or to put it more descriptively, of a resource external to themselves contributing significant input to the construction of thought and life. The issue then becomes whether human beings have correctly or incorrectly identified a resource of informational input external to themselves, and whether they have appropriately or inappropriately characterized it theistically.

A point that needs to be emphasized is that many of those who have engaged seriously with the possibility of theistic reality external to themselves have found that that externality has apparently engaged with them—and engaged in such a powerfully self-authenticating way that their initial ideas and concepts about 'god' have been broken down. The ideas and concepts which have been culturally transmitted and inherited may well serve many people as they stand; or they may, to others, seem so implausible or defective that they no longer function as informationally resourceful at all. In between are a more disturbed and disturbing group, for whom the ways in which traditional concepts have hitherto been expressed break down, but who work through the experience to a new characterization of theistic reality, and to a new realization of the way in which externality, theistically characterized, continues to be a resource and a goal in the construction of human life.

That category of people is probably a large one. It is impossible to quantify it, but it is probable that a large number of those who continue to construct their lives intentionally within the boundary of a particular theistic system have worked through, or lived through, some such crisis. But the issues raised can be much better focused by concentrating on particular examples. So the purpose of this book is to look at four religious systems, in which senses of God have come into such severe crises that they have led to a completely new characterization of the possibility and nature of God. In three cases, the possibility of God has seemed to be renewed and enhanced; in one, it was reduced, though not altogether eliminated. The four examples are Judaism, Christianity, Islam, and Buddhism. In each of these traditions we can find figures (and in the case of three of them formative figures) who were reduced to silence in the crisis of plausibility which occurred in their existing sense of God. The four are Job, accepting silence before the apparent majesty of God, Jesus, choosing silence before his accusers, Muhammad in silence on Mount Hira (a silence later recapitulated by alGhazali when he stood in front of his university class and found himself completely unable to speak), and Gautama, the Buddha, electing silence after his Enlightment.

Four quadrant points of silence, in each of which a transaction occurred in the prevailing characterizations of God: what can we learn from them about the ways in which human consciousness forms its senses of God, and at the same time is formed by them? And to what extent will this help us to comment on the contemporary dilemma of explanation in the area of religious behaviour—the dilemma exemplified in all the behavioural sciences in *The Sense of God*: methodological atheism in the behavioural sciences insists that there cannot be religious determinants of religious behaviour, if by religious determinants are meant unseen entities such as gods, spirits, etc. But phenomenological evidence (i.e., the accounts which people give of their experience) suggests that there may be determinants of religious behaviour which are not yet identified within the scope and description of a natural scientific approach. The rejection of the possibility that there may be religious determinants of religious behaviour tends to issue in reductionism (explaining religious phenomena in terms of something else), and the acceptance of that possibility (even though the claimed ground and nature of the determinants may have been described naïvely, or inadequately, or mistakenly) tends to issue in theology—and it is essential to note that theology is not, and never has been, uncritical of its own subject matter. Methodological atheism holds that it is not possible to move so simply from the private to the public, and that phenomenological evidence is not evidence but testimony. But a phenomenological anthropology holds that it is premature to delimit the possible determinants of religious behaviour: there may yet be, for example, a Copernican revolution in our understanding of information flow in the universe, which may do better justice to such edgy phenomena as telepathy and ESP.

But is it the case that the present state of the evidence or testimony makes it possible that we may yet have to extend the identification of causation in religious behaviour to include not the invariable but the possible contribution of the claimed resources of input? This does not confer automatic truth on all such claims, nor is it an insistence on an either/or: either sociological, psychological, etc., determinants, *or* religious determinants. It is a suggestion that we may need both/and, a suggestion at least that it is premature to eliminate the latter, although majority opinion at the present time would unhesitatingly do so, and would probably claim that the behavioural sciences can only proceed coherently if that is done. But majorities are not always right, even in scientific matters: the majority for more than a thousand years (from Galen to Harvey) thought that there were two blood systems, the venous and the arterial, and that blood flowed from one to the other through invisible pores in the septum of the heart, and through 'anastomoses', minute openings between the veins and arteries which allowed exchange;[34] the majority, for roughly the same period, maintained a geostatic understanding of the universe. The majority views produced explanations of phenomena of great sophistication and persuasion, but in the end they were inadequate to contain the development of further observation and evidence. We are only at the very beginning of the study of religious belief and behaviour.

It became a serious subject of study little more than a century ago. The question is, at the very least, whether the study of religion does not require (as Ninian Smart has put it) methodological agnosticism while sitting down, a little more patiently, before the evidence—a posture in which contemporary theoreticians of religion are not always to be found. But if that is so, it would be as well to turn to more detailed evidence ourselves before commenting further on this issue.

I

JUDAISM

1. SHEMA ISRAEL

THE year 135 of the Christian era: the year in which Judaism ceased to exist—or should have ceased to exist, by any human reckoning. It was the year in which the final and most disastrous of the Jewish revolts against Rome was defeated. Three years earlier, great hopes had been focused on the quasi-Messianic figure of Simon bar Cochba. They were hopes that the theocratic kingdom of the future might actually be inaugurated here and now, 'in the midst of time, under the eye and by the strength of God'.[1] But those hopes were now eclipsed. From this point on, whatever future the Jews might have as a people, defending in the construction of their lives their belief that God had given them long ago in Torah the conditions of renewal and success, they were now compelled to become reconciled to the fact that the future would not immediately contain a land, a *polis*, a *civis Judaicus*, of their own. In other words, they would no longer have an obvious geographical context of their own in which to express their allegiance to God and to his word.

At the end of the bar Cochba revolt, the Romans did not simply burn the Temple. Hadrian implemented his plan to eradicate the Jewish Jerusalem and to build on its site a pagan city, Aelia Capitolina. The Temple site was ploughed, a temple to Jupiter was built in its place, and Jews were forbidden to enter the new city. Aqiba, the great father in wisdom, the guide to the Jewish community, was executed. He died reciting the Shema, a kind of basic affirmation of Jewishness: *Shema Israel, adonai eloheynu adonai ehad*; Hear, O Israel, the Lord our God, the Lord is one. He died with the Shema on his lips. But he died nevertheless.

Beyond Aelia Capitolina, the study of Torah (the first five

books of Scripture) was forbidden for the Jews, and observances such as circumcision were also forbidden. But what could not be eradicated were the mind and the faith which continued to form the words, 'And to Jerusalem, your city, return in mercy . . . and build it soon in our days as a building which will endure.'[2] Those words come from the Shemoneh Esreh, one of the oldest formal prayers of the Jews (outside the Psalms) which has survived. It continues to be prayed to the present day, though in detail it has of course changed during the two thousand years of its existence. But the defeat of bar Cochba created a new agony within the prayer. From the Roman point of view, this revolt had occurred a mere sixty years after another major insurrection of the Jews— one that had taken more than five years to subdue; consequently it seemed to them essential to make sure that nothing similar occurred in the future. They were in search of a final solution. As a result, the Jews had to find a means of continuing their identity, through obedience to the word of God (which they believed had been spoken to them in Torah) in pagan or gentile contexts.

They had some precedent to guide them. Jews had been living outside Jerusalem and Palestine, in the so-called Diaspora, or Dispersion, for centuries, and there were strong Jewish communities in Rome, Mesopotamia, and Alexandria. But the Jews in the Diaspora had always had a home base, Jerusalem, even if they had never lived there. Furthermore, the concept of Jerusalem as the centre of the world and the focus of God's promise and redemption was by no means vague. Jewish identity was tied to Jerusalem though the *sheqalim* (the tribute money paid to the Temple, when not appropriated by the Romans), through pilgrimage festivals, through prayer (for some Jews) corresponding to the Temple services, and even for Jews who were not particularly observant of those practices through the plain bond of affection. But without Jerusalem, the diaspora faced a more difficult problem of identity. Jewish communities could certainly continue in Palestine, but the failure of the Bar Cochba revolt, only sixty years after the massive defeat of the earlier revolt in the year 70, wrote the words 'not yet'—or alternatively, the words, 'How long, O Lord, how long?'—into the construction of Jewish self-consciousness.

As a result, much that can be observed now in Israel, just as much that could have been observed in the growth of Zionism at the end of the nineteenth century, is a living commentary on the dilemma of how and where it is possible to be fully and authentically Jewish. How and where is it possible to live within the boundary and under the authority of Torah? What does it mean, what does it involve to be Jewish? For many Jews at the time when Jesus was alive, to be Jewish did require a land, or at least an enclave, not just for its own sake, but as an area within which the details of Torah could be lived out without compromise. The reason goes back to a fundamental command in Torah: 'You shall be holy to me, as I, Yahweh, am holy' (Lev. 20:26). A case might be made for regarding this, not simply as *a* fundamental command, but as *the* most fundamental. Thus Leo Jung, summarizing the essentials of Judaism, claimed: 'The key to Judaism is *Kedushah* (holiness)'.[3] And Sifra, an early rabbinic commentary, states of the section of Leviticus beginning with the same command (Lev. 19:2 ff., 'Be holy, for I, Yahweh your God, am holy'): 'Why was this section of Torah to be said before all the congregation? Because most of the important commands of Torah are to be found in it.' The command to the Jewish people is that they should be as far removed from everything which corrupts or contaminates as is God himself. Leviticus, therefore, immediately continues, in 20:26: 'I have separated you from other people that you should be mine alone.' Consequently, the earliest rabbinic commentaries on the verse, including Sifra, extend the verse so that it reads: 'You shall be holy and separated, even as I am holy and separated.'

Because of the emphasis on separation, it has often been claimed that the essential meaning of holiness is separation. But from the Jewish point of view, the essential meaning of holiness is closeness, albeit closeness *involving* separation. It is closeness to God, which cannot be attained without separation from everything which might compromise or destroy that union. The basic point was made by Schechter, when commenting on the rabbinic conception of holiness:

Diverging as the ideals of holiness may be in their application to practical life, they all originate in Israel's consciousness of its intimate relation to God, which is . . . the central idea of Rabbinic theology. In fact, in its broad features, holiness is but another word for *Imitatio Dei*, a duty dependent upon Israel's close contact with God. 'You shall be holy, for

I the Lord am holy' (Lev. xix. 2). These words are explained by the ancient Rabbinic sage, Abba Saul, to mean, 'Israel is the *familia* (suite or body-guard) of the King (God), whence it is incumbent on them to imitate the King' (Sifra 86c). The same thought is expressed in different words by another Rabbi, who thus paraphrases the verse from Leviticus . . . 'You shall be holy, and why? because I am holy, for I have attached you to me, as it is said, "For as the girdle cleaves to the loins of a man, so I have caused to cleave to me the whole house of Israel" (Jer. xiii. 11)' (Tanhuma Qedoshim 5). Another Rabbi remarked, 'God said to Israel, Even before I created the world you were sanctified to me; be therefore holy as I am holy'; and he proceeds to say, 'The matter is to be compared to a king who sanctified (by wedlock) a woman to himself, and said to her: Since you are my wife, what is my glory is your glory, be therefore holy even as I am holy' (Tanhuma, *ibid.* 2). In other words, Israel having the same relation to God as the *familia* to the king, or as the wife to the husband, or as the children to the father (see Lev. R. xxiv. 4), it follows that they should take him as their model, imitating him in holiness.[4]

Without separation there cannot be closeness to God. Israel is called to a practical transcendence of the mundane while still experiencing an unequivocally terrestrial life. Holiness implies closeness, nearness, but it involves separation, and that is the paradox of Israel. Without separation, the basic command that Israel should offer itself in holiness as a dedicated offering to God cannot be fulfilled.

But does that kind of separation require *geographical* separation? It is obvious that not *all* uncleanness, as Torah defines it, can be avoided, no matter where a person happens to live. But for the minor details of life there are provisions of cleansing and separation within Torah itself. What surely would have to be avoided would be the gross occurrences of uncleanness which would inevitably occur in a pagan, uncaring, idolatrous environment. How could they be avoided? Or how, conversely, could the Jews observe their own dietary and other laws? Only, responded some Jews, by setting up geographical boundaries within which perfect observance of Torah could be made.

In this way the pressure for a land developed. It did not have to be the whole of the promised land, though obviously the very fact of the promise designated that area as ultimately the most appropriate. But various sects at the time when Jesus was alive isolated much smaller geographical areas within which a perfect condition of holiness might be attained—or at least aspired to. Some went into the desert, others went to the shores of the Dead Sea. It did not even have to be within the promised land at all. At about the time (*c.* 160 B.C.E.) of the Maccabean revolt, for example, an extreme conservative group had actually established an alternative temple at Leontopolis in Egypt, as a protest against corruption in the Temple at Jerusalem.[5] But even within the Temple itself at Jerusalem, there was a different kind of geographical isolation to emphasize the necessity of separation within the concept of holiness. Gentiles, women, laymen, priests, all were successively excluded by actual divisions in the Temple: first, there was the wall beyond which gentile visitors could not proceed, with its famous 'no entry' notices in at least three languages, 'Anyone who is apprehended (beyond this point) will be killed, and he will be responsible for his own death'; then the wall and the gate beyond which women could not proceed; then the gate and veil, or curtain, beyond which laymen could not proceed; and finally the overlapping or double curtains which divided the sanctuary, beyond which lay the holy of holies. Here no one could go except for the high priest, and even he only entered once a year, on the Day of Atonement—on the day when the separation between God and his people caused by rebellion or sin, was healed, and they were made once more 'at one'.

So even the Temple itself offers another, quite different, example of geographical necessity within the concept of holiness. How else can separation from uncleanness be achieved unless a formal boundary is set up which will keep contamination as Torah defines it at bay? It is the same question of geographical necessity which stirred in the revival of Zionism in the nineteenth century. In the Haskalah (Enlightenment), the revival of Jewish confidence led some to propose, not geographical separation, but assimilation, with Judaism becoming a private religious confession: 'Be a Jew at home, but a man in the street', as the poet Judah Gordon put it. But the feeling against a private Judaism was far stronger, and as early as Kalischer the argument was being advanced that the Jews should not rely for their salvation on a gratuitous, messianic intervention, but should advance it for themselves by a more strictly literal attention to the conditions of the covenant, which would necessarily include a resettlement of Palestine and a restoration of the sacrificial system. The political impossibility at that time of a return to Jerusalem simply meant that some other area would have to be found as an interim measure, and Argentina, Uganda, and el Arish in Egypt were all seriously proposed and considered for Jewish colonies, right up to the time of the near-schism at the sixth Zionist Congress. In fact, when Herzl, one of the important founders of Zionism in its modern form, published in 1896 his brief essay *Der Judenstaat* (which has been regarded as 'the beginning of modern political Zionism'),[6] he left it open whether the Jewish state should be in Palestine or Argentina: 'Shall we choose Palestine or Argentina? We shall take what is given us, and what is selected by Jewish public opinion.'[7]

As that opinion formed, it became obvious that any settlements outside Palestine (and a settlement *was* established in Argentina) could only be regarded as staging-posts on the return to Jerusalem. At the Sixth Zionist Congress, Herzl tried to reconcile those who argued for a cautious return via settlements established elsewhere, and those who were determined on Jerusalem or nothing. At one point he withdrew from the conference, almost broken by the conflict. But then he returned to make a final and decisive speech, ending with his right hand raised high in the air, and with the words of Ps. 137:5 on his lips: 'If I forget you, O Jerusalem, let my right hand wither away.' From then on, there was no serious alternative to Palestine.[8]

It is something to have room and space to be Jewish (i.e., to be obedient to the command of God), but the promise and the goal toward which the Jewish route through time progresses is Jerusalem. This is even true of the predecessors of the rabbis who, while the Temple was still standing, developed ways of being authentically Jewish for those who lived outside Palestine, and for whom the Temple might be a thousand miles away. Yet they too still regarded Jerusalem as central. The predecessors of the rabbis are usually referred to as Pharisees, but the term is misleading: since 'pharisees' are attacked as violently by the rabbis as they are by the Gospels, and since the rabbis did not refer to their predecessors as Pharisees, it is better to refer to them by one of the words which the rabbis themselves used, and for that reason they are referred to here as the Hakamim (the Wise, or the Sages). As the predecessors of the rabbis, the Hakamim were in many ways the builders of what would be now recognized as Judaism. For them, the issue of holiness and its attainment was absolutely crucial.

In the book, *Jesus and the Pharisees*, I have emphasized that the great vision which brought the Hakamim into being, in the century before Jesus was born, was the realization that holiness *cannot* be identified with, or confined to, geographical isolation. Of course the Temple and Jerusalem were important. But they argued that it must be possible for *all* Jews—not just for a minority who can opt into a Dead Sea Sect, or who can live near the Temple—to understand and obey the commands of Torah. What God commands *for* his people must be able to be implemented *by* his people, even though they are living a thousand miles away from Jerusalem, or even if the Temple itself has been destroyed.[9] That in itself is a major reason why the rabbinic understanding of what it means to be Jewish was able to survive the destruction of the Temple, where other understandings (like that of the Sadducees, for example, the priests who depended on the Temple) could not. The Hakamic vision was thus a vivid leap of conceptual imagination, insisting that holiness is a condition which can be attained anywhere. In *Jesus and the Pharisees* I summarized it by saying that 'where others built walls on the shores of the Dead Sea, or within the Temple, they built a fence around Torah'.[10] The reference to a fence around Torah, a boundary condition within which all Jews can live, goes back to Pirqe Aboth, and to the three traditional principles which lie at the root of the rabbinic enterprise: 'Be deliberate in judgement, establish many disciples, and make a fence for Torah.'[11]

On this basis the Hakamim and the rabbis were able to project a Jewish route through time, which like love, like *agape*, for Paul, could bear all things, endure all things, and never fail. They mapped this route with increasing precision and detail. They built into it procedures of transmission and control which enabled its stability and its informational alertness in the scan of any particular compound of limitation which they encountered. In practical terms they established schools, they developed new methods of exegesis so that they could actually build a bridge between the resource in the past (Scripture) and the needs of the present, and they created in the Synagogue a means of transmission and participation week by week.

In these ways, the Hakamim and the rabbis established that the commands of God, the conditions on which his promises of a land and of Jerusalem depend, *can* be obeyed even when one is absent from the land, or even when the land is occupied by Roman invaders. But obedience to those commands *does* require a

separated way of life. So they denied singular geographical isolation, but they did not deny (indeed they affirmed) geographical
necessity within the concept of holiness. It is this which has created
the tension which is characteristic of so much of Jewish life: the
conditions on which the fulfilment of the promises of God depends
(including the promise of the land) are well known: they are
included in the legal parts of Torah which were unpacked and interpreted by the rabbis. Those conditions can be kept even outside
the land, even while living in the midst of gentiles. But they can
only be kept if the idiosyncrasy of those conditions is preserved by
at least a degree of separation from the gentile environment. This
is the tension of Jewish life, once it becomes recognized that
Torah, the guidance of God to men, includes specific requirements—once it is recognized, in other words, that it includes
'statutes, ordinances and commands'—*huqim*, *mishpatim*, and
mizwot. They are not the whole of Torah, and for that reason the
term Torah should not be translated as Law. The narratives of
Genesis and Exodus are as much a part of Torah as the legal
commands. Nevertheless, statutes, ordinances, and commands
are a part of Torah, and they were recognized as a constitutive
necessity in the construction of Israel's life very early on.

All four terms (those three plus Torah itself) are linked together
in 2 Kings 17:34 and 17:37, in a passage which reveals a great deal
about Israel's sense of itself, and of its relation to God's word. The
passage, briefly, is part of a Jewish account of how the bitter schism
developed between Samaritans and Jews. It is not historically
accurate, and there is no doubt that the Samaritan account would
be different; but this is the Jewish account of how the northern
tribes (the northern 'sons of Jacob', descendants from the same
father) broke away from Yahweh and became an apostate people:

They do not pay homage to Yahweh, for they do not keep his statutes
and his judgements, the law and commandment, which he enjoined
upon the descendants of Jacob, whom he named Israel. When Yahweh
made a covenant with them, he gave them this commandment: 'You
shall not pay homage to other gods, or bow down to them or serve them
or sacrifice to them, but you shall pay homage to Yahweh who brought
you up from Egypt with great power and with outstretched arm; to
him you shall bow down, to him you shall offer sacrifice. You shall
faithfully keep the statutes, the judgements, the law and the commandments which he wrote for you, and you shall not pay homage to other

gods. You shall not forget the covenant which I have made with you; you shall not pay homage to other gods. But to Yahweh your God you shall pay homage, and he will preserve you from all your enemies.' However, they would not listen [*welo shameu*, they did not hear] but continued their former practices.

And they continue to do so, the writer adds in a dismissive comment, down to the present day. In practical detail, the fault of the northern tribes (according to this southern account) was that they failed to implement the hammer-like refrain of that passage, 'You shall not pay homage to other gods'. But the essential fault which led to the practical offence was that 'they would not listen': *welo shameu*—they did not hear. In contrast, what constitutes Israel as a people (in their own self-consciousness) is, first, a genetic relation, a recognition of common genealogies, whereby it can be known who are the legitimate 'bene Jacob', sons of Jacob (and the books of the Bible, from Genesis to Chronicles, pay very careful attention to the question of genealogy); but second, it is the creative act and the promise of God, responded to by their own obedience and willingness to hear. In contrast to the northern tribes who refused to hear, they have continued to respond to the command, *Shema Israel*—Hear, O Israel.

The creative act of God was eventually believed to run back to whatever the beginning of space and time as a consequence of God is conceived to have been: *bereshith bara elohim*, in the beginning God created. The act and promise of God, preceding any act or response of men, is the *sine qua nihil*, or, to mix languages, the *sine qua tohu wabohu*, that without which all would be waste and void, as the second verse of Genesis describes it.

So what constitutes Israel is the gratuitous, creative act of God, which becomes focused on a particular family and people, the 'bene Jacob', the sons of Jacob. Yet what *also* constitutes Israel is their response, their willingness to hear and to fill out the substance of their life with the guidance, the instruction, and the command which God has entrusted to them for the construction of their life. It is a willingness, in other words, to allow their lives to become Torah-informed, so that the words of Torah become (at least potentially) a constraint over the outcomes in the subsequent construction of life. It is in the realization of these conditions that the covenant bonding between God and men is established.

Why, then, *Israel*? Why the focus on one particular people? It is ultimately for the repair of the whole human condition. What Israel displays, in hearing and in implementing what they hear, is a proleptic representation (a representation in miniature and in advance) of what will ultimately be the entire human case, when 'the earth shall be full of the knowledge of the glory of Yahweh as the waters fill the sea' (Hab. 2:14). When Israel hears and obeys and fills out her life with that obedience, she is representing in the midst of time what God intended at the beginning, in the paradisal conditions of unbroken harmony which Genesis describes and which God still intends to realize through the faithfulness of this one particular people.

As will be seen in greater detail, the opening chapters of Genesis describe the progressive disintegration of man's relatedness to God, to his environment, to his wife, to his family, to his fellow-men. The rest of Scripture then describes the gradual repair of this disintegration, through the covenants beginning with Noah and running through to David (in a sense, even to Ezra and Nehemiah, at the very end of the Biblical period). Israel is thus the focus and the means of God's repair. So from the Jewish point of view the offence of the northern tribes collectively, and the root of the passionate and angry hostility which developed between Jews and Samaritans, lies, exactly as the writer of 2 Kings so succinctly summarized it, in the fact that the northerners were no longer prepared to attend to the words and conditions of the covenant: *welo shameu*, they did not hear. Conversely, this is why the *Shema* (hear, O Israel), which Aqiba was reciting as he died, is so profoundly important in Jewish life and practice. In its present form the *Shema* is made up of three separate passages[12] and it is recited daily, morning and evening; and, of course, by that recital it is written deeply into the construction of the Jewish route through life and through time: *shema Israel, adonai eloheynu adonai ehad*: 'Hear, O Israel: Yahweh our God, Yahweh is one'. The *Shema* then continues:

You shall love Yahweh your God with all your heart and with all your soul and with all your strength. These words which I command you this day are to be kept in your heart. You shall repeat them to your sons, and speak of them indoors and out of doors, when you lie down and when you rise. Bind them as a sign on the hand and wear them as a phylactery on the forehead; write them up on the doorposts of your houses and on your gates.

There could scarcely be a better summary of the designated informational resource from which Jewish life must be constructed: God—not as a vague concept, but with a name and in a relation to his world which he has made known and which would not otherwise be known—offers to this people, Israel, words which are intended to flow into their lives. They are to be in their hearts, at the very root of behaviour and belief; they are to flow into every detail of life, in private, or in public, waking or sleeping. There are to be formal and deliberate reminders (mechanisms of transmission and control): 'Bind them as a sign on the hand and wear them as a phylactery on the forehead; write them up on the doorposts of your houses, and on your gates'—an example of precisely those customs which were later to seem to so many non-Jews eccentric or bizarre.[13]

But to a Jew such customs, like those of circumcision or of the great festivals of his year, represent the means of faithfulness. They are the language of response. They offer the means of creating, in the midst of time, a representation of obedience and community—a demonstration of community in a world which is otherwise full of hatred and division. It is a sense of community which is forged by obedience even to commands which to others seem ridiculous. Deuteronomy goes on, immediately after the section recited in the *Shema*:

In times to come, when your son asks you, 'What is the meaning of the decrees and laws and customs [*eydoth, huqim, mishpatim*] which Yahweh our God has laid down for you?' you shall tell your son, 'Once we were Pharoah's slaves in Egypt, and Yahweh brought us out of Egypt by his mighty hand . . . He brought us out from there to lead us into the land he swore to our fathers he would give us. And Yahweh commanded us to observe all these laws and to fear Yahweh our God, so as to be happy for ever and to live, as he has granted us to do until now. For us right living will mean this: to keep and observe all these commandments before Yahweh our God as he has directed us.

If the son had then asked, 'What is the purpose of keeping the commands?' he would most probably have been told, 'For their own sake'—'because they are there', as a consequence of God's initiative. He would certainly *not* have been told that they should be kept for the individual's benefit, or for the sake of reward in heaven. It is one of the most extraordinary facts about Jewish Scripture that almost the whole of it was written without a belief that there would be any conscious continuity of life with God after death. With the exception of a few passages right at the end of the biblical period, all the material in Scripture was written with the knowledge that death was absolute and final. At the most, a thin filtered shadow, a faint trace of a person, might go to Sheol. But the point about Sheol was that it severed all contact with life as lived on earth, and with God. In the Israelite anthropology, there was nothing that *could* survive: man was made from dust, and into him was breathed the breath of God. When he died, the body returned to dust (that was observably the case) and the breath returned to the air. What was there that could survive death? Nothing.

When one considers the powerful descriptions of the reality of God's effect in, for example, the Psalms or Job or Genesis, and when one also considers the urgency of the plea in the Prophets that people should respond to God and condition their lives by what they claimed to be his word, it is all the more extraordinary that it was believed that death would break the relationship completely. It points to a deep and profound experience of God *in this life* which was, so to speak, its own reward. The commands of Torah become the language of faith and love, the means through which a response to God can be articulated. In a sense, the more bizarre the commandment might appear, the more unequivocal it is as a language of assent. The purpose of obedience is thus not for an individual reward after death, but for the continuity of a community which incarnates the restoration of God-relatedness in the world. The promises were made to the fathers, but they did not live to see them fulfilled; Moses saw the promised land from afar, but he did not enter in.

So when Aqiba was executed at the end of the Bar Cochba revolt, that seeming destruction of Israel, he suffered and died as an individual, but with the absolute conviction that in the faithfulness of his death the life of the community would certainly continue. He therefore died with the words of the *Shema*, the epitome of obedient faith, on his lips. What is more, as he recited those words in final agony, he realized that only at this moment of a faithful death had he been able to implement the fullest detail of Torah. Superficially, that was surely absurd. Aqiba was a scrupulously attentive scholar. He had unlocked new riches of learning in Torah by developing better methods of exegesis, and

he had even refused to eat in prison because he did not have
enough water to carry out the required cleansing of the hands.[14]
Yet he who had paid so much attention to Torah felt that he had
not fully responded to the command *Shema*, Hear, until he made
of his death a faithful offering:

When Rabbi Aqiba was being tortured before the evil Turnus Rufus,
the time came to recite the Shema. He began to recite it and laughed
for joy. The Roman said to him, 'Old man, are you one who weaves
spells [*harash*] or are you making light of your sufferings?' He answered
'Woe to that man! I am not one who weaves spells, nor am I making
light of my sufferings. No: all my days I have recited this passage, but
I felt deeply sad when I came to these words, 'You shall love the Lord
your God with all your heart and with all your soul and with all your
strength.' I have loved him with all my heart, and I have loved him
with all my wealth: but with all my soul was not clear to me. But now
that all my soul is demanded, and the time for reciting the Shema has
come, and I have not wavered, while I recite it, should I not laugh for
joy?' He had not even ceased speaking when his soul departed from
him.[15]

Finkelstein commented—and these are the words with which
he ended his life of Aqiba:

The scene, indelibly impressed on the eyes of Joshua haGarsi, became
part of Jewish tradition. The association of the *shema* with the great
martyr's death made its recitation a death-bed affirmation of faith,
instead of a repetition of select verses; and to this day the pious Jew
hopes that when his time comes he may be sufficiently conscious to
declare the unity of his God, echoing with his last breath the words
which found their supreme illustration in Akiba's martyrdom.[16]

How, then did Aqiba come to this moment of grateful joy in the
agony of a vicious and painful death, with his flesh ripped and
shredded from his body with iron rakes? Why indeed did he come
to this death at all? How did the Jewish people come to this sense
of God breaking into their history, separating them from all other
nations, creating in their obedience a sign of hope and promise in
the world, summoning them always to this instrumental obligation with the command, *Shema Israel*? How and why did it come
about, as we reach the edge of tragedy far beyond the death of
Aqiba, that they constructed so different a universe of meaning
that the first stones were placed on the walls of what eventually

became the ghettoes of Europe, not by gentiles, but by Jews? The point is put graphically by Eliezer Livneh:

If the Gentile authorities had not surrounded the ghetto with physical walls, it would have been defended by invisible but impenetrable Jewish walls. The forests and fields, the rivers and lakes, the hills and valleys that surrounded the *städtel* were fertile countryside, but for the Jews they breathed a spirit of their own, aroused different associations, produced different symbols. When the fields of Europe lay under deep snow and the soil and plants were frozen, Jews would celebrate their festival of trees.[17]

What Livneh is pointing out here in conceptual terms is what Nehemiah established in practical terms, when he rebuilt the walls of Jerusalem, and when the people excluded those of foreign descent from Israel.[18] This happened on the return of the Jews to Jerusalem after they had been taken into exile by the Babylonians in the sixth century B.C.E. On their return, they asked themselves, How can we avoid another catastrophe like that? Only, they felt, if they could tie themselves in even *closer* obedience to what Yahweh required of them as a people, by excising all other resources of effect in the construction of their route through time. So one of the first actions of Nehemiah when the Jews were restored to Jerusalem after Cyrus' defeat of the Babylonians, was to set about rebuilding the walls of Jerusalem.[19] But in addition to that, marriage with foreigners was forbidden,[20] and Ezra actually required that where such marriages existed, there should be a divorce. Those of foreign descent were excluded from Israel.

Both the literal and the metaphorical walls were thus set up between Israel and 'all that is foreign' (Neh. 13:30), and it is in this sense, harsh though it may seem to say it after the bitter Jewish experience in the so-called Christian centuries, that the first stones of a self-imposed ghetto were set up, not by Gentiles, but by Jews. Did this have to be so? Could there have been a Jewish universe of meaning without this literal construction at its heart? Is Zion necessary for the authentic construction of Jewish life? How did they come to this sense of a God who requires separation if they are to have a discernible and saving knowledge of himself? To answer these questions, we will have to go back to that basic command, *shema Israel, Adonai Eloheynu Adonai ehad*, Hear O Israel, Yahweh our God, Yahweh is one, and explore it in even greater detail. As Rosenzweig once put it: 'There is no such thing as an essence of Judaism, since that is an abstraction. There is only, Hear, O Israel.'[21]

If we try to enter into an understanding of Judaism through this opening verse of the *Shema*, we shall in fact be following very closely the advice of Maimonides (one of the most important intellectual figures in Judaism, *roughly* the equivalent in Judaism of Aquinas in Christianity and alGhazali in Islam, all of whom lived within two hundred years of each other). Maimonides was once asked: 'When should a father begin to instruct his son in Torah? As soon as the child begins to talk, the father should teach him the words, Moses commanded us Torah; and also the opening sentence of the Shema.'[22] Let us, then, attempt to become as little children, and enter, so far as it is possible, into the Jewish kingdom of heaven—or enter, to use less attractive language, into the universe of meaning constructed from the resources which Jews regard as legitimate and of authority.

2. ADONAI ELOHEYNU ADONAI EHAD

'You shall be holy to me, as I, Yahweh, am holy. I have separated you from other people that you should be mine alone' (Lev. 20:26). It seems straightforward enough as a command, but it implies underlying questions: first, who is this strange sounding 'Yahweh', and how did he come to the position of being entitled to demand the obedience of this particular nation? And second, who are these people? How did a kinship group of Semitic tribes come to a sense that they had a uniquely significant history and a uniquely distinctive destiny as a consequence of God's action in relation to themselves?

To answer those questions, we must return to the basic command, *Shema Israel, Adonai Eloheynu Adonai ehad.* But that is a very strange combination of words. *Adonai* means 'my Lord', and it represents a way of reading (or, to be more accurate, a way of avoiding reading) the four letters (i.e., the Tetragrammaton), Yhwh. It is now customary to write this name of Israel's God as Yahweh, but no one knows what its original pronunciation was. The original text of Scripture contained no vowels, only consonants; the vowels of the existing text were added by the Massoretes many centuries after the time of Jesus. Even if the early worshippers of Yhwh pronounced the name, it is impossible to know how they did so: in the course of time, it became an assertive arrogance to pronounce the name Yhwh on lips which also bear the profanities of life. The Massoretes decided that wherever the letters Yhwh occurred, the reader should be reminded to convert the name to Adonai. They therefore inserted the vowels a.o.a. and produced the impossible and hybrid form Yahowah—hence Jehovah, a bogus name which is certainly not original. If the name is pronounced Yahweh (and many Jews would certainly *not* pronounce *haShem*, the Name, in that or any other way), it is simply a guess at the original, but as a guess, it has become the conventional spelling.

Eloheynu is the word *elohim* (God) with the pronominal suffix, 'our'; so it means 'our God'. *Ehad* is the word meaning 'one'. So the sentence is literally, Yahweh our elohim, Yahweh is one. Since the verb 'to be' is understood and not actually written into the sentence, it is obvious that the sentence can be differently translated. But the main point remains clear: Yahweh is claimed as 'our God' and is claimed also to be unique and single.

How, then, is Yahweh related to Elohim? Elohim is a far more common and general term for God throughout the ancient Near East. And how is Yahweh related to El, a second major term for God in the Semitic world? El is a term which extends virtually over the whole Semitic world, both geographically and chronologically. Precisely because it is so extensive, the possible meanings it may bear—the possible intended reference in any particular usage—may well vary. But certainly in the early period, most graphically in the Ugaritic texts (Canaanite texts of the fifteenth to thirteenth centuries B.C.E.), El is a term for the supreme god, the god above gods, the father of the gods, the head of the council of gods. In the Ugaritic texts it seems clear that the position and some of the functions of El were being invaded and taken over by Baal-Hadad, the god of the storm.[1] The possibility of an invasion of one god's territory and position by another was highly important for Israel, because that in effect is what Yahweh, their own God, had to do. But even though El was under repeated threat of being displaced as an object of immediate concern by gods of more dramatic effect, El remained a very widespread term with which to refer to hierarchical supremacy in the domain of active reality which exists above the dish-cover dome of the sky which is placed over the earth. In order to bring El into a more significant and direct relation to the world, it was then necessary to specify his action or his relation to a particular place more precisely. El was therefore delimited as El Bethel, El Shaddai, El Olam, El Roi, El Berith, El Elyon.[2] All those are terms which occur in Scripture; and they lead into the complicated phrase, in Gen. 33:20, El Elohe Israel, El the Elohim of Israel, El is the Elohim of Israel.

What, then, of the term *elohim*? In contrast to El, the word *elohim* is in appearance a plural word—the 'im' at the end of a word in Hebrew indicates a plural. So this word could, quite legitimately, be translated, not god, but gods; and there are in Scripture some instances where that is exactly what it means.[3] For example, it can refer quite straightforwardly to gods in the form of actual images: the teraphim which Rachel stole from

Laban are called *elohim* (Gen. 31:30); Micah, in Judg. 17:5 has a
house of gods, a *bet elohim*;[4] the images of Egypt cast in metal are
called *elohim* in Dan. 11:8. Or again, *elohim* means 'gods' in the
plural, in Scripture, in the reported speech of non-Jews, who,
because they are polytheists, refer quite naturally to the many
gods whom they accept as being potentially resourceful in their
own case. Thus Goliath cursed David 'by his *elohim*' (1 Sam.
17:43), and Cyrus returned to the Jews the Temple treasure which
Nebuchadnezzer had dedicated 'to his *elohim*' (Ezra 1:7).[5]

But what is obvious in Scripture is that the plural uses of *elohim*
are comparatively rare. Almost invariably the word *elohim*, despite
the plural appearance and its possible plural sense, is constructed
with a singular verb. It is clear that the term has come to represent
not gods, but the gathering into a single figure of all that the gods
might be for men. 'Hear, O Israel, Yahweh our Elohim Yahweh
is one'—*ehad*, one, gathering into this single figure all possible
significant effect, all that the many gods constructed by men (and
often literally constructed out of wood and stone) might be for
men. There is only one other major way of using the word *elohim*
in a plural sense, and that is in order to denounce the *so-called
elohim*, the so-called gods, of other people and of other nations.

There are in fact about 300 passages of that sort, and the point
of them is obvious: it is to establish the absolute contrast between
Elohim as he is (as he is made uniquely known to Israel in his
name and nature as Yahweh) and the so-called *elohim* of other
people. In other words, passages which denounce a plural sense of
what looks like a plural word, are emphasizing that Israel must
never themselves invest the word *elohim* with plural meaning:
Yahweh our Elohim is *ehad*, one, utterly distinct. It is this figure
who, according to Scripture, is Yahweh. Elohim (what God is) has
created in the midst of one particular people (the kinship group of
tribes descended from Jacob, the bene (sons of) Jacob) a unique
knowledge of his name and nature: our Elohim is Yahweh.

It follows that the so-called *elohim*, gods, of other nations are
really *elilim*, and that is exactly what Ps. 96:5 calls them. *Elilim*
is another word which may also have meant 'gods', being akin,
as Koehler argued, to the South Arabic *alaalah*.[6] But there is not
really any serious doubt that because the word *al* also means 'not'
in Hebrew, the Hebrew word *elilim* implies exactly that—*alilim*
not-nesses, nonentities, nothingnesses,[7] and that is exactly what

Ps. 96 says: 'The *elohim* of the nations are *elilim*, but Yahweh made the heavens.' The argument is very similar to Blake's, when he produced his Nobodaddy, a combination of 'nobody' and 'daddy'. 'Old Nobodaddy aloft' was derided by Blake, because he was totally unable to take any saving or significant part in human life. Once again it is the issue of effect:

> Why art thou silent and invisible,
> Father of Jealousy?
> Why dost thou hide thyself in clouds
> From every searching eye?[8]

It is almost exactly the same attack which is launched against the gods in Ps. 82. In that Psalm, Israel's God appears as prosecuting counsel against the gods, the *elohim* and derides them: all right, God challenges the gods, if you *are* gods, let the weak and the orphan have justice, be fair to the wretched and destitute, rescue the weak and needy, save them from the clutches of the wicked. But they cannot do it: they are impotent, and for that reason the Psalmist agrees with Mencken that they should go straight down the chute. The Psalm in fact goes on to describe an absolutely literal death of gods:

> This is my sentence: *elohim* you may be,
> Sons of Elyon all of you may be,
> But like Adam [or, 'like men'] you will die:
> The strongest princes fall, without exception, so will you.

The *Shema*, therefore, summarizes the pressure that developed among the bene Jacob to recognize only one source of possible theistic effect. It was a pressure which led to the supremely assertive formula, that Yahweh is not only Elohim of Israel, but Elohim of the *elohim*, Lord of the Lords, the great El, as Deut. 10:17 puts it.[9] Even so, we have still to ask, *why* that pressure? What was it that required of them that they should look no more for a wide and varied range of theistic realities? We can answer those questions by focusing first on a narrower issue: the bene Jacob and later the Israelites and the Jews were constantly reminded that there is only one God, one source of theistic input—the worship of so-called 'other gods', *elohim aheyrim*, is suicidal, because it destroys the close bonding they have with Yahweh, through which alone they prosper. And yet, despite that emphasis of Scripture and the *Shema* on the word *ehad*, an early memory of

Israel's origin as a people (in Josh. 24:2) states very clearly that
the patriarchs (the forefathers and ancestors of this kinship group)
did actually worship *elohim aheyrim*: 'Long ago,' says Joshua, to
the assembled people, 'your forefathers, Terah and his sons
Abraham and Nahor, lived beside the Euphrates, and they worshipped *elohim aheyrim*.'

There is no particular guilt or recrimination about that memory.
The question, therefore, has to be asked: how did they make the
transition from *elohim* in an unequivocally plural sense to Elohim
as alone of significant effect in the construction of life and of the
world, and to Elohim whose name they alone know as Yahweh?
The answer according to Exod. 6:3 is simple: because God—
that to which Elohim correctly refers—made known his name and
nature within the history of Israel, and supremely to Moses in the
Exodus from Egypt. When Moses was summoned by God to
return to Egypt and lead out the enslaved people, only then,
according to Exod. 6:3 was the name Yahweh made known: 'I am
Yahweh. To Abraham and Isaac and Jacob I appeared as El
Shaddai; I did not make myself known to them by my name
Yahweh.'

Here, then, appears to be the origin of the Jewish sense of God.
Before this date the ancestors of the Hebrews participated in the
wide range of possible senses of God which obtained in their
environment. But at this dramatic moment which changed their
life-way so completely, the name and nature of God as he is
beyond and apart from the shadowy confusion of gods chose its
own moment to become known, and to lay claim to the allegiance
of one man, and beyond him, of one people. It is an idealized
picture, but it is not, at least in poetic terms, incredible—not,
except for the familiar fact of exactly that self-contradiction or
inconsistency in the Pentateuch (in Torah) which led Astruc in
the eighteenth century to suggest that Genesis must have been put
together from four main sources, or what he called 'memoirs'.[10]

Even the most cursory glance at Genesis makes it clear that the
name Yahweh was known to Abraham, Isaac and Jacob, and that
Yahweh was the name of their god. Indeed, Gen. 4:26 states
specifically: 'It was at that time [the time of the birth of Adam's
grandson] that men began to call on the name of Yahweh.'

It was the contradiction between Gen. 4:26 and Exod. 6:3,
together with the fact that the name Yahweh *was* known, according

to many Genesis narratives, to Abraham, Isaac and Jacob, which
led Astruc to suppose that Moses must have used two main
memoirs (supplemented by two others) in putting together the
book of Genesis: what he called the A memoir used only the name
Elohim, and what he called the B memoir used the name Yahweh
throughout. There is no need to follow the tangled way in which
that suggestion was developed into the modern documentary
hypothesis of two separate accounts of Israel's origin (the Yah-
wistic J and the Elohistic E), which were fused and formed with
other traditions, and which were reworked by later writers with
Deuteronomic interests (promise and threat and holy war) and
with Priestly interests (temple and ritual), resulting in the familiar
J E D and P. Astruc well foresaw the battles which lay ahead:
the opening words of his Preface make that entirely clear.[11] But
there is no need to make a further tour of these ancient fields of
battle. From the point of view of understanding what lies at the
root of the Jewish sense of God, it is enough simply to observe
that almost the earliest Jewish exegesis to which we have access
recognized that there is a conflict between Gen. 4 and Exod. 6.
But that exegesis also recognized that no one apparently saw any
need to eliminate the elementary and very obvious contradiction.
A careful (not to say inspired) writer could surely have avoided
inconsistency if he had wished to do so, not least because inconsistency was avoided in the change of names of Abram and
Sarai:[12] once the names Abram and Sarai are changed to Abraham
and Sarah, the earlier names are not used. There is a careful consistency.

Consequently, later exegesis concluded that the apparent contradiction must originally have had a different and intended
significance: although it has always been Yahweh who has been
God and therefore *could* be known (so that it was Yahweh as El
Shaddai who appeared to the fathers and established his covenant
with them) those earlier covenant relations were established in
very general terms: it was only in the Exodus and in the Sinai
covenant that Yahweh became fully known once more, and that
the covenant conditions became established in detail. Jewish
exegetes, therefore, looked more carefully at Gen. 4:26, and
observed that the word translated 'began' ('men began at that time
to call on the name Yahweh') also means (in a different form of the
verb) 'to profane', or 'rebel'.[13]

The verse was therefore translated: 'At that time men profaned [or 'rebelled'] in calling on the name of Yahweh.' According to Ber. R. xxvi. 4, the same meaning is to be found in Gen. 6:1 and 10:8. As a result of man's profanity and rebellion, the name of Yahweh ceased to be generally known, but since obviously it remained the name of Elohim (the only actual theistic reality) it was occasionally known and made use of by the fathers. It is highly unlikely that this exegesis bears any relation to the historical way in which Yahweh became known as *the* Elohim among the bene Jacob. But from the point of view of the Jewish understanding of God, that is scarcely relevant. Much more to the point is the fact that that exegesis coheres completely with the Jewish understanding of the nature of man. According to Jewish anthropology, there was no single 'fall of man' as the Christian tradition has tended to suppose from Genesis. What Genesis portrays is a progressive disintegration of man's relatedness and security—his relatedness to God, to his wife, to his environment, to his family, to his fellow human beings. This progressive disintegration culminates in the Tower of Babel. If there is one single moment of catastrophe (or near catastrophe) in Genesis, it is the moment in Gen. 6:5 when God repents of his mistake in creating men and prepares to obliterate them. But that is also the moment at which Genesis begins to portray the progressive repair of disintegration. The bonds are gradually re-tied through the long sequence of covenants, beginning with Noah, and extending through Moses to David, and indeed to Ezra and Nehemiah.

The first steps back are expressed in very general terms: the covenant with Noah is to be 'between God and living things on earth of every kind' (Gen. 9:16). Again, the first covenant promise to Abram has external reference, beyond himself and his own descendants: 'All the families on earth will pray to be blessed as you are blessed' (Gen. 12:3). Yet here already the proleptic importance of Israel is obvious: by their demonstration of the harmony between God and man and of its consequences, they can help others as well to find their way back to the lost paradisal conditions. But the covenant to which Exod. 6 refers has become focused entirely on Israel, on the descendants of Abraham, on the tribes who can claim descent from him, from Isaac, and from Jacob. Here the seeds of that other theme, equally recurrent in Scripture, become apparent, the theme of Israel in distinction from other nations,

alone safeguarding the name and honour of God, in advance of
all the rest, and understanding themselves as *chosen* by God to do
this. The seed of this theme is also apparent in the first covenant
promise to Abram: 'Those that bless you I will bless, those that
curse you, I will execrate.' It is in adherence to the honour of
this name, Yahweh, that this group of tribes becomes, out of all
possible tribes, Isra-el.

Scripture therefore portrays a progressive fall of man, and also a
progressive rebuilding and repair. What this means, in summary,
is that when Adam chose to know, he chose; and that meant the
possibility of choice with evil consequence. This is exactly where
men still stand, but now their choices are, or can be, informed,
through the covenant conditions, with the signals which determine
what constitutes a choice for good. This means, as I have suggested
elsewhere, that the Jewish 'fall of man' is, in some ways, a fall
upwards, 'a move into new structures and new opportunities of
knowing, but structures now attendant with pain'.[14] This basic
anthropology came to be summarized in the ideas of the two
yazrain, or inclinations, the evil *yezer*, and the good *yezer*, which
represent the pull within the construction of human life toward
opposing poles of consequence. So from the Jewish point of view,
men are not 'bound' to sin.[15] Indeed, one could say that there is
bias, in Jewish anthropology, to the side of good, because the
conditions which establish what will count as a choice for good
are specified in Torah and in the covenant itself. This eventually
was the rock on which Paul's Jewishness foundered, because he
was compelled, by what Jesus had been within the Jewish universe
of meaning, to ask a radically disruptive question of this anthropology, and he was compelled to ask it both by retrospective and
by introspective evidence. What that question was, and why Paul
had to ask it, we will come to in due course.

In contrast to Paul, the Jewish universe of meaning sets forth a
relatively optimistic anthropology; and this explains why the
family is so critically important in that universe, and why a father
is under such emphatic obligation to instruct and educate his sons,
as can be seen implicitly in the question put to Maimonides
(p. 45). It is because the construction of a human life-way can,
from the Jewish point of view, be well-informed of the conditions
of appropriateness, that the son must be instructed, so that his
scan of any situation will always draw on those particular resources

of interpretation; and it is because the construction of human life-ways can be thus well-informed, that a family can represent a kind of return in miniature to the paradisal state, even here, in the midst of time—a kind of Eden, a kind of fruit-bearing oasis, in the midst of the deserts of disobedience.[16]

Obviously, Genesis and Exodus, in their present form, are composite. They draw on varied traditions in order to construct this picture of paradise lost and of the gradual rebuilding by God of a route by which men can find their way back, if not to paradise itself, at least to a land in which the conditions of friendship can be re-established. Equally obviously, the sources and the traditions are organized to create the picture. But it *is* this picture which is fundamentally resourceful in the Jewish universe of meaning. So in order to understand the Jewish sense of God, it is relatively unimportant to adjudicate in strictly historical terms on the conflict between Gen. 4 and Exod. 6. It is relatively unimportant where God came from in Jewish prehistory—whether Yahweh was a God literally unknown among the bene Jacob (the sons or tribal descendants of Jacob) before the Exodus from Egypt, as Exod. 6 appears to state, and as modern theories, such as the Kenite hypothesis, reinforce—the Kenite hypothesis coming, for some, as near as is possible to 'certain probability';[17] or whether Yahweh had always been known, at least by a part of the bene Jacob, but only became extensively and exclusively the God of the whole tribal group as a consequence of the Exodus—as, of course, the tenacity of the tradition about a prior knowledge of Yahweh asserts and as Exod. 3 makes explicit. What *is* important for the Jewish sense of God is the recognition of the obvious, that no matter what Yahweh had been before, in the consciousness of men in the interval between Adam and Moses, and no matter where he had come from, it was in and through the Exodus that he was established unequivocally as God.

So the bene Jacob could remember without embarrassment that there had been a time when their fathers had worshipped *elohim aheyrim*, other gods, exactly as Josh. 24:2 puts it. But Josh. 24 also summarizes the supremely formative moment when the kinship group, the descendants of Jacob, undertook to tie themselves in a formal covenant bond to Yahweh and to each other, as a consequence of his demonstration of effect within the Exodus, and to regard him alone as the resource of theistic effect.

It is now a matter of much dispute whether Josh. 24 is based on a very early account, close to the historical events, or whether it is an imaginative reconstruction from a much later period. That issue will be taken up shortly (pp. 69–70). What is not in dispute is that, whether sooner or later, the bene Jacob made the transition from many gods to one God because of the demonstration of his effect in their communal and individual life.

But how did they make the other transition, from being a fairly loose-knit kinship group, to being, in their own estimate, a chosen people? How did they make the transition from bene Jacob to Israel? Obviously they were not made into a people by the Exodus. The bene Jacob already had a strong sense of kinship affinity, based on a recognition of a common genealogy, long before the Exodus. So how did they become a nation, taking over the land of Canaan, a transition and a conquest which is intricately tied into their developing sense of God?

The answer to that, like almost everything else in this early period, is much disputed. One major theory picks up the history of a nomadic background and suggests that the Israelite tribes were originally followers of flocks and herds, who came from Mesopotamia. As they increased and found that the desert could no longer support them, they began to press into the agricultural land of Canaan, although for centuries they were confined to the mountainous uplands and could make little impact on the richer land of the valleys. They were not desert nomads in the later Badu sense, but in origin they had no settled place of abode.

That reconstruction picks up the hints which some of the earliest fragments of Israelite tradition record. One of these we have already seen in the summary in Josh. 24 of Israel's origin: 'Long ago your forefathers . . . lived beside the Euphrates, and they worshipped other gods.' The memory of having no settled place of abode is stated exactly in the basic credal confession which Deuteronomy requires of all Israelites at the ceremony of first fruits: 'My father was a homeless [or "a wandering"] Aramaean who went down to Egypt with a small company and lived there until they became a great nation' (Deut. 26:5). It is this picture, of the tribal groups acting to a great extent independently and only gradually forcing their way into the land, which is portrayed in Judg. 1. There is a different pattern and history of settlement for different parts of the land.[18]

That picture of relatively incoherent chaos was in fact *too*
coherent for Mendenhall. His radically different theory of the
origin of Israel was based on the observation that 'hebrews' are a
well-attested and well-defined group in ancient near Eastern texts
—or if not exactly 'hebrews' (*ibri*), then certainly in the form
apiru. The Tel el Amarna letters gave the first clue of this. These
letters were written to inform the Pharaoh of Egypt that a people,
identified as *habiru*, were invading Palestine. More extensively the
letters make it clear that the *habiru* were in revolt against Egyptian
suzerainty, and that kings, princes, local leaders, cities, and wider
areas had joined up with the *habiru* in revolt. Could not this be a
reference to an invasion by a new people, the Hebrews, which
would thus correspond to the Genesis and Joshua accounts of
dramatic invasions? So clear did this identification become that
when, in 1928, Erith summarized the current understanding of
Israel's history, it had become 'undoubted':

Many of these [Tel-el-Amarna] letters show that Palestine was being
invaded by a people called Sa-Gaz, whom Arad-Hiba, the governor
of Jerusalem, designates as Habiru. Of the identification of Habiru with
Hebrews there is no longer any doubt; and so we learn that during the
period of Egyptian weakness in Palestine the country was being over-
run by Hebrew invaders, who, as Arad-Hiba says, 'are capturing the
fortresses of the king'.[19]

But then came more evidence which made it clear that the term
apiru did not refer to a people or a nation at all, but to people in a
particular social situation—or to be more exact, to people who
had no assured place in society. The term refers to military con-
scripts, to slaves, to servants; it refers also to mercenaries who
hire out their services, and it refers to land-pirates, plundering
bands completely outside whatever law obtained at the time and in
the relevant situations.

It was this observation which formed a point of departure for
Mendenhall's reconstruction. He accepted the *apiru-ibri*-Hebrew
identification, and consequently rejected the argument that the
Hebrews, as a people, invaded from the outside. On the contrary,
they represent a takeover bid from within, a bid which was
successful, in the sense that this suppressed part of the existing
population destroyed the Canaanite city-state system and replaced
it with their own loosely federated alliance. The seizure of the

promised land was not an invasion from without, but a takeover from within: it was if anything a peasant's revolt.[20]

But this conflict between invasion from without and uprising from within is in fact unnecessary: it is not a question of 'either/or', but of 'both/and'. Mendenhall in isolation does not do justice to the extreme tenacity with which Israelite tradition asserts that their origins lay outside Canaan, and that their distinction from the native people of Canaan was absolute. Nor does his argument do justice to the equal tenacity with which the tradition maintains that the groups or tribes which came to make up Israel were linked in an affinal kinship bond. The details of the kinship bonding may well have been reworked at various stages, but no account which ignores the extent and tenacity of this tradition of affinal bonding is convincing. What is therefore a possible reconstruction combines the two conflicting accounts. The origins of Israel lay in a kinship group of a pastorally nomadic kind. The search for suitable areas in which to live meant that the smaller groups which made up the whole affinal bonding could, and often did, pursue different histories, exactly as Judg. 1 represents, and as more detailed narratives portray—for example, the decimation of Simeon and Levi as a result of their dealings with Shechem, in Gen. 34. This meant also that the reality of the affinal bonding in the whole kinship group was often latent, but that in a crisis it could be summoned into being. The Song of Deborah, in Judg. 5, is an obvious and very early example of this, where it is clear that the families or tribes of the kinship group can be summoned with an expectation that they must respond. Reuben, Gilead, Dan, and Asher are taunted and mocked because they failed to come to the battle against Sisera. By the time Reuben had finished debating the matter, the battle was over and the victory won.[21]

An even clearer example occurs a little later, at the time of the very great threats posed to Israel, in general by the Philistines, and more immediately, in this case, by the Ammonites. When Saul heard that Nahash was about to capture Jabesh-gilead, Saul summoned the kinship group by hewing a yoke of oxen into pieces and by sending the pieces 'all through Israel', with the message: 'If anyone will not march with Saul, this shall be done with his oxen.' Then the narrative continues: 'The fear of Yahweh [not of Saul, but of Yahweh] fell upon the people, and they came out, to a man' (1 Sam. 11:7).

It is therefore entirely possible that this kinship group came from without, and that the memory of invasion is correct, and yet also that in its quest for *lebensraum*, living space, it linked with indigenous *apiru* unrest to such an extent that some of its elements were indeed identified with it. The origins of Israel do not have to be identified with one theme, and one only, from Israel's memory of itself. On the contrary, the varying histories of the clans, or family groups, mean that many themes were undoubtedly in play. Some were themes of conflict, some of alliance. In this affinal bonding, it was certainly possible for the different family or tribal groups to have different histories. It was possible for many different covenant or treaty relationships to be developed, through which those who were not genetically related were nevertheless bonded into the family group. Reference has already been made to one example, the bond which was established with the Kenites, whereby the Kenites linked themselves under the worship of Yahweh. But whether through conflict or alliance, whether with separate histories or at times in partial combination, the central tradition is pervasive and insistent, the tradition of a kinship group, depending for its formal bonding on affinity. The bonding is often latent but always potential. It is a social system which is found in almost identical form much later among the Arabs. It was this kinship group, attentive to its genealogies, but willing to admit others into them through affiliation, which agreed to accept the god Yahweh as the single resource of theistic effect in its own case. It is the formality of that decision which Josh 24 records and summarizes. Of course it remained the case that some (perhaps many) individuals and local settlements within the kinship group continued to regard other gods as resourceful in the construction of their lives. But once allegiance had been formally offered to Yahweh, it was possible for other individuals and other groups to emerge to protest that the reference to other gods is treacherous, and that those people, those traitors, really know that they have undertaken to have reference to Yahweh alone. Prophets can emerge with this as one of their most insistent themes; Rechabites can emerge, tradition literalists who, when the tribes did establish living space in Canaan and settled down to an agricultural life, protested against innovations which took the tribes away from the literal conditions which Yahweh had laid down in the desert: they protested, for example, against planting vines, and certainly, therefore, against drinking wine, because that kind of agriculture could not possibly have been undertaken in the wilderness.[22]

What Josh. 24 asserts is that the whole kinship group assented to this undertaking, that Yahweh alone was to be the source of theistic effect in their case. Consequently, Amos could come as a prophet from a tribe in the south, and could know that his protest on behalf of Yahweh would be intelligible in the north; it would be intelligible, even though rejected. It is the formality with which this kinship group undertook their obligation to Yahweh which created the powerful reach of Yahweh into their history, even though they frequently in subsequent years became casual about their obigation or even tried to evade it. There have been many Jews who have shared the hesitation of Moses by the burning bush, and have argued, Why me? or even, Why us, as a people? It is the prayer of Solly Gitnick in the shipping room in the army: 'O Lord we are thy chosen people: for Christ's sake choose somebody else.'[23]

> Solly Gitnick said a prayer
> Standing on the washroom stair:
> Lord, we are your chosen race,
> For Christ's sake choose another, in our place.
> God did so. Or so some others thought.
> In God's name, they pursued and caught
> Young Solly Gitnick in his prayer,
> And killed him on the washroom stair.

It is this which creates the 'aristocracy of suffering' of which Zunz wrote, and which George Eliot quoted for Daniel Deronda to read:

If there are ranks in suffering, Israel takes precedence of all the nations —if the duration of sorrows and the patience with which they are borne ennoble, the Jews are among the aristocracy [*mit den Hochgeborenen*] of every land—if a literature is called rich in the possession of a few classic tragedies, what shall we say to a National Tragedy lasting for fifteen hundred years, in which the poets and the actors were also the heroes?[24]

But Deronda did not agree with the defeatist irony of Pash the watchmaker, the 'small, dark, vivacious, triple-baked Jew'. Despite Deronda's inclination by nature 'to take the side of those on whom the arrows of scorn were falling',[25] he agreed with Mordecai in rejecting Pash's belief that Judaism is an antique superstition which cannot be made credible by the pruning of a few useless rites and literal interpretations:

'As plain as a pike-staff,' said Pash, with an ironical laugh. 'You pluck it up by the roots, strip off the leaves and bark, shave off the knots, and smooth it at the top and bottom; put it where you will, it will do no harm, it will never sprout. You may make a handle of it, or you may throw it on the bonfire of sacred rubbish. I don't see why our rubbish is to be held sacred any more than the rubbish of Brahmanism or Buddhism.' 'No,' said Mordecai, 'no, Pash, because you have lost the heart of the Jew. Community was felt before it was called good. I praise no superstition, I praise the living fountains of enlarging belief.'[26]

Community was felt before it was called good: that has remained the persistent vision of the Jews, that they are called as people to make of themselves a whole offering to God, and the roots of that go back almost to the origins of themselves as a people. If it had been left as a matter of vague rhetorical appeal it might have perished as a consequence of the suffering of the people in generation after generation. But it was not left as a matter of vague appeal: it was formulated precisely, economically, and dramatically in the concept of the covenant; and it is to that concept that we must now turn.

3. THE COVENANT

IT was pointed out in the last chapter that, however much individual parts of the kinship group may have been independent or even isolated at different times, there persisted a strong sense of the underlying kinship bond. The *actual* affinity was known to obtain in different degrees, by direct descent, by lateral descent, or by affiliation. The stories of the patriarchs, particularly of their marriages, illustrate different ways in which outsiders could be attached to the kinship group. The consequent sense of affinity was extremely strong, even though particular tribes were separated geographically and were often compelled to follow different histories. The most serious geographical separation was caused by the Jebusite occupation of central Palestine. Communication between the settlements in the north and those in the south was minimal until David captured the Jebusite capital, Jerusalem. Yet despite the separations which occurred, the latent sense of bonding did not diminish, and on occasion it could be called into actual realization.

The most important illustration of the reality of separation and yet of the possibility of the latent bonding being subsequently reaffirmed is the settlement of part of the kinship group in Egypt which was followed by their escape and linking up once more with the rest of the group on their return to Canaan. It was on this occasion that the God Yahweh, who made possible the escape, was locked into the existing sense (which obtained in the clans who had remained in Canaan) of God bound in a covenant relationship to particular people or places.

The exact details of this reconstruction are, like all else in so early a period, disputed. It is not even known how many of the family clans of the whole kinship group were in Egypt. The narrative makes it clear that eventually *all* the sons of Jacob were in Egypt, but equally the narrative makes it clear that the significant history belonged to the Rachel tribes (Joseph and Benjamin), and to Levi of the Leah group. The obvious inference has become a commonplace, that it was predominantly the Rachel group which was in Egypt, while the greater part of the Leah group never left its foothold in the hills of Canaan. Appeal is then usually made to the absence of any conquest tradition for the central area of Palestine, where a part of the kinship group was nevertheless settled. That is, by definition, an argument from silence: the silence is there, because no conquest took place; it was unnecessary because the tribes never left the area. But it is perhaps equally a reminder that since the narratives combine the ideal and the actual in their references to all Israel in the Exodus, it will never be possible to say with certainty who actually did belong to that event. Two midwives, for example, were sufficient for the needs of the people in Egypt (Exod. 1:15–22), but on the march they numbered over 600,000 men of fighting age (Num. 1:46; 26:51), which would mean a total company of over two million people. It was that kind of observation which offered to Colenso (the Trinity mathematician who became bishop among the Zulus) so many targets in the nineteenth century. He calculated, for example, that if this number of Israelites stood before the door of the Tabernacle, as it is said that they did, and if they stood nine abreast (a fair calculation since the Tabernacle was 18 feet wide), the resultant queue would be nearly 20 miles long.[1] Similarly, if the priests alone had to eat the sin-offerings for the birth of children, each priest would have had to eat 88 pigeons a day.[2]

There is no need to take the calculations seriously. Colenso had to do so, because they involved a deep pastoral problem, the veracity of the foundations of the faith which he was encouraging among the Zulu people: 'my heart answered in the words of the Prophet, Shall a man speak lies in the name of the Lord? I dared not do so.'[3]

But the calculations are at least a reminder that where the narratives combine both the theoretical and the actual, the reconstruction of detail is elusive. In general terms, however, what the narrative represents in Jewish consciousness is clear: in the period when this kinship group was pressing for living space, one part of it, Joseph, found its way to Egypt, and was compelled to find its life-support in *apiru*, Hebrew, bondage, as the tradition of the selling of Joseph into Egypt suggests. But the establishing of a sufficient foothold meant that when life-support in Canaan became even more precarious through famine, other parts of the kinship group found their way there as well. It was this group which, reduced to bondage again, sought and found their escape under Moses, and supremely under the guidance and power of Yahweh.

Whether Yahweh was a newly discovered, or a newly reasserted, god is scarcely of moment, though the latter is obviously what the tradition as a whole maintains. What became obvious to their own reflection was that Yahweh was sufficient to disrupt and break the bonds of their Egyptian situation, and to construct for them an entirely new life-way, in this case a literal way across the wilderness, first to settle at Kadesh, and then eventually to return to Canaan.

Once again, we have to observe that the question of how much of the tradition of the wilderness goes back to any single sequence of original events is a matter of conflict. For von Rad, it was 'obvious' (his own word)[4] that the tradition of the divine revelation at Sinai was inserted into already extant traditions concerning the wanderings in the wilderness, since Kadesh traditions precede the Sinai period and Kadesh traditions follow it; and for him it was equally obvious that the Sinai tradition was inserted into the saving history at a comparatively late date, because the earliest poetic credos make no mention of it: J, E and P associate quite different kinds of law with Sinai, and this suggested to von Rad that Sinai was introduced in a cultic situation as a peg on which to hang fundamentally constitutive laws, but that the nature of the laws changed because of the changes in Israel's situation and need as a people. In other words, what was required was historical justification for the changes, or innovations, and that is why a Sinai pericope was tied into the saving history. On that basis it would, of course, be possible to argue that when the Jahwist came to put together his account of Israel, he knew virtually nothing about the wilderness period, except for the quite separate Sinai tradition complex; he therefore filled in the long empty period with any traditions which seemed to have a wilderness flavour or background. If that seems a somewhat drastic extension, it is nevertheless almost exactly the methodology and general argument of Volkmar's recent *Israel in der Wüste*.

The whole argument has been strongly contested, not least by Beyerlin. One of the important strands of his argument is that the Decalogue, the basic law of the Sinaitic covenant, is itself formally tied into the saving history by its brief historical prologue: 'I am Yahweh, your Elohim, who brought you out of Egypt, out of the land of slavery' (Exod. 20:2). It is gratuitous to assume that this is a tag inserted in order to tie the Decalogue into the wilderness traditions. On the contrary, the careful analysis of the forms of the Hittite covenant treaties, initiated by Korošec, but popularized by Mendenhall and subsequently developed in even greater detail, suggests that the argument must be reversed. The earliest Hittite covenant forms, of the late second millennium B.C.E., almost invariably open with a historical prologue, summarizing the situation up to that point. The later Hittite covenant forms, of the period when the compilers of the Pentateuch were supposed to have been doing their work, scarcely ever, if at all, have a historical prologue—though admittedly far fewer examples from the later period have been found, and of those which *have* been found, some are mutilated at the point where a prologue might have occurred. Nevertheless, some of the covenant contexts of the Israelite tradition reflect very closely, in the sequence of their construction, the form of the early Hittite treaties, including the historical prologue. Beyerlin, therefore, concluded:

The traditions of the deliverance from Egypt and of the events on Sinai were connected at a very early date under the influence of an old covenant form going back to the pre-Mosaic period. This is true of the earliest stages of the growth of Israel's tradition and not simply of the later period of literary fixation, and is the reason for the union of history and law which is characteristic of the Old Testament.[5]

The point where this becomes unequivocally clear is in Josh. 24, the account which summarizes the way in which the whole kinship group bound themselves in a formal covenant agreement, and *by* a formal covenant agreement, to adhere only to Yahweh. Josh. 24 records a fusion or contribution of resources in memory and in tradition. There is the contribution of the earth-disturbing way in which a god, Yahweh, has broken into the sequences of their existing situation and transformed them, not only in the Exodus but also, as Josh 24:13 puts it, by giving them land on which they had not laboured, cities which they had never built, produce of vineyards and olive-groves which they did not plant. It is this transformation which establishes the claim that Yahweh is not *a* god, but the only God from whom significant effect on such a scale can possibly be expected; so, effectively, he is claimed as the only God: Yahweh *is* Israel's God (Josh. 24:2, 14, 16 ff., 23).

But there is also the contribution of earlier resources of tradition, the memory of the forefathers of this kinship group, who had worshipped other gods beyond the Euphrates, but who had found, as they moved from beyond the river toward new pastures and new settlements in Canaan, an equally significant effect from El on their behalf. El, in the traditions which eventually found their way into Genesis, was diversely characterized: sometimes he was bound to a place, but equally—and not surprisingly for a nomadic people—he could be bound to a people in movement. The point is that there were several *different* resources of covenant memory, of covenants with Abraham, Isaac, and Jacob, among the bene Jacob. But what occurs in Josh. 24 is a fusion or contribution of those resources from which senses of God were available and alive within the component elements of the kinship group. There is a deliberate pooling of covenant memory and Yahweh experience so that Yahweh, interpreted in a covenant relation, became and was intended to become the only resource of theistic construction and interpretation, so far as Israel is concerned.

The formal structure of Josh. 24 follows very closely the formal structure of the early Hittite covenant treaties. That does not in any way establish the authenticity of Josh. 24 without further discussion, but it certainly emphasizes the extreme deliberation with which this kinship group reinforced its unity—the unity which was always latent, but was now realizable in a new way, first, because of the actual return into geographical proximity of those who had been in Egypt, and second, because of the continuing geographical penetration which the group (sometimes separately, sometimes in combination) was achieving. What was creatively so important was the way in which what was primarily a political form so far as the Hittites were concerned (the treaties were mainly with other kings or vassals or other political entities) was transformed into a means of binding the kinship group into a covenant treaty with God: it was a treaty with conditions, and with expectations which depended on those conditions being observed. So, whereas the Hittite treaties begin with a heading which identifies the author and usually senior partner of the covenant (the king), the Josh. 24 covenant begins with exactly the same kind of heading, identifying the author and the senior partner, but here the author is Yahweh: Thus says Yahweh, Israel's Elohim.

A closer comparison of a particular Hittite covenant with Josh. 24

will show how close the two are, and yet what a profoundly different use Israel made of the basic form. The example taken is the treaty between Duppi-Tessub and Mursilis.[6] After the opening statement identifying the author of the covenant, the Hittite treaties then continue with a survey of history up to the point where the treaty is being made: 'Aziras was the grandfather of you, Duppi-Tessub. He rebelled against my father, but submitted again to my father. When the kings of Nuhassi Land . . . and the kings of Kinza rebelled against my father, Aziras did not rebel.' And so it goes on. In Joshua we find exactly the same: 'Your fathers dwelt of old time beyond the River, even Terah, the father of Abraham, and the father of Nahor. And I took your father Abraham and led him throughout all the land of Canaan' (vv. 2 f.). In exactly the same way, it summarizes what has happened down to the point where the tribes are about to enter into the agreement.

Next comes the basic statement of what the treaty is to involve: 'When you [Duppi-Tessub] take a wife, and when you beget an heir, he shall be king in the Amurru land likewise. And just as I shall be loyal toward you, even so shall I be loyal toward your son. But you, Duppi-Tessub, remain loyal to the king of the Hatti land . . . forever!' In Joshua: 'Now, therefore, fear Yahweh and serve him . . . and put away the gods which your fathers served beyond the River . . . Choose you this day whom you will serve; whether the gods which your fathers served . . . or the gods of the Amorites, in whose land you dwell: but as for me and my house, we will serve Yahweh' (vv. 14 f.).

The basic stipulation is that Yahweh alone is to be Elohim in the newly re-evoked alliance of the affinal group, the bene Jacob. After the basic statement, the specific conditions are laid out: in the Hittite treaty they are too numerous to quote in full, but they include, by way of example, that Duppi-Tessub is to pay the same tribute (300 shekels of gold), what military help is to be given and when, relations with other countries, and extradition agreements. In Joshua the conditions are not detailed in that way, but they are alluded to in the solemnity with which Joshua warns the people, in v. 19, that perhaps they really ought not to undertake this treaty: perhaps they will simply not be able to keep the necessary conditions; for Yahweh, he continues, is not just Elohim, but Elohim qedoshim, a *holy* god, 'a jealous God who will not forgive your transgressions or your sins' (v. 19). Here the implication of detail is inevitable: what does holiness mean, and what does transgression mean? That precisely is what the laws in Torah define, laws which were constantly to be extended and developed from generation to generation, but which remain conceptually uniform as an elaboration of the term *qadosh*, holy. 'Be holy to me, as I, Yahweh, am holy. I have set you apart from all these peoples, so that you may be mine' (Lev. 20:26). The harvest of detail is contained in the seed of holiness, so that even the most bizarre instruction is justified by the necessary conditions of obedience; and that is exactly the interpretation which Rashi summarizes for the verse in Leviticus, based on Sifra:

If you separate yourselves from them, then you are mine. If not, then you will be the possession of Nebuchadnezzar and his kind [lit., 'companions']. R. Eleazar b. Azariah said:' On what basis should a man not say, with all my being I hate pig's meat, or, I have no desire to wear *kilaim* [clothes with mixed wool and linen, Lev. 19:19], but rather *should* say, I do desire it, but what shall I do? My Father in heaven has imposed all this on me. Scripture states, 'I have set you apart from all these peoples, so that you may be mine.' This means that your separating yourselves from them is for my name's sake—separating [*poresh*] oneself from sin and taking upon oneself the yoke of the kingdom of heaven.

The Hittite treaties then invoke long lists of gods to witness the treaty: '. . . the gods and the goddesses of the Hatti land, the gods and the goddesses of the Amurru land, all the olden gods, Naras, Napsaras, Minki, Tuhusi, Ammunki, Ammizadu, Allalu, Anu, Antu, Apantu, Ellil, Ninlil, the mountains, the rivers, the springs, the great sea, heaven and earth, the winds and the clouds, let these be witnesses to this treaty and to the oath.' That list represents only a brief excerpt. But anything like that was, of course, impossible in Joshua: the whole point of the treaty was to abolish recognition of other gods in favour of Yahweh. There is, therefore, a variation of great interest: 'And Joshua said to the people: You are witnesses against yourselves that you have chosen Yahweh to serve him' (v. 22).

Then the Hittite treaties conclude with a formula of curses on those who break the treaty and blessings on those who sustain it. In Joshua the curses and blessings occur earlier, in v. 19 and 20, where the people are warned of the solemnity of what they are undertaking. Finally, the Hittite treaties frequently include a formal deposition of the covenant in the vassal's sanctuary, and provision for the reading of the covenant terms if necessary. This too is reflected in Joshua:

Joshua wrote these words in the book of the law of God: and he took a great stone, and set it up there under the oak that was by the sanctuary of Yahweh. And Joshua said . . . 'This stone shall be a witness against us: for it has heard all the words of Yahweh which he spoke to us: it shall be therefore a witness against you, lest you deny your God (vv. 25 ff.).

So what is summarized in Josh. 24 is a reaffirmation on the part of the kinship group of the latent affinal bonding which has persisted, even though a part of the group has been geographically separated for some centuries in Egypt. What Josh. 24 suggests is that when those family groups returned, there was a formal reaffirmation of the bond between them and those who had remained in Canaan. There is no real reason to doubt the authenticity of that suggestion. There would be nothing particularly unusual in reaffirming fundamental obligation through some form of covenant, since the concept and practice of covenant was already deeply established in the traditions and memory of the tribes. But what was unusual—what was indeed a dramatic innovation— was the insistence of the refugees from Egypt that they had been brought back to this land and to this point in time by a god of total and irresistible, but conditional, power: there are conditions which must obtain if the continuing effect of Yahweh is to be discerned in the construction of Israel's life-way.

It is here that the covenant form proved to be so profoundly creative in Israel's life. It is structurally an almost perfect vehicle for information transmission and control. Formally, within the structure which made it what it was, it summarized the history which reinforced the worth of looking to Yahweh for effect in the present; and it summarized also the boundary conditions on which that effect depends. The covenant form could be allusively simple, feeding an immediate and direct input into the scan of any situation, or it could be extended almost indefinitely, both in its historical recital or in its specification of the conditions, as happens in the book of Deuteronomy. But whether on a small scale or a large, the effect was the same: the covenant form tied together paradigmatic accounts of theistic effect and the conditions which must obtain for the continuity of that effect to be obtained; and since the covenant form is so basically economical, it could potentially feed those inputs into the construction of thought and action with very little signal loss or distortion. It was this which unlocked the inspiration of Israel's vision in which history and behaviour become the working out of God's purpose and man's destiny.

It is much contested how early the covenant understanding of Yahweh's relation to Israel became important. Perlitt in particular has argued that the strong covenant understanding must be late (seventh century B.C.E.), since otherwise it is impossible to account for the apparent silence of the eighth-century prophets about the Sinai covenant. They certainly did not elaborate their message on the basis of an explicit appeal to the covenant. According to Perlitt, law and covenant were first linked and emphasized in Deuteronomy, which understood the promise of the land to the fathers to be conditional. On this view, Josh. 24 does not rest on an old covenant tradition preserved in Shechem, but was composed as an appeal to keep faith with Yahweh during the threat from Assyria in the seventh century. However, the argument depends to some extent on eliminating contradictory indications, on the ground that they have been added by a later editor. Thus, Hos. 8:1b is eliminated and attributed to a Deuteronomic editor. Or again, the last two chapters of Micah (6 and 7) are disintegrated and parts are regarded as late (e.g., the reference to the covenants with Abraham and Jacob in the last verse, 7:20) despite the fact, as will be seen in detail, that the two chapters as a whole reflect very closely the pattern of the Hittite covenant form.

It may, therefore, be better to take the clues of antiquity for what they appear to be—clues of antiquity—rather than designating them invariably as editorial additions, particularly since there are other indications connecting the eighth-century prophets with formal treaty ingredients. The most obvious is the adaptation of the curses of ancient Near Eastern treaties (pronounced on those who break the treaty) to the threat pronounced by the prophets against those who break the known boundary conditions of Yahweh's agreement with his people.[7] Even in general terms it is obvious that a saving history tradition is sufficiently well known for prophets, not simply to refer to it, but to engage in direct exegesis of it; and this occurs as early as Hosea (ch. 12, which included a deliberate play on the name Jacob; cf. Jer. 9:4) and as late as

Jeremiah (e.g., 4:23–8, though needless to say that is usually excised as a later addition) and Deutero-Isaiah (who juxtaposes Abraham and Cyrus). The position is thus not unlike the position of Paul, in relation to the tradition concerning the words and acts of Jesus. On the one side, Paul makes virtually no direct appeal to the tradition to reinforce his own teaching or advice, yet on the other, he apparently presupposes the tradition (as when he distinguishes between his own word and the Lord's), and occasionally refers to it, as in the case of the last supper (1 Cor. 11:23). The prophets similarly presuppose that the people know the basis on which their behaviour is being judged, without the necessity for a particular argument to establish the point—as Clements has effectively summarized:

The prophets did not regard themselves as introducing a new doctrine of God in Israel, or as teaching a new morality. On the contrary their ethical teaching appears incidentally in their condemnation of the people for unrighteous and immoral behaviour, and the prophets clearly expected their hearers to know what they were talking about.[8]

So, although it is necessary to be cautious in attaching the prophets to a specific covenant tradition (the Sinai covenant), there is no doubt that the tradition, which combines reference to Yahweh's action in the past with conditions which the people know very well must be met if that action is to continue for good, was a fundamental basis of their activity as prophets.[9] The importance of this will emerge again in I.4. It follows that the general point being made here, about the informational significance of the covenant form, does not depend on a decision being reached on the question of antiquity, although the indications of antiquity do, as a matter of fact, seem to be stronger than the counter-indications. The point remains that, at whatever stage the covenant form was articulated as a means of summarizing what was already believed to be the case (the bonded relation between Yahweh and his people), it would serve as a powerful vehicle in the transmission of that belief, and in the construction of particular actions or thoughts.

The consequence of a covenant understanding of man's relatedness to God were liberating and creative, particularly when the conditions became increasingly defined and elaborated—paradoxical though that may sound. But in fact the gradual codifying of the *huqim*, the *mizwot*, and the *mishpatim* (the 'statutes, ordin-ances, and commands') made it possible for people to know the constraints which were expected to obtain over their own be-haviour. In contrast to Cleon in the Mitylene debate, who lamented the fact that men are always 'looking for something else, so to speak, than the terms on which we live', the Jews could know exactly the terms on which their lives were to be established. And that is liberating, because (to revert to Ashby's point), 'where a constraint exists, advantage can usually be taken of it'—in other words, one is set free from anxiety—or at least one is released into a different anxiety, about the extent, perhaps, to which one is living within the boundary condition.

It is not possible to do more than hazard a broad guess at the stages by which the laws of Torah were accumulated and drawn together in their present form, though it is clear that the final form became fixed in and after the Exile, when, in effect, some Jews asked themselves how they could prevent such a catastrophe happening again. An obvious answer was to draw the boundary of Torah so unequivocally that there could be no possibility of care-less or unthinking offence in the future which might justify such punishment. New reference and authority figures were designated or reinforced (as with the scribes and priests), and Neh. 9 and 10 exemplify the formality with which the covenant became an infor-mational resource.

But although the covenant came to represent a very powerful mechanism of information transmission in the construction of Israel's life-way, it also created very acute conditions of conflict. The first and most obvious, which can be seen very clearly in the prophets, was the conflict between the conditions (now able to be known and understood) and the actual behaviour of people who were unwilling, or who failed, to accept those constraints. For example, not all the bene Jacob were prepared to give up their traditional view that there are other resources of theistic effect in addition to Yahweh: some of them continued to make offerings to the *baalim* (the heavenly proprietors, or absentee landlords, of particular pieces of land),[10] others continued to worship Chemosh or to keep a few teraphim (little idols) in the house.[11] Even at a date toward the end of the biblical period, there was a Jewish community which seems to have accepted that it was appropriate for Yahweh to have a wife.[12] At an earlier time, the Song of

Deborah (Judg. 5:8) accused the people of giving their allegiance
not simply to other gods (*elohim aheyrim*) but actually to new gods
(*elohim hedashim*).

Consequently, it is not surprising to find in the prophets, who
understood themselves to be spokesmen of Yahweh and channels
of his communication into the world, a savage denunciation of
other gods: if gods, then not Yahweh: if Yahweh, then not gods.
The classic instance of this is in the story of Elijah challenging the
prophets of Baal to demonstrate the effect of their god by leaving
it to him to kindle the wood on the altar. When the prophets fail
to induce Baal to kindle the fire, Elijah asks exactly the same questions as the crowd asked of Nietzsche's lunatic (p. 2): 'Has he
got too much to do? Or is he busy? Or has he gone on a journey?
Or perhaps he's fallen asleep and will shortly wake up.' (1 Kgs.
18:27).[13] The same challenge, focused on the issue of effect,
appears in Hos. 2:4-15:

> Israel's mother has played the whore,
> she who conceived them has disgraced herself.
> 'I am going to court my lovers' she said
> 'who give me my bread and water,
> my wool, my flax, my oil and my drink.'
> She would not acknowledge, not she,
> that I was the one who was giving her
> the corn, the wine, the oil,
> and who freely gave her the very silver and gold
> of which they have made the Baals . . .
> I mean to make her pay for all the days
> when she burnt offerings to the Baals
> and decked herself with rings and necklaces
> to court her lovers,
> forgetting me.
> It is Yahweh who is speaking.

This literal war on earth between those who regarded Israel as
dependent on Yahweh's effect alone, and those who continued to
look for theistic effect from other gods, is reflected in a metaphorical war in heaven, in a conflict between Yahweh and other
gods as he invades their domain. An instance of the same kind of
invasion has already been pointed out (p. 47) in the Ugaritic
texts, where Baal-Hadad is portrayed as invading and usurping
the functions of El. Similarly, it was essential for Yahweh to take

over the position of El if he was to become the single resource of
theistic effect and the unique object of worship and belief. The
conflict could not, in this case, be so absolute as it was with the
Baalim (as in Hos. 2), because El in various modes of relationship
was deeply established among the bene Jacob, as Ahlstrom has
emphasized.[14] Nevertheless, one can certainly see traces of the
way in which Yahweh did invade the domain of El and take over
his functions, until, of course, in the end the two are so indistinguishable that El becomes a name for what Yahweh is—
namely, God.

A few traces remain of the early stages of this process. In Deut.
32:8, for example, a much simpler relationship is envisaged, in
which the supreme God, El Elyon, divides up the nations of the
world according to the number of the lesser gods (*elohim*) and
allocates Israel to Yahweh:

> When Elyon divided out the nations,
> when he dispersed all mankind,
> he laid down the boundaries of every people
> according to the number of the sons of God;
> but Yahweh's share was his own people,
> Jacob was his allotted portion.

It is possible that Ps. 82, to which reference has already been
made (p. 49), also reflects this situation. As the text stands the
first verse reads:

> Elohim takes his stand in the council of El,
> To deliver judgement among the Elohim.

But this Psalm is in the so-called Elohistic psalter, that section of
the Psalms (42–83) in which an attempt appears to have been made
to replace the name of Yahweh by El or Elohim. Thus Pss. 14 and
53 ('The fool has said in his heart, There is no God') are identical,
but where Ps. 14 has Yahweh, Ps. 53, in the Elohistic psalter, has
Elohim. So it is probable that Yahweh was originally the subject
of the first verse in Ps. 82. That would at once make much better
sense of the whole psalm, and it would sharpen the distinction of
the opening verse. It would then read:

> Yahweh takes his stand in the Council of El,
> To deliver judgement among the *elohim* (gods).

Then follows the charge against them which has already been
quoted: if they are what they are claimed to be, *elohim*, then they

ought to be powerful on behalf of the weak and the orphans, and
they ought to be the benefactors of the destitute and downtrodden:

> You ought to rescue the weak and the poor,
> And save them from the clutches of wicked men,
> But you know nothing, you understand nothing,
> You stumble about in the dark
> While earth's foundations are giving way.

Then Yahweh pronounces sentence:

> 'This is my sentence: *elohim* you may be,
> Sons of Elyon all of you may be,
> But like Adam [or 'like men'] you will die:
> The strongest princes fall, without exception, so will you.

That brilliant psalm is one of the great classics of ironic invective,
and it is an important reminder that traces of a war in heaven
reflect much more than traces of the same struggle on earth, as
people abandoned reluctantly, if at all, the possible resourcefulness of other gods. It was a struggle: and in that struggle with the
'godness of God' (with what must be the case if God is truly to be
God where Israel is concerned) the covenant eventually proved to
be a decisive aid. If the isomorphic conditions are known and
sufficiently agreed within any projected universe of meaning or
discourse (however much the conditions may themselves be involved in the process of structural change), there can develop a far
greater confidence in what a participant within that universe
undertakes. The clearer the existing landmarks are, the more confident the traveller can be of his position, and of the next stage in
the journey, even though it be toward the unknown.

The covenant came to summarize in the construction of Israel's
life-way something approaching an isomorphic map, against which
the appropriateness or the inappropriateness of projected action
could be tested. It was this which enabled a constant series of
transformations to take place—transactions in the available conceptual grammars of Israel's environment, until a wholly new
theistic grammar was produced, a new set of rules and conventions
governing and controlling the articulation of theistic intuition
and private experience into novel ritual, textual and symbolic
outcomes, and into intelligible utterance. It is a function of a
grammar of theistic concepts that it enables the 'godness of God'

(what God must be if God is indeed to be God) to be construed, and that certainly happened in Israel's case.

When the various religious traditions of the ancient Near East developed their conceptual grammars (the rules governing the formal articulation of belief in text and ritual) they operated, in part, on materials which were available in common. Component features of ritual, mythology, institution, and personnel appear very widely. But they are transacted into different outcomes in each case. The same is true of Israel. Many of the basic materials for the construction of Israel's belief and ritual were drawn from the environment, but in their transaction into Israel's articulation of them, they were transformed into totally divergent and novel outcomes. They have the same story of a flood as the Babylonians, but it is used to make a very different theological point; they have prophets who look the same as other prophets in Canaan, but they become entirely different; they have sacral kings like those of other nations, but they develop into something unique; they have agricultural festivals like those of others, but they are soon celebrating through those festivals something more than the seasons and the fruits of the earth. As will be seen (with reference to those examples) in the next chapter, the more one identifies resemblances between Israel and the surrounding peoples, the more impressive the differences become.

There is in fact, a tremendous irony in this, because at the very time when Nietzsche was writing about the Christian creed having become incredible (p. 3), one of the standard arguments which was used to reinforce that incredibility was to point to the parallels in other religions and argue that there was nothing original in Israel or in Christianity. That observation was used to establish a kind of reductionist argument: Judaism and Christianity claim to be a consequence of God's initiative in revelation which distinguishes the truth of those religions from other religions; but everything in Judaism and Christianity can be paralleled in other religions; therefore, one must reduce these two religions to the level of all other religions, to the level of human speculation in a pre-scientific age, because they are nothing but examples of the same basic beliefs.

The irony lies in the fact that the more parallels or points of contact are found (as, for example, more evidence is unearthed), the more the reductionist argument has to be reversed. It becomes apparent that what has to be explained is not similarity, but why, from commonly available resources, differentiation occurred— why, for example, some theistic construction moved toward extinction, as Mencken observed, and why some (at least two from the Semitic world, the Jewish and the Zoroastrian) did not.

If, then, we wish to understand the Jewish sense of God, we need to focus our attention on the question of how and why those remarkable transformations took place when the Israelites transacted the materials available in their environment into a totally novel outcome. To do this extensively would require an entire book on its own. But the point can be illustrated by taking three examples, the emergence of the prophets of Israel, the introduction of kingship, and the transformation of festivals—examples which one might summarize as 'prophets, priests, and kings'; even then, they cannot be discussed in detail, but they can at least illustrate the importance of what happened.

4. PROPHETS, PRIESTS, AND KINGS: THE TRANSFORMATION

IT has been argued so far that the specific sense of being related to a particular God, who has demonstrated his effect (in much more than simply the Exodus) and who has made known the conditions for the continuity of that effect for good, fed into the bene Jacob a simple but powerful constraint in the construction of their lifeway. When that sense of relatedness was articulated in the various forms of covenant, the informational strength of the signals from that resource was magnified greatly. The consequence of regarding Yahweh as the only significant resource of theistic effect (whose nature and demand are known) can be seen in the transformation which took place as Israel transacted materials which were commonly available in the environment into the articulation of their own belief.

An example of this can be seen in the transformation of the prophets. In the Canaanite environment, prophets were a part of the cultic apparatus through which a connection between unseen realities (gods and spirits) and men was established. They were a part of the opportunity which cult and ritual provided in several different ways of securing additional help in coping with the unknown or with a particular problem. Thus prophets might be consulted about the future, or they might be hired to control an event in the future by, for example, cursing an enemy. The prophets were designated as prophets by the fact that they were visibly possessed by a spirit or god: they went into seized or ecstatic states, in which the pressure of what they believed were god-given words within them was irresistible: 'The lion has roared, who can but tremble? God has spoken, who can but prophesy?' (Amos 3:8). Jeremiah called it a fire burning in his bones, and he also begged that Yahweh would leave him alone and not compel him to be a prophet (Jer. 20:7 ff.).

Although the evidence for prophets in the ancient Near East is not particularly extensive, Scripture alone makes it clear that they were not uncommon in Canaan. There is a good description of the prophetic bands and of the ecstatic state which they manifested and sometimes induced through rhythm and chant in the accounts of a saying which became proverbial, 'Is Saul also among the prophets?' The question had to be asked, because Saul was infected and fell into a similar trance. Samuel instructed Saul to go to Gibeah: 'As you come to the town you will meet a group of prophets coming down from the high place, headed by harp, tambourine, flute and lyre; they will be in ecstasy. Then the spirit of Yahweh will seize on you, and you will go into ecstasy with them, and be changed into another man' (1 Sam. 10:5 f.). Saul obeyed the command: 'From there they came to Gibeah, and there was a group of prophets coming to meet him [Saul]; the spirit of God seized on him and he fell into ecstasy in their midst. When all who knew him previously saw him prophesying with the prophets, the people said to each other, "What has happened to the son of Kish? Is Saul also among the prophets?"' (1 Sam. 10:10–12). The second account also describes an ecstatic appearance:

Saul went on from there to the huts of Ramah and the spirit of God came on him too, and he went on his way in an ecstasy until he came to the huts at Ramah. He too stripped off his clothes and he too fell into an ecstasy in the presence of Samuel, and falling down lay there naked all that day and night. Hence the saying, Is Saul also among the prophets? (1 Sam. 19:23 f.).

The fact that the question ('Is Saul also among the prophets?') was evoked emphasizes how clearly the prophets were marked off *as* prophets: there were unmistakable signs, in ecstasy, which were surprising if they were observed in somebody outside the obvious category. The prophets were often organized in bands, and precisely because they were so clearly designated as being possessed, or in-filled, by a god, they were well worth consulting. But consulting about what? Certainly about the future, one of the most intransigent of limitations on the construction of a human life-way. So, for example, in the story of Micaiah ben Imlah, the two kings wish to know the outcome of their battle against the Syrians, and it is to the prophets that they turn (in an episode which is of great importance in understanding the emergence of Israel's prophets):

He [the king of Israel] said to Jehoshaphat, 'Will you join me in attacking Ramoth-gilead?' Jehoshaphat said to the king of Israel, 'What is mine is yours: myself, my people, and my horses.' Then

Jehoshaphat said to the king of Israel, 'First, let us seek counsel from the Lord.' The king of Israel assembled the prophets, some four hundred of them, and asked them, 'Shall I attack Ramoth-gilead or shall I refrain?' 'Attack,' they answered; 'the Lord shall deliver it into your hands.' Jehoshaphat asked, 'Is there no other prophet of the Lord here through whom we may seek guidance?' 'There is one more,' the king of Israel answered, 'through whom we may seek guidance of the Lord, but I hate the man, because he prophesies no good for me; never anything but evil. His name is Micaiah son of Imlah.' Jehoshaphat exclaimed, 'My lord king, let no such word pass your lips!' So the king of Israel called one of his eunuchs and told him to fetch Micaiah son of Imlah with all speed. The king of Israel and Jehoshaphat king of Judah were seated on their thrones, in shining armour, at the entrance to the gate of Samaria, and all the prophets were prophesying before them. One of them, Zedekiah son of Kenaanah, made himself horns of iron and said, 'This is the word of the Lord: "With horns like these you shall gore the Arameaeans and make an end of them." ' In the same vein all the prophets prophesied, 'Attack Ramoth-gilead and win the day; the Lord will deliver it into your hands.' The messenger sent to fetch Micaiah told him that the prophets had with one voice given to the king a favourable answer. 'And mind you agree with them,' he added. 'As the Lord lives,' said Micaiah, 'I will say only what the Lord tells me to say.' When Micaiah came into the king's presence, the king said to him, 'Micaiah, shall we attack Ramoth-gilead or shall we refrain?' 'Attack and win the day,' he said, 'the Lord will deliver it into your hands.' 'How often must I adjure you,' said the king, 'to tell me nothing but the truth in the name of the Lord?' Then Micaiah said, 'I saw all Israel scattered on the mountains, like sheep, without a shepherd; and I heard the Lord say, "They have no master, let them go home in peace." ' The king of Israel said to Jehoshaphat, 'Did I not tell you that he never prophesies good for me, nothing but evil?' Micaiah went on, 'Listen now to the word of the Lord. I saw the Lord seated on his throne, with all the host of heaven in attendance on his right and on his left. The Lord said, "Who will entice Ahab to attack and fall on Ramoth-gilead?" One said one thing and one said another; then a spirit came forward and stood before the Lord and said, "I will entice him." "How?" said the Lord. "I will go out", he said, "and be a lying spirit in the mouth of all prophets." "You shall entice him", said the Lord, "and you shall succeed; go and do it." You see, then, how the Lord has put a lying spirit in the mouth of all these prophets of yours, because he has decreed disaster for you.' Then Zedekiah son of Kenaanah came up to Micaiah and struck him in the face: 'And how did the spirit of the Lord pass from me to speak to you?' he said. Micaiah answered,

'That you will find out on the day you run into an inner room to hide
yourself.' Then the king of Israel ordered Micaiah to be arrested and
committed to the custody of Amon the governor of the city and Joash
the king's son. 'Lock this fellow up', he said, 'and give him a prison diet
of bread and water until I come home in safety.' Micaiah retorted, 'If
you do return in safety the Lord has not spoken by me' (1 Kings 22: 4–
28).

But it is not only the unknowness of the future that the prophets can help to penetrate. They can resolve more immediate
problems. When Saul was sent out to find the lost asses of his
father, it was to a prophet that he turned for help. It was this
incident which evoked the illuminating comment, 'Formerly in
Israel when a man used to go to consult God he would cry "Come,
let us go to the seer" [the *roeh*, literally, the one who sees], for a
man who is now called a "prophet" was formerly called a "seer" '
(1 Sam. 9:9).

So when anyone consulted a prophet of this kind, he was in fact
consulting God, because the god had manifestly taken possession
of the prophet. The state of seized possession is precisely why a
number of taunts in Scripture say that the prophets look like
drunken men, and frequently talk like them as well. A dramatic
example occurs in Isa. 28:7 ff.:

> They are reeling with wine,
> staggering from strong drink.
> Priest and prophet are reeling
> from strong drink,
> they are muddled with wine;
> strong drink makes them stagger,
> they totter when they are having visions,
> they stumble when they are giving judgement.
> Yes, all the tables are covered with vomit,
> not a place left clean.
> Who does he think he is lecturing?
> Who does he think his message is for?
> Babies just weaned?
> Babies just taken from the breast?
> With his
> *sav lasav, sav lasav,*
> *kav lakav, kav lakav,*
> *zeer sham, zeer sham.*

Attempts used to be made to translate those last lines, as, for

example, 'Precept upon precept, precept upon precept; line upon
line, line upon line, here a little, there a little.' But the attempts
were mistaken. The lines were meant to represent, not sense, but
nonsense. They imitate the gurgles of infants or the gibberish of
drunken men; and that is all the worth which, in Isaiah's view, the
ecstatic 'speaking in tongues' of the cultic prophets has.

Since the prophets now referred to as canonical are linked to
this context and background, it has long been argued that many of
the oracles in the Prophetic Books (and some of the Psalms as well)
were in origin cultic oracles. Equally it has been suggested that
some of the canonical prophets were themselves cultic prophets.
But the argument at once creates a problem. Let us assume that all
the arguments which connect the so-called canonical prophets with
the cult are sound—the argument, for example, that several prophets have visions of God in a temple (not just the famous vision
of Isaiah, in Isa. 6; even Amos (9:1 ff.), one of the earliest of the
prophets whose oracles were preserved under his own name, had
a vision of God standing beside the altar); or the argument that
Jeremiah (1:1) and Ezekiel (1:3) came from priestly families; or
that the Book of Lamentations, traditionally associated with Jeremiah, was brought together for a cultic festival of remembrance
(an argument which to Eissfeldt was 'certainly' the case[1]); or the
argument that the prophecy of Joel may have been delivered
during a cultic ceremony,[2] and that Nahum and Habakkuk could
have been written in a liturgical form.[3] Those are simply examples
of the kinds of argument which are advanced (and they range,
obviously, from matters of speculation to matters of fact, so far as
fact can be disentangled in sources of so fragmentary a nature).
Let us accept, for the moment, that they do establish some sort of
continuing connection between the later-called canonical prophets
and the cult; and let us also accept that the later-called canonical
prophets have developed from the cultic prophets. But then it
immediately becomes a question, how and why did some prophets
develop out of that background to such an extent that oracles
attributed to them could be preserved and eventually become
canonical? And even more to the point (since it may well be the
case that in the Psalms and the Prophetic Books oracles have been
preserved from otherwise unknown cultic prophets, so the distinction would not be so absolute), how did it come about that in
the oracles in the Prophetic Books there is a fierce and often angry

rejection of those 'other' prophets, those cultic prophets, those 'prophets over there', those prophets summarily described as false?[4]

The distinction occurs, not as a matter of later observation, but within the prophetic material itself. How and why did that distinction occur? What governed the transaction from the generality of prophets to the distinctive prophets whose oracles became canonical? An obvious suggestion might be that it depended on the different gods for whom the prophets claimed to speak. That was clearly the issue between Elijah and the four hundred prophets of Baal (p. 72). But it was not the issue between the later-called canonical prophets and the other prophets whom they denounced, because *all* those prophets claimed to be spokesmen of Yahweh. So it is not the god who compels a distinction among them. Nor is it the appearance. In outward appearance and in the kind of actions they undertook, they were indistinguishable. They all *looked* like prophets, they all claimed to be vehicles of Yahweh's word, and they all performed the prophetic actions, which constrained the future.[5] So what compelled a distinction between them?

Another rudimentary test occurs in the same story of Elijah. The true prophet—the prophet who is true in his claim to be the spokesman of Yahweh—is the one whose words in the name of Yahweh take effect. That solution to the problem of the true and the false is very clear in the story of Micaiah ben Imlah (quoted on pp. 78 ff.). All the prophets are accepted as being prophets of Yahweh. But Micaiah—and he only under pressure—delivered a prediction completely opposed to that of his fellow-prophets. Who was right? They looked the same, they spoke in the same way, and in the name of the same god. It was Micaiah who expressed the rudimentary test of consequence and effect: 'If you come back safe and sound, Yahweh has not spoken through me.'

But that test really makes the prophets superfluous: if no one can ever know which of two conflicting prophets is true (when in form and appearance they are identical) until the event occurs or does not occur, he might just as well not consult them. He is no better off having done so. Even worse, one would have to conclude (as the story does conclude) that since the prophets who are subsequently defined by outcome as false look and sound the same as the true prophets, and since they claim to be inspired by the same god, they must indeed have *been* inspired by the same god, but by a lying spirit sent from him.

So the story of Micaiah is not really a solution; it is a graphic articulation of the problem. However, this story does in fact come to the very edge of what *did* cause the distinction between the Prophets and the prophets, that is, between the true and the false. This dramatic shift is summarized in two passages in Deuteronomy, which comment on the issue of who is the true or the false prophet. The first is in ch. 18:20 ff.: 'The prophet who presumes to say in my name a thing I have not commanded him to say, or who speaks in the name of other gods, that prophet shall die. [But] you may say in your heart, "How are we to know what word was not spoken by Yahweh?" When a prophet speaks in the name of Yahweh and the thing does not happen and the word is not fulfilled, then, it has not been spoken by Yahweh.' That is the simple and rudimentary test of Micaiah. But in the other passage, in Deut. 13:2–6, one can observe the profound structural shift which created the prophets of Israel: 'If a prophet or a dreamer of dreams arises among you and offers to do a sign or a wonder for you, and the sign or wonder comes about . . .' (at which point the Micaiah test would say, 'That prophet is a true prophet of Yahweh'; but Deuteronomy in contrast goes on) 'and if he then says to you, "Come, then, let us follow other gods (whom you have not known) and serve them", you are not to listen to the words of that prophet or to the dreams of that dreamer. Yahweh your God is testing you to know if you love Yahweh your God.'

Here, in miniature, is the all-important shift, from the form to the content of the message. Even if the prophet authenticates himself in the formally appropriate ways, he can still be determined as false if he says anything which destroys the boundary conditions within which Israel must live if Yahweh is to be Yahweh for them. And Deuteronomy is very specific on the point as it goes on:

Yahweh your God you shall follow, him you shall fear, his commandments you shall keep, his voice you shall obey, him shall you serve, to him shall you cling. That prophet or that dreamer of dreams must be put to death, for he has preached apostasy from Yahweh your God who brought you out of the land of Egypt and redeemed you from the house of slavery, and he would have made you turn aside from the way that Yahweh your God marked out for you.

The prophet is now designated by the extent to which his word can be matched to the paradigmatic recital of God's effect and to the conditions which have been established for its continuity, the way that Yahweh has marked out. Exactly the same appears in another Deuteronomic passage, Judg. 6:7–10:

When the Israelites cried to Yahweh because of Midian, Yahweh sent a prophet to the Israelites. This was his message: Thus Yahweh speaks, the God of Israel: 'It was I who brought you out of Egypt and led you out of a house of slavery. I rescued you from the power of the Egyptians and the power of all who oppressed you. I drove them out before you and gave you their land, and I said to you: I am Yahweh, your God. Do not reverence the gods of the Amorites in whose land you now live. But you have not listened to my words.'

It is Yahweh himself who has marked out the way and who has thus established the boundary conditions within which Israel must construct its route through life and time. The boundaries are specifically marked in terms of command. What became the determining issue among the prophets in Israel was not the *form* of a prophet's appearance or message (because those remained largely indistinguishable) but the extent to which that message or word was controlled into its outcome by the degree of its match or mismatch to the informational resource of Israel's past. That past was not a generalized memory: it was a specific articulation of Yahweh's effect in word and event, which eventually came to be summarized formally in the covenant.

So the prophets emerged from a general background of visionary and ecstatic figures, and they remained exactly the same, at least to some extent. But they became also very different indeed because they conceived their function as spokesmen of Yahweh to be spokesmen of *Yahweh*! In other words their message (what they believed Yahweh was giving them to speak) was controlled by what Yahweh was known to have been and to have demanded in the past and they then applied that to what they saw around them in the behaviour of individuals, or of society, or of the nation. Their authenticity came to be determined by the degree of match or mismatch between their particular words and what was known of the effect of Yahweh in word and action; and the authenticity (or the value, almost) of the behaviour of the people was constantly scanned by the prophets and tested for a similar degree of match or mismatch.

'Son of man,' says God to Ezekiel (3:17), 'I have made you a *zopheh* for the house of Israel', a watchman, one who watches out like a sentry for the defence and early warning of Israel. One can find a similar idea running back through Jeremiah to Hosea.[6]

The argument has sometimes been pressed further, and the prophets have been regarded as watchmen of the covenant with Yahweh, not simply in a general way, but perhaps in very specific terms as well. It has long been argued that some of the oracles in the Prophetic Books were originally delivered at an annual ceremony in which the people renewed the covenant, and in which the prophets played a vital part in pronouncing God's judgement on the way in which the people have (or have not) been keeping the conditions. Like almost everything in the Scriptural period, that particular suggestion is disputed. While there are certainly descriptions of ceremonies of covenant renewal on particular occasions, from Josh. 24 to Neh. 9 and 10, there is no specific description of an annual covenant renewal ceremony. Reference has already been made (p. 69) to the problem of determining at what time the covenant became formally important. But whether there was such a ceremony or not, it is certainly the case that the Prophetic Books frequently presuppose the covenant background, and occasionally reflect its formal structure.

The concluding two chapters of Micah are a clear example. The context is a formal judgement on Israel's behaviour (6:1–3). Exactly like the covenant in Josh. 24, it begins with a summary of Yahweh's known effect. As the text stands, the summary has been over-summarized: when the account reaches Balaam and Balak in 6:5, it breaks off and leaps on to a conclusion which cannot be attached grammatically. One can almost imagine a scribe on a fine day, at some stage in the transmission, thinking that the story was well enough known and putting '. . .'. After the historical recital, exactly as in the Hittite covenant form, there is a reference in summary form to the known boundary conditions within which Israel must live. It is certainly not human sacrifice ('Shall I give the fruit of my body for the sin of my soul?'). That is an unmatched innovation, and Micah bursts out, almost angrily: 'He has shown you, O man, what is good; and what does Yahweh require of you, but to act justly, and to love mercy, and to walk humbly with your God?' (v. 8).

Justice (*mishpat*) is not vague: it is mapped in detail in the informational resources which are known and available to all. So after the basic stipulation of the covenant agreement, attention is turned to the detailed terms which the prophet accuses the people of breaking (vv. 9 ff.). It is in relation to the known demand that the behaviour of the people is assessed, and their failure is summarized by saying that they have constructed their lives, not within the boundaries set by the law of Yahweh, but within those set by the laws of Omri, not with reference to the customs of the fathers, but with reference to the customs of the house of Ahab (v. 16). They have, therefore, in terms of the covenant, constructed a life-way which leads to the effect of Yahweh in curse and not in blessing; and the curse in 6:15 exactly reverses the blessing of Josh. 24:13. There it was a gift of a land for which they did no work, towns which they did nothing to build, vineyards and olive-groves which they did not plant. But in Micah this is exactly reversed. They will do all the work, but get nothing for it: 'You will sow, but never reap, press the olive but never rub yourself with oil, press the grape but never drink wine from it.'

And so in 7:1–6 the judgement and the curse are accepted and described. It is, in summary, the disintegration of Israel. But then this is counterbalanced by a description of the blessing which can still obtain for these who look to Yahweh and put their trust in him. It used to be said, in critical scholarship, that the verses promising a blessing must be a later addition: surely no one would utter a curse and then take it away by immediately promising a blessing.[7]

But in fact it is obvious that in the context of a covenant understanding as an informational resource, the promise *must* accompany the judgement. The articulation of consequence in the construction of Israel's life-way must be the articulation of consequence in both directions, for blessing and for curse, and the issue depends on the extent to which Israel constructs its life-way within the boundary conditions which the covenant summarizes. It is, therefore, entirely appropriate that these two chapters in Micah should end with a specific reference to the promise which God made to Abraham and Jacob.

The prophets are thus an example of how the transmission of information from a designated resource can occur in practice. But they are also a consequence of the same process: that is to say, they were constrained away from the generality of prophets in Canaan (and initially in Israel) into a novel outcome as a consequence of the constraint imposed by the designated and accepted resource—the tradition, as far as it had been developed at any particular point in time. And since the fundamental resource, even behind the tradition, was believed to be Yahweh, the prophets were led into a constant succession of attempts to extend the conceptual implications of Yahweh's known effect. In lurching, visionary, and sometimes unbelievably paradoxical ways, they constantly extended their understanding of the range of Yahweh's possible effect, until in the end prophecy passed away into apocalyptic—into visions of what will finally be the case when Yahweh exercises his authority over the whole cosmos.

It is the quintessence of the prophetic achievement that they put constant pressure on the obtaining sense of God's effect and extended the conceptualized range of that effect, until eventually they could enunciate visions of Yahweh's effect being discernible everywhere: visions, not of Yahweh's effect in Israel alone, but of all men joining the Jews in acknowledging that there is no other resource of theistic effect but Yahweh alone; the day, in other words, when ten men out of each of the nations of the world will catch hold of a Jew by the sleeve, and say, 'We will go with you; for we have heard that God is with you' (Zech. 8:23).

Inevitably, they came to regard all things, every aspect of time and space, as the work and creation of his hands. By them the possibility was established of shifting the serial occurrences of life into a new and totally different perspective of interpretation: annals (year by year accounts) became history. Even more to the point, they found it possible to read, not only their own traditions or their own history, but also the whole universe as a book written by the hand of God.

> The heavens are telling the glory of God,
> The vault of heaven proclaims his work;
> Day tells of it to day
> Night to night hands on the knowledge.
> No utterance at all, no speech,
> No sound that anyone can hear;
> Yet their voice goes out through all the earth,
> and their message to the ends of the world.[8]

Of course that requires a special way of seeing: the bush-fire which Moses saw burning in a thorn (Exod. 3:2) is not necessarily (is not unequivocally) eloquent of God. The language through which the possibilities of theistic meaning arise (or even more

openly, the possibilities of varied interpretation in human consciousness) are mediated through the cues of interpretation which
arise in the universe, but few of these are plain or unequivocal.
'That language', as de Caussade put it,

is a cypher in which nothing is apparent but confusion; it is a thorn-
bush from which no one could imagine God speaking. But faith makes
us see, as in the case of Moses, the fire of divine charity burning in the
midst of the thorns; faith offers a key to the cypher and enables us to
discover in that confusion the possibilities of another kind of wisdom.
Faith gives a face as of heaven to the whole earth, and by it our hearts
are seized and transported to converse with God.[9]

That we can venture to see at all in that way owes much to the
prophets of Israel. But they are not the only example of the way in
which familiar and commonly available material was transacted in
Israel into a novel outcome. It can be seen also in many of the
festivals, where the original elements can often be discerned, but so
also can the totally new significance which has been developed
later. Of this, Passover is perhaps the clearest example. The feast
of Passover and Unleavened Bread became a celebration of the
escape from Egypt and from the plagues which overwhelmed the
Egyptians. Yet in origin it was a plain agricultural festival—indeed,
the two parts (Passover and Unleavened Bread) seem in origin to
have been two separate festivals: the Passover was a shepherd's
ritual to ward off destruction from the flocks, and Unleavened
Bread was a festival for a more settled agricultural community, an
act of trust in God to secure a new harvest in the ensuing year.
Passover was originally a home ritual, celebrated wherever the
flocks happened to be, but Unleavened Bread was celebrated
centrally, where the whole settled community could attend. It
was only much later that the two were fused together and made
into a celebration of Yahweh's saving effect in the Exodus which
had taken place (or was believed to have taken place) at that time.

But the transformation of feasts did not simply take place in the
early days. Long after the Exile, the Book of Esther was written
primarily to legitimize the festival of Purim. The origins of Purim
are obscure, but there is little doubt that it originated in the
Eastern diaspora of the Jews, and that it was taken over by them
from a Persian festival; Ringgren's guess may well be right, that it
was taken over from a Persian New Year Festival.[10]

The adaptation of concepts more widely diffused in the Near East can be seen equally well in the transformation of kingship. The early bene Jacob were not ruled by kings. They gave their allegiance to more local and less extravagant forms of authority. However, in a crisis they gave their allegiance to whatever man or woman seemed best able to meet the crisis. That is exactly the situation described in the Book of Judges. After the crisis the emergency leadership subsided. There was no permanent leadership of that sort, over-arching all the tribes in the kinship group, unless the crisis (or the opportunity of booty or conquest) persisted. At the end of the crisis the tribes simply withdrew their allegiance and returned to their more local forms of communal authority and administration.

Exactly the same pattern appears in the Arab tribes at the time of Muhammad. They gave him their allegiance (or were constrained into it by conquest) until he died. When he did so, many simply withdrew and went back to their customary way of life. However, Muhammad had had a vision of all men united under God as the single family of one father. It was a vision of a tribe transcending the tribal divisions of men. Consequently, the first events of Islamic history after the death of Muhammad were the wars of the Riddah, the campaigns in which Abu Bakr went out to bring the tribes back into a permanent condition of allegiance. The word 'riddah' means apostasy, yet in fact it is obvious that the tribes in question were not 'apostatizing'. They were simply following their time-honoured custom of returning home when the party was over.

Much the same tension appeared at the time of Saul and David. Saul emerged as a leader in the crises posed by the Ammonites and even more by the Philistines. In fact, one can say that under Saul the crises were permanent, so that correspondingly his own leadership seemed as permanent as that of a king. There is no doubt that Saul and some others pushed in that direction, much as other attempts had been made to establish kingship in the period of the Judges (Judg. 9).

The tension for Saul was that while he wanted his son to succeed, the tribal method of recognizing leadership in a crisis discerned in David a better man for the job. David, of course, did become the leader; and it was David who captured Jerusalem, that awkward wedge dividing the northern settlements from the southern;

and it was David also who converted his authority into a deliberate
form of kingship.

So here with David we have a clear example of innovation. But
we have also a spectacular example of conservative constraint.
When David captured Jerusalem, he instituted a form of kingship
through which he hoped to hold together the people who for the
first time were working and fighting together, and were achieving
great success. There is little doubt that he based this novel
institution on the sacral kingship which he found in Jerusalem,
'after the order of Melchizedek', as Ps. 110 puts it. The outrage
was considerable, particularly on the part of those who were conservative of the tradition of Yahweh's saving effect. They had
done very well without kings so far: why introduce them now?
Equally disastrous, from the same point of view, was David's
determination to build a temple for Yahweh in Jerusalem, another
unmatched innovation. Nathan the prophet, therefore, in the
name of Yahweh protested: ' "Are you [David] the man to build
me a house to dwell in? I have never stayed in a house from the
day I brought the Israelites out of Egypt until today, but have
always led a wanderer's life in a tent" ' (2 Sam. 7:5 f.).

However, to the same prophet are attributed the words which
legitimized David's innovations, by saying that they are in fact a
continuation of the long sequence of covenants which God has
made with the fathers and is now making with David: 'Your House
and your sovereignty will always stand secure before me and your
throne be established for ever' (2 Sam. 7:16). In a similar way, it
was carefully pointed out in the narrative now standing in Gen.
14 that, however much Abraham may have had to fight against
pagan kings, and however emphatically he dissociated himself
from the king of Sodom (vv. 21 f.), he received gifts from Melchizedek and offered tribute to him. The inference is obvious: no
general principle of assimilation or recognition of pagan gods is
implied in David's adaptation of Jerusalem customs and institutions, but at the same time some innovation has always been
possible: what was good enough for Abraham should be good
enough for his descendants.

Even so, the innovation was too much for the northern tribes.
Although they continued to give their allegiance to David's
successor, Solomon, they refused to do so to Solomon's son
Rehoboam:

What share have we in David?
We have no inheritance in the son of Jesse.
To your tents, Israel!
Henceforth look after your own house, David! (1 Kgs. 12:16).

Yet even the north had seen the enormous advantage of a single continuous leadership which brought the tribes into concerted action, and they introduced their own form of kingship in the north. What they were not prepared to do was give their allegiance for ever to the house of David. They therefore followed tribal precedent and simply withdrew. The south wrote this up as a great apostasy, exactly as the Muslims described the campaigns against the Arab tribes, who had done the same at the death of Muhammad, as the wars against apostasy. In fact, in neither case is the word appropriate. Nevertheless, the withdrawal of the northern tribes meant that David's brief but brilliant experiment was over—the experiment in which he had tried to draw the *whole* kinship group together by giving them a new and neutral centre (Jerusalem had not been captured by any of the tribes) and by giving them a new form of leadership which would transcend any ancient rivalries.[11]

What, then, was the kingship which David introduced? All over the Near East there were forms of kingship which differed greatly from each other but which had one feature in common: they all linked the king closely to the gods. The way in which this was done differed from nation to nation: in Egypt the king was an incarnation of the gods, in Mesopotamia the king represented the god on earth, particularly in playing the part of the god in the New Year Festival, in which the death and new life of the seasons was acted out. There are many indications that the ideation of the Davidic kingship was drawn from this background. Indeed, it is commonly argued that a New Year Festival was developed on the foundation of the existing festival, Sukkot (Booths or Tabernacles), which occurred at that time of year, and that the king played an important part in the ceremonial. This would certainly accord well with the central importance of the king in the Psalms, which, from this point of view, are appropriately connected with David.[12] The counter-argument that the New Year character of the feast (with an emphasis on the return of rain and new life to the earth) does not appear in descriptions of Sukkot in Torah, is not convincing, partly because those descriptions were finally

edited at a time when the Jews believed that the kings had led
them into such dire error that they had been punished by exile in
Babylon, but much more because even as late as the time of
Alexander, the actual ceremonial at Sukkot was following, not the
text, but the tradition; and the traditional celebration included
a rain-making ceremony: when the Hasmonaean high priest
Alexander decided to follow the advice of the biblical literalists,
the Sadducees, he decided to cut out the water libation, because
there was no description of it in Torah. But the people knew perfectly well how the feast had been celebrated since time almost
literally immemorial, and they pelted him with *ethrogim* (citrus
fruit which were used in the ceremonies) until he restored the
customary way of doing things. So an attempt had clearly been
made to eliminate New Year elements from the biblical text, but
the people had a more tenacious memory and insisted on the
traditional celebration—no doubt because they believed that the
fertility of their crops was involved.[13]

There is really little doubt that the kings in Judah *were* closely
linked to God, and that this accounts for the close association of
the two in the Psalms—indeed, the most natural interpretation of
Ps. 45:6 (in conjunction with v. 7) is that the king is actually on
that occasion (a royal wedding) addressed as God.[14] But how
close was the link to God? Did the king, for example, play the part
of God on some ceremonial occasions, so that he was regarded as
representing God on earth? It is here that one can see the difference
in the Davidic kingship: Davidic kingship did not escape the controls established over the repertory of possible outcomes by the
informational resource (the Yahweh tradition) in the past. Specific
attempts were made to establish the match between David's
projected innovation and that resource, as has been pointed out
already. Even so, individual kings could not escape the constant
scan of their condition which was maintained by precisely those
who were coming to believe themselves to be the guardians and
transmitters of that tradition—namely, the prophets. It was always
possible for prophets to challenge the kings and to prevent any
tendency to autonomy based on an appeal to the divinization of
the king—and this challenge was possible in both north and south:
Nathan, ending his story to David of the rich man and the poor
man's lamb, 'You are the man' (2 Sam. 12:7); Elijah confronting
Ahab, and Ahab who thought there was no check on his career,

crying out, 'Have you found me, O my enemy?' (1 Kgs. 21:20);
Micaiah ben Imlah, of whom king Jehoshaphat said, 'I hate him,
for he does not prophesy good concerning me, but evil' (1 Kgs.
22:8).

So there is an apparent paradox in the status of the king: on the
one hand, there is the extravagant language applied to him, connecting him closely to God:

> Give the king your judgements, O God,
> and your righteousness to the king's son.
> He shall judge your people with righteousness,
> and your poor with judgement. . . .
> He shall come down like rain upon the mown grass,
> as showers that water the earth. . . .
> His name shall endure for ever:
> his name shall be continued as long as the sun,
> and men shall be blessed in him:
> all nations shall call him blessed (Ps. 72:1 f., 6, 17).

On the other hand, there is constant and stark criticism of the
king, based on the extent of the degree of match or mismatch
between his conduct and the resource of Israel's constraint. What
has happened is that the institution of kingship has been constrained into a novel outcome, an outcome which A. R. Johnson
once summarized by saying that whereas in the civilizations
around them the king was usually regarded as representing God
before the people, in Israel he was regarded as representing the
people before God. 'Hear, O Israel, Yahweh our God, Yahweh is
one.' Too close an association of a human figure with God would
diminish or compromise that absolute insistence. But at the same
time the king could be regarded as one of the ways in which the
effect of Yahweh can be mediated into the world, and he could
certainly be regarded as summarizing in his own person the hopes
and well-being of the people—and also their sins, hence the formula, 'Such-and-such a king did evil in the sight of Yahweh and
caused Israel to sin.'

The focus of the people's well-being in the king can be seen in
the so-called messianic oracles of the pre-exilic period:

> The people that walked in darkness
> have seen a great light.
> They that dwell in the land of the shadow of death,
> upon them has the light shined (Isa. 9:2).

Why has this happened?

> Because unto us a child is born,
> unto us a son is given,
> and the government shall be upon his shoulder (9:6a).

An actual royal child has been born in the palace, and the continuity of succession has been secured; and with the succession, the prosperity of the people has also been secured, because of the mediation of theistic effect through him. The divine protocols are therefore recited of the new-born infant with enthusiasm:

His name shall be called Wonderful, Counsellor, The Mighty God, The Everlasting Father, The Prince of Peace. Of the increase of his government and peace there shall be no end, upon the throne of David, and upon his kingdom, to order it, and to establish it with judgement and with justice from henceforth even for ever. The zeal of Yahweh Sabaoth will perform this (9:6b–7).

In the strictest sense, these are certainly messianic oracles, in the sense that they have to do with *haMashiach*, the anointed one, the messiah. But they are not messianic in the later futuristic sense, of looking for a final coming figure in the future. Before the Exile, such oracles are concentrating on actual royal figures. But gradually it became obvious that the kings were betraying the high hopes invested in them, and the Exile confirmed that adverse judgement. Already by the time of Jeremiah, at the very beginning of the Exile, one can observe a further transformation taking place in Judah's idea of kingship. In Jer. 23:5 f. there is an oracle focused on Zedekiah (Yahweh my righteousness), which claims that a king will be born who will actually live up to that name; in 33:15 f. the hopes invested in the king have been so destroyed by the events leading up to the Exile that the title has been transferred, not to a person, but to the city of Jerusalem.

But the hopes concentrated on a messiah (an anointed king) could not be wholly destroyed by the Exile, without implying that Yahweh had changed his mind, or that his promises and his covenant with David were vacuous. A brief attempt was made after the Exile to revive messianic hope in an actual king (as in Haggai and Zechariah), but the Exile had really destroyed such faith in realized messianism. For that reason, messianic hopes began to be transferred to a future figure, one in whom the covenant promises to David and his house would be fulfilled.

Even so, that was only *one* way in which transformation occurred in the concept of a messiah. It was still possible to revert to a realized messianism, as the Hasmonaeans attempted, and others developed a view that the priestly anointed figure (priestly 'messiah') was equally important. But the central point remains the same: the conceptual materials available in the environment (or more particularly in Jerusalem) were transacted in Israel into a totally novel outcome (a concept of kingship entirely different from any in the environment despite the many points of connection and similarity), which led eventually to the idea of the Messiah.

Such transactions, if they are to endure and develop consistently through time, require strong transformational constraints in the information system in question, since otherwise they become arbitrary and rapidly lose connection with their point of departure. There is no necessary harm in that, as the innovation and experiment of contemporary art and music show (though it runs the risk of becoming unintelligible, because of the absence of cues of understanding derived from a stable tradition): it is simply a different way of proceeding through time. But Israel did not proceed in that disjunctive way. Instead, the transformations of available material were controlled in a bounded system with a designated resource of fundamental information. As and when the covenant understanding of their relatedness to God came to be formulated, they possessed a very powerful mechanism of informational transmission and control: the formality of the system was enhanced.

This did not lead, as is often assumed at the present time, into an arid subservience to tradition. Creativity can be inspired and liberated within bounded systems, as the achievements of religious cultures make clear. But the covenant understanding of relatedness to God contained within itself a major problem—a problem which threatened a real crisis in the Jewish sense of God. It was this crisis which reduced Job to silence, and which evoked from Jesus an entirely new response. And since Christianity, although it started as a part of Judaism, spread most rapidly in the Hellenistic world, it is important to understand the way in which the Hellenistic world had come into a similar crisis in its own senses of God. The Greek 'death of God' was very unlike the Jewish, because obviously the senses of God in each case were very different. But because both crises were focused on the issue of theistic effect, and because Jesus was believed to have offered a new solution to that problem, Christianity was able to meet the Hellenistic form of the problem although it had originally been addressed to the Jewish. For this reason, Christianity could take root without strain or distortion in Hellenistic soil. But to understand this, it is necessary first to look briefly at what the problem was.

5. THE DEATH OF GOD IN THE GREEK AND JEWISH WORLDS

According to Jose b. Joezer, those who wish to imbibe wisdom should begin by sitting in the dust at the feet of the Hakamim, and by drinking in their words with thirst.[1] Let us therefore join two young boys as they do this, a little before the year 300 of the Christian era. The boys in question are Abaye and Rabha, who subsequently became the epitome of meticulously detailed talmudic argument. The *hawayoth deAbaye weRabha* became almost proverbial for the intricacy of their construction.[2] But at this much earlier stage, when they were being taught by Rabbah bar Nahmani, they were being instructed in far more basic matters. On this particular day, Rabbah asked them:

'To whom do we address the prayers of blessing?' They answered, '*LeRahmana*, To him who is merciful.' 'And the All-Merciful, where does he abide?' Rabha pointed to the ceiling; Abaye went outside and pointed to the sky. Rabbah said to them: 'Both of you will become rabbis.' This illustrates the saying, 'Every pumpkin is known from the sap in its stem.'[3]

There could hardly be a more effective summary of precisely that assured perspective in the universe—God's in his heaven—which to us seems so problematic. For us, it is precisely 'up there', where Abaye and Rabha pointed, that God is not: there is no literal place 'up there' where God is to be found; whereas for Abaye and Rabha, there was obviously no great difficulty in visualizing a world of super-natural reality, above the ceiling, the dish-cover dome, of the sky. Yet for us, or at least for many in the contemporary world, the death of God occurs because there do not seem to be comparably effective imaginative terms with which to locate—and the term *locate* must be stressed—the transcendence of God. This exact point is summarized by Wilder, in an article on 'Art and Theological Meaning':

If we are to have any transcendence today, even Christian, it must be in and through the secular . . . If we are to find Grace it is to be found in the world and not overhead. The sublime firmament of overhead reality that provided a spiritual home for the souls of men until the eighteenth century has collapsed.

So far, so *ad tedium* familiar. But the point of drawing attention to the contemporary dilemma of transcendence is to draw attention to a comparable dilemma in the Greek and Jewish worlds which threatened, just as much, to lead to a death of God—indeed, in some cases it led to exactly that consequence. This was the dilemma, not of transcendence, but of immanence.[4] It was the problem of discerning and specifying the difference which God ought to make, if he *is* God as he is claimed to be. It was, in other words, the problem of specifying the effect of God—the difference which he is supposed to make—in the world and in the lives of men.

It remains, of course, a searching dilemma. If it can never be said what discernible and accessible consequence God has which humans can apprehend, then from the human point of view (which is not the only point of view, of course, but the only one with which we can sensibly deal) we are involved in a pseudo-hypothesis whose truth or falsity makes no observable difference. To what, then, can the theologian point as constituting a differentiating effect? Certainly to examples of cultural behaviour, to people, for example, praying, worshipping, and attending church, chapel, temple, and mosque; certainly also to very extensive testimony to the consequences in experience for those who attend faithfully to the possibility of God. But can he argue that through and within the web of sociological, anthropological, and psychological constraint God contributes to the sense of God? We can all, like Nietzsche's lunatic, light lanterns in the early morning brightness of our enlightened post-positivistic age and say that we are looking for God. But what would count as a demonstration that we had found him, or conversely that there is nothing to be found? To feel one's heart strangely warmed within one may well be irrefutable evidence for the man who feels it, even though the dilemmas of subsequent behaviour may remain great as they did for Wesley.[5] But can one ever point more extensively (on the basis, maybe, of that individual assurance) to the difference which might be made by God, supposing he exists? If not, then perhaps the death of God *can* be dated even more precisely than Nietzsche supposed: he died in 1969. It was in that year that an American lawyer, Russell Tansie, filed a damages suit for $100,000 against God for 'careless and negligent' control of the weather, after the house of his client, Miss Betty Penrose, had been struck and destroyed by lightning:

Plaintiff is informed and believes that the defendant [God] . . . is responsible for the maintenance and operation of the universe, including the weather in and upon the state of Arizona, and that on or about August 17, 1960, defendant so maintained and controlled the weather in, around and upon Phoenix, Arizona, in such careless and negligent manner as to cause lightning to strike the plaintiff's house, setting it on fire and startling, frightening and shocking the plaintiff.[6]

The process of the law followed its course: 'The Sonoma county clerk issued a summons for the deity and returned it to the attorney for service. Tansie said he hopes to win a default judgement when the defendant fails to appear in court.'

Here, immediately, the issue is focused on effect. Lightning is exactly what would have been regarded as an act of God, or as evidence of his effect. As Gibbon put it: 'Places or persons struck with lightning were considered by the ancients with pious horror, as singularly devoted to the wrath of heaven.'[7] Yet Gibbon was himself already sceptical. In this case, it is not just the characterization of God which has died, which is relatively unimportant, despite the recent drama of the image of God which must go. It is the effect of God which, in this example, is no longer discernible as it was believed to be. Lightning no longer counts as a discernment of that effect; and this is a more serious issue, because if God is of no discernible or specific effect, it is hard to know what difference it could make whether he is or is not. Perhaps God, like ex-President Nixon, regards himself as above the Constitution, and under no obligation to appear in court. But perhaps then he is so far removed from the world, and so transcendent, that he is under no obligation to appear anywhere. In *that* case, how can he be claimed to be resourceful in the construction of human life, or in the construction of the universe? In this way, the issue of specification becomes acute, very much as Henry James argued that the air of reality depends on the solidity of specification.[8] But one ought perhaps to remember, even so, that James was writing, in that passage, on The Art of Fiction.

The dilemmas of immanence and transcendence are not divorced from each other. But the focus in the ancient world was much more

on the problem of immanence. With a quite different understanding of the universe, there was no particular problem in locating
the transcendence of God, up there, where Abaye and Rabha
pointed. But the problem of discerning the effect of God was in
one respect far more acute for the Jews: they had no doubt whatsoever that it was precisely the effect of God which had constituted
them as a people. What had been manifestly the case in the past
should surely be manifest now. And if not, then why not?

This form of the problem was reinforced by a covenant understanding of the relation between God and men. As has been
pointed out already, the covenant supremely summarizes the conditions of Israel's life as 'the people whom God has chosen': it
summarizes the paradigmatic effects of God in the past, and it
refers to the fact that there are necessary conditions if that bonding
with God is to continue. But that could easily be inverted, and it is
the inversion which created the problem of immanence: if the
conditions are known which must obtain if in their case God is to
be in effect God, and if those conditions obtain, then the effect of
God should be specifiable and discernible, as it has been in the
past. There can be, and indeed ought to be, a high content prediction, which is exactly what one finds characteristically in the
prophets, and then later in apocalyptic. 'You know, O man, what
is required of you: to act justly, to love mercy, and to walk humbly
with your God' (Mic. 6:8). It has already been pointed out that
Torah maximizes information about what counts as justice, what
counts as mercy, what counts as walking attentively with God. But
what if the conditions are kept as faithfully as possible, and the
effect of God, is *not* discernible? 'Well, you may see the righteous
suffer—and that may be a test of their faithfulness. But in the end
they never fall, and at least you never see the children of the
righteous begging for their bread.' So at least says the Psalmist in a
somewhat desperate plea (Ps. 37:23–6). But we *have* seen the
children of the righteous suffer, and their children's children, not
least in the recent history of Europe—as in that terrible passage
from Hay which is quoted in my own *Problems of Suffering* (pp.
37 f.). So: where can the effect of God be discerned when those
who are defined as innocent suffer—defined as innocent in the
sense that they have kept the conditions so far as, in the case of
children, they are able or expected to?

It is in this way that the peculiarly Jewish problem of suffering emerged, as I have summarized and discussed it in the book on *Problems of Suffering*. But it is summarized also, within the Jewish tradition itself, in the figure of Job, who is deliberately and artificially defined at the very opening of the book, *as innocent*: 'A man perfect and upright, one that feared God and eschewed evil' (1:1). Yet he suffers. Furthermore, Job emphatically refutes the Psalmist's plea that at least the children of the righteous will be secure. It is Job's children who suffer first, long before he does so himself (1:18).

The importance of Job being defined as innocent is that it also refutes the otherwise irrefutable argument of Eccles. 7:20, that no man *is* innocent. The Ecclesiastes argument (though it is far more extensive than Ecclesiastes alone) agrees that if a man lives within the boundary conditions then he should discern Yahweh for blessing and not for curse. But, the argument goes on, man is 'born to trouble as the sparks fly upward' (Job 5:7), and no man does live within those conditions; therefore all suffering is deserved: 'where you see suffering, there you see sin' (B. Shab. 55a). Job's suffering proves that he must have broken the boundary, even though he may have been unaware of it himself.

But that argument is academic, not real. The distribution of suffering cannot be construed satisfactorily, least of all in emotional terms, by that paradigm. The distribution of human suffering is not commensurate with individual offence. Job is much closer to the paradigm which often does obtain in human experience, that the distribution of suffering does *not* correspond to individual offence; and in this crisis of plausibilty in the Jewish sense of God, Job was reduced to silence:

> My words have been frivolous: what can I reply?
> I had better lay my finger on my lips.
> I have spoken once—I will not speak again;
> More than once—I will add nothing (Job. 40:4 f.).

There is indeed no answer in the terms in which the problem is stated in Job. There are at least five *suggested* answers in the Book of Job, some explicit in the speeches of his friends or 'comforters', some implicit in the Prologue and the Epilogue. But they are not in the least convincing—or at least, Job did not find them so; and in the end, when contemplating such extraordinary features of creation as the hippopotamus and crocodile, and when challenged by God to say whether he could design and control such weird extravagances, Job has to admit that his understanding is too limited to comprehend the whole design. Yet what *never* comes in question (indeed this is exactly what is reaffirmed) is the possibility that the universe is a language of theistic utterance, or at least an expression of theistic effect. And that is because the underlying support and reinforcement of the Jewish sense of God lies so profoundly in a this-worldly and present life experience of theistic reality. A realization of God-relatedness is simply a possible fact of human experiencing, from which no inference was drawn at this early stage to the possible continuity of that relatedness through death (as already pointed out on pp. 41–2). But then the unevenness of consequence and distribution in events and human affairs was bound to become a critical problem—a problem posing a crisis in at least the individual relation to God.

To some extent the problem could be alleviated when some Jews began to believe that there *would* be a conscious continuity of life with God after death. But that did not come in until the very end of the Biblical period, and even at the time when Jesus was alive, Biblical literalists, such as the Sadducees, refused to accept that belief, because in their view there was no scriptural warrant for it. Certainly there is no hint of it in Job: Job does not appeal to life after death as a possible solution to his problem; and attempts (no doubt under the influence of Handel's *Messiah*) to find such an appeal in Job 19:25 f. are mistaken. The reality of death is absolute, as chs. 7 and 14 make clear. The passage 14:13–17 even makes the plea for God to hide Job in Sheol and then call him forth:

> But no! soon or late the mountain falls,
>   the rock moves from its place,
> water wears away the stones,
>   the cloudburst erodes the soil;
>   just so do you destroy man's hope . . .
> Let his sons achieve honour, he does not know of it,
>   humiliation, he gives it not a thought.

Consequently, it is here and now that the effect of God must be discerned; and if it is not discerned rewarding the faithful and those who endeavour to respond to the command, Hear, O Israel, then what is the point of such obedience? It was this which created the peculiarly Jewish problem of immanence. Eventually, of course, the Jews could come back to their earliest realization, that it is *not* for the individual that life comes and goes, but for the whole community and for the whole process of the world. That answer should not be underestimated. It has meant that when individual Jews have been doubtful about speculative pictures of an after-life, they have nevertheless kept their faith, and this was as much true in the Holocaust as in the Biblical period. For this reason, the Jewish crisis in plausibility must not be exaggerated. It is unlikely that large numbers despaired of the effectiveness of God, though the exact numbers who did so will never be known. Nevertheless, conceptually there was a real issue here, where individuals were concerned, an issue which threatened, in practical terms, a very real death of God: a death, not 'up there', in heaven, from which, as Ps. 14:2 puts it, Yahweh looks down at the sons of men, but down here—down here, where it may indeed be the fool who says in his heart 'There is no God', in that same Psalm; but the fool has at least this justification for what he says, that although the poor man is entitled to live in hope (v. 6), he nevertheless remains poor.

This means that for the Jews the death of God, the atheism, which threatened through their particular dilemma of immanence, could not possibly resemble the atheism attributed to Diagoras, who, as Athenagoras (*Plea* 4), put it 'chopped up a statue of Heracles in order to boil his turnips, and proclaimed outright that God did not exist'. In fact, we know very little of what Diagoras thought; we know simply that he became a *tupos*, a type, of outright atheist in the anecdotage of the classical world. Cicero's account of him (in *De Natura Deorum* iii, 89) became particularly well known:

You say that a good man often dies a good death? Yes, we seize upon examples of this and then attribute them without any reason to the beneficence of the gods. Diagoras the Atheist once visited Samothrace and a friend there said to him, 'You think the gods have no care for man? Why, you can see from all these votive pictures here how many people have escaped the fury of storms at sea by praying to the gods, who have brought them safe to harbour.' 'Yes, indeed,' said Diagoras, 'but where are the pictures of all those who suffered shipwreck and perished in the waves?' On another occasion he was on a voyage and the crew became anxious and alarmed about the bad weather and began to mutter that it served them right for taking an atheist on board.

Diagoras just pointed out to them a number of other ships on the same
course which were in equal difficulties and asked them whether they
thought that there was a Diagoras on the passenger-list of every one of
them. The fact is that a man's character or way of life makes no difference at all to his good luck or his bad.[9]

In one sense, of course, there is a superficial resemblance between Diagoras and the Jews: Israel, like Diagoras, had chopped
up the statues of their gods and of the so-called gods of other
nations long ago: 'Moses seized the calf they had made and burned
it, grinding it into powder which he scattered on the water' (Exod.
32:20). Even more to the point, when the Jews came to reflect on
the great divide which was established between Abraham their
father and the other nations of the world, they saw the division as
concentrated in the issue of idolatry, and they told many stories of
Abraham literally smashing and chopping up the images and idols
that he found.[10] But when *they* smashed the idols and mocked the
gods, it was not because they had become sceptical, as some Greeks
were to become, about the discernible regularity of theistic effect in
general. On the contrary, when *they* smashed the idols, it was not
an act of *general* scepticism: it was an act of faith that Yahweh's
effect was real and possible through this very action of destroying
other gods.

The crisis of plausibility in the sense of the Olympian gods was
quite different from that. And yet there is an important link, which
proved crucial for the spread of early Christianity: both are focused
on the issue of effect. Because the Olympian gods were so bound
up in their own affairs and their own histories they could not be of
any regularly discernible or accessible effect in the world of men.
Their effects were, if anything, more like the richochet effect of
bullets belonging to a different battle, golf balls landing on the
first fairway when they were aimed at the eighteenth green.
Furthermore, as Xenophanes (and many other Greeks) observed,
those histories are scarcely edifying: 'Homer and Hesiod have
attributed to the gods all manner of things that are shameful and
reproachful among men—stealing, adultery, deception of each
other.'[11]

Obviously, it would be an absurd error to give the impression
that the Olympian gods were the only potential resource of theistic
effect to which the Greeks looked. Exactly the reverse is true: the
possible resources of theistic effect for the Greeks were very varied

indeed, ranging from 'the divine something' (*to daimonion*) which Plato and Xenophon record of Socrates, to the kind of mantic seers and formal divination which, according to Plutarch, were the ultimate ruin of Nicias (the Athenian general who led the fatal and disastrous expedition to Sicily). Here, once again, the 'Diagoras issue' of effect recurs, as Plutarch records it in comparing Nicias with Crassus: 'Nicias scrupulously observed, Crassus entirely slighted, the arts of divination; and as both equally perished, it is difficult to see what inference we should draw.'

All the same, a particular crisis of plausibility in the Greek sense of God *was* focused on the Olympian gods. The death of those gods was well in hand long before the fifth century B.C., the century of the great tragedians. But certainly for Sophocles, however expectant he himself may have been of theistic effect (if, for example, that is the implication of his giving house-room to the snake image of Asclepius), the ways in which the world of the gods and the world of men are linked had become difficult to discern. Do the gods reward the just and punish the wicked? It is the famous question of the Chorus in *Oedipus Rex* (ll. 873, 883–96):

If any man walks arrogantly in deed or word, with no fear of justice [*dikas afobetos*], having no reverence for the habitation of the gods, may an evil fate seize him for his ill-starred pride, if he will not win his goal justly [*dikaios*] . . . What man, in such a case, can hope to ward off the arrows of the gods? Indeed, if such deeds are held in honour, why should I dance before the gods?

What Sophocles seeks, if the gods are to be worthy of reverence —if, that is, he and others are to dance in honour before them—is *dike*, the word (or root) repeated twice in that passage. *Dike* represents justice and order; it signifies an equitable balance of consequence in time and space. The roots of this fundamental concept lie very deep in the Greek structural process, not least because, as Segal has argued, 'the early Presocratic thinkers still use hymnic language to describe their new physical principles, thus transferring to them terms traditionally applied to the gods.'[12] This can be illustrated from the early sentence of Anaximander: 'From whatever is the genesis of things that are, into these they must pass away according to necessity. For, they must fulfil the appropriate penalty [*dike*] and make restitution [*tisis*] to each other for their injustice [*adikia*] according to the order of time.'[13]

But what then became problematic, as the plays of Sophocles

exemplify, is the discernment of *dike*, that balancing consequentiality in the tangled affairs of men. The thread of cause and effect, by which the *dike* of the gods and of the world is worked out, may be very long indeed—far too long for any individual to comprehend—and other threads of *dike*, consequence, may well be interwoven. Thus the blight on Thebes, which the Priest and Suppliants ask Oedipus to examine and appease (ll. 14 ff.), was certainly bound up with the coming home to rest of *dike* in Oedipus' own life; but the thread of consequence, of cause and effect, in which Oedipus was caught was one of which, when he stumbled into it, he could not possibly have had any knowledge whatsoever. *That* is what creates the tragedy: the thread of *dike*, of consequence, *is* being worked out, but to Oedipus it is hidden. Furthermore, although the effect of the gods may well be to establish eventually equitable consequence in the world, already in Sophocles they are beginning to work this effect through the feelings and passions of men. The dramatic intervention of the gods, such as one might associate with the *deus ex machina* (which Cicero claimed was simply 'a divine intervention to unravel the intricacies of the plot'),[14] is not prominent in that way, and in Sophocles the gods, or at least the effect of the gods, is already descending into the ground or depth of our being. Consequently, *in effect*, the Sophoclean hero is acting in what Knox called 'a terrifying vacuum', in which the hero cannot discern the thread of consequence, even if it exists, and in which, therefore, the effect of the gods is remote. So, continued Knox, in what is admittedly an extreme statement.

Sophocles presents us for the first time with what we recognize as a 'tragic hero': one who, unsupported by the gods and in the face of human opposition, makes a decision which springs from the deepest layer of his individual nature, his *physis*, and then blindly, ferociously, heroically maintains that decision even to the point of self-destruction.[15]

Euripides makes exactly the same point, though he expresses it in a different way. Euripides used to be held up as the great example of rational scepticism and enlightenment, a late Victorian intellectual before his time. That was a misreading of Euripides. In many ways, he is far more conservative than Sophocles of existing senses of God, and because he took them seriously he was able to pose, just as effectively, the Greek problem of immanence. Certainly Euripidean characters criticize the habits and histories of the gods, but the effects of the gods are expressed in traditional terms as very real and direct: the gods still descend literally from the machine, they walk the stage, and they effect consequences in the lives of men for reasons which seem to belong, at least in part, to their own nature alone. Thus in *Hippolytus*, Aphrodite condemns Hippolytus to death, at the very opening of the play, for the reason, apparently, that he honours Artemis more than herself, and she causes Phaidra to become the means through which her intention is effected. In *Heracles*, Hera sends the madness directly on to Heracles which makes him kill his wife and sons; and when, after the madness is withdrawn, he sees no course open but suicide, Theseus dissuades him precisely on the grounds that the gods do not escape from *tuche*, if we can believe the poets; *they* sin often enough, but they still live in Olympus; he should not feel guilt in such circumstances. Thus analogy is proposed, not from earth to heaven as with us, but from heaven to earth. In *Andromache*, Apollo allows the plot of Orestes to succeed, whereby the people of Delphi kill Neoptolemus, despite the fact that Neoptolemus has gone to Delphi to make amends to Apollo:

> In this way has the Lord that gives men oracles,
> The judge of what is just among all men,
> Dealt with Achilles' son who only came to him
> To make amends [*dikas didonta*]. Like an evil man
> The god remembered only his grudge of old—
> How then could he be wise? (1161–5)

In *The Bacchae*, Dionysus appears in human form in order to effect the destruction of Pentheus, and he makes the mother of Pentheus the agent of his terrifying death. Not surprisingly, the Chorus conclude *The Bacchae* by saying:

> In many different ways the will of the gods is wrought,
> Much that they do, no man can know in advance.
> What men thought certain, they bring to nothing,
> What no one thought possible, they bring into effect.
> This is where this story has led.

It is, of course, possible to comment on all this that Euripides was only conservative of existing senses of God in order to expose their absurdity; or again, that he introduced the gods only in order to feed in information which was needed for the plot. In other words, he paraded caricatures and straw figures in order simply to knock them down. But the reality is not in fact so simple. Taking the *deus ex machina* alone, Spira has argued that it is by no means a device for sustaining a plot, or for rescuing a plot which would otherwise have got 'bogged down', as Cicero suggested. He has pointed out that the gods, in these technical appearances, often rescue the characters from situations into which their human limitations have led them, and that what 'rescues' them (if that is the appropriate word) is the recognition of the far more extensive purposes of the gods. The effect of the gods is by no means one that can be regarded as negligible or absurd. It is frequently of Kafka-like opaqueness and terror, in which the human characters involved undergo what Krieger called 'a cosmic shock'.[16]

So it is precisely because the effects of the gods within the world are derived at least in part from their own nature, and are therefore unpredictable and irresistible on the part of human beings (so that Helen, for example, in *The Trojan Women*, is accused by Menelaus of causing the war, but pleads that she could do nothing to resist the power of Aphrodite), that the Greek version of the problem of immanence was posed quite as effectively by Euripides as it was by Sophocles. It is not a *reductio ad absurdum*. Both of them, though in very different ways, pose the same question: if the effect of the the gods in the sequential constructions of human life is so difficult either to predict or at times to discern, would it not be wise to discount the possibility that there is any *regularity* of effect which is available to that construction, and simply to live heroically and with reverence—to join hands, like Theseus and Heracles, and make what way they can, as friends, in the world? The immanent effect may indeed be there: neither Sophocles nor Euripides deny it. But what they question is whether that effect is immediately available or accessible for the construction of life, from the human end.

This is a problem of immanence, and it involves a death of gods. Quite how extensive in its consequences that death could be, can be seen clearly in yet another contemporary, Thucydides. What Thucydides himself believed in, or did not believe in, is as impossible to discern as it is in the case of, say, Shakespeare. But what is certainly the case is that when Thucydides came to acccount for the Peloponnesian War and for its eventual disastrous outcome, he did not attribute causative effect to the gods. In those terms, they are, effectively, dead. Indeed, when people in desperate circum-

stances appeal to the gods to intervene, they are, in general, dis-
appointed: the Plataeans beg for mercy in the name of heaven and
are destroyed;[17] two hundred and twelve alone escape the massacre,
and as Thucydides succinctly commented: 'This was the end of
Plataea, in the 93rd year after she became the ally of Athens' (iii. 68).
Or again, when Nicias tried to rally his troops on the disastrous
Sicilian expedition, he argued that the gods surely could not allow
their fortunes to continue in such an evil way from beginning to
end.[18] But evidently they could because, as Thucydides put it,
'Their losses were as they say, total; army, navy, everything was
destroyed, and out of many, only few returned' (vii. 87).

In fact, if one had to specify a single instance of what counted
for Thucydides as a cause of the eventual defeat in the Peloponnesian War, a very strong candidate would have to be the decision
to send the expedition to Sicily. But not in any specific way did
Thucydides suggest that the men who made up the Assembly
which took that decision were acting as they did as a consequence
of theistic effect, even though he had a real opportunity to make
that connection: on the eve of the expedition, the Hermai (the
statues of the protective god) were mutilated. The connection and
the inference of theistic effect were surely obvious: the expedition
failed because the god took his revenge. We know that others
made exactly that connection between cause and effect: Timaeus
wrote specifically: 'The Athenians taken in Sicily paid the penalty
for their impious outrage on Hermes in mutilating his statues.'[19]
But Thucydides made no such connection. In that sense, the death
of gods is absolute.

Thucydides, therefore, attempted to find natural explanations for
human acts and historical events. Of course he accepted that the
aetiology (the reflection on causes) of some events requires *tuche*,
chance; in other words, he accepted that there are causes and occurrences completely out of human control and prediction: 'Consider,
before you come to it, how much is unpredictable [*paralogos*] in
war. As it is long drawn-out, so more and more things occur by
tuchai.'[20]

But Thucydides never developed the loose existing theistic
associations of *tuche*, nor did he exploit the gaps of *tuche* in order
to insert a theological explanation. On the contrary, he insisted
that a *paralogical*, not a *theological*, inference is all that is appropriate. *Paralogos* means 'beyond reason', and Thucydides accepted

that some events are *paralogoi*, beyond the comprehension and control of men, as in the passage above.[21] Thus in vii. 55, the Athenian defeat by the Syracusans at sea is to themselves totally paralogical, because previously they had been strongest at sea. But a paralogical event in Thucydides is never to be identified with a theological effect.

Thucydides may well have been an exceptional character—no doubt he was; and Xenophon is perhaps more representative of aetiological speculation in this period than Thucydides. It is certainly true that Xenophon admitted a greater supernatural effect than Thucydides. He accepted (as did Plato, though with differences in detail) a supernatural effect in the life of Socrates; and equally, in the *Historia Graeca* (the continuation of Thucydides' History) the further Xenophon gets from the end of Thucydides' narration, the more he introduces supernatural explanation. It is not a great deal in any case, but it is certainly more than Thucydides would have allowed, as Soulis has analysed. Yet even in Xenophon theistic effect is marginal. His aetiology of defeat (for example, the defeat at Cunaxa) is as prosaic and humanistic as it is in Thucydides. In one respect, Xenophon was a more realistic historian: he recognized that individuals *are* expectant of theistic effect, and he therefore recorded that expectation as a part of the scene to be portrayed—as in the password at Cunaxa (*Zeus soter kai nike*, Zeus, saviour and conqueror, i. 8), or in the appeal of Clearchus to Tissaphernes (ii. 3), or even in Xenophon's own comment at the end of the retreat that the omens at the first sacrifice had proved correct, and that he himself was well pleased with the god (vii. 8). But although, in Xenophon's opinion, the construction of human lives can certainly be informed from *to daimonion*, a certain divine something, the gods do not directly create the visible consequences of history. They can be approached through sacrifice, but they cannot be discerned as the authors of the totality of historical events in any consistent fashion. And *that* is why Xenophon put to the Delphic oracle a question which as early as Socrates was recognized as being very odd: how could he best and safely make the journey *hen epinoei*, which he already had in mind? The initiatives in creating events are human, not divine, but the effects of the gods may well stand as markers and constraints on the route (*Exped.* iii. 1), although one cannot actually be sure of them.

This is the death of God which Plato came to recognize among at least some of his contemporaries, not a naïve atheism which denies that the gods exist at all, but the problem of discerning and specifying a regular effect of God. Naïve atheism is simply, in Plato's view, an aberration of youth which no one of intelligence maintains when he gets older. But he continues (or at least, the Athenian continues):

It is true that some men (but not many) do persist in labouring under the impression either that although the gods exist they are indifferent to human affairs, or alternatively that they are not indifferent to human affairs but can easily be won over by prayers and sacrifices. Be guided by me: you'll only see this business in its truest light if you wait to gather your information from all sources, and then see which theory represents the truth. In the meantime, do not venture any impiety where gods are concerned (*Laws*, 888).

But where, in that crisis of plausibility, with the death of those particular gods, does one go? Does one accept the constraint of rationality and ask what sense of God does one's constructed universe require or demand? That, or something like it, was the transformation in the grammar of God which Aristotle transacted. Aristotle certainly took seriously the death of the gods, and Merlan has argued that Aristotle anticipated Epicurus in holding that even if the gods exist, they are so bound up in their own order that their real concern cannot be for human welfare or affairs.[22]

But as Whitehead once drily observed, the consequent sense of God was not very available for religious purposes.[23] So if the existing gods had in fact failed in effect, then another response would be to develop gods of real and discernible effect. This explains what to Dodds was one of the unsolved riddles of western civilization, why the great Age of Reason in Greece (or at least, the beginning of what might have been such an age) did not lead to an even greater edifice being built on those foundations, but why instead it was followed by an increase of what he called the irrational:

A prevision of this [following] history would have surprised an observer in the third century B.C. But it would have surprised him far more painfully to learn that Greek civilisation was entering, not on the Age of Reason, but on a period of slow intellectual decline which was to last, with some deceptive rallies and some brilliant individual rear-guard actions, down to the capture of Byzantium by the Turks; that in all the sixteen centuries of existence still awaiting it the Hellenic world would produce no poet as good as Theocritus, no scientist as good as Eratosthenes, no mathematician as good as Archimedes, and that the one great name in philosophy would represent a point of view believed to be extinct—transcendental Platonism. To understand the reasons for this long-drawn-out decline is one of the major problems of world history.[24]

But in fact it is no problem at all. It is exactly what one would expect: *les dieux sont morts; vivent les dieux*. If claimed theistic effects collapse, one response will be to discern and specify other means and resources of theistic effect. So in the Greek case, there is no doubt that a very real death of gods occurred, but it did not lead to a naïve atheism. It led to a very wide range of further theistic construction beyond it. Any attempts to guess the motives for those reconstructions are idle speculation, because we have no access, in the evidence, to the motives of those concerned. Psychoanalytic guesses are likely to be right, that some of those concerned could not continue their lives without illusory figures on to which to project their frustration and fears. But at the same time, it must be possible that others recharacterized the sense of God because theistic externality continued to impress the sense of its own reality on their consciousness, despite the collapse of traditional descriptions.

The Greeks solved the problem of immanence at two extremes. At one extreme, it was dissolved by removing God from directly immanent discernible effect and by making him the unmoved mover. At the other, it was resolved by bringing God into much *more* accessible effect through mysteries, magic, oracles, astrology, the divinization of great men, the postulation of intermediaries between heaven and earth—the range of possibilities was vast. No doubt the universe of experience of Aristotle was very different from the universe of experience of the Greek soldier of Qolophon (as he spelled it) who sailed up the Nile and carved his name on the leg of the Pharaoh's relief at Abu Simbel. But what they both shared in common was the problem of immanence: where can the effect of God be discerned and how can it be mobilized on my behalf?

For the Greeks, the Olympian gods were too bound up in their own affairs. But for the Jews, in contrast, God is *not* so bound up with his own nature or with his own affairs that no concern of his for the world can be discerned. He is bound up with his people, and the bond which ties them is the covenant; and if his people live within those boundary conditions, the effects for good will be specific and manifest. The contrast is stark and obvious if one looks at the aetiology of defeat in Josephus. Josephus was certainly well enough educated to know Thucydides' work, and in writing his *Histories* of the Jews and of the Jewish revolt, he used Thucydidean terms and vocabulary. But his understanding of history is entirely different. 'Speaking generally,' as Josephus put it at the opening of *The Antiquities*, what one can discern in Jewish history is that those who conform to the will of God, articulated in specific law, prosper, and those who 'depart from the strict observance of the laws . . . end in irretrievable disasters' (i. 14).

The consequence for Josephus is that far from the effect of God being opaque in historical events, it is so luminously clear that proper attention to history is a way of disentangling appropriate and inappropriate senses of God. It can illuminate, in other words, exactly what to the Greeks seemed past knowing, the *ousia* (essential being) and the *phusis* (nature) of God. The passage just quoted continues:

At the outset, then, I entreat those who will read these volumes to fix their thoughts on God, and to test whether our lawgiver has had a worthy conception of his nature [*phusis*] and has always assigned to him such actions as befit his power, keeping his words concerning him pure of that unseemly mythology current among others.

Similarly, the last words of *The Antiquities* (xx. 268) carry the same theme over into another projected work: 'It is also my intention to compose a work in four books on the opinions that we Jews hold concerning God and his essence [*peri theou kai tes ousias autou*] and concerning the laws, that is, why according to them we are permitted to do some things while we are forbidden to do others.' This means that according to Josephus, Greek problems of *phusis* and *ousia*, even if they cannot be completely solved (because what God is *kat ousian*, in his essential being, as Josephus put it in *Contra Apionem* ii. 67, is *agnostos*, beyond human knowing), can certainly be reduced by an attention to Jewish evidence; and the reason why lies in the fact that Jewish evidence—Jewish history—demonstrates, according to Josephus, a unique relation of God to this people *en dunamei*, in power, in effect:

Moses persuaded all the people to regard God as the cause [*aition*] of all good things, both those which occur to all men in general, and also those which they had brought to themselves by prayer in crises; he persuaded them that no action or thought of any kind could be hidden from him. He represented him as One, unbegotten, and without change through the entire course of time, in beauty exceeding the furthest human conception, made known to us in his effect [*dunamis*] however much he is *agnostos kat ousian*.

Nothing could be much further removed from Thucydides, where the intervention of divine effect in the construction of divine events is precisely what is *not* illustrated. Josephus was just as well aware as Thucydides that there are paralogical occurrences —indeed, he is capable of putting them in the superlative, as in the case of Cestius' withdrawal: 'Cestius, who did not appreciate the despair of the besieged or the feelings of the people, suddenly called off his soldiers . . . and, *paralogotata* [most paralogically], withdrew from the city' (*War* ii. 540; cf. iv. 49).

But although Josephus could recognize the paralogical, the whole of his history is held together in a bracket of divine purpose, and so of divine cause and effect—or as he would have put it, history demonstrates the *pronoia*, the providence and working out of God's purpose.[25] Thus the issue between Thucydides and Josephus is put very succinctly in *War* iii, 391 (in at least part of the manuscript tradition), where Josephus asks of a particular incident: 'Should one say by *tuche* or should one say by the *pronoia* of God?' The working out of *pronoia*, which of course goes back to the Deuteronomic 'I set before you this day a blessing or a curse', for Josephus belongs unequivocally to the absolute truth, the *aletheia*, of history.[26]

But *does* history exemplify the Deuteronomic theme? *Can* the *pronoia* of God be discerned in effect? That is clearly the precise issue of the failure of the Jewish war against Rome, and Josephus summarized his understanding of the apparent absence of the effect of God in rescuing his people in the famous speech which he put into his own mouth as he walked round the walls of besieged Jerusalem—by that time Josephus had already deserted to the Romans and was making an attempt to parley with the Jews: 'Josephus, accordingly, went round the wall, and, endeavouring to keep out of range of missiles and yet within earshot, repeatedly implored them to spare themselves and the people, to spare their country and their temple, and not to display towards them greater indifference than was shown by aliens.'[27]

The speech which follows is divided into two quite separate parts. In the first part (v. 363–74) the arguments are expressed in entirely open terms: there is nothing specifically Jewish in the argument at all. Indeed, one could put the point more strongly: the first speech depends specifically, not on Jewish, but on Greek resources: 'There is an established law, as supreme among animals as among men, "Yield to the stronger" and "The mastery is for those pre-eminent in arms" ' (*War* v. 367). That is a Hellenistic commonplace: 'By nature ruling belongs to the stronger.'[28] Or again: '*Tuche* has from all quarters passed over to the Romans, and God, who goes the round of the nations, bringing to each in turn the rod of empire, now rests over Italy.' (*War* v. 367). That again is a Hellenistic commonplace. But it is not the understanding of God's relation to the nations which we find in Isaiah or Jeremiah; there indeed God has power over the nations, and he uses them as instruments of his purpose. But it is not by *tuche*, but by *pronoia* (to revert to Josephus' term), that God brings up the Assyrians, or uses even an evil people, like the Babylonians, to correct Israel, or makes Cyrus his messiah (Isa. 45:1).

The sort of rota system which Josephus envisages has some counterpart in apocalyptic, but in the more fundamental resources of Jewish construction, the intervention of God is more specific, direct, and immediate. So Greek, in fact, are the arguments of Josephus in the first half of the speech, and so far removed from the resources of Jewish construction, that he himself emphasizes their total failure of impact: 'Josephus, during this exhortation, was derided by many from the ramparts, by many execrated, and by some assailed with missiles. Failing to move them by this direct advice [*tais phanerais sumbouliais*], he passed to reminiscences of their nation's history' (*War* v. 375). It is at that point that Josephus proposes, in the second half of the speech, an explanation of the absence of God's effect which is constructed from Jewish resources of interpretation, and the examples extend far beyond what was already coming to be understood as scripture. In this part of the speech Josephus has no difficulty in locating the reason for the absence of immanent effect.

How much more impious are you than those who have been defeated in the past. Secret sins—I mean thefts, treacheries, adulteries—are not beneath your disdain, while in rapine and murder you vie with each other in opening up new and unheard of paths of vice . . . And after all this do you expect God, thus outraged, to be your ally? (*War* v. 401 f.).

So the reason for the defeat, according to Josephus, is very simple: the Jews had to be punished because, even in comparison with Jews who had suffered defeat in earlier times, they were more impious—*asebesteroi*. Thucydides used exactly the same term, *asebema*, in connection with the mutilation of the Hermai (vi. 27), but whereas for Josephus *asebeia* is central to the aetiology of defeat, for Thucydides it is important for the aetiology of people's attitudes to the expedition: it is not a *cause* of defeat, as it is for Josephus.

The second speech of Josephus, appealing to history as paradigmatic of the blessing and the curse, did have some effect. It did not lead all the Jews to surrender, but at least it led some of the Jews to desert (v. 420 ff.). However, this paradigmatic use of history brings us at once to the very heart of the Jewish, as opposed to the Greek, problem of immanence. Josephus had no difficulty exemplifying the Deuteronomic covenant theme and using it as an explanation of the absence of effect on behalf of the Jews in the Jewish war. But what of those situations where the events could *not* be declined acccording to the paradigm? Where then is the effect of God to be discerned? Take this obvious example:

Yahweh, you are the only one,
You made the heavens, the heaven of heavens, with all their array,
the earth and all it bears,
the seas and all they hold.
To all of these you give life
and the array of the heavens bows down before you.
Yahweh, you are the God who chose Abraham,
brought him out from Ur in Chaldea . . .
You saw the distress of our fathers in Egypt . . .
you worked portents and miracles against Pharaoh . . . (Neh. 9:6–10).

And so the recital in Neh. 9 continues, an almost perfect expression of the paradigmatic effect of God in creation and history in the past. But what of the present? How, at this time, will God be apparent for us? That is exactly the note on which that Psalm ends (vss. 36 f.):

> Here are we now, enslaved;
> Here in the land you gave our fathers
> to enjoy its fruits and its good things,
> we are slaves . . . Such the distress we endure.

In the recital the people admit that the distress is deserved
(v. 33): 'In all that has befallen us, you have been just, you have
kept faith, but we have done wrong.' But what, then, can be done
to restore the blessing of the covenant, as opposed to the curse?
There is only one conceivable answer: to keep the conditions
which belong to the covenant agreement. That is exactly where the
paradigmatic recital of Neh. 9 leads: it leads, in ch. 10, to a formal
and sworn renewal of obedience, and to the specific statement of
particular laws which require very careful attention for the repair
of that situation, above all the avoidance of marriages to non-Jews,
and the avoidance of trade with non-Jews on the sabbath. The
answer to distress is to repair the fence of Torah and live within it.
What other answer could possibly be given in the terms of the
covenant itself? But what that failed to solve was the problem of
why the effect of God is sometimes indiscernible even when the
fence of obligation and holiness *has* been secured and when people
are trying conscientiously to live within it. Here again one must
remember that the classical answer (that all suffering is a punishment for sin, since there is no man who does not act wrongly at
some time) was made of less effect by the fact that Torah itself
contains the means of repair, forgiveness, and renewal—not
least in its sacrificial system, for which the Rabbis rapidly found
equivalent actions when the Temple was destroyed. It was at this
point of strain that there occurred in the Jewish case the crisis of
plausibility, summarized at the beginning of this chapter, which
reduced Job to silence. The problem was inevitably acute, because
however much Josephus might analyse[29] the fall of Jerusalem and
the terrible destruction of Masada in terms of *asebeia*, offence
against God, the writer of 2 Baruch could still cry out, Surely the
offences of Jerusalem are not commensurate with this degree of
destruction? Should not the obedience of the godly have counterbalanced the sins of the ungodly?

> Again I will speak in your presence:
> What have they gained who had knowledge before you,
> And have not walked in vanity as the rest of the nations . . .
> See! they have been carried off,
> Nor on their account have you had mercy on Zion.
> And if others did evil, it was due to Zion,
> That on account of the works of those who did well
> She should be forgiven,

And should not be overwhelmed on account of the work of those
who wrought unrighteousness (xiv. 4 ff.).

The problem here is the inscrutability of God's relation to those
who *are* attempting to observe the conditions of his covenant. The
only possible response, unless the Jewish sense of God was to be
extinguished, was to remember that the *pronoia* of God works out
its purpose, not for the accountancy of the individual, but for the
eventual and ultimate good of the whole. At the same time it was
clearly essential to work with, and not against, that purpose, by
attempting to define even more exactly the boundary conditions
of Israel's life and of Torah, and by attempting to live within
them.

Thus the *extinction* of Israel's sense of God was never a serious
or extensive possibility. The Jews in general had no doubt that
they could still point 'up there' (p. 97), and could have good
reason for doing so, because their history would not have been
what it had been without their bonded relation to God, whose
name and nature had been disclosed within that history. So Abaye
and Rabha could still point to the ceiling and to the sky. Some
Greeks could not even do that: 'Of reasoning man,' Democritus
observed, 'few hold up their hands in that direction, to what we
Greeks now call air, saying, Zeus considers all things, and knows
all things; he gives and he takes away: he is king of all.'[30]

Although, therefore, one can say that the problem of immanence,
the problem of the apparent absence or irregularity of the effect
of God, was as pervasive in the classical Hellenistic world as in
the Jewish, the lineaments and features of the problem varied
greatly. Certainly in the Jewish case the problem of effect was very
different indeed; yet in the way just summarized (as in the case of
Job) it could be very acute. How then did they attempt to solve
the problem? At one extreme, there was a range of solutions which
were virtually indistinguishable from those occurring in the
Hellenistic world at large. Some Jews were quite as capable as the
Greeks of looking for new and more dramatic modes of theistic
effect, in magic, in astrology, in divination, in pagan temples, and
in pagan mysteries. At the opposite extreme stands, not Aristotle,
not metaphysical analysis, but the *practical* analysis of the term
qadosh (holiness). The only solution which would defend the construction of *Jewish* life would be one which paid more, not less,

attention to the analysis of the boundary conditions which will enable the condition of holiness to be attained: then, and then only, will the effect of God be manifest for good. But how can that condition of holiness be obtained? Perhaps by creating 'holy communities', or baptized communities, perhaps by building literal geographical enclosures, little enclosures of holiness, like those of the community on the shores of the Dead Sea; or again, perhaps by insisting rigidly on the absolute sanctity of one place on earth, the Temple, from which law and its consequences in holiness could go forth to Israel and the world. 'As the Shekinah stretches from the Temple to Jerusalem, so the Shekinah will one day stretch from one end of the world to the other' (Est. R. i. 4). But all those responses tended to restrict holiness to an élite, a remnant, which indeed had good biblical precedent. But the biblical command is for the people *as a whole*, and it was the supreme vision of the Hakamim, the founders of rabbinic Judaism and of what we have come to know as Judaism, to see that somehow the requirements of Torah must be able to be understood and applied by *all* the people, and that all the people must be helped to that understanding and obedience. It is for that reason that they built schools and developed synagogues, and that they produced new methods of exegesis in order to build a bridge from Scripture in the past to life in the present. No matter where people lived, it had to be possible for all people to understand Torah, and to implement it in their lives. When, therefore, the Temple was destroyed by the Romans, they were already prepared for an authentically Jewish life without the Temple, and they alone could survive the catastrophe almost without disturbance.

Those, then, represent two poles of response to the Jewish crisis in the sense of God: at one extreme, there were those who looked for more immediate and dramatic effects of God, for the individual more than for the ultimate good of the community. At the other were those who believed that the effect of God could not be for good unless they made a more thoughtful effort to define the boundaries of Torah and live within them. But among the Jews there was another, highly idiosyncratic solution, or claimed solution, to the problem of the apparent absence of God's immediate or regular effect. It was the solution which Jesus proposed and as a consequence of which he died. Jesus had much to say (or is reported as having had much to say) about the nature of

God and his relation to men. There is no possibility of understanding why his claims about God were so disturbing and yet so compellingly memorable unless we understand first what was problematic about the nature of God at the time. To what problems did Jesus offer solutions? This, in barest outline, we have begun to see: the most searching problem was that of discerning regularity in the distribution of God's effect, not least in relation to reward and suffering. What solutions did Jesus offer to that problem?

II

CHRISTIANITY

1. JESUS AMONG THE JEWS

WHEN the Jews faced the problem of discerning the effect of God in the catastrophes that overwhelmed them, whether as individuals or as a nation (as in the fall of Jerusalem), a consistent element in their response was to attend more carefully to the boundary conditions of Torah. It was that which led to social or even geographical isolation, in order to ensure that at least a nucleus, or a remnant as Isaiah had put it, would be able to offer itself in perfect holiness to God. The Essenes, the Therapeutae, the baptizing communities, all emphasized the need for serious attention to the demands of holiness. The Dead Sea Sect withdrew into the remotest possible isolation, no doubt in part to escape their enemies, but also to ensure an area free from contamination. Even Philo, who made an extensive attempt to interpret the inner meaning of the commands of Torah through Hellenistic categories, insisted that actual obedience to the external command was still necessary. How, indeed, would it be possible to discern the inner meaning of a custom or practice unless one preserved every detail of the external sign? That at least was Philo's argument, in *de Migratione Abrahami*, 89–93:

There are some who, regarding laws in their literal sense in the light of symbols of matters belonging to the intellect, are over-punctilious about the latter, while treating the former with easy-going neglect. Such men I for my part should blame . . . It is quite true the Seventh Day is meant to teach the power of the Unoriginate and the non-action of created beings. But let us not for this reason abrogate the laws laid down for its observance, and light fires or till the ground or carry loads or institute proceedings in court or act as jurors or demand the restoration of deposits or recover loans, or do all else that we are permitted to do as well on days that are not festival seasons. It is true also that the Feast is a symbol of gladness of soul and of thankfulness to God, but we should not for this reason turn our backs on the general gatherings of the year's seasons. It is true that receiving circumcision does indeed portray the excision of pleasure and all passions, and the putting away of the impious conceit, under which the mind supposed that it was capable of begetting by its own power: but let us not on this account repeal the law laid down for circumcising ... It follows that, exactly as we have to take thought for the body, because it is the abode of the soul, so we must pay heed to the letter of the laws. If we keep and observe these, we shall gain a clearer conception of those things of which these are symbols.

There were, then, different ways in which Jews attempted to ensure that the commands of Torah and the conditions of the covenant promises were kept at least by some. But by far the most enduring of those responses to what was summarized in the last chapter as the problem of immanence was that of the Hakamim, the predecessors of the rabbis. (It has been pointed out already, on p. 36, that there are great problems of reference in the term 'Pharisees', and that consequently it is better to refer to them by one of the terms which the rabbis themselves used, the Hakamim, or Wise of old). The great vision of the Hakamim was that Torah must be within reach of all men: it was not simply for an élite, in the Temple or in a sect: it was meant by God for *all* his people. The Hakamim came into being to extend the possibility of Torah to all Jews, no matter how far they were dispersed across the world.

To do this, they produced new methods of exegesis (which in themselves were very carefully controlled and which were derived from principles implicit in Scripture itself),[1] and in that way they were able to establish a direct link from the informational resource in the past to the present circumstances of life, many of whose details had obviously not been envisaged in the original text. They also developed means of informational reference and transmission in synagogues and schools, and in the eventual designation of rabbis as the only authentic transmitters of tradition.

But at the same time that they were affirming the continuity of God's effect by securing the fence around Torah, they were also denying claims to the effect of God which were located outside the boundary. On the one hand, they developed new means of relating the whole people to God, but on the other, they denied the continuity into their own time of traditional modes of revelation through, for example, prophets. Thus they affirmed that God is still directly present to the world through his *shekinah* or through his *bath qol*. The *shekina* is the kind of 'after-glow' of God's presence, the sometimes visible and usually specific mode of God's presence in the world: 'Where two are gathered together in the study of Torah, my *shekinah* is present with them' (B. Ber. 6a). The *bath qol* is, literally, the daughter of the voice, not the face to face speech of God, but the audible communication which had replaced the direct inspiration of the prophets by the holy spirit: 'After the death of Haggai, Zechariah and Malachi, the last prophets, the *ruach haQodesh* [the holy spirit] ceased from Israel, but there were still communications to Israel through the *bath qol*' (T. Sot. xiii. 2).

But in that passage we have the statement of the other side of the rabbinic emphasis, the statement that prophecy has ceased. They then rationalized the disappearance of the holy spirit, focused in the cessation of prophecy, by saying that the holy spirit was withdrawn after the exile as a punishment for Israel's sin. So the cessation of prophecy is in itself an example of what the Hakamim and the rabbis had to eliminate if their own proposal for the continuity of Israel was to succeed: on the one side God *is* still of discernible effect: he still communicates his word dramatically through the *bath qol*. But on the other side, he does not communicate as he once did, through the direct inspiration—the inbreathed spirit—of the prophets.

Why not? The reason is obvious: it is because visible ecstatic possession remained very common in the ancient world. There were many people who claimed to be prophets, and who gave the authentic appearance of being inspired, or ecstatically seized, by extra-human reality. If that reality were believed to be God, then anyone with that appearance could stand up, look like a prophet, and say, Thus says the Lord. But that would clearly threaten to destroy the *raison d'être* of the Hakamim in establishing, communally and traditionally, the boundary conditions of Israel. There cannot be any stability in the rabbinic field of information if any prophet can stand up and perhaps contradict an opinion or ruling of the Hakamim, particularly since these were derived from, and controlled by, scripture. The Hakamim had to deny that the appearance of spirit possession established the proof of an authentic relation to God. And this was not just an amiable theoretical argument in the area of religious epistemology. The rabbis knew perfectly well that at least two schismatic groups in Israel had done exactly this: they had claimed that their interpretation of what Judaism should become was proved to be authentic because of the visible return of the holy spirit to their respective communities. The two groups were the early Christians and the sect of the Dead Sea documents, both of whom claimed to identify the return of the holy spirit to their own communities.[2]

So the way in which the Hakamim tried to solve the Jewish problem of immanence, and the way in which they became a living solution to that problem, is very complex. They had to affirm that God is still of effect where the boundary conditions of Israel (as they understood them) are observed. But they had also to affirm that claims to the effect of God which do not observe or fall within those boundary conditions are to be disregarded. For this reason they opposed (and eventually excised from their own modes of discourse) apocalyptic, since apocalyptic often claimed to be based on a personal vision of God, or of heaven, or of the future, or of the interpretation of history. The rabbis held that innovations cannot be established in Israel on the basis of a claimed personal vision. They must be tested, if they are allowed at all, against the isomorphic map being established with such detail in the rabbinic universe of meaning. So the rabbis even came to excise *merkabah* visions (visions induced by concentration on the opening chapters of Ezekiel). They decided that such visions were aberrant, even though they were scripturally based, and even though one of the great founding fathers of rabbinic Judaism, Johanan b. Zakkai, had practised that kind of contemplation.[3]

In line with this they also held that individual teaching could not be maintained if the majority opinion decided against it. Thus on one occasion R. Eliezer tried to establish a *halakah*, or legal ruling, on a disputed matter of cleanness or uncleanness, but the other rabbis refused to accept his arguments. He then brought various miracles to his support, but they remained unimpressed:

He said: 'If the *halakah* agrees with me, let this stream prove it.' At once the stream began to flow back uphill. They said: 'A stream of water is no proof at all.' At last [after other miracles] he said to them: 'If the *halakah* agrees with me, let it be proved from heaven.' At once a *bath qol* proclaimed: 'Why do you argue with R. Eliezer? In all

matters the *halakah* agrees with him.' But R. Joshua stood up and said:
' "It is not in heaven" (Deut. 30:12).' What did he mean? R. Jeremiah
said: 'He meant that Torah had already been given on Mount Sinai,
therefore we take no notice of a *bath qol*, since it was long ago written
in Torah, "Follow after the majority" (Exod. 23:2)' (B.B.M. 59b).

Because R. Eliezer was in a minority of one, not even the direct
intervention of God could establish his teaching against the
majority. This, of course, had good biblical foundation, not only
in the texts appealed to by R. Joshua and R. Jeremiah, but in the
fundamental passage in Deut. 17:8–13, which deals with the case
of the contumacious or rebellious man who refuses to accept the
final decision of the highest authority of the time—'the judge then
in office' (v. 9):

When the issue in any lawsuit is beyond your competence, whether it
be a case of blood against blood, plea against plea, or blow against blow,
that is disputed in your courts, then go up without delay to the place
which the Lord your God will choose. There you must go to the
levitical priests or to the judge then in office; seek their guidance, and
they will pronounce the sentence. You shall act on the pronouncement
which they make from the place which the Lord will choose. See that
you carry out all their instructions. Act on the instruction which they
give you, or on the precedent that they cite; do not swerve from what
they tell you, either to right or to left. Anyone who presumes to reject
the decision either of the priest who ministers there to the Lord your
God, or of the judge, shall die; thus you will rid Israel of wickedness.
Then all the people will hear of it and be afraid, and will never again
show such presumption.

There could scarcely be a clearer statement of the boundary
condition of Israel's continuity. A teacher who insists on his own
opinion when the majority or the locus of authority in his time has
decided against him must be excised from Israel, because nothing
could be more destructive of Israel than the development of
schismatic interpretations of Torah. Almost any offence could
perhaps be forgiven if the offender confessed his fault and made
due reparation, but not the offence of the person who holds out
against the final locus of authority. If such a person insists on his
own judgement or interpretation, even when he has been brought
to the highest prevailing authority of the time, he must be executed,
and some of the later rabbis said that even if he disowned his
interpretation on the way to the place of execution, he must still

be executed, as a warning against this most destructive of all offences in Israel. It is possible, as will be seen later, that this is exactly the problem which Jesus posed to at least some Jews.

The Hakamim and then the rabbis established a structural sequence in the continuity of Israel's life-way, which became what we would now regard as Judaism. They mapped with great clarity and precision the boundary conditions within which the construction of Jewish life could continue, even though the Temple was destroyed and even though in a crude sense it might have seemed as though God had hidden his face from Israel. They enabled Israel to keep faith. But although theirs was the solution which endured, they were, when Jesus was alive, only one among many suggested solutions to the problem of continuing the covenant relationship and of discerning God's effect in the world.

Among the other proposed solutions was that of Jesus. But the solution which Jesus claimed to the problem of the apparent absence of God's effect in the world or in individual life was so idiosyncratic and so aberrant that in the end it could not be contained within Judaism at all. Indeed, one can say that it was literally idiocentric. For what is clearly suggested by the surviving evidence is that Jesus offered his own self as the solution to the problem; or perhaps more accurately one should say that Jesus seems to have located the solution to the problem first and foremost in his own person, and that it was in and through his own person that he claimed to be mediating God's effect in the world.

If this argument is correct, it makes Christology inevitable. Indeed, one can invert this slightly and say that this is the reason why there are Christological reflections in the Christian tradition: precisely because Jesus located a solution to the Jewish problem of immanence in his own person in a way which apparently claimed a direct relatedness to God, and because that solution seemed dramatically persuasive to at least some others, there had to be some account of that person and of its relation to God. Those accounts are not the introduction of a later development, although they obviously became increasingly elaborate and sophisticated. But in principle they go back to Jesus himself, who first located the effect of God in his own person and shared it with others, and who was constrained by this into the novel outcome, the figure who evoked allegiance as the *locus* of theistic effect in the world and

who produced the unusual accounts of a human figure of that sort
which now stand in the Gospels.

But is that account correct? It is certainly the basic picture
given of Jesus in the Gospels. In a book of this scope, it is not
possible to examine all the Gospels. But the point can be seen
most clearly in Mark, and without commenting for the moment
on the issue of whether his portrayal of Jesus has any historical
foundation, it may be as well to examine exactly what figure it is
that Mark portrays. Mark is at least consistent. What he portrays
both in general and in detail is one who restored the direct and
visible effect of God to the world, and he portrays the one who did
this as unmistakably human. What occurs in Jesus is not the effect
of an angel: angels may minister to him but they are not confused
or identified with him (Mk. 1:13, cf. 8:38). Nor is it the effect of
a special creation, of a heavenly resemblance of a man or a new
Adam, or anything of that kind. It is the effect of a man, a carpenter,[4] the son of Mary, the brother of James and Joseph and
Judas and Simon—'and are not his sisters here with us?' (6:3).
In the context of that passage, it is the dramatic nature of the
effect which Jesus was making manifest in the world which led
the people to ask how he was doing it and from what resource he
was drawing this power, this *dunamis* as Mark calls it (6:2, 5),
using a word which was also important to Josephus (pp. 113 f.):
'They were astonished saying, *Pothen touto tauta*? Whence to this
man these things?' (6:2).

What kinds of effect were they, which seemed to restore the
effect of God to the world? The most familiar are the many accounts
of healing. But in Mark it is obvious that the words, or teaching,
of Jesus were equally an issue of effect. Indeed, on occasion they
are the *prior* issue of effect. This is true in the passage just referred
to in ch. 6: it is the teaching which makes them ask the question.
But it is equally true in 1:22 and 27: it is his teaching, his *didache*,
which causes astonishment, and the issue is immediately raised of
the authority, the *exousia*, on which it is issued. On what possible
ground could he issue judgements in his *didache* which differed so
sharply, not just from one interpretation of what it means to be
Jewish (the interpretation, say, of the Sadducees or the Hakamim
or the Baptizers) but from all of them in different ways, and at
different points of strain. 'They came to him and said, "By what
authority [*exousia*] are you acting like this?" ' (Mk. 11:28).

The problem posed by the teaching of Jesus lies in the peculiarity of its configuration when it is superimposed on other proposed maps of Jewishness. If one takes issues which were controversial among the Jews (some of which appear in the Gospels), such as the status of the existing Temple in Jerusalem, the authority of the actual high priest, the necessity for sacrifice, the fate of the dead, the means of exegesis, the permissibility and terms of divorce, attitude to the Roman occupation, the *kelal* of Torah (which command is it that summarizes all the commandments?), what it is that makes a man unclean; and if one lays them out giving a spatial location for the alternatives on each issue, one can then establish the different configurations for each of the different Jewish groups, according to where their answers fall. For example:

	Resurrection of the dead	
	Yes	*No*
Hakamim	✓	
Sadducees		✓
Dead Sea Sect	✓	
	Acceptance of Temple as it exists	
Hakamim	✓	
Sadducees	✓	
Dead Sea Sect		✓

If one then maps the configuration for each group and superimposes the maps on top of each other, it is possible to see that although each map is different they overlap with each other in some parts of the grid, but not in others. If one then superimposes the teaching of Jesus on to the other maps, there is still overlap, because Jesus is profoundly and deeply involved in the interpretation and continuing construction of the Jewish universe of meaning, and it is obvious from Mark that Jesus was living within the boundary conditions of Israel.[5] But the configuration is unique —even bizarre—and it is of course individual. It is not attached to any of the other collective proposals: it is locked up in the person of this Jesus, this carpenter, this man.

It has already been pointed out (p. 125) how unforgivable the offence of individuality in teaching was in Israel, on the basis of Deut. 17:8–13. The issue, therefore, became inevitable of how this individual configuration of teaching could be justified, linked as it was with effects which in *any* Jewish construction of meaning were believed to belong to God—healing and the forgiveness of sins, as one finds in Mark 2:7: 'Why does this man speak thus? He blasphemes. Who is able to forgive sins but God alone?' One can well imagine Jesus answering, No one. For he did not apparently claim to be a substitute for God, but to be a mediation of what was still God's effect, not his own.

Jesus is thus one who teaches. That is what those closest to him, the disciples, most often call him: *didaskale*, teacher.[6] Once he is called the more technical 'rabbi' (11:21), formal and authenticated teacher, but even if that is not an anachronism, as some have argued, it does not do more than juxtapose Jesus to the Hakamic tradition as an alternative. Otherwise, he is more usually referred to as 'teacher', and not only by the disciples, by others as well.[7] He is the one who teaches[8] about the nature of God, whose teaching is authenticated by the consequences which flow out of him—consequences which were believed, in the connection between sin, suffering, forgiveness and healing, to belong to God alone.

If Jesus had not stayed so obviously within the boundary conditions of Israel, then his unique configuration of teaching would not have been so disruptively problematic. There were plenty of other miracle-workers, ecstatic prophets, and eccentric teachers around the place, particularly in Galilee, which had retained a considerable geographical and social independence from Israel.[9] But so long as they stayed eccentric (literally ex-centric, out on the edges of the circle) then there was no great problem. Judah b. Durtai refused to give up his individual teaching on the Passover, but he went far away to the south.[10] Jesus, in contrast, insisted, first maybe on the edges, but then at the very centre of Israel, eventually in the Temple itself, that what he knew, and what could be discerned in his life and word, of the nature and effect of God, was an authentic representation of that nature and its effect in the world of God's creation.

It is not possible, in a book of this length, to illustrate the powerful confidence with which Jesus spoke of God, and of the manner and the range of God's effect—the kingdom of God, in more poetic language. According to Mark, the assurance of Jesus' teaching derived from a direct relatedness to God which he summarized in his account of the Baptism and the Transfiguration. Thus, what Mark implies is that it was in his own self that Jesus solved the problem of immanence—or that this at least was the ground which Jesus explored and tested in his own life. He seems to have claimed, not just verbally, but in practice, that God (externality theistically characterized as Abba, Father) is directly available to the construction of life for those who have the faith that it can be so. Faith becomes the new boundary condition. Jesus asserted this first and foremost through the construction of his own life, moving constantly into each new encounter (and apparently bringing to the construction of consequence in each encounter) the sense of his own relation with God, and of God's relation to himself, to all men, and to the whole created order:

Very early next morning he got up and went away to a lonely spot and remained there in prayer. But Simon and his companions searched him out, found him, and said, 'All men are seeking you.' He answered, 'Let us go elsewhere, to the towns nearby, in order that I may proclaim there also; for, for this reason I came forth.' So he went throughout the whole of Galilee, proclaiming in their synagogues and throwing out demons (Mk. 1:35–9).

There was no denying the dramatic nature of what Jesus was doing, in word and work, any more than one could have denied dramatic effects in the case of Honi, the maker of rain. And just as there was great confusion about how to treat Honi (should he be executed or excommunicated, or should he be tolerated because clearly there was some kind of unique relation between Honi and God?),[11] so also there was great uncertainty about Jesus. But Jesus created a far greater problem than Honi: it was impossible to ignore Jesus, because he insisted on the issue of what he was claiming and making manifest closer and closer to the literal and the conceptual centre of Israel. He insisted on the journey to Jerusalem,[12] which for Jews who were not sectarian in a divisive sense was the centre, not only of emotional attachment (p. 32), but also of final decision and authority.

So what could one say or do about him? What account or what interpretation could be given? Mark records a number of different and conflicting interpretations. At one extreme, he records an interpretation which accepted the factual reality of what Jesus was doing, but which claimed that the resources of effect were not God but the opposition to God: only with Beelzebub's consent could Jesus throw out the spirits who lie under the authority of Beelzebub: 'by the ruler of the demons he casts out the demons' (Mk. 3:22). But Jesus was quite capable of dealing with *that* manœuvre, and in fact reserved his most frightening threat for those who, when they see the effect of God (the holy spirit, in mythological language) say 'Not-God' (3:29).

So the question of resources remained open, the question of Mark 6:2, *pothen touto tauta*, whence to this man these things? Mark makes it clear that there were other speculative answers to that question. An obvious possibility was that the holy spirit had been given to him in so obvious and direct a way that he could best be interpreted as a prophet. Herod thought he must be John the Baptist risen from the dead, 'and that is why the *dunameis* [powers] work in him. But others said, He is Elijah; yet others said, He is a prophet like one of the prophets' (6:14 f.).

It is obvious from the Markan account of Jesus that what people at that time would have referred to as the spirit—the introspective sense that men can be moved and stirred and inspired to construct particular words and actions, in contrast to other hypothetically possible words and actions—was a part of Jesus' understanding of how God can be related to men and can reach, not only into their nature and into the construction of their lives, but also through that nature into the world, creating further ripples of effect. 'I have baptized you with water; he will baptize you with the holy spirit' (Mk. 1:8). The summary of this is articulated in the account of a visible gift of the spirit at his baptism (1:10), but that only dramatizes what Jesus seems to have sensed in the construction of his life. That is why the saying in Mark 3:28, 'I tell you this: no sin, no slander, is beyond forgiveness for men; but whoever slanders the holy spirit can never be forgiven', is connected, very appropriately, to what has just gone before, 'It is by the ruler of demons that he throws out demons.' To deny the effect of God when one sees it, and to deny that God *is* of effect through the spirit which moves in men, is to excise oneself from any possible relation with God. God is then—and then only—absolutely dead. How can one be related to God if one denies the means of that relation? And then again Mark was perceptive in concluding this sequence with the anecdote, 'Your mother and your brothers are outside' (3:32); to which Jesus responds, 'Here are my mother and my brothers. Whoever enacts the will of God is my brother, my sister, my mother.' The issue is one of effect and action.

But apart from this, Jesus, in the Markan account, is very reticent about the holy spirit, and about the spirit in general. The holy spirit occurs in the collection of apocalyptic material in Mark 13 as the one who will give words to Christians to speak when they are on trial (v. 11). The only other usage is a perfect example of the way in which the Hakamim were attempting to restrict the holy spirit to the past, to the inspiration of scripture or of prophets in the past. 'How can the scribes maintain that the Christos [the Messiah] is the Son of David? David himself said, *in the holy spirit*, "The Lord said to my Lord: Sit at my right hand" ' (Mk. 12:35 f.). Obviously in the argument of Jesus it is a brilliant and subtle bit of polemic: 'All right,' he says in effect: 'you accept that *those* words were a consequence of the holy spirit (no matter what has happened to the spirit since then), so you can't deny their implication.'

But in general, in the Markan account, Jesus does not argue that his words and works are evidence of a restoration of the spirit as of old: the spirit may lead him (1:12), he may see in his spirit, and sigh in his spirit (2:8, 8:12), he may observe that the spirit is eager, but the flesh is weak (14:38), but those are very general terms. They are not used to suggest that Jesus was doing and saying what he did because he was directly inspired, as were the prophets of old. There are at best remote hints that Jesus understood himself in a prophetic role—that his mission, for example, had the effect described by Isaiah (Mk. 4:12; cf. 8:18);[13] or perhaps more specifically, when those who knew him and his family well were scandalized at him, he replied: 'A prophet is not without honour, except in his own country' (6:4). But that is almost proverbial in character and it is scarcely enough to establish that Jesus understood the effect of God in and through himself in exclusively or primarily prophetic terms. The nearest relation to that interpretation lies in those of his actions which resemble the technical *oth* of the prophets—the technical symbolic acts which summarize a future event and make its occurrence certain (p. 82).

There are two places where particular actions of Jesus may have been intended as prophetic actions, not least because the actions, or the events which took place, are interpreted through a quotation from the prophets. There is an obvious question whether the early Church made the connection, and illustrated the appropriateness of what he was supposed to have done (or what was supposed to have happened) through a text from a prophetic book. But let us accept that Jesus *did* make the connection himself, in order to make the strongest case possible that Jesus interpreted himself as a prophet 'like one of the prophets of old'—i.e., that he saw the restoration of the *dunamis* of God as being a consequence of the return of the holy spirit, as it had been in the days of old. The first episode is the cleansing of the Temple (Mk. 11:15–19) based on Jer. 7:11. Although only v. 11 is quoted, the context of the verse in Jeremiah makes the point of Jesus' action even more dramatic: 'Now go to my place in Shiloh where at first I gave my name a home; see what I have done to it because of the wickedness of my people Israel . . . I will treat this Temple that bears my name, and in which you put your trust, and the place I have given to you and your ancestors, just as I treated Shiloh.' It is possible that Jesus deliberately enacted a prophetic *oth* in order to express his certainty that the destruction of the Temple was already a *fait accompli*.

The second and even more probable example of Jesus expressing a deep conviction through the form of a prophetic action is the Last Supper. Once again, a prophetic word interprets the conviction: 'Jesus said to them, "You will all lose faith, for the Scripture says: I shall strike the shepherd and the sheep will be scattered" [Zech. 13:7].'[14] In the context of teaching and authority, there is no doubt that Jesus could have realized the danger to himself of coming to Jerusalem—and in fact it seems likely from the record that others knew it, just as well as he did. By doing so he was bringing his affirmation about the way in which God's effect can be found in the world to the very *locus* of authority and decision in Israel, to Jerusalem; furthermore, as will be seen, there is little doubt that he realized that the issue must necessarily be focused on his own death, since if his claim to the effect of God was absent there, then the worth of that effect was ultimately of passing moment. Nevertheless, so unequivocal had the *dunamis*, the effect, of God been in and through his life, that he insisted to his closest friends that even if he died, the effect of God (what they had seen of God in him) would still be mediated to them. The urgency of this he summarized in the prophetic action of taking bread and wine and saying (as it was later to be interpreted), In this sign I will still be with you, even to the end of the world. The only difference between this prophetic action and all others was picked up by Paul, in his account of the appropriation of the action in 1 Cor. 11:23 ff.: whereas other prophetic actions are appropriated in the future once, and once only, (Jeremiah enacted an exile and some particular people had to appropriate the action by going into exile), Paul makes it clear that this action was intended to be appropriated again and again. Twice over he repeats: As often as you do this, as often as you do this (vv. 25 and 26).[15]

But even if those two examples are accepted as prophetic actions, they do not establish that Jesus interpreted the restoration of the *dunamis* of God in prophetic terms. At the most, they suggest that Jesus did not limit himself to one category only within the Jewish resource of interpretation, but drew on whatever was most appropriate for a particular issue or occasion. Thus when the issue of divorce was raised (Mk. 10:2 ff.), Jesus did not confront his questioners with an alternative word directly inspired, 'Thus says the Lord'; he argued with him in the terms which *they* regarded as appropriate. In general terms, the Markan Jesus did not attempt to explain or justify the effect of God in and through his own person as being a return of the spirit which was known—or believed—to have created the words and actions of the prophets of old. In fact, exactly the reverse: that is exactly the opportunity which was offered to Jesus (after his so-called trial) which he refused. The Markan account of the trial suggests that it was nothing of the kind, but that it was a preliminary investigation to see whether Jesus would count as an aberrant teacher of the kind envisaged in Deut. 17:8–13 (see p. 125). Jesus himself drew attention to his teaching at his arrest (14:49), and the initial charge against Jesus focused on his threat to the Temple, the final *locus* of authority (14:58). When Jesus refused to respond to the high priest at all, let alone explain what his suspect teaching about the Temple meant, that silence was enough to condemn him as contumacious—as refusing to accept the decision of the 'judge who shall be in those days'. The high priest's subsequent question may have confirmed the aberration: the high priest, confronted by silence, and thus by a refusal on the part of Jesus to submit his individual teaching to the authority of 'the judge then in office', challenged him to state whether he believed he was justified because of a direct relation of himself to God as an anointed figure, the Christos. Jesus replied that he does stand in a direct relatedness to God, but not of the kind the high priest suggests: he is related to God as 'the son of man'—and what that means (since it is not a messianic title) will be discussed in due course.

Thus by refusing to submit the unique configuration of his teaching to 'the judge who shall be in those days' he made it certain that he should be excised from Israel, unless his teaching could be regarded as directly inspired, or unless it could be held that he was not actually a qualified teacher (which would certainly have been the opinion of the Hakamim). But in the terms of the actual investigation, as I have put it elsewhere, 'the real offence of Jesus lay, not in the fact that he said "I am", but in the fact that he said nothing. Silence was the offence, because it was a contempt of court which made him, in effect, a rebel against it.'[16]

On that basis, 'they therefore condemned him to be deserving of death' (v. 64)—though it seems likely, in view of the transfer to the Roman court, that the word 'they' is an inaccurate simplification, and that the majority of Jews involved did *not* accept that Jesus was sufficiently authenticated to count as a qualified teacher from the Deuteronomic point of view. The record in Mark then immediately continues: 'Some began to spit on him, blindfolded him, and struck him with their fists, crying out, *Profeteuson*, Prophesy' (v. 65). For those who *did* believe that he came in the category of a resistant person, the only other way (if he was not directly designated by God by anointing) in which the unique and rebellious configuration of his teaching could now be justified would be by some visible and unmistakable sign that the holy spirit had been given to him and had created his words and actions by a direct inspiration, or in-breathing, from God; and that would require some sign of the prophetic gift. But Jesus again remained silent. He did not take up the opportunity to interpret himself in a prophetic role. Indeed, he had long before given answer to those who specified what authenticating signs must obtain before they will recognize a dissolution of the problem of immanence before their own eyes. 'To test him they asked him for a sign from heaven. He sighed in his spirit and said, "Why does this generation ask for a sign? I tell you this: no sign shall be given to this generation." And with that he left them . . .' (8:11 ff.).

There were, then, *some* clues in the life of Jesus which might have justified interpreting Jesus as a prophet in the classic sense of that term—one to whom the spirit has visibly returned; so that people could say of him, in Mark 3:21, he is *exeste*, a suitable word for describing the ecstatic appearance of a classical prophet. But Jesus did much more than could be contained within that interpretation. He did not really fit the category, though he came close to it; and when it was reported to him that people were speculatively attempting to account for him as a prophet (in Mark 8:28) he did not pick up the speculation as correct.

But if Jesus was not wholly contained within the category of prophet, what other category would account for the visible effect of God manifest in him? Could he be the Christos, the anointed one, the Messiah?

It has been pointed out already (p. 95) that at the time when Jesus was alive there was no single concept of 'the Messiah'. There was not even a unanimous concept of a single messiah, since some thought there would be two, one on the priestly, the other on the kingly side. There was not even a consensus in regarding the Messiah as an exclusively eschatological figure, a figure only at the end of days. Provided the signs described in Scripture of the ideal ruler's age obtained, that moment or that situation could be regarded as 'messianic' in a reduced sense. The later Hasmonaeans made an attempt to interpret their reigns (or at least that of Simon) as messianic, and the Hakamim came close to regarding the reign of Salome Alexandra in that way.[17] But of course the critical factor lay in the phrase 'provided the signs obtained'. Did the manifest effects in the case of Jesus justify that interpretation? Did the signs obtain?[18]

Once again there are hints of a pressure toward that interpretation in the Markan account. There is obviously the so-called confession of Caesarea Philippi where Peter calls Jesus 'Christos', and there is the assent of Jesus to the question of the high priest in Mark 14:61 f. But as we have just seen, that question is one which shifts the ground: it is no longer about his teaching (what, if anything, he had said about the Temple) but about his person and the resources of his life: is he really claiming a direct link with God to justify his attitude? Jesus replies that he is, though he immediately modifies the claim by saying that it is *not* in the messianic sense usually associated with the term, but only as 'the

son of man'; in *that* sense, according to Mark, Jesus accepted
the designation of a direct relatedness with God; and that links
also to the two occasions, the Baptism and the Transfiguration,
when the *bath qol* calls Jesus, 'My beloved (or only) son'.

As with the category of prophet, Mark allows that there were
some indications in the life of Jesus which suggested that 'the
Messiah' might be an appropriate interpretation of how the effect
of God was manifest in him. The entry into Jerusalem in 11:7 ff.
makes that explicit; and the argument in 12:35 ff. against the
Scribes at least establishes that the Messiah does not have to be a
descendant of David. But the argument is not developed or applied
in Mark at all. In fact, exactly the reverse: as with the category
of 'prophet', although there are traces of a pressure toward the
interpretation of Jesus through those categories, the overwhelming
record of Mark is of an extreme reticence about them.

The places where there is no reticence, and where there are what
one might call 'high titles' applied to Jesus (titles which attribute
almost superhuman relation to God) are the two instances of a
voice from heaven (at the Baptism and the Transfiguration), and
the words attributed to those who have experienced the effect of
God mediated through Jesus in their own case (or who hope to do
so). So we find 'the Holy One of God' (1:24), 'the Son of God'
(3:11), 'the Son of the most high God' (5:7), 'son of David'
(10:47).

But those are the unclean spirits or the diseased crying out.
They are terms wrenched out of those who need the effect of God
for their own healing; and the response of Jesus can be an even
more emphatic reticence—a command (as in 1:25 and 3:12) that
they should be silent. The same note of retience (of commanding
silence) is explicit elsewhere, in 1:44, 5:43, 7:36, 8:30, 9:9. It
culminates in the head-on collision of Mark 11:27-33, where the
chief priests, the scribes, and the elders ask him the question of
resource outright: in what authority do you do these things? or
who gave you this authority in order that you may so act? According to Mark, Jesus completely turned the argument against them
and avoided a direct response: 'Neither do I tell you in what
authority I do these things.'

The reticence which comes so strongly through the Markan
record is all the more remarkable if one takes the view that by the
time Mark's Gospel was written Jesus was believed to be the

Christ, the Messiah. But in Mark, even where there is a pressure to interpret what was happening in Jesus through that category (or through the category of prophet) the interpretation is never developed; and in some instances Jesus is recorded as repudiating it. So it has long been obvious that this reticence about fairly obvious categories of interpretation is one of the basic and characteristic features of Mark's Gospel. It was this indeed which formed the basis for the theory of the so-called messianic secret, the theory that Jesus held back the knowledge of himself as Messiah until the appropriate moment. It was this which led Wrede to consider 'the messianic self-concealment of Jesus, in the clearest and most obvious sense of that term, as the essential subject with which we have to deal'.[19]

Wrede attempted to find a reason for the messianic self-concealment in a background of Jewish ideas about a hidden messiah, which in fact are not really applicable to the New Testament period. But in any case there is a much simpler reason for the reticence about high titles, or about other categories of interpretation. It lies in the fact that Jesus *did* use a category of interpretation (according to Mark), but it was entirely different from the more obvious ones available in the Jewish environment. He referred to himself (again, according to Mark; some maintain, as will be seen shortly, that Jesus historically never used the phrase of himself) as *ho huios tou anthropou*, the son of man. In a sense Jesus was saying, It is *not* as messiah, *not* as prophet, *not* as son of David, *not* as an angel, that I do what I do. It is as the son of man that these effects of God are manifest in me. In fact, one can say that his own solution to the problem of discerning God's effect in life depended absolutely on those *other* interpretations of his person being wrong. They may be accepted as illuminating, but as accounts of his person they are wrong. It is not as an extraordinary figure, but as the son of man, that he demonstrates the *dunamis* of God in their midst. Why, then, was this description important to Jesus, and what might he have meant by it?

2. THE SON OF MAN[1]

THERE are thirteen 'the son of man' sayings in Mark. There are two (2:10, 27) which speak of his present activity.

> 'But to prove to you that the son of man has authority on earth to forgive sins'—he said to the paralytic—'I order you; get up . . .'

> 'The son of man is master even of the sabbath.'

There are a larger number which speak of his suffering, death and rising again (8:31, 9:12, 31, 10:33, 45, 14:21, 41). Of these, three are the so-called Passion predictions (not quoted here in full):

> And he began to teach them that the son of man was destined to suffer grievously [lit., 'that it is necessary (*dei*) for the son of man to suffer many things'] (8:31).

> 'The son of man will be delivered into the hands of men; they will put him to death; and three days after he has been put to death he will rise again' (9:31).

> 'Now we are going up to Jerusalem, and the son of man is about to be handed over to the chief priests and scribes . . .' (10:33).

In 8:31 the word *dei*, it is necessary, has caused problems because it is uncertain from what the necessity derives. A similar problem arises in two further sayings in this category, 9:12 and 14:21, because they say that the sufferings of the son of man are exactly as scripture has described and foretold. But it is generally held that scripture does not describe the sufferings of 'the son of man' anywhere (a view which will shortly be contested):

> 'How is it that the scriptures say about the son of man that he is to suffer grievously and be treated with contempt?' (9:12).

> 'The son of man is going to his fate, as the scriptures say he will, but alas for that man by whom the son of man is betrayed' (14:21).

The two other sayings in this group are expressed in more general terms:

> 'The son of man did not come to be served but to serve, and to give his life a ransom for many' (10:45).
> 'The hour has come. Now the son of man is to be betrayed into the hands of sinners' (14:41).

Finally, there is a group of four sayings (8:38, 9:9, 13:26, 14:62) which refer to the son of man as a future figure yet to come. One of these (9:9) is closely connected to a saying (9:12) which refers to suffering, and the two together resemble the Passion predictions, although in an inverted order:

> As they came down from the mountain he warned them to tell no one what they had seen, until after the son of man had risen from the dead.

Two of these sayings draw their imagery directly from Dan. 7:13, 'I saw in the night visions, and, behold, one like a son of man came with the clouds of heaven, and came to the ancient of days, and they brought him near before him':

> 'Then they will see the son of man coming in the clouds with great power and glory' (13:26).

> 'I am', said Jesus, 'and you will see the son of man seated at the right hand of the power and coming with the clouds of heaven' (14:62).

One other saying is reminiscent of Daniel, though not so explicitly connected:

> 'If anyone in this adulterous and sinful generation is ashamed of me and of my words, the son of man will also be ashamed of him when he comes in the glory of his Father with the holy angels' (8:38).

These sayings, together with those in the other Gospels, have posed endless problems of such complexity that a recent writer has speculated that they may perhaps be insoluble—even though, as he pointed out, the correct solution may actually exist among the many widely divergent proposals which have already been made.[2] It is a dramatic change from the situation in 1931, when

Hoskyns and Davey posed 'the riddle of the New Testament', and found that 'the Son of Man description', which they regarded as a fundamental Christological title, was sufficiently unproblematic to be used to solve other parts of the puzzle. But it can now be seen that what they proposed as the meaning and use of the title is in fact an extremely lucid description of the nature of the problem which the phrase poses (Hoskyns and Davey did not actually justify their assumption that the phrase *is*—or was—a title). They recognized that the phrase in the Gospels is used by Jesus in direct speech—neither he nor anyone else is described outside direct speech as 'the Son of Man'; they noted that the phrase refers to the Son of Man in very different modes of activity, sometimes in the present, sometimes in the future, sometimes suffering, sometimes in glory; and they observed (though without drawing out the significance of what they had observed) that in Q (the supposed source used by Matthew and Luke) there are sayings about the present condition of the Son of Man, but none about his suffering and death.[3] Their solution was to unite these disparate features into a single Christological title which predates Mark's employment of it:

The very remarkable 'Son of Man' Christology is not a creation of Mark, and is not the result of his manipulation of the tradition. The whole tradition concerning Jesus, as it is presented by a critical separation of sources, emphasizes two Comings, the first in humiliation, and the second in glory. These are held together by the application of the title 'Son of Man' to Jesus Himself.[4]

That is what may be referred to as the classical solution. Yet at the very moment when those words were being written, Bultmann was working by an opposite method to an opposite conclusion—the enlarged edition of his book, *Die Geschichte der synoptischen Tradition*, appeared in exactly the same year as *The Riddle of the New Testament*.[5] He took seriously the basic observation that in the Gospels only Jesus talks of the Son of Man, *always* in the third person, and he argued that Jesus was talking not of himself, but of another, of an eschatological figure whose coming Jesus was looking for and whose advent he perhaps believed that he was initiating. Only later did the early Church come to regard Jesus *as* that figure, and thus to apply the title which Jesus had used of another to Jesus himself in his this-worldly and suffering activity. Thus, instead of uniting the sayings and regarding them as authentic self-references, he drove a wedge between them and regarded as authentic only those sayings which referred to a figure (different from Jesus) coming in the future; the other sayings he took to be creations of the early Christian communities. This may be referred to as the radical solution.

Since the time of Bultmann the radical solution has been taken even further, to the extent that it is now maintained (for example, by Vielhauer and Conzelmann)[6] that Jesus never used the phrase at all. It was entirely the creation of the early Christians as they tried to interpret the life of Jesus:

The unconnected juxtaposition of the three groups of sayings about the Son of Man can be explained from the structure of the Christology of the early community. They believed in the death and resurrection of Jesus; they waited for the parousia. Both points are formulated independently, as the evidence of the confession shows. The one who was expected, and imagined with the help of the idea of the Son of Man, was identified with Jesus. So his appearance on earth was also interpreted with the title Son of Man.[7]

That proposal is extremely improbable, if not absurd. It depends on '*the* idea of the Son of Man' being so well known and well established as a title ('with *the* title Son of Man': 'mit *dem* Menschensohntitel') that the community would turn to it for help in interpreting Jesus. The German original is even more specific than the English translation, since it has an additional adjective in the penultimate sentence: '. . . mit Hilfe der jüdischen Vorstellung vom Menschensohn'.[8] But that is exactly what the background does *not* supply. Only six pages before, Conzelmann stated (correctly) that the phrase in Aramaic is not a title, and he alluded to the fact that no evidence has yet been found to establish that 'the Son of Man' was a known and recognized *title* in any form of Judaism; it follows that Jesus could not have referred to himself by means of a well-known title, since it did not exist. Yet apparently a title *has* emerged in the period between the death of Jesus and the formation of the Gospel tradition which was sufficiently well known for the early Church to make extensive use of it in interpreting Jesus by it. Needless to say, Conzelmann did not produce evidence that this totally new title *had* been introduced in Judaism in the brief period in question. Nor would it be possible to do so.

Between the classical and radical solutions, a whole range of intermediate solutions has been produced. The basic strategy has been *divide et impera*: it has been to take the three categories of sayings (present activity, suffering, future coming), to designate one group as fundamental and authentic (except, of course, for the extreme radical solution which does not accept any as authentic to Jesus), and then to explain how the other two groups were introduced in the history of the early Church. The strategy has been effectively summarized by F. Hahn:

There is a certain consensus of critical opinion that the prophecies of suffering, at least in their present form, arose only in the community, and as a result the sayings about the dying and rising again of the Son of Man are placed at the end of the development. It is debated whether the words about the coming Son of Man or those about his earthly work must be regarded as primary and so referred back to Jesus himself; it is not very probable that both are equally original.[9]

On this basis, it is obviously possible to come up with diametrically opposed solutions, depending on which category is accepted as basic. Thus some regard the 'present activity' sayings as fundamental, and regard the 'future figure' sayings as a later addition under the influence of the Book of Daniel, when the early Church believed that Jesus would shortly be returning: having been one sort of 'son of man' on earth, they believed that he would shortly be returning as the other, and so added that belief to the tradition. However, others regard the futuristic sayings as fundamental, and maintain that Jesus identified himself with the apocalyptic agent who would appear on earth and inaugurate the final rule of God.[10]

One of the few points of agreement to emerge in the last half-century of debate is (as has already been observed) that there was no title 'the Son of Man' in any form of Judaism which was so well-known that Jesus could have used it with a reasonable assurance that people would have understood the references. On the other hand, there are five background contexts, mainly in Scripture, in which the phrase occurs, and which might therefore have supplied the use attributed to Jesus in the Gospels.

The first and most obvious (since it is numerically the most frequent) is in the Book of Ezekiel, where the prophet is repeatedly addressed as 'Son of Man'. It occurs nearly a hundred times, but it is extremely improbable that this can be connected directly with the New Testament use (because Jesus is never addressed by this title, and because it does not in any way help to explain the content of the phrase where it refers to a suffering and glorified figure); but it should be borne in mind more carefully than it sometimes is that any audience who had heard the Prophets read in synagogue or elsewhere would be familiar with the phrase as a mode of address and might, therefore, not find it surprising or novel to hear it applied to a human figure, albeit one with a particular function in relation to God. The book of Ezekiel at least ensures that the phrase would not have been totally bizarre or unfamiliar.

The second main use (numerically) in Scripture occurs in Hebrew poetry, where 'son of man' appears as a parallel to 'man'. Hebrew poetry was constructed basically by means of stress and parallel meaning:

> What is man that thou art mindful of him:
> And the son of man that thou visitest him? (Ps. 8:4).

It is one of the few points of almost unanimous agreement in debates about 'the son of man' that, since the phrase in those instances is simply another way of saying 'man', it cannot supply a sufficiently distinct use to be of any help in determining possible meanings in the New Testament. But that judgement carries with it a possible distortion of historical perspective: the fact that scholars since the time of 'the eminently learned' Lowth[11] have been able to recognize parallelism as a device of poetry does not mean that exegetes in the more ancient world could not have attempted to discern additional significance in the second half of a verse, or in particular words within it. In fact, we know that exegetes, both Christian and Jewish, *did* find significant meaning in the parallel words. In particular, it will be argued shortly that the Targum translators of Hebrew poetry undoubtedly discerned a significant meaning in the phrase 'son of man', which was established by the comparably similar nature of the contexts in which the majority of instances occur in Scripture; and it will be argued further that the particular nuance of meaning which they discerned is congruent with the uses attributed to Jesus in Mark. It is familiar that rabbinic exegesis did not regard even the traditional aberrant orthographies in the text of Scripture as idle: they would certainly not be deterred by *parallelismus membrorum*.

The third important use in Scripture is Dan. 7:13 f.:

I saw in the night visions, and behold, with the clouds of heaven there came one like a son of man [*kebar enosh*] and he came to the Ancient of Days and was presented before him. And to him was given dominion and glory and kingdom, that all peoples and nations and languages should serve him. His dominion is an everlasting dominion, which shall not pass away, and his kingdom is one that shall not be destroyed.

In v. 18, reference is made to 'the saints of the Most High (who) shall receive the Kingdom, and possess the Kingdom for ever, for ever and ever'. The original meaning of that passage is disputed.[12] In general terms, is 'the one like a son of man' to be identified with the saints of the Most High, so that this particular figure symbolizes a corporate entity, namely, the persecuted faithful of Israel, who are, in this vision, being vindicated beyond their persecution and death? Or is the figure in the vision separate from the saints, coming *from* God as an agent of the final vindication and restoration of the martyrs? For present purposes there is no need to decide between those two possible interpretations, because what remains in common to both is that Daniel envisages a vindication of the faithful in Israel beyond their persecution and death, either because they are themselves identified with 'the saints of the Most High' (strong association), or because the nations will be subordinate to the angels, and Israel will benefit from the ensuing peace (weak association). The vindication is most specific in vv. 21 f., and is a necessary consequence of the judicial nature of the scene envisaged: it is focused on the figure of 'one like a son of man' in vv. 13 f., no matter whether that figure is understood as a symbol or as an agent.

The fourth background use begins to move outside Scripture, and is to be found in apocalyptic works. The instances occur in the Similitudes of Enoch (Eth. Enoch xxxvii–lxxi) and in 4 Ezra xiii. Those at least establish that interpretations of Dan. 7 were made in apocalyptic works, but they cannot establish that such interpretations were commonly or extensively known at the time when Jesus was alive. The problem of dating the works is notoriously difficult; and while it remains the case that no parts of the Similitudes are found among the Qumran texts (in contrast to the discovery of fragments of other parts of 1 Enoch), the presumption must be that the Similitudes are an independent work subsequently incorporated into the whole. That would not necessarily prove that such a work is late in date: Lindars has argued that since the Similitudes identify Enoch with the Son of Man, it is hard to suppose that the work was written by a Christian; consequently, the work may have been extant at or before the time when Jesus was alive.[13] But even if the problem of date were solved, the apocalyptic use is insufficient to establish that there was a widely known figure in Judaism known as 'the son of man'. As Lindars put it, 'It has now become embarrassingly obvious that the Son of Man was not a current title in Judaism at all'.[14] But what Lindars also illustrated in his article is that Daniel was available, and was used, for *different* exegetical interpretations, and that Jesus might very well have made his own use and interpretation of it. Therefore, where Leivestad (one of those who takes the 'present activity' sayings as fundamental) had attempted to eliminate pretentious and apocalyptic connotations from the phrase, so that its designation becomes 'a humble one, denoting solidarity and identification with the sons of men',[15] Lindars rightly asked:

We are entitled to ask what the evangelists thought they were doing when they picked up this designation from the sayings tradition, and incorporated it in apocalyptic sayings of coming glory, in a way which recalls, and sometimes is clearly intended to recall, the one like a son of man of Dan. vii.[16]

A possible answer would be that they were incorporating their knowledge of the resurrection, and that they therefore extended the humble self-designation to include the vindication, and that they did so by means of the exegetical opportunity afforded by Daniel. But in that case, it has to be pointed out that the suffering and the vindication are *already* linked in Daniel, and that it is not in the least improbable that Jesus himself could have made the connection as a means of expressing his understanding of his own situation and his trust in the Father. The strength of Lindars' argument is that it reinforces that possibility.

Fifth, and again outside Scripture, but influencing and contributing to scriptural ideas at different points, are the ideas of a primal or primordial man, which occur in ancient Near Eastern material and continue into Gnostic beliefs. The possible links between those beliefs and the New Testament have been explored,[17] but it is even more difficult to establish a direct connection between them and the New Testament than it is to establish a direct connection between the New Testament and the apocalyptic uses. This is not to deny the possibility of an indirect influence, through the effect of those ideas on, for example, Dan. 7.

In addition to those five background contexts which might have supplied a well-known sense of the phrase, and which might, therefore, have established its intended meaning, G. Vermes has recently suggested an entirely different background context.[18] He has suggested that the phrase, *bar nash* (a son of man) or *bar nasha* (the son of man) might have been derived from colloquial Aramaic, the language spoken by many ordinary people at the time of Jesus and apparently (to judge from the Aramaic phrases attributed to him in the Gospels) by Jesus himself. It is well known that *bar nash* and *bar nasha* can mean 'someone', and 'man', 'a human being'. But Vermes has attempted to exemplify and establish an earlier suggestion that the phrases were also used as a circumlocution for 'I'; in other words, that people used the phrase to refer to themselves and to mean 'I' when they were being modest or not wishing to draw attention to themselves. It has frequently been suggested that this was the original meaning of at least some of the instances in the Gospels, and that this innocent phrase was converted into a title by the later Church. Thus, for example, Bultmann commented on Mk. 2:10, 28, Mt. 8:20, 11:19, 12:32: 'This . . . group owes its origin to a mere misunderstanding of the translation into Greek. In Aramaic, the son of man in these sayings was not a messianic title at all, but meant "man" or "I".'[19]

Vermes's argument takes a slightly different form. Having argued that the circumlocution existed in Aramaic, he then distinguished between those sayings in the Gospels which are and are not connected with Dan. 7. He then concluded:

To sum up, there is no evidence whatever, either inside or outside the Gospels, to imply, let alone demonstrate, that 'the *son of man*' was used as a title. There is, in addition, no valid argument to prove that any of the Gospel passages directly or indirectly referring to Daniel vii. 13 may be traced back to Jesus. The only possible, indeed probable, genuine utterances are sayings independent of Dan. vii in which, in accordance with Aramaic usage, the speaker refers to himself as the *son of man* out of awe, reserve, or humility. It is this neutral speech-form that the apocalyptically-minded Galilean disciples of Jesus appear to have 'eschatologized' by means of a midrash based on Dan. vii. 13.[20]

Part of this proposal is clearly assertion, not argument, since it can equally well be said that 'there is no valid argument to prove' that Jesus did not make his own exegesis of Dan. 7, as a means of interpreting his situation and person in relation to God. It is arbitrary to exclude passages connected with Dan. 7 when it cannot be proved that Jesus did not make the connection with Dan. 7 himself. If someone did it in the early Church, it must be possible that Jesus could have done it himself.

However, the more fundamental part of Vermes's argument, in favour of a circumlocutionary use of *bar nash(a)* in Aramaic, is independent of that speculation. Where the more important argument is concerned, it is obvious that almost all suggested solutions to the problem of 'the son of man' would be helped, in different ways, if his argument is correct. For if that argument is correct, it helps to explain how so unusual a phrase ever came to be used or attributed as a self-designation, even if it was also understood to have additional meaning: if it was colloquially characteristic to refer to oneself in that way in certain circumstances, then the possibility of doing so with what Vermes calls *double entente*[21] is made very much more straightforward and unsurprising. But precisely because the argument would be so helpful, it is all the more important to be clear whether the evidence is in fact strong enough to bear the weight being placed on it.

In the article 'The Son of Man' I have looked at the arguments in some detail and it would be superflous to repeat the exercise here. But in summary, I have suggested that the arguments advanced are not sufficient to establish a circumlocutionary use beyond doubt. Vermes has found only nine examples on which to base the claim that *bar nash(a)* was used as a circumlocution, and although he is undoubtedly correct in pointing out how little *colloquial*, spoken, Aramaic has survived in the written texts, the fact remains that even within the nine examples, it cannot be said that more than two (possibly only one) make a strong case for a circumlocutionary use. The others are *congruent* with such a use, in the sense that they are coherent with that sense, but they cannot on their own *establish* that sense, because other interpretations of their use are possible.

In putting forward those criticisms, I stated at the time that they were not advanced in any negative or defensive spirit, as though, for example, Vermes's argument for circumlocution is inimical to traditional New Testament exegesis. On the contrary, if his argument does establish such a use, it would be extremely helpful to more interpretations of the 'son of man' sayings in the Gospels than his own—indeed, it would probably be helpful to all of them. But for that reason, it is important not to grasp the assistance offered before it has been sufficiently well established that the use was easily and widely understood. It is a question whether nine examples are sufficient when it is recognized that not all the examples establish the use, but are simply congruent with it, while at the same time being open to other possible interpretations. These are, of course, early days, and other examples may well be forthcoming. At present, the case *does* seem to be established that the phrase could carry with it a generic reference, and that a speaker could include himself within the reference. That argument is an important gain, and is a direct consequence of Vermes's work.

This summary of the six main areas in which the phrase '(the) son of man' occurs indicates how complicated this aspect of the problem of reference is, since all of them have been used, sometimes in combination, to answer the question whether there was a use which was sufficiently well known at the time of Jesus to establish what he might have meant by the phrase (supposing he used it).

One of the few points of almost total unanimity in this tangled discussion is that the second area of scriptural use summarized above (the use in poetry, p. 144) can be eliminated from reference to the New Testament because its use as a parallelism in Hebrew poetry gives it nothing more than a synonymous sense: it can only be a surrogate for 'man'. Yet at the risk of creating even further confusion, it may be questioned whether this almost unanimous verdict has not been arrived at too fast. It is possible that Jewish exegetes of Scripture *did* discern a significant meaning in the use of this phrase, because in the places where it occurs in Scripture it usually (though not invariably) does so in contexts which carry with them the same general meaning. 'Son of man' occurs in contexts which refer to man's weakness in contrast to God and the angels, because he is subject to death. This is the case in Ps. 8:4 (which, although it celebrates the extraordinary status of man in creation, does so by emphasizing that he may be godlike in his command of some aspects of creation, but he is certainly less than God [*meat me-elohim*]), 144:3 f., 146:3 f., Job 16:21 f., 25:6, Isa. 51:12). The four uses in Jer. 49:18, 33, 50:40, 51:43 cannot really be taken as expressing much more than the phrase 'no one', *lo . . . ben adam*, but they undoubtedly reinforce the contextual association of 'son of man' with death, since all four instances occur in parallel conjunction with *ish* (man) and all four refer to a situation of total desolation and destruction, in which 'man' and 'the son of man' will no longer be found. Less explicit, but certainly expressing an absolute contrast between man and God, is Num. 23:19. The exceptions to the contextual association are Ps. 80:17 (though even there the *total* context of the Psalm makes it clear that the reference is to 'man under threat of destruction', the people of Israel who have suffered and who plead for help), Job 35:8, Isa. 56:2. Thus anyone who had read all these passages with care (and Jewish exegetes certainly had an eye for detail) might well conclude that the predominant sense of 'son of man' was man subject to death, in contrast to God and the angels, but that it was not the invariable sense of the phrase. Furthermore, the equivalence of Pss. 8:4 and 144:3 (cf. Job 7:17) would itself suggest that the comparison of passages was justified.

This is exactly the understanding of the phrase which occurs in the Targum translations of Psalms and Job. They are medieval translations and have no direct relevance to the New Testament of any kind whatsoever. But reference is made to them here, because they use the phrase 'son of man' so consistently with the association of 'man subject to death', 'man born to die', that they make it clear that to recognize this sense of the phrase, established in the original biblical contexts, is not idiosyncratic. It is clear that the Targum translators recognized that the nuance associated with the phrase 'son of man' in the majority of biblical contexts is 'man born to die', and they therefore used that phrase to translate 'man' in other contexts where man's subjection to death is referred to.

Details of this are given in the article, 'The Son of Man'. It is not, of course, a surprising understanding of the phrase. It is the literal implication of it: 'son of man' is by definition man born in the sequence of generations, and therefore destined to yield his own place to a subsequent generation in due course. This, in turn, goes back to Genesis, where the first man (Adam, which in itself is a word which means 'man') was subjected to the penalty of death. The *bene adam*, the sons of Adam/man, remain subject to the same penalty, so that man in the succession of generations is by definition subject to death. Since *ben adam* (the Hebrew for 'son of man') occurs in Scripture predominantly in contexts associated with death, it is not surprising that the obvious linguistic connection was developed exegetically into the tendency to use *bar nash* in comparable contexts. This can be seen in the Targums on Genesis. *Bar nash* is particularly common in the creation narratives (see, e.g. NGen. i. 2, 27, ii. 18, 23, vi. 6mg, 7mg, viii. 21, TJ2 Gen. i. 26); in vi. 6 and 7 the margin (mg) corrects to *bar nasha* in contexts where the connection with man's subjection to death is obvious:

'Behold I have given my spirit to the sons of man [*bene enasha*] because they are flesh and their works are evil . . .' And there was regret before the Lord that he had created man [*adam*, mg. *bar nasha*] on the earth . . . And the Lord said: 'I will blot out man [*adam*] whom I have created [mg., 'And the word of the Lord (said): 'I will blot out *bar nasha* whom I have created'] from above the face of the earth . . .'

In Gen. 9:5 f. the association with death is particularly clear and explicit:

'For your life-blood I will demand; from every beast I will demand it; from the son of man [*bar nasha*] from the brothers of the son(s) of man, I will demand the life of the son of man. Whosoever sheds the blood of a son of man [*bar nash*], by the hands of a son of man shall his blood be shed, because in a likeness from before the Lord he created man [*adam*; mg., *bar nasha*].'

Two examples of particular interest occur in Genesis, which indicate that *bar nash(a)* was indeed sufficiently associated with man's subjection to death for the translators to use it to express that association. The first is Gen. 40:23, a verse in which the translators incorporated an explanation of the fact that the chief butler forgot his promise to Joseph, who therefore stayed in prison for two further years: why had that happened? TJ1 interpreted it as follows:

Joseph forsook his trust in heaven and put his trust in a son of man, and said to the chief butler, 'Remember me when it is well with you . . .'. And because Joseph forsook the favour that is from above and put his trust in the chief butler, in flesh which passes away, therefore the chief butler did not remember Joseph . . .

In TJ2 the phrase 'son of man' is not used, but the interpretation is expanded:

He put his trust in the chief butler, in flesh which passes away, and in flesh which tastes the cup of death. He did not remember the scripture as it is written and interpreted, 'Cursed is the man [*gwbra*] who trusts in flesh and makes flesh his trust . . .'

However, in Neof. *both* parts of the interpretation are locked together:

Joseph forsook the favour that is from above and the favour that is from below and the favour which had accompanied him from his father's house, and he trusted in the chief butler, in flesh that passes, in flesh that tastes the cup of death. And he did not remember the scripture, for it is written in the book of the Law of the Lord which is like the book of the Wars: Cursed be the son of man (*bar nasha*) who trusts in flesh and who places his trust in flesh.'

A similar introduction of *bar nasha* in connection with death occurs in the comment which TJ2 and N add to Gen. 49:22: 'The daughters of the kings of the rulers said to one another: "This is Joseph the righteous man: he has not gone after the sight of his eyes, nor the imagination of his heart. Those are what destroy the son of man from the world." '

Obviously, those Targum uses cannot establish a direct connection with the New Testament on their own. What they can establish is that at least some translators recognized the contextual association and took it to be the main implication of the phrase 'son of man'. Not surprisingly, therefore, the same association of the phrase with 'man born to die' can be found elsewhere, particularly in connection with Genesis. A neat example of this occurs in J.Ter, viii. 3 (5), J.A.Z. ii. 3, which record the saying of R. Jose bar R. (A)boun: All sweat (*zya*) which falls from a son of man is deadly poison except that which comes from his face.' This is exegesis by a very literal pressure on Gen. 3:19: the Aramaic *zya* is the direct equivalent of the Hebrew, in the verse which emphasizes, dust you are, and to dust you will return.

But quite apart from any connections with Genesis, the phrase in connection with man's subjection to death occurs elsewhere, and it occurs at least as early as Ecclus. 17:30: 'All things are not able to be among men, because a son of man is not deathless.' Indeed, one might say that the earliest occurrence outside Scripture, Sef. iii. 15 ff., reinforces the *natural* association of the phrase with death: man as son of man is in the sequence of generations, and is therefore bound to die: 'If the idea should come to the mind of the Kings of Arpad, in whatever way a son of man shall die, you will have been false to all the gods of the treaty which is in this inscription.'

Similarly, in the Dead Sea Scrolls, although the plural use is more common (as in Scripture), the singular 'son of man' certainly seems to reflect the biblical associations of the phrase in 1QS xi. 20–3, where the whole psalm is constructed to draw out the contrast between the *bene adam* (the *sodh basar* (ll. 6 ff.), who cannot see the true design of God and who have not been cleansed from sin) and the *bene shamaim* in l. 8:

> Who can contain your glory,
>> and what is the [lit., 'a'] son of man
>> in the midst of your wonderful deeds?
> What shall one born of woman
>> be accounted before you?
> Kneaded from the dust,
>> his abode is the nourishment of worms.
> He is but a shape, but moulded clay,
>> and inclines towards dust.
> What shall hand-moulded clay reply?
>> What counsel shall it understand?[22]

The same is also true of 1QH iv. 29 ff., where the contrast is clear between 'the creature of clay', a son of man in whom there is no perfection, and the righteousness which God establishes:

> But what is flesh (to be worthy) of this?
> What is a creature of clay
>> for such great marvels to be done,
> Whereas he is iniquity from the womb
>> and in guilty unfaithfulness until his old age?
> Righteousness, I know, is not of man,
>> nor is perfection of way of the [lit., 'a'] son of man:
> to the Most High God belong all righteous deeds.

It may, of course, be maintained that those passages are so biblical in their style that 'son of man' simply slipped in as an obvious phrase, without a conscious recognition of its original contextual meaning. But that is really to make the same point in a different way: the connection between 'son of man' and death *is* obvious and it *is* biblical, and was, consequently, a natural phrase to introduce in these contexts.

In the later literature, the phrase with this association is more common. Some of the possible examples are those which Vermes claimed as circumlocutions. In itself, this is not surprising, because one of the reasons suggested for circumlocution is that a speaker

might not want to refer to his own death. However, if the phrase
was established as appropriate through its scriptural connection
with death, the circumlocutionary reference is no longer necessary:
the speaker may be referring to man's subjection to death, 'man
born to die', and including himself (obviously) in the same condition. This seems an entirely natural interpretation of J.Ket.
35a (xii. 3), one of the examples offered by Vermes: 'It is related
that Rabbi was buried wrapped in a single sheet, for he said: "It
is not as *bar nasha* [the son of man] goes that he will come again."
But the rabbis say: "As *bar nash* [a son of man] goes, so will he
come again." '

The dispute is about the form and appearance of the resurrection
body: will it appear in the same clothes (as the rabbis maintained)
or will it be in an entirely different guise or clothing (as Rabbi
maintained)? The point is a general one, but there is obviously no
doubt that Rabbi was including himself in the genus of men who
have to die.

The same sense of 'man subject to death' comes through in one
of the other examples quoted by Vermes, the story of R. Simeon
b. Yohai in the cave:

R. Simeon b. Yohai hid in a cave for thirteen years with the support of
carob-beans until sores came on his body. At the end of those thirteen
years he said to himself: 'I will go and see what is happening in the
world.' So he went and sat in the mouth of the cave, where he saw a
trapper trapping birds in his net. He heard the *bath qol* saying, 'Go
free,' and the bird escaped. He said: 'A bird, apart from heaven, does
not perish; how much less the son of man' (J. Sheb. ix. 1 (38d), Ber. R.
lxxix. 6).

This could also be true of another of Vermes's examples, J. Ber. 5b:
the disciple of 'man born to die' is as dear as a son, because the
disciple—to whom R. Hiyya in this instance has actually bequeathed his goods—*is* the succession and continuity beyond
death, as is a son: 'When R. Hiyya bar Adda died . . . R. Levi
received his valuables. This was because his father used to say,
The disciple of *bar nasha* is as dear to him as his son.'

But the general association of this phrase with the sense of
'man subject to death' makes sense in other passages, and in
some, it makes sense of them. For example, B. Sukk. 53a records
the elliptical saying of R. Johanan bar Nappaha: 'The feet of a son

of man [*bar eynash*] have charge over him: they bring him to the
place where he is required.' This saying can only be understood
without elucidation if 'a son of man' was known to carry with it
the nuance, 'man who has to die'; and a story is told in B. Sukk. to
illustrate that that is exactly what the phrase means. It is a story
about Solomon, who one day observed the angel of death, and
noticed that the angel was sad. When Solomon asked the angel
why he looked so sad and heard that the angel had come to gather
in two Cushite scribes of Solomon, Solomon at once sent the
Cushites to Luz in order that they might escape death—there being
a tradition that the angel of death has no power in Luz. But at the
very gate of the city, the two Cushites died. So when Solomon
saw the angel of death next day, he found the angel looking much
more cheerful. 'Why are you so cheerful?' he asked, 'Because', the
angel replied, 'to the place where they were wanted you sent them.'
Solomon immediately responded, 'The feet of a son of man have
charge over him: they bring him to the place where he is required.'

Or again, in the story in J.Yom. 42c (v. 2) of how Simon the
Just predicted his own death, the point of the final sentence is
dramatically reinforced if the phrase was well known to bear
this association with death. In this story, the people ask Simon
how he knows that his death is about to occur. He replies that
each year when he approaches the Holy of Holies, an old man
has appeared in order to accompany him, but that in this particular
year, the old man has not appeared. R. Abbahu heard a man
objecting, on the basis of Lev. 16:17, that no man could possibly
have appeared there; nor could it have been an angel, because, as
Ezek. 1:10 puts it, their faces resemble those of men. It follows
that if they had appeared in the Holy of Holies they, like men,
would have suffered the penalty of death, because they *look* like
men. For this reason the explanation was recorded: 'I am not
saying that it was a son of man [*bar nash*, i.e., one subject to death,
whether angel *or* man]: I am saying that it was the Holy One,
blessed be he.'

Despite Ezek. 1:10, it is more usual for *bar nash* to be contrasted
with angels, on the basis of Ps. 8:5(6). It is this, for example,
which creates the pun in J.Peah, iii. 7(8):

According to R. Phinehas, there were two brothers in Ashkelon, who
had gentile neighbours. They said, 'When these two Jews go to Jerusalem on pilgrimage, we will take all that belongs to them.' But when

the time came for them to go, the Holy One, blessed be he, put two angels in their place, who, in their coming and going, were exactly like them. When the brothers returned, they sent gifts to their neighbours, who asked them, 'Where have you been?' They replied, 'In Jerusalem.' They said: 'Then whom did you leave in the house?' They answered, 'Not a son of man.'

The phrase (as in the passages of Jeremiah) can clearly mean 'no one', but it is also intended to convey, 'not "man born to die" in contrast to angels, but angels themselves.'

The point of this argument has not been to suggest that *all* occurrences of the phrase carry with them this association, since that is certainly not the case: the phrase can mean simply 'someone' 'anyone', 'no one', or even 'a human being'. What is being suggested is that the phrase was recognized as being associated with man's frailty and subjection to death in the main biblical contexts, and that this recognition was not surprising, because the phrase itself in Hebrew, *ben adam*, draws attention to the connection with Adam's penalty of death in Gen. 3:19, and to the consequent succession of generations.

If that is correct, it can then further be suggested that the occurrences of the phrase, 'the son of man', in Mark are entirely congruent with the biblical senses of the phrase, but that in Mark the two main senses (from the poetic association and from Dan. 7) of man born to die who will nevertheless be vindicated by God, have already been combined. It is worth noting that Heb. 2:6–9 has exactly this understanding of the phrase, strongly associating it with death, but also drawing attention to vindication. Having quoted Ps. 8:4 in 2:6 f., Hebrews goes on: 'At present, it is true, we are not able to see that "everything has been put under his command", but we do see in Jesus one who was "for a short while made lower than the angels" and is now "crowned with glory and splendour" because he submitted to death: by God's grace he had to experience death for all mankind.' Here, the association of the phrase with the main biblical sense and with Jesus is explicit. If the argument of Vermes is right, it is then not surprising to find such a phrase used in self-reference; but even if that argument is not correct, the third main use in Scripture, the address to Ezekiel, at least helps to explain how such a phrase used of a particular person, would not have seemed impossibly bizarre.

But why the phrase? We have already seen how the opening chapters of Mark portray Jesus as one who restored the *dunamis* of God to the world and to the lives of men. This evoked questions about the *exousia*, the resource, from which he did this, culminating in the incredulity of 6:1-6, where the known and certainly human origins of Jesus are emphasized. But precisely because the people *do* know the family of Jesus—'and are not his sisters here with us?'—they are compelled to ask the question which remains the fundamental question from which all Christological reflection begins: *pothen touto tauta?* Whence to this man these things?

As we have seen, many answers (according to Mark) were projected toward Jesus, ranging from those who affirmed that he was doing what he was doing through the prince of devils, to the confession of Peter. In this respect, the works and the disturbing words of Jesus were not at issue: the issue was to know from what resource Jesus derived them. Many possible answers were floated toward Jesus: perhaps he did it because he was directly inspired by God, as a prophet; perhaps because he was Elijah; perhaps because he was the Christ. According to Mark, Jesus either repudiated those descriptions, or else accepted them (or at least the last of them) only with an extreme emphasis that no one should be told about it. Similarly with the so-called 'high titles' (1:24, 3:11, 5:7; cf. 1:34), which are evoked from those who have felt in their own case the *dunamis* of God mediated through Jesus: the usual reaction of Jesus is to command silence. It was this observation of reticence which led to the theory of the messianic secret.

But if the phrase 'the son of man' was used by Jesus with reference to himself in a way which combined the fundamental biblical senses (man born to die who nevertheless will be vindicated beyond death by God) then the explanation of the reticence is obvious. In effect, according to Mark, Jesus insisted that it is *not* as an extra-ordinary or super-natural figure that he does and says what he does; it is not even as a specially inspired person, a prophet: it is himself, as a man among men, as the son of man, the one whom they all know about, man who has to die; and yet he also affirms through the same phrase that it is as man who will be vindicated beyond an unevaded and totally real death: 'He warned them to tell no one what they had seen, until after the son of man [man who has to die but who can and will be vindicated] had risen from the dead' (Mk. 9:9).

Applied to the reported sayings in Mark (pp. 139–40), it can be seen that sometimes the vindication theme dominates (8:38, where the transition from 'me' and 'my' to 'the Son of Man' is a transition from relation to Jesus here and now, to relation to Jesus, the one who has to die but who will be vindicated; 13:26; 14:62), sometimes it is the theme of suffering and subjection to death (9:12, where it now becomes obvious instead of puzzling exactly *where* it is written that the son of man must suffer and be treated with contempt; 14:21, with which cf. J.Kil. ix. 3 (6), J.Ket. xii. 3, Ber.R.c. 2 (see p. 154)—here again the enigma of *where* it is written that 'the son of man goes' is solved; 14:41). On this argument it is consequently possible that the so-called Passion predictions originally combined a reference both to the necessity of dying and to his vindication through resurrection (through resurrection because Jesus took the side of the Hakamim against the more strictly biblical Sadducees, 12:18–27), however much details may have been filled in *post eventum*. Furthermore, the word *dei* in 8:31 (it is necessary), concerning which there has been a difficulty in determining from whence the necessity is derived, becomes obvious: it is indeed necessary that the son of man, man born to die, *should* die; the Genesis penalty of death is virtually universal, and although Enoch and Elijah may have been taken straight to heaven, Jesus, as the son of man, as the one who is not extra-ordinary, must also die.

These considerations, which begin to foreshadow Pauline interpretations through Adam, suggest a possible interpretation of 10:45. The most probable background for the term *lutron*, 'ransom', lies in the area of *lex talionis*, since the applicability of *lutron* in order to alleviate the strict interpretation of that law, may have been an issue before 66 c.e. If so, it would make Jesus' use of the term unsurprising, since it is clear that he was sensitively aware of other issues between Hakamim and Sadducees (for example, issues concerning divorce and resurrection); he would simply have been developing and reapplying a conceptual issue in order to claim that as man born to die, his death could be interpreted as being a ransom or redemption payment for many who are otherwise subject to the Genesis penalty of death.[23] As Mk. 3:28 implies, *all* the sons of men are liable to death. But in this man who equally has to die, the substitutionary payment is made, and a new God-relatedness (a new covenant, in the language of the time) is established. It is evidenced in the effect (the holy spirit) of God—an effect which the early Church undoubtedly claimed and experienced.

Could Jesus have made so Pauline a leap of imagination? Or may it be the case that Paul could be so imaginative about the death of Jesus and its effects because it was anticipated in Jesus' own understanding of himself as 'the son of man'? If the latter, it implies a very profound understanding by Jesus of his relation to God whose *dunamis* was being mediated through him. This is equally implicit in 2:10 and 27, which assert that it is as *man* born to die that he nevertheless has authority on earth to forgive sins, and is 'lord of the sabbath'.

The point of this argument is not to assert that all the sayings attributed by Mark to Jesus are authentic, or that none of them have been developed or modified in the course of transmission. The point has been to show that if the phrase originally represented a fusion of the two main biblical senses of the phrase, all the sayings are coherent and possible. Whether any *particular* saying is authentic depends on a careful evaluation of its status in Mark and in relation to the other Gospels. But fundamentally it seems possible that Jesus was aware of the contextual meaning of the phrase 'the son of man', as 'man born to die', 'man subject to death', and that he applied this to himself in order to emphasize that the mediation of God which was discerned in his case was *not* mediation through an extraordinary or supernatural or superhuman figure: it was through a man who, as much as any other, was subject to death; and yet he insisted through the other biblical (or at least traditional) association of the phrase that it was also through a man who would be vindicated by God in a dramatic and death-defeating way.

Whence, then, to this man these things? These suggestions lead at once into Christology, for they imply a self-consciousness in Jesus of his own relatedness to God sufficient for those affirmations to emerge—in act as much as in word, in the insistence on going to Jerusalem as much as in the prediction of the likely outcome. In all the Gospels, not simply in Mark, the theme of Jesus' determination to go to Jerusalem is fundamental, and there is no reason to assume that it is simply a structural device (p. 130). It may indeed have been a basic thread on which to hang incidents and teaching which had become detached from a specific location

in the transmission of the tradition. But if the argument advanced
here is at all correct, there is an obvious and necessary reason for
the insistence on the journey to Jerusalem. Mark portrays Jesus
as someone who was unequivocally human and who was therefore
subject to death. Yet he realized, according to Mark, so powerful
a transformation of his own experience as a consequence of the
effect or *dunamis* of God that he had the confidence to mediate
that *dunamis* to others. Indeed, he claimed that even greater
effects would be possible for others if they had the faith that it
could be so. To put it in jargonistic language, but language which
does justice to the evidence which has survived in the Gospels,
Jesus gave the impression of existing in an information net of
stable communication with a reality external to himself which he
characterized theistically (as Abba, father), and of then extending
the information net to include others. So unequivocally powerful
was the consequent *dunamis* of theistic input into the contruction
of life that it led, not simply to the transformation of life, but, in
a more dramatic word, to its transfiguration (Mk. 9:2 ff.).

Jesus, then, is portrayed as claiming that relatedness to God is
not remote or esoteric. It is simple—or at least, it can be initiated
with the child-like simplicity of faith, even though to continue to
live in a God-related and God-realizing way is extremely demand-
ing, to say the very least. Jesus therefore solved the problem of
locating theistic effect in the most direct way possible, by simply
claiming its realization as a prosaic human possibility. But that
was potentially in conflict with any other claimed solution which
insisted that the realization of theistic effect must at the very least
be accompanied by attention to the boundary conditions of
Israel's covenant. It is not that Jesus, according to the record,
militated against the covenant conditions *per se*, but he certainly
left the impression that the boundary conditions were not indispensably necessary. It seems that initially Jesus expressed his
convictions about God *within* the boundary of Israel, and that it
actually proved to be a hard lesson for him to learn that the new
boundary condition of faith could be evoked among and expressed
by Gentiles. But the more Jesus recognized that fact, the greater
became the developing strain between his own account of the
condition of theistic effect and that of other expressions of Jewishness. Jesus did not even seem to demand the minimal links of
sociological connection, such as circumcision. That this remained

a problem in the early Church indicates how tense the issue was.

So in the end—literally in the end—the issue of the validity and authenticity of Jesus' claim was bound to be focused on his own death. Jesus undoutedly believed (with the Hakamim against the Sadducees) that there would be a continuity of conscious relatedness to God after death. But he differed from the Hakamim in linking that continuity to the realization of God's effect here and now, and not to the covenant condition. If the argument advanced above is correct, Jesus went to Scripture for a self-description which would emphasize that he made this claim and manifested its consequence, not as a superhuman or extra-ordinary figure, but as a man subject to death; yet at the same time he affirmed through the same self-description that it was as a man subject to death who will nevertheless be vindicated by God. There was no way of avoiding the issue; was Jesus right or not? Or at least, there was no way of avoiding the issue *if Jesus insisted on it in Jerusalem*, because there he would be challenging the *locus* of authority in Israel. Jesus was claiming that relatedness to God depends on the condition of faith, not on the conditions in the covenant. He did not argue that relatedness to God *cannot* occur within the covenant conditions: it is clear (not least from his use of Scripture) that Jesus had too profound a sense of God's effect in creating Israel to say anything so naïvely absurd about his fellow-Jews as that. But he certainly gave the impression of regarding the conditions in the covenant as being neither a sufficient nor a necessary condition of relatedness to God.

There is, therefore, no reason to doubt the Gospel account, at least in outline, that Jesus went to Jerusalem because he himself understood very well the seriousness of the issue involved and because he intended to insist on his understanding of God-relatedness and of its realization in effect, both in life and in death. For this reason, as has been suggested already (pp. 133 f.), when he believed that the issue was unlikely to be postponed, he tried to convey to his disciples that what they had seen and experienced of the effect of God in his company would not be destroyed by death—the son of man must go as it is written (14:21), but in the kingdom of God (Dan. 7:14, Mk. 14:25, 62) the restoration and vindication will be manifest. He therefore adopted the most dramatic language possible, the language of the prophetic action, and he claimed through it that he would continue to mediate the new relatedness to God (the new covenant, in the language of the time) as much after his death as before it, whenever they appropriate this sign in the continuity of their own lives. He may have been entirely wrong in supposing that this can happen (though the experience of at least some Christians in subsequent generations suggests that one should hesitate before drawing that conclusion on *a priori* naturalistic grounds of its impossibility). But in the total context of the time there can be little doubt that this is what he believed and intended, and that this explains why anyone should do anything quite so bizarre, even by the standards of the ancient world, as to take a piece of bread and say, 'This is my body'; it also explains why those who continue to find in Christ the means and the realization of God-relatedness in their own case *must* make the appropriation of the sign in bread and wine the centre and the foundation of their life.

It would seem, then, that Jesus regarded his own death as focusing the issue of effect: he had offered in and through his own self a solution to the problem of discerning the effect of God, but it was a solution which bypassed much of the resourcefulness of traditional institutions and customs. Those who were sensitive to the religious necessity of those institutions, or (at a quite different extreme) to the political consequences of a threat to those institutions, would certainly have found Jesus disturbing. It is consequently possible that Mark has recorded an entirely accurate note in 3:6, that the initiative to silence Jesus came from an otherwise wholly improbable combination of Herodians and *pharisaioi* (pharisees). It has already been pointed out that the *pharisaioi* in the Gospels share the same characteristics as the extremist *perushim* (pharisees) of the much later rabbinic texts, where *perushim* are attacked as unequivocally as are *pharisaioi* in the Gospels, as hypocrites.[24] It is therefore highly probable that those who took initiatives against Jesus were extremists, but at opposite extremes: at one extreme were those who were attentive, not to the conditions of the covenant, but to the continuity of the political *modus vivendi* with Rome (and the accounts of Herod's investigations of Jesus may well reflect that concern); and at the other were those who were so attentive to the exact detail of the covenant conditions that in the end those who succeeded them in that attitude were denounced by the rabbis as being no part of authentic Judaism. Potentially, action could be taken either on the political side (through the courts established by the Herodian dynasty or through Roman courts), or on the religious side, particularly through the Great Sanhedrin, which had been set up to retain jurisdiction in religious matters when the Hasmonaeans designated themselves as high priests although technically they were not qualified.[25] But action on the religious side would of course require commitment on the part of the Temple authorities. The attempt to secure that commitment may well explain the tentative and probing exploration of Jesus' attitudes on the part of those authorities which Mark and the other Gospels record.

But if extremists for the detail of Israel's law felt that they must mobilize action against Jesus, on what grounds could they make the case for such action to be taken? The most secure ground would be to proceed on the basis of Deut. 17:13 (see p. 125): if it could be established that he was a contumacious teacher of that kind, he would certainly have to be excised from Israel. The chance of establishing a charge based on a particular aspect of his teaching, such as blasphemy, was out of the question: Jesus had shown far too subtle an ingenuity in evading specific and culpable statements when he had been probed on such issues as divorce or resurrection or the resource of his own authority (11:27-33). Yet it did seem possible to establish that he rejected the final authority of 'the judge who shall be in those days', and that is why the initial charges against Jesus related to his challenge to the Temple itself (14:58), although the exact nature of the charge was later obscured in the Christian tradition by taking the saying as a reference to the resurrection.

It is thus possible (as was suggested earlier) that the so-called trial of Jesus was an investigation to see whether he came into the category described in Deut. 17:8-13, of one who refuses to submit to the authority of the final court of appeal. Despite the note in v. 64 that they 'all' regarded him as worthy of death, it is highly improbable that such unanimity was forthcoming. The refusal of Jesus to respond to the high priest would certainly put him in the category, because *ipso facto* he was refusing to subordinate his judgement to that of the designated authority. However, there was a preliminary point which quite clearly it might not be possible to establish, without which the whole action in the opinion of some would fail: was Jesus a teacher at all? He was certainly referred to most commonly as 'teacher' (p. 129), but the mere title would not establish him as a formal, recognized teacher, either from the Sadducaic or from the Hakamic point of view. So a possible inference of the transfer of the action to the Roman court is that the Jewish action failed because Jesus could not be established unequivocally as being the kind of teacher envisaged in Deut. 17, although for some his silence before the high priest was sufficient. Consequently some (*tines*, 14:65) took the formal precaution of testing whether Jesus could legitimize his idiosyncratic teaching by manifesting a return of direct inspiration through the gift of the holy spirit, which would make him a prophet (p. 135). When he still remained silent, that served to reinforce and justify their determination to proceed against him, and for that reason they transferred the action to the only court which might now assist their purpose, the Roman. It is true that Mk. 15:1 states that the whole council and all the officials were involved in the transfer, but on any showing that looks like a generalizing over-simplification. None of the other officials makes any further appearance in the narrative, except for the scribes in v. 31, who may in any case simply be the scribes of the court.

If this account is at all correct, it follows that the much later understanding that 'the Jews' were responsible for the death of Jesus is completely incorrect. Some Jews, who held such an extremist understanding of Torah that their successors in the same general attitude were repudiated by the rabbis, certainly took initiatives against him, but in the end they could only sustain their action outside the boundary of Israel, in a Roman court.

When these arguments were advanced in outline in *Jesus and the Pharisees*, one reviewer dismissed them with the question, 'But is this anything more than mere speculation?' But the counter-question then has to be asked, 'What turns speculation into *mere* speculation?' *All* accounts of the trial of Jesus are speculative, since there is no record of the trial outside the Gospels, and our knowledge of legal procedures and the actual administration of Jerusalem and the Temple in the period before the fall of Jerusalem is almost non-existent. The interpretation proposed here at least makes sense of the evidence which has survived, and it offers a completely coherent and consistent account of what, according to the surviving evidence, was at issue in the life and teaching of Jesus, and of why he insisted on going to Jerusalem, and of what happened there. A dominant alternative at the present time is to explain the transformation of the evidence (i.e. of the tradition) by attributing it to the theological needs and interests of early Christian communities, concerning whose beliefs, nature, and even (in some putative instances) existence there is even *less* evidence. Yet apparently those hypothetical reconstructions are not speculative—a conclusion which seems to me improbable.

What is undoubtedly true is that no record survives of action being initiated in this period, before the fall of Jerusalem, under the heading of Deut. 17, but there is no reason in principle why it could not have been. It is a procedure fundamentally established in Torah, and it is well known that after the fall of Jerusalem, the rabbis went to considerable trouble to designate exactly how the procedures envisaged in Deut. 17 should work. Certainly one cannot read back their understanding of what should have been the case into the historical situation, but the account they gave at least bears witness to the fact that Deut. 17 was taken seriously. This is confirmed by the further fact that the silence in the period before the fall of Jerusalem is not absolute. Both Josephus and Philo drew attention to the importance of Deut. 17, and both designated the officials whom they believed (in their different situations) counted as 'the judge who shall be in those days'; in other words, neither of them was dealing with a piece of theoretical antiquarianism. So in *Ant.* iv. 176 ff., Josephus put in the mouth of Moses a farewell speech to his people, at the end of which Moses gives to the people 'the laws and the constitution recorded in a book' (iv. 193). At this point Josephus decided to give a brief summary of the laws, 'to enable my readers thereby to learn what was the nature of our laws from the first'. He then went on: 'All is here written as he left it: nothing have we added for the sake of embellishment, nothing which has not been bequeathed by Moses' (iv. 196). The summary is based primarily on Deuteronomy, but it is certainly not an 'unembellished' account. When Josephus came to paraphrase Deut. 17:8 f., he wrote: 'But if the judges see not how to pronounce upon the matters set before them—and with men such things oft befall—let them send up the case entire to the holy city and let the high priest and the prophet and the council of elders [*he gerousia*] meet and pronounce as they think fit' (iv. 218).

In effect, that is a practical exegesis of the phrase 'the judge in those days', because it specifies who the judge is. It is exactly parallel to Josephus' expansion of Deut. 16:18, which occurs immediately before (iv. 214). In that passage, the original injunction, 'You are to appoint judges and scribes in each of the towns that Yahweh is giving you', has become: 'As rulers let each city have seven men long exercised in virtue and in the pursuit of justice; and to each magistracy let there be assigned two subordinate officers of the tribe of Levi.' That again is a local and practical interpretation of the original phrase, making it specific; indeed, *so* local is the interpretation that it is difficult to find other examples of courts constituted in that way.

Philo's interpretation can be seen in *de Spec. Leg.* iv. 190:

Since a vast number of circumstances slip away from or are unnoticed by the human mind, imprisoned as it is amid all the thronging press of the senses, so competent to seduce and deceive it with false opinions, or rather entombed in a mortal body which may be quite properly called a sepulchre, let no judge be ashamed, when he is ignorant of anything, to confess his ignorance. Otherwise in the first place the false pretender will himself deteriorate as he has banished the truth from the confines of the soul, and secondly he will do immense harm to the suitors if through failing to see what is just he pronounces a blind decision. So then if the facts create a sense of uncertainty and great obscurity, and he feels that his apprehension of them is but dim, he should decline to judge the cases and send them up to more discerning judges. And who should these be but the priests, and the head and leader of the priests. For the genuine ministers of God have taken all care to sharpen their understanding and count the slightest error to be no slight error, because the surpassing greatness of the king whom they serve is seen in every matter . . . Another possible reason for sending such cases to the priests is that the true priest is necessarily a prophet, advanced to the services of the truly Existent by virtue rather than by birth, and to a prophet nothing is unknown since he has within him a spiritual sun and unclouded rays to give him a full and clear apprehension of things unseen by sense but apprehended by the understanding.

Philo, like Josephus, saw that the phrase in Deut. 17:9 demands interpretation, and in this passage he has stated that 'the judge in those days' is 'the high priest'. The high priest was also included by Josephus as a part of the meaning of the phrase, although Josephus added a wider range of judicial functionaries. An even more interesting point of connection between the two is that they apparently saw in the judiciary the continuing work of the prophets. The exact line of succession of the prophets had long since ceased (*Cont. Ap.* i. 41), but the responsibility of pronouncing the judgement of God had continued. It was, therefore, recognized that the phrase, 'the judge in those days' required definition, but the actual content given to the phrase inevitably varied as circumstances changed. To some extent it depended on who the judges actually were, or who the particular exegete wanted them to be. Of this last point, a good example is the sect of the Manual of Discipline, because in a sense that sect is a practical exegesis of the text, defining its own authorities and dismissing those outside. In IQS v. 2 f. the 'judge who shall be in those days' is in effect defined, though without explicit reference to Deuteronomy (cf. CDC xiii. 2, IQSa i. 2 f.).

So in the few places where the silence is broken, it is clear that Deut. 17 was not a dead letter, but that it was actually important in the divided situation of the Jews for each party to define the final *locus* of authority as envisaged in general terms in Deuteronomy. Yet even though this offers a very possible context for the investigation of Jesus, the interpretation being offered here of Jesus does not depend on it. Even if that particular suggestion is held to be unjustified speculation, the argument can still be put forward that, as a consequence of his experience of theistic input into the construction of his life here and now, Jesus was convinced that death would yield, not defeat, but vindication. But it is clear from the Gospel records that he had no idea *in detail* what form that vindication would take. According to Mk. 14:62 he continued to express it in Danielic terms, but it is one thing to quote inspired poetry as an expression of faith, quite another to stake the reality of one's own death on the underlying truth of the image. It is clear that in Gethsemane Jesus did not know how in detail the vindication would occur (except that according to Luke and Matthew, it was not to be by angels or by the sword). For this reason he said that his soul was in bitter distress (*perilupos*) until the moment of death, when perhaps the vindication would become manifest, not of his effect, but of God's.

This makes the agony of the cross all the more profound. For in the end the vindication seemed opaque. 'My God, my God, why did you forsake me?' And yet *after* the reality of that unevaded and unequivocal death which Jesus had insisted through the phrase 'the son of man' must apply to him, a vindication did apparently occur which not only took the close friends of Jesus by surprise:

according to Mark, it filled them with fear (16:8). It seemed to them that Jesus continued to be present to them, although they knew that he was dead, and that he continued to mediate the effect of God as he had promised at the last supper.

One of the most searching implications of the interpretation suggested here on the basis of Mark is that nothing short of a dramatic effect could possibly count as the vindication of 'man who has to die', on which Jesus had also insisted through the same phrase, 'the son of man'. For one who has, unequivocally, died, the vindication must be correspondingly unequivocal, since otherwise it cannot possibly count as vindication. So the least probable explanation of the 'resurrection' is the suggestion that somehow the disciples retained a vivid sense of Jesus' continuing word and presence with them, and that they mythologized it into a bodily resurrection. If Jesus focused the issue of his claim to the immediacy of the effect of God on his own death, then the effect of God in vindicating Jesus' claim would have to be sufficiently definite to meet the point. Indeed, the only interpretation which makes sense of the historical evidence as interpreted here is that Jesus rose from the dead, in some sense that passed the comprehension of his associates as much as it passes ours. Nothing less than some actual re-presentation of Jesus could possibly pick up his claim, focused on his own person, that the effect (the *dunamis*) of God so obviously manifest in the transfiguration of this life will be equally manifest in the transfiguration of death— a point which Luke (9:31), in particular, noticed. This may seem to be a highly improbable historical judgement, to put it mildly. But the very least that has to be said is that some of the early associates of Jesus had no doubt that it *was* that kind of vindication which had taken place, and on that basis they came to understand themselves as outposts in the world of the continuity of theistic effect which they had first seen and experienced in the person of Jesus. Only this will account for the extraordinary innovations in language and experience which suddenly appear in the documents now known as the New Testament—language and experience of being 'in Christ' (a phrase which has become so familiar that we sometimes forget how *very* odd it is to talk of a relationship in that way, particularly if Jesus, to their knowledge, had simply died) and of the Spirit (the continuing and transforming effect of God) being in them.

Whence, then, to this man these things? It remains the necessary question arising from the tradition, to which the early Christians attempted to give an answer. Before attempting to answer it ourselves, it may be as well to look at one of those early answers, that of Paul, in order to establish the connection and the coherence between the Markan portrayal of Jesus and the Pauline discussion of the implications. They are by no means so far apart as used once to be supposed, and together they show why Christology is inevitable.

3. THE DEVELOPMENT OF CHRISTOLOGY

In the last two chapters, it was pointed out how emphatically Mark portrays Jesus, not as an extra-ordinary figure (such as an angel), nor even as in-breathed character (such as a prophet), but as a man among men. It is as an unequivocally human figure, as much subject to death as any other man, that he nevertheless manifests the *dunamis* of God in and through his own person. However much he might have resembled a Galilean wonder-worker, or a prophet, or a messiah (and there are traces of all those resemblances in the evidence) he nevertheless eluded *all* those categories and could not actually be contained within them, in terms of what he said and did. One consequence of this was that he evoked the *sui generis* literary forms of the Gospels. There was apparently no existing category of literary production which would contain the novelty of this phenomenon.[1] This means that when we attempt to account historically for the life of Jesus and its consequences, we are in effect attempting to discern and specify the constraints obtaining in the life of Jesus which controlled it into its eventual outcome, namely, the life which evoked the testimony to it which issued in the documents which now constitute the New Testament. In that respect we are in exactly the same position as the early Christians, who asked the same question, but in a rather more succinct form: *pothen touto tauta*—whence to this man these things?

But if, as the record asserts, Jesus seemed to carry within an observable life a demonstration, not simply whether God is (which was hardly controversial) but what God is in effect in relation to men, so far as a human life can bear and make that manifest, then it is not surprising that the quest of early writers like Paul or John was not primarily for the historical Jesus, but for an account which would adequately convey the truth and consequence of that history. Nor was the matter quite so academic as that lengthy sentence makes it sound: they would not have embarked on that or any other quest in relation to Jesus if they had not been possessed in their own experience by a continuity of the effect of God which had first been seen in Jesus and which they believed he had promised would continue. The New Testament writers consistently maintain that a new spirit has been let loose in the world, a spirit which issues characteristically in *agape*, love, and one which would not have been apprehended in that way at all if Jesus had not lived and died as he did.[2] They were caught up in such a powerful transformation of character that in the end it is that which becomes the criterion of authenticity in any claim to God-relatedness: by their fruits you shall know them (Matt. 7:20); if a man says, I love God, and hates his brother, he is a liar: for he who does not love his brother whom he has seen, how can he love God whom he has not seen? (1 John, 4:20).

Paul (or more accurately Saul) was literally 'caught' by the vision of Christ. It is now reasonably clear that when Saul was on the road to Damascus, he was practising what other deeply religious and highly trained Jews in the Hakamic (Rabbinic) tradition also practised, namely, *merkabah* mysticism. *Merkabah* mysticism is mysticism based on intense concentration on the visionary chapters in Ezekiel, in which the prophet saw the chariot of God. Accounts have survived of the *merkabah* visions which Johanan ben Zakkai (a contemporary of Saul's who was one of the great founding fathers of Rabbinic Judaism) also saw on a journey. Points of detail in the accounts of Saul's vision and of Johanan's are sufficiently similar to suggest that Saul saw a vision because he was attempting to induce one through techniques which were current for the highly trained in Israel,[3] and which are not uncommon in other religions and cultures. What remains completely beyond historical explanation (and will remain so, short of going back in time and taking up residence inside Saul's head) is why he was suddenly convinced that it was *Jesus* who was communicating to him through the vision.

But that certainly was his conviction. And as a consequence of that change in direction Paul became quite clear that a new spirit had been let loose in the world as a consequence of Jesus—a spirit which informs and *must* inform all lives which claim to be related to God through Christ; a spirit whose character is summarized as *agape* (love). Thus when Paul wrote to the Christian communities at Corinth he did so, not only because he had been an instrument of God in founding them, but also because (as he put it) he too has the spirit of God which is the resource of all Christian judgement and action, and which is the continuing 'mind of

Christ' (1 Cor. 2:15 f.). The basic problem in Corinth was that the behaviour of the Christians there did not seem to be exemplifying the new transfiguration of life which is (or should be) a consequence of the gift of the spirit—the new mediation of theistic effect as a consequence of Christ. Thus even the very focus of the continuity of that effect, the appropriation of the prophetic action of Jesus at the last supper, through which God-relatedness or covenant is maintained, had been debased by the Corinthian Christians (1 Cor. 11:17–29), and they had apparently tolerated behaviour which even gentiles would have condemned (1 Cor. 5:1). Yet there was an even more fundamental fault: they had actually taken cases to pagan law courts! (1 Cor. 6:1 ff.). But they had been given a new spirit as a consequence of Christ which supplies them with an entirely new basis on which to form all judgements —the spirit of *agape*, love. There should be no need to go to pagan courts: they have a new spirit which will give them insight and judgement which will extend into their case, as into Paul's, the mind of Christ. Exactly as Jesus had affirmed in his own person, so Paul also repeats: the manifestation of God as God, the difference which God should make if God is God, is not a matter of talk but of power, of *dunamis*, of discernible effect; or to put it back into Paul's own language, 'I will come shortly to you, if the Lord wills, and I will know not the speech of those who have been puffed up, but the power [*dunamis*]; for the kingdom of God is not in speech but in power' (1 Cor. 4:19 f.).

Then, indeed, all the questions came flooding in on Paul which have exercised the Church ever since: how does one know which is the true spirit and which is the false? Must the spirit have a visible effect, and is ecstatic appearance, or speaking with tongues, a superior work of the authentic spirit? How *do* Christians arrive at moral or other judgements on this rather vague basis of 'the spirit'? And what are those judgements in particular cases?

In 1 Corinthians Paul wrestled with those problems, and in chs. 7 ff. he actually took specific case issues to show what *agape* means in practice in particular situations, such as the relation between husband and wife or between servant and master, the question whether or not to eat meat offered to idols, the behaviour of congregations, the identification of authentic effects of the Spirit. But then almost in irritation at their failure to implement all this spontaneously, Paul broke off and wrote: Look, let me tell you all you need to know—'a more excellent way'—to solve all problems: provided you embody and translate into life the controlling constraint of *agape*, all else will look after itself. And then follows the famous ch. 13, 'Though I speak with the tongues of men and of angels . . .'

Is that too abrupt a summary of what Paul derived from Jesus? Certainly. But it draws out what was absolutely fundamental in the transformation of Saul into Paul, that he recognized in Jesus a return of the effect of God to the world, a *dunamis*, a power which without Jesus had not existed and could not have done so. There were many prophets, many workers of miracles, many gods, many religions in the world in which Paul lived (1 Cor. 8:5); there were myths of dying and rising gods, mysteries which opened, or claimed to open, a way through death. But Jesus was open to a kind of prosaic observation. He was tangled up in the human situation. And in Jesus the knowledge of God characterized as father is established: 'For even though there are so-called gods in heaven or on earth, just as there are gods in profusion and lords in profusion, yet to us there is one God, the father, from whom are all things, and we in him, and one Lord, Jesus Christ, through whom are all things, and we through him' (1 Cor. 8:6).

The theme of a figure establishing all this, who was open to acquaintance and observation here and now, is perhaps even more specific in 1 John: 'What we have seen with our own eyes, what we have looked upon and what our hands have touched . . . we declare to you' (1 John 1:1 ff.). But Paul was equally clear that however much Jesus subsisted in the *morphe*, the form, of God, he was discerned in the *schema* of men, and that he accepted the condition of that *schema* up to and including death (Phil. 2:6 ff.). He was not an extraordinary figure: he was born out of the seed of David on the human level, but designated son of God in power (*en dunamei*) according to the spirit of holiness by resurrection of the dead. Those are a part of the opening words of Paul's letter to the Romans. And Romans, therefore, constantly implies the recurrent question: what was there about the human condition which required Jesus for something to be done about it?

The opening two chapters of Romans give the immediate answer: what made Jesus necessary is the kind of behaviour which makes it impossible for people to live with each other in the same world in any kind of bond of trust or love. It was that

observation which compelled Paul to ask the radically disruptive
question of Jewish anthropology to which reference was made
earlier (p. 53). Jewish anthropology did not deny the reality of
human failure, or sin as it would then have been called. But it
claimed that the nature of that failure could be met, controlled,
and redeemed by attending to the words which God has given to
the world for the purpose of that repair—by attending, in other
words, to Torah, and by living within the boundary conditions
which are there established, and which tell one what to do when
things have gone wrong, and which will thus repair the damage.

But Paul asked, Does Torah achieve this? Is Torah capable of
going to the root and changing the realities of human life-construction? Is it capable, as Jesus (and Jeremiah long before) had
posed the question, of going *en tais kardiais*, into the hearts of men?
One has only to observe behaviour, so Paul argues, to know that it
does not: 'You are named a Jew; you take your stand in the law',
says Paul in Romans (2:17). 'You who forbid stealing, do you
steal? You who prohibit adultery, do you commit adultery?' Law
alone does not change men *at heart*; and the truth of this, Paul
argues, we know really beyond doubt, by awareness of the conflict that occurs within the construction of our lives: 'the good that
I would I do not; but the evil which I would not, that I do'
(Rom. 7:19). We do not particularly have to define what will
count as evil, or what will count as good—though Paul did in fact
sketch in, in very general terms, what count as the fruits of the
spirit and what count as the reverse (Gal. 5:19–23). But what is
enough to explain the necessity of Jesus is the fact of conflict
itself—the fact of *antistrateuma*, to coin a noun from Paul's verb
(Rom. 7:23), within our own experience. All men have sinned and
come short of the glory of God (Rom. 3:23); all men are therefore
rightly subject to the penalty of the first Adam, death. If Torah
had been sufficient to guide, to control, to inspire, to resist, then
Jesus would not have been necessary. But Torah had not, so Paul
believed, delivered the goods. It had not, more specifically,
delivered man from his dilemma. Torah simply designates what
counts as sinful. It does not give to men a spirit within them with
which to turn away from what they know to be evil.

Do we then make the Law of no effect (Rom. 3:31)? *Me genoito*,
God forbid; we are in fact establishing why Torah was necessary
as an interim measure, which might theoretically work. But what

was really required was a cutting through to the root, a radical innovation, a new Adam from whom men can now derive a spiritual life, as from the old Adam, our common humanity, we derive a life in this apparent body which leads to death. And yet it is *in* this body in which sin abounds, not in a docetic illusion of a body, that this transfiguration is wrought—and wrought by the action of God, not by our merit. 'What shall we say then? Shall we continue in sin, that grace may abound? *Me genoito*, God forbid, because . . .' (Rom. 6:1 f.). But it is not necessary to go on. We are now simply following through the argument of Romans, and that is better done by reading the letter itself.

Even from those extremely brief pointers it is obvious that Paul's thought was controlled by a single dominant input, the fact of Jesus as Christ (i.e., as one designated by God as being in a special relatedness to himself). It is that which transforms the human situation and restores to all men a serious hope. Obviously acute questions are raised by this concerning the relation between the new community derived from Christ and the old derived from the Law, which Paul continued to emphasize was God-given; and Paul faced those questions in chs. 9–11. Yet still the fact—or what Paul took to be the fact— remained, which had constrained him into becoming a follower of Christ. The resurrection of Christ demonstrates, in Paul's belief, that the power of death and the associated rule of sin have, in his case, been defeated; hence the Law becomes irrelevant—it has no bearing on this new and completely different situation (7:1 ff.). That victory is not a private matter: others can share in it by coming into union with him (6:3—11). Paul took great care in this passage to point out that since sin no longer reigns or commands obedience (6:12), and since equally the Law has authority only over those in the old situation (7:1), this is indeed 'a glorious liberty' (8:21), but it is not unbounded licence. On the contrary, it is, to put it extremely, the exchange of one slavery for another (6:18); and this is intended to have visible consequences (6:12—14, 19), 'bearing fruit for God' (7:4). Hence by repeatedly using strong terms of authority in this passage (*douleuo, kurieuo, basileuo, hupakouo*) Paul emphasized that those who are dead to the Law 'through the body of Christ' are not made thereby a lawless body (see especially 6:15 ff.): 'The reason therefore, why those who are in Christ Jesus are not condemned, is that the law of the spirit of life in Christ Jesus has set you free from the law of sin and death' (8:1). This is a genuine freedom; but the word *nomos* (law, constraint) is used of *both* conditions. In the rest of ch. 8 Paul endeavoured to state in greater detail what this 'law of the spirit of life' (8:21) actually means. In brief, it means living as a son of God (8:14–17,) as a middle term between the love already known to be embodied in Christ (8:39) and the salvation yet to be made manifest in the entire creation (8:18–25). Thus love, *agape*, becomes the governing characteristic.

Exactly as in 1 Corinthians, so here: if *agape* is the governing characteristic, all other means of determining what is the will of God fall away in significance. 'We know that by turning everything to their good God co-operates with all those who love him, with all those that he has called according to his purpose. They are the ones he chose specially long ago and intended to become true images (*summorfous tes eikonos*) of his Son, so that his Son might be the eldest of many brothers' (8:28 f.). But then the Corinthian question has to be asked: how in practice *does* the Christian 'discover the will of God and know what is good, what it is that God wants, what is the perfect thing to do' (12:2)? In general, Paul suggested, it is by offering up the bodies (*ta somata*), in which sin has previously reigned, as a living sacrifice, and by allowing the consequences of union with Christ to work their own effect by creating an entirely new outlook and expression (lit., by the renewing of the mind, 12:1 f.). Those in whom this occurs are not left in isolation: 'So all of us, in union with Christ, form one body, and as parts of it we belong to each other' (12:5).

On this basis, Paul then went on to suggest a scheme of complementary activities in which each person will contribute whatever the freely given effect of God has given him to do, and in which every other person will respect that activity for what it is: 'Love each other as brothers should, and have a profound respect for each other' (12:10). Paul was well aware that by making *agape* the governing characteristic and, in a sense, the final court of appeal, he was resting everything on his belief (and experience) that there is a theistic effect (the Spirit), which *does* work in human lives to transform them. Nevertheless, he knew perfectly well that in any community the real exists with the false, the genuine with the counterfeit, the wheat with the tares. There is a necessary precondition of the structure which he envisaged, and this precondition he expresses tersely in the appeal: *he agape anupokritos*, let love be without hypocrisy (12:9). But granted that precondition, Paul clearly argued that in the one body, in the new community, authority is a matter, not of hierarchy, but of respect for a number of complementary activities, all of which contribute to the whole. Wherever *agape* is allowed, genuinely, to dictate all activities, there cannot be doubtful cases. Hence in 13:8-10 Paul reverts to the example he had taken in 7:7 ('You shall not covet') and adds to it all other commands and states that the whole lot are summarized in the single principle, 'You shall love your neighbour as yourself.' The basis of his vision is then summarized: 'Love works no·evil to any you encounter [lit., to the neighbour]. Therefore, love is the *pleroma* of the law'.

The words of the New Testament have become so familiar that it is almost impossible any longer to hear them. It is particularly hard to imagine what must have been happening for Paul to have felt that Torah (for which he maintained an undiminished status as God-given and necessary revelation) had been displaced by love. It is one of the most extraordinary transformations imaginable in the conceptual grammars of God's effect. And yet the constraint which governed this transaction and controlled it into its novel outcome was extremely simple: it was the conviction that an unequivocally human figure had transmitted the differentiating effect of God into the world in and through his own person. Therefore if any adequate account of that person and its nature is to be given, it must accept a close relatedness between Jesus and the resource of theistic effect external to himself. Consequently, it was inevitable that the early Church would be led in the direction of Christological statements which attempt to state the apparently impossible, that Jesus is wholly and unequivocally man, but that the nature of God is wholly and unequivocally present in him as well. The attempted statements proliferated in wild variety, like hedgerows in summer before County Councils found it cheaper to buy weed-killer than employ men with scythes. But the important fact to grasp is that this mental activity would not even have begun if Jesus had not presented himself evidentially in the first place as one who solved the problem of discerning the effect of God in and through his own person.

In no way can this be attributed to the invention of Paul (who, according to a prevalent account, took a simple Palestinian teaching and corrupted it into a Hellenistic mystery of salvation).[4]

There was no need for Paul to do anything of the kind, because the simple teaching (of faith as the boundary condition of God-related-ness—of the new covenant—and of the manifestation of God's effect) solved the fundamental Hellenistic problem as effectively as it did the Palestinian without any essential modification being needed. In I.4 it was pointed out that in both worlds (the Hellenistic and the Palestinian) the crisis in the sense of God was focused on the problem of effect—it was the same problem phenomenologically, although the *way* in which it posed itself as a problem differed radically in each situation. If Jesus had, as was claimed, dramatically restored the manifest effect of God to the world, and if that effect had not been defeated by death, then Jesus as the focus of God's particular action and effect met Hellenistic problems just as much as it met those of some Jews. Certainly new pictures of the continuity and consequences of God's effect in Jesus were developed, but there was no need to modify the basic foundation on which the elaborations were based. What Greeks as well as Jews needed was a renewed confidence that God, when attended to seriously, actually does make a difference in the construction of life; and Paul knew that he could promise and demonstrate a new spirit which had been let loose in the world as a consequence of God's effect in Christ, which would make a difference—a happy difference—not only to life, but also to death.

If, then, it is recognized that Mark portrays Jesus as one who restored the effect of God to the world (a figure who was himself so convinced that it was the effect of God, not of himself, that he was emphatically reticent about his own status); and if it is borne in mind that that effect of God seemed to be continuing despite the death of Jesus (or as they come rapidly to say, *through* the death of Jesus, which was unable to break what he was in relation to God), then it is obvious how completely consistent Mark and Paul are. There is (or can be) a *dunamis*, a new Spirit, alive in the lives of men, transforming their character into the expression of love—a building and sanctifying Spirit which, without Jesus, would not have been released or realized in that way. That Spirit and its consequent character of love is, in the end, the single criterion of authenticity. Anyone can lay claim to the name of Christ and cry, 'Lord, Lord' (Matt. 7:21). But in the end, in the *telos*, in the direction and the conclusion of a human life, that life is either shown to have been instrumental of love—or it is not. And if not, then claims to God-relatedness, or to a saving knowledge of God, are spurious (Matt. 25:31–46).

So even here the supposed conflict between Paul and Jesus on the issue of faith and works turns out to be no conflict. Both insist that there should be visible consequences: by their fruits shall you know them. But both equally insist that a God-bearing agapeistic quality of life is not easy to attain: it requires, to release it, that internal and acquiescent alertness to the informative possibility of God which they summarize as faith. Faith, therefore, precedes works, when looked at from that perspective; but faith without works, justification without sanctification, is a contradiction of the renewal which Christ was believed to offer.

It is because, according to the surviving evidence, Jesus gave the impression of solving the problem of God's effect in and through his own person, and because others also discerned the extension and continuity of that effect in their own experience and in their observation of others, that Christological and Trinitarian reflection was inevitable. Given the acceptance of those fundamental pro-positions (an acceptance which was constrained by evidence and testimony, of which some parts eventually ended up as New Testament), it was inevitable that the questions would be asked which led directly into classical Christian doctrines—such ques-tions as: what must have been the case about Jesus for Jesus to have been what he was and to be what he continues to be in the construction of human lives? What must have been the case about the human condition for Jesus to be necessary? What does the restoration of effect in Jesus imply about the essential nature of God? And what are, or should be, the consequences of all this in subsequent human lives?

The first question led to the exploration of an adequate Christ-ology—to the exploration, that is of a statement, adequate to the evidence, of the relation between the human and the theistic realities in a single person; the second question led to doctrines of atonement—and, incidentally, to the eventual revision of Jewish anthropology; the third question led, with equal necessity, to the development of Trinitarian theology; and the fourth led to the working out of the pattern of justification and sanctification. If Jesus located in his own person the restoration of God's effect and mediated it to others through his own person, as Mark undoubtedly portrays, then the line of development in all four areas is continuous from Jesus himself.

But how well founded is that account of Jesus historically? Did Jesus actually do what he is portrayed as having done? The question of historical authenticity in detail is at the present time insoluble: unless other accounts of Jesus are recovered as improbably as the Dead Sea Scrolls were recovered, there is nothing against which to check the Gospel accounts. *Some* details can be checked against the little—extremely little—that is known of the different forms of Judaism at the time when Jesus was alive. In point of fact, contrary to majority academic opinion at the present time, it can be shown that the details in Mark which *can* be checked show a remarkably sensitive authenticity to the situation before the Jewish revolt in A.D. 66; and the probability is that the authentic details in Mark's record are there, not because Mark was a diligent antiquarian, but because they were simply there in the traditions as Mark received them.

But even when that exercise of checking detail has been completed, it is almost peripheral to the more fundamental issue of the historicity of the *general* portrayal of Jesus—though it is not peripheral, of course, to other issues, such as the question (which still seems to be lucrative for journalistic copy) whether Jesus ever existed, or whether the tradition as recorded is wholly and completely divorced from any Judaism known to us. Even if, as seems to be the case, details in Mark are authentic, the fact remains that Mark has organized his material to tell a particular story, and we have no means of knowing to what extent—if at all—he modified, or for that matter invented, material for his own purposes. On the other hand, we have to bear in mind that something exactly like the Markan portrayal of Jesus in its essential nature (i.e. an unequivocally human figure who gave the impression of claiming to locate and mediate theistic effect in and through his own person) is a necessary historical inference to account for the consistency with which the New Testament in extremely diverse ways believes itself to be derived from such a figure. It does not in the least mean that Jesus was correct in making that claim. But that he gave the impression of making—or rather manifesting—the claim seems to be a necessary inference in order to account for the coherence between, for example, Paul and Mark (and between other New Testament writers as well): in utterly different languages, their work is nevertheless derived from the same point of departure, their belief that an unequivocally human figure (who as such had to die) nevertheless manifested the effect of God in a way that has life-giving consequences for all men.

This means that the historical question remains, as it was posed before, of the extent to which it is possible within the surviving evidence to discern and specify the constraints which controlled Jesus into the single outcome, the figure who evoked the testimony about him which stands in the New Testament. Where Christology is concerned, it is of course obvious that Christian statements have until recently accepted the account as historically reliable and have therefore been able to pose the question, as did Anselm, in the form *cur Deus homo*, why did God become man? The fact of the incarnation was established; it was simply a question of asking why it had to happen. It follows that when Anselm posed and attempted to answer that question, he could do so without reference to the historical details of Jesus' life. His argument was concerned to establish that the very notion of incarnation belongs to any adequate sense of God. It is not possible, so Anselm argued, to think about the nature of God adequately without coming to the realization that at some point, given the human situation as it is, it would belong to that nature to become incarnate. Otherwise 'the human race, God's precious creation, would have utterly perished, and it is not fitting that the intentions of God for man should suddenly be frustrated, nor could his design have been carried out unless the human race had been delivered by the creator himself.'[5]

But the problem now is different, not *why* but *whether* it happened (and if so, in what—probably reduced—sense). In other words, Anselm's question has been inverted, and it has become, *cur homo Deus*, why did a man become God? At a naïve level, that question is frequently answered euhemeristically: Euhemerus maintained that the gods had evolved from the veneration which people offered to heroes and conquerors. So it is suggested that a simple Palestinian teacher was promoted into the dying-rising god of a Hellenistic mystery religion. That is the least probable account of the New Testament evidence, not least because it distorts the fundamental coherence between all parts of the tradition. But the question, *cur homo Deus*, can be put more seriously: why and how did it come about that one who was unequivocally human and who went out of his way to insist on that, nevertheless came to be regarded, and apparently had to be so regarded if justice was to be done to the evidence, as *deus verus de deo vero*, very God of very God, consubstantial with the Father?

If the root of that development lies, as has been argued, in the fact that Jesus located the solution to the problem of God's effect first and foremost in his own person, then the question can be rephrased: out of what informational resources could he have attempted so radical and so God-claiming a solution? There were two major resouces in the environment: the Jewish traditions including Scripture, and the universe itself, from which Jesus frequently derived insight into the possible nature of God. But Jesus also implied a *direct* input from theistic externality as being resourceful in his own case, and he claimed that it could also be resourceful for others. Was he justified or was he misreading experience in doing so?

There is no doubt that the Jewish emphasis on the externality and independence of God (for which transcendence is not a synonym, but another aspect of putative theistic reality) created the condition in which that claim might occur, because it created a *sui generis* expectation of theistic possibility and of the possible information flow between God and the world. It was pointed out in Part I that the continuity of Israel's life-way (constructed as historically it was constructed) depended on the postulation of God as wholly other, and as being the single and only point of theistic reference, and yet as contributing from that externality to the construction of individual and communal life-ways significant effect. The nature and the condition of that relatedness was eventually summarized in the covenant. What that created in Israel was an almost perfect condition of information: a postulated wholly independent resource of stable signal strength, existing prior to, and quite apart from, any action of their own, combined with an increasingly articulate and elaborate statement of the boundary conditions within which signal loss will be minimal—until, indeed, the day may come, when each man will sit under his own vine, when the signal loss will be nil.

So independent—so other—was God to Jeremiah, as the one from whom by definition the word of the Lord comes, that Jeremiah wished profoundly that God would let him alone, and not compel his word through Jeremiah into the world; and yet so unequivocal was the signal strength of that 'word' within the construction of Jeremiah's sequences of speech in at least some instances, that it was as though a fire was burning in his bones (p. 77). Were Jeremiah and others like him mistaken in supposing that there was an external resource of that effect? Behavioural accounts of believing behaviour would have no hesitation in accepting the dramatic nature of that experience, but in order to contain the explanation of men within the natural order, they have minimized the issue of externality because they have needed to excise what they would otherwise regard as a *super*-natural or other than natural cause of it. Confusion has then arisen because 'supernatural' and 'other than natural' have been identified with the issue of externality, and thus the issue of the grounding of the signal source has become undiscussable. So behavioural accounts have been able to emphasize the importance of beliefs in brain behaviour without adjudicating on any issues of ontology, and they have actually felt it none of their business to interfere in nebulous topics of that sort; such concerns are dismissed as metaphysical, despite the fact that many behavioural explanations are themselves extremely metaphysical. The result is that much behavioural analysis has been content to ask how it is that any belief that there is an external resource of effect in the construction of life, history, or the universe becomes coded for retrieval in brain behaviour, whether that belief is justified or not; and behavioural analysis can then quite profitably attend to such questions as why, for example, the initiative in God-retrieval in the scan of any situation has a higher priority for some people than it does for others; or why, in other words, the coded God-symbols which are commonly available in the history of cultural transmission are stored and retrieved more extensively and more immediately in response to a new situation or stimulus by some people than by others. In this way, it has seemed possible to bypass completely issues of truth or falsity in theistic belief: don't ask for the meaning, ask about the user.

But put in those terms and linked to the informational issue of externality, there is no need for this sort of account of believing behaviour to be at issue in the justification or otherwise of theistic belief. *All* externality is mediated to the brain-process through *some* mechanism of coding, storage, and retrieval, of which, at present, we know very little indeed. But as the Indian tradition has always made much more explicit in its reflections on epistemology, what occurs to the conscious subject in brain-process cannot, in relation to externality, adjudicate finally on what it is, nor even absolutely, as a particular, on whether it is. What remains at issue is what one regards as a necessary condition to create the effects in consciousness which do in fact obtain. Is externality and independence a necessary condition for the sense of God which developed in the consciousness of at least some in Israel and which led to the unique sequence of theistic construction which occurred in Israel's case? No one doubts presumably that Elohim was coded as having that characteristic. But what was necessary for the reinforcement of that coded expectation within the symbol, Elohim, in the continuity of Israel's theistic construction? Would it not have to be the at least occasional realization within that brain-behaviour of exactly what was expected, an independent resource of signal effect, able, within certain conditions, to be realized in the construction of life, mediated initially through external details of transmission, but extending, in actual appropriation and behaviour, beyond the limits which those details might suggest?

To take a manageable and therefore small example: Amos (8:1 ff.) saw a basket of summer fruit and by the coded verbal connection between *qayiz* (basket) and *qez* (end), he transacted through that connection a theistic interpretation which not only extended the signifying weight of those words, but also extended the characterization of what was theistically resourceful in the construction of Israel's life-way. But the very enterprise of continuing to participate in a theistic transaction of that sort depends on a sufficient signal strength from that postulated and characterized resource of theistic effect into the construction of brain-process and behaviour; otherwise—perhaps—there would not be an Amos to look at a basket of fruit through *prophetic* eyes. For what enables the life of *some* God-suggestive symbols, as opposed to the death and extinction of others, is their plausibility; and what supports their plausibility is the degree of match between what they suggest and what is discovered when they are incorporated in the construction of a particular life. Many die and become implausible; but some live.

So the issue of externality can be put very directly: when we look at a theistic tradition, are we simply looking at a history of God-suggestive symbols, or can we ask within that history whether the death of some symbols and the continuing life of others occurs because some symbols are better matched to what is in reality the case, and because they better enable the incorporation of information-reference to that reality in the construction of at least some human life-ways? The impasse and the nagging irritation of theistic assertion (and therefore also of philosophical theology) which worries like a terrier round the heels of more fashionable epistemologies, is that that question cannot be answered *either way*. It cannot be answered because we have no access, short of death, to what may in reality be the case theistically, except through the history of those symbols. So we are committed to a circle (or a treadmill depending what view one takes of theology).

On the other hand, it is obvious that differentiation does occur within the history of God-suggestive and God-enabling symbols; and the study of information process makes it clear that some die because they fail to evoke informational expectancy and consequence, while others live and are extended creatively because they do. It is also clear from the surviving evidence that there occurred in Jesus a drastic and transacted revision of available symbols (of available God-suggestive and God-enabling words and actions) in order to create a better informational match between those symbols and what he believed to be the external resource which contributed to the construction of his observable and public life. That Jesus had problems conveying this even to his disciples is not exactly surprising. Nevertheless, if one surveys the evidence which surrounds the elusive figure of Jesus (the writings and the lives which were evoked by him, whoever or whatever he was), there really is no doubt that his route through life was constructed in the way which resulted in that evidence because he accepted the informational frame which has just been summarized: theistic reality as a wholly other and external resource in the construction of life, yet available within certain (but now newly defined) boundary conditions. And equally, there is really no doubt that he gave the impression of the construction of his life and actions being constantly informed from that external resource at a stable and self-authenticating level of signal strength.

To say 'there really is no doubt' is to use extravagantly strong language. But the earlier discussion of historicity will have made it clear that that language is not used in order to claim a reconstruction in detail of the historical Jesus. It is used to claim that the surviving evidence would not be as it is unless Jesus had believed that the major constraint over the outcomes of his life was direct input from externality which he characterized theistically as Abba, Father. That evidence could not have been evoked in Judaism as it then was without a figure at the root or at the heart of it who regarded God as independent and other, and yet as constantly available to the construction and transformation of life, a claim which the Gospels make clear was located and tested first and continuously in his own person.

That is what traditional Christology has constantly tried to explicate and defend: the distinction between the two natures in Christ, the human and the divine, and yet their congruence in a single and undivided person, in which neither nature is diminished or lost. It culminated eventually in the definition at Chalcedon which became orthodoxy:

One and the same Christ, Son, Lord, only-begotten, acknowledged in two natures, without confusion, without change, without division, without separation, the difference of the two natures being in no way destroyed through the union, but rather the unique character of each nature being preserved, and concurring in one visible appearance and underlying nature . . .[6]

One may well think with Tristram Shandy, 'What a pudder and racket in Councils about *ousia* and *hypostasis*. What confusion from words of little meaning and as indeterminate a sense.'[7] But what Chalcedon establishes in the Christian universe of meaning is the boundary condition within which the appropriateness or the inappropriateness of any proposed Christological utterance can be judged, when matched against the fundamental informational resource (the evidence in the New Testament).

What is therefore impressive about a Christology based on the process of information in the construction of human utterance, is that it requires a Chalcedonian frame for its expression. It requires that the resource of input remains independent, but allows that it could be wholly expressed through, and become totally informative of, another. Phenomenological evidence makes it clear that the externality which presents itself to human consciousness as though it should be characterized theistically, does so in a way which suggests that if it exists and is not a misreading of experience, it relates to us as a kind of field or independent net of information. The phenomenological impression may of course be mistaken, but that is how the impression of theistic effect seems to occur, or at least is reported as occurring. This is clearly so in the case of Jesus, according to the surviving evidence. Externality theistically characterized (Abba, Father) remains independent of himself and yet is not other than himself, in the sense that it mediates effect to the construction and expression of his life, and through him to the lives of others. The themes of independence and yet of identification are already apparent in Mark, although they receive their consummate expression in the Fourth Gospel.

This means that it is credibly and conceptually possible to regard Jesus as a wholly God-informed person, who retrieved the theistic inputs coded in the chemistry and electricity of brain-process for the scan of every situation, and for every utterance, verbal and non-verbal. We cannot, of course, say with absolute certainty that that *is* what happened historically. But we can say—with absolute certainty—that it could have happened, and that the result would have been the incarnating (the embodying) of God in the only way in which it could possibly have occurred. No matter what God may be in himself, the realization of that potential resource of effect would have to be mediated into the process and continuity of life-construction through brain-process interpreted through the codes available at any particular moment of acculturation. There is no other way of being human, or indeed of being alive, because otherwise consciousness ceases. 'For men can but proceed from what they know, nor is it for the mind of this flesh to practise poiesis, *ex nihilo*.'[8]

That is as true of Jesus *de humanitate* as of anyone else. But what seems to have shifted Jesus into a different degree of significance in making manifest, and in recreating in others the desire to realize, the possibility of God as an available resource of effect (and thus shifted him also into being regarded as a different kind of signifying of that possibility in relation to the lives of men) was the stability and the consistency with which his own life-construction was God-informed. To use that phrase does not mean anything casual, as, for example, that Jesus kept God more or less in mind, and every now and then tried to teach a few parables about him. The possibility is far more precise, that externality theistically characterized was internalized as a constant and stable resource in the construction of life, and became an invariable constraint over the outcomes in his case. That would undoubtedly yield a

Christology in which God is wholly present within and through the human without modifying or destroying the human in any respect.

This means that this proposal does not repeat Sanday's mistake when he formed 'A Tentative Modern Christology' seventy years ago. Sanday picked up the slowly forming language of the late nineteenth century of there being, in human nature, a subliminal consciousness (a subconscious part of the mind) and suggested, 'first . . . that the proper seat or *locus* of all divine indwelling, or divine action upon the human soul, is the subliminal consciousness, and . . . that the same, or the corresponding, subliminal consciousness is the proper seat or *locus* of the Deity of the incarnate Christ'.[9] The Chalcedonian objections to that are so obvious that they do not need rehearsing; and even if they are of no moment, the psychological objections are insuperable: the proposed creature is impossible. But to talk in informational terms is *not* to talk, as Sanday did, of the insertion of God-items into aspects, or perhaps even into delimited locations, of brain behaviour. Exactly the reverse, it is to talk about the consistency with which the codes of theistic possibility are retrieved in the scan and construction of *all* thought and action; and this is not in any way to confine the nature of God in Christ to intellect or concept alone. Again exactly the reverse: what is retrieved for the formation of action is or can be manifest in *every* aspect of behaviour, literally from top to toe: nor is it in any way limited to *conscious* retrieval; it may be a constant, because actual, presence.

It is possible on this basis to talk about a wholly human figure, without loss or compromise, and to talk also, at exactly the same moment, of a wholly real presence of God so far as that nature (whatever it is in itself) can be mediated to and through the process of life-construction in the human case, through the process of brain behaviour by which any human being becomes an informed subject—but in this case, perhaps even uniquely, a wholly God-informed subject. Whatever the godness of God may be, it could only be established and mediated through a *human* life by some such process as this. There may indeed be immediacies of experience of God-relatedness beyond word and language, but they cannot be locked into the construction of a human life without a translation into the means, whatever they are, of life-construction.

It is neither conceptually nor intrinsically impossible that some such occurrence obtained in the case of Jesus, which gave to his claims about the nature of theistic reality their independence and extraordinary conviction. But even supposing, for the sake of argument, that that is an accurate account of the transaction which occurred in the person of Jesus in the Jewish sense of God, would it say of Jesus anything more than might be said (potentially) of any other human being? If Jesus was a God-informed man, surely others can be so as well? And in that case, the traditional claim that Jesus was different not simply in degree but in kind must surely fail. To the question whether other human beings can be similarly God-informed, Jesus answered unequivocally, Yes. That was the whole point of claiming that the *dunamis* of God is open to those with sufficient faith in its possibility. If it was contingently desirable, one could no doubt ask Mount Everest to take a walk to the Indian Ocean (Mk. 11:23). We have already seen that Paul regarded others as being able to be drawn into the same status as Jesus, so that he is the first-born of many brothers (p. 176), and John 14:12 recorded Jesus as believing that greater works than his own would ensue. But it may be that the traditional claim was attempting to articulate an important insight, that, because Jesus in his own person unlocked this access to a new relatedness to God (one which would not have obtained if he had not lived and died as he did), his person is essentially, not casually or accidentally, related to God and to the expression of God's effect. At the very least it may be necessary to say that the difference of degree in Jesus' case amounts to a difference in kind.

There is nothing particularly remarkable in that possibility since we have become familiar with the transcendence of types in the structural sequences of human process. For example, it has seemed possible to some to argue that the human brain is simply a complicated computer: the differences are differences of degree. Thus in 1952 Bar-Hillel summarized the argument: 'If a human being can do it, a suitable programmed computer can do it too'. But later he came to express a quite different point of view, that although analogues between brain and computer exist, and although the two undoubtedly function in some respects in a very similar way, the difference of degree between the two in the realization of ability is so vast that the differences of degree amount to a difference in kind. In a comment on television on the machine translation programme (where it was once hoped that one would be able

to feed into a computer a book in French and extract it in reflec-
tive and intelligible English) he said:

It became more and more clear to me that man's ability to translate
and, in the course of time and with more experience, to translate better
and better, rests on some kind of innate organisation. At the moment
there are no indications that we shall understand this innate organisation
in the foreseeable future to such an extent that we shall be able to make
use of this understanding for building models and for programmed
simulation. To put it into somewhat more philosophical terms: it seems
that we human beings in order to acquire that particular disposition
of the first kind, which is called 'competence' in a given language, make
use of an innate disposition of the second kind whose anatomical and
physiological aspects are as yet completely unknown to us.[10]

Whether or not we eventually understand more of the human
ability and translate it into machines does not alter the basic point,
that the present situation exemplifies differences of degree amount-
ing to differences of kind. The same could be true of the person of
Jesus. The analogues and the potentials of behaviour obtain, but
the realization in the case of Jesus, although it is simply a difference
of degree (in the stability, for example, in the retrieval of theistic
input), nevertheless amounts to a difference in kind.

But is this what happened in the construction of Jesus' life? Was
this direct theistic input one of the constraints which controlled
him into the outcome of the figure who evoked the teaching and
experience which now stands in the New Testament? We have
no way of knowing, at least this side of the grave. We have no glass
of Momus set in the human head, 'through which to view the soul
stark naked . . . her motions, her machinations . . . her frisks, her
gambols, her capricios . . . This is an advantage not to be had by
any biographer in this planet.' Yet we do have the consequences in
Mark and Paul and John and other New Testament writers, and
we do have the continuing consequences in subsequent experience
(not necessarily our own) of claimed theistic effect mediated through
and from the focus of Christ. But in the end it becomes a matter
of individual judgement of the evidence, of whether that evidence
suggests or even demands such a figure to have brought it into
being. At the very least it is hard to say less than this, that Jesus
was himself possessed by the either/or nature of what he was
claiming about the nature of God in his own person, and that he
recognized the conflict with other obtaining senses of God. With-

out that recognition of issue, Gethsemane and the voluntary choice of confrontation in Jerusalem become inexplicable in that Jewish situation. It would seem that Jesus was constrained to Jerusalem and to the cross by the consistency with which his claim to the accessibility of God was vindicated in his own experience of himself; and in the perspective of information-process and energy-flow it is entirely credible that God (the resource of theistic effect external to the human subject) could take the initiative in creating this particular consequence in the case of Jesus, as some theologies (for example, the Barthian) have emphasized. But without a glass of Momus, that cannot be other than a guess.

But certainly the early Christian interpretation of Jesus had no doubt that the issue of Jesus in relation to God remained one of effect, of fruits of the spirit, of translating into life the mind and spirit of love. Yet when Muhammad looked at the condition of Christian life in his time (five and a half centuries later) his comment was not, 'Behold, how they love one another.' He used the verb *ihtalafu*, they fell into conflict. The condition of Jewish and Christian life unquestionably posed a new and quite different crisis in the sense of God, one which drove Muhammad into silence, into an impossibility of words, as well. It is to that crisis that we can now turn.

III

ISLAM

1. ALGHAZALI

DURING the summer of 1095, while men in England, according to the Anglo-Saxon Chronicle, were lamenting a typical summer in which the crops had to be abandoned unharvested, preparations in Europe were being made for those expeditions against the Muslim empires of the East which are now referred to as the First Crusade. That same summer in Baghdad, one of the most eminent teachers among Muslims of the time was preparing to teach a class of students. His lectures were always well attended, because he was, as near as could be, an absolute master of his subject—not simply *fiqh*, jurisprudence, but also philosophy, theology, and those subjects which would now come within the scope of natural sciences. So there should have been no complication or worry about giving this particular lecture. And yet when he stood up to speak he found that his voice was paralysed: he was completely unable to speak, and he stood before his class in silence.

The man was alGhazali; and this occasion on which he was reduced literally to silence will lead us to the third of the four quadrant points of silence, the silence of Muhammad on Mount Hira, through which we are exploring the variety of ways in which particular senses of God came into crises of implausibility, and why it is that sometimes in those crises, senses of God go to extinction, yet sometimes, equally, they lead to a reconstruction of what God must be to *be* God beyond the ruins of that particular disintegration.

In alGhazali's case, the crisis in the prevailing intellectual characterization of God did not lead so much to reconstruction as to reaffirmation of what Muhammad had established; but there is no doubt of the severity of the crisis. According to alGhazali's own account, in the *Munqid min adDalal* (iii. 4), 'God shrivelled [or "parched"] my tongue until I was prevented from giving instruction. So I used to force myself to teach on a particular day for the benefit of my various pupils, but my tongue would not utter a single word.' Not surprisingly, the crisis affected his whole life and he moved into an increasingly deep depression. He was virtually unable to swallow anything, or to digest it with any comfort if he did: 'The doctors despaired. They said: "This matter [or, "affair"] has descended into his heart, from where the poison has spread into his whole body. There is no possible treatment except that he be delivered from the anxiety which overwhelms him." '

It is doubtful whether a doctor in the twentieth century would give a diagnosis much different from that. He would conceivably use the word 'psychosomatic', and he would probably put that word in inverted commas, because it is not in the least explanatory. It is simply descriptive of the complex relation between brain and body, as a consequence of which the kind of paralysis which alGhazali suffered is by no means uncommon. So it scarcely matters whether one says that one of the features of 'psychosomatic' disorder is 'intracranial vasomotor instability' as a recent introduction to psychiatry puts it,[1] or whether one says with the Arabs that the matter descended into the heart (*bilqalb*), the reality of the situation remains the same and the Arab description is no worse than the other. Similarly, the Arab prescription (the prescription of the doctors, that is, who attended alGhazali) is correct, that there is unlikely to be a cure for this condition unless the root cause of the anxiety is removed.

What, then, *was* the crisis which reduced alGhazali to paralysed silence? The underlying causes, in terms of the formation of alGhazali's person, will never be known, because no evidence survives which gives access to that kind of inquiry. Carlyle claimed that the purpose of biography is 'to know our fellow creature; to see into him, understand his goings-forth, decipher the whole heart of his mystery: nay, not only to see into him, but also to see out of him, to view the world altogether as he views it, so that we can theoretically construe him, and could almost practically personate him'.[2] But that is to set a standard almost too high for *auto*biography, let alone biography, seeing how little a man knows of himself, let alone of others.

Why was alGhazali an anxious person? There is no means of

knowing, and certainly no means (despite its popularity) of pyscho-
analysing the characters of the past. But in terms of surface-mean-
ing, in terms or precipitation and of what immediately triggered
the particular crisis, much more can be said, because alGhazali
has left us considerable evidence of what it felt like to him.

First and foremost it must be emphasized that there is no question of alGhazali's stature and achievement in the intellectual and
spiritual history of Islam. In extremely general terms one can say
that he is *roughly* the equivalent of Aquinas in Christianity, and of
Maimonides in Judaism—in the sense that all three (though in
completely different ways) had a profound effect on the subsequent
development of their respective religions. The effects were not
necessarily beneficial. In the opinion of some, alGhazali's 'achievement' was to rescue orthodoxy at the expense of rationality, and to
create (or at least powerfully influence) the divorce between faith
and reason which persists in Islam to the present day. In fact, as
will be seen, that is not intrinsic to alGhazali's position, but it was
certainly an inference drawn from it. Superficially, it can be seen
most obviously in the fact that it was he who, having achieved such
pre-eminent acclaim in philosophy and theology, turned on philosophers and academic theologians and wrote the famous *Tahafut
alFalasifah* (*The Refutation of the Philosophers*).

The *Tahafut*, as will be seen in greater detail, is a critique of
metaphysics, which shares one important method with Kant's
critique (though the two in general are very different indeed),
namely, that one of the arguments of the *Tahafut* is designed to
exhibit the inability of metaphysical philosophers to establish
certainty in their propositions. In fact the phrase 'metaphysical
theologians' became a term of abuse for alGhazali, much as the
term 'theological' became a term of abuse for Harold Wilson—
'that which is totally obscure and of no practical use to anyone', a
distortion of words, incidentally, which illustrates graphically the
poverty of British socialism under that particular Prime Minister,
for whom the consequences of reflection on the nature of God for
the worth of human beings were never very apparent. There is a
sardonic entry in the *Jewish Encyclopedia* which catches beauti-
fully this pragmatic contempt for metaphysics. In the article on
Solomon Maimon (a Jewish philosopher at the end of the eighteenth century), the writer says of him at the time when he was
twenty-one: 'Maimon had now an excellent opportunity to begin

an honourable career; but his mind, fed on metaphysical problems, had become inadaptable to any regular occupation.'

AlGhazali also came to mistrust the pretensions of metaphysical philosophy and theology, though for much more substantial reasons. He summarized them in the *Tahafut* (*The Refutation of the Philosophers*), and six months after writing that work he was reduced to paralysed silence in front of his university class. So in immediate terms, the paralysis was not surprising: having just exposed with ruthless acuteness the limitations of philosophy and theology, he was compelled to stand up in front of his class and encourage his pupils to see the worth of those disciplines. In a tension of that sort, the paralysis is dramatic but not altogether surprising. He at once resigned his university lectureship and withdrew into the greatest possible isolation and solitude (almost literally into the desert, but actually up the tower of the mosque of Damascus) in order to become a Sufi. The term 'Sufi' is applied as a collective name to the main traditions of Islamic mysticism and contemplative experience of God through direct intuition, which coexisted in an often uneasy relationship with more formal religious orthodoxy.

So far, the silence of alGhazali must seem relatively straight-forward: alGhazali would seem to be a kind of Muslim Malcolm Muggeridge, who toward the end of his life looked back on the supposed achievements and pleasures of youth and found in them nothing of enduring value: having mastered the many areas of knowledge and the many modes of inquiry in Islam; having set his mind to the limits of inquiry in physics, in metaphysics, and in theology; and having even exposed the uncertainty of metaphys-ical argument, alGhazali felt that this accumulation of knowledge and technique in argument and demonstration amounted to noth-ing—nothing, if it did not bring him into a direct experience of that which he could describe externally with such fluency, the nature of God and of man's relatedness to him.

That feeling in general terms is not uncommon. In fact, one might say that it is almost a commonplace of theistic traditions, '. . . lest by any means, after that I have preached to others, I my-self should be rejected' (1 Cor. 9:27). That was Paul's way of expressing it. AlGhazali put it this way: 'My feet were standing on a sand-bank which was slipping beneath me, and I saw that I was in danger of hellfire if I did not do something to change my ways.'

AlGhazali was thus experiencing the difference between what
William James described as a menu with one raisin on it and a
menu with the word raisin on it: one raisin may not be much of a
meal but it is at least a commencement of reality. The point (and
the edge of alGhazali's anxiety) was put succinctly by de Caussade:

As it is fire and not the philosophy or scientific knowledge of fire that
warms us, so it is the will and designs of God that produce sanctity in
our souls and not intellectual speculation about this principle and its
effects. If we wish to quench our thirst, we must lay aside books which
explain thirst, and take a drink.[3]

Are we then to interpret alGhazali as an ageing man, yielding to
the theology of fear and rejecting the barren intellectual achievements of his youth in order to make sure of his salvation? It is not
difficult to find this interpretation of alGhazali. Bertrand Russell,
for example, summarized alGhazali in that way, in his *History of
Western Philosophy* (p. 444):

There was a sect of completely orthodox theologians, who objected
to all philosophy as deleterious to the faith. One of these, named
Algazel, wrote a book called *Destruction of the Philosophers*, pointing
out that, since all necessary truth is in the Koran, there is no need of
speculation independent of revelation.

But that passage is an example of the kind of ignorant prejudice
which has bedevilled the western understanding of Islam since the
Middle Ages. The Anglicized and traditional spelling of the name
as alGazel is not important, or at least it is far less important than
the distortion of alGhazali into a mindless fideist (relying solely on
faith) who saw 'no need of speculation independent of revelation.'
In fact, alGhazali saw every need of speculation independent of
revelation in many, perfectly proper, areas of human inquiry. However, it is doubtful whether Russell actually read much of what
alGhazali wrote, since it is almost entirely in Arabic and very little
was available to Russell in translation. But even among those who
certainly could consult the original sources, a similar estimate of
alGhazali can be found. R. A. Nicholson, for example, in *A Literary History of the Arabs* (p. 382), wrote: '. . . Often in his discussion of the philosophical schools, Ghazali's religious instinct breaks
out. We cannot imagine him worshipping at the shrine of pure
reason any more than we can imagine Herbert Spencer at Lourdes.'
Should we then accept that interpretation of alGhazali, as one

who turned away from the worth of intellectual achievement, and devoted himself instead to mysticism and religious devotion? We cannot in fact do so, because it is a false account of what happened in alGhazali's case. However reluctant he may have been to worship at the shrine of *pure* reason, he never ceased to reverence the exercise of reason in its proper spheres and in relation to appropriate subject matter. The simplest illustration of this lies in the fact that it was in the very period of his withdrawal from university teaching and of his exploration of Sufi mysticism that alGhazali wrote his greatest work by far, *Ihya Ulum udDin* (*The Reviving of Knowledge of the Faith* or, *of Religious Knowledge*). In writing that work, he did not compromise in any way at all the radically empiricist theory of knowledge which he had established already in his earlier philosophical work. Indeed, he actually reinforced in the *Ihya* his convictions about the way in which worthwhile public knowledge is established in the human community on fundamentally empiricist grounds. What is even more to the point, alGhazali recognized as a consequence of this, that if theological propositions are to be publicly intelligible and genuinely informative, they must be reinstated, not on the basis of fideism (by being accepted simply on the basis of faith) but in terms which accept the constraints of empiricism.

What kind of empiricism? That will emerge in the later discussion. But to anticipate, we can say that it is an empiricism with a surprisingly modern flavour to it, an empiricism which post-Humean philosophy in the west rediscovered for itself. What is important about alGhazali (and here the relation to Kant is by no means remote) is that when he came to the limits of reason at the bounds of sense, he sought in the *Ihya* to give an adequate and secure value to the further construction of interpretation set up on the foundations of perception. He is thus one of the few theologians who have tried, not to defend theology in relation to empiricist challenges, but to reconstruct theology on the basis of an empiricist theory of knowledge.

How successful he was in the endeavour is for the moment less important than the fact that he made it. For it means that it is certainly wrong to interpret alGhazali as an old man who turned on the achievements of his youth and regarded them as having no abiding status. In fact it would have been almost impossible for alGhazali to have done that, because it would have involved repudiating a fundamental emphasis in Islam, the emphasis on the high value of *ilm*, or 'knowledge'. The universe and this world within it are the creation of God. Consequently, to explore it is to listen to the language of God. The Quran itself is emphatic in claiming that there are in the universe innumerable *ayat*, cues of theistic reality. This emphasis on the worth of *ilm* has been effectively summarized by Rosenthal:

Ilm is one of those concepts that have dominated Islam and given Muslim civilization its distinctive shape and complexion. In fact, there is no other concept that has been operative as a determinant of Muslim civilization in all its aspects to the same extent as *ilm*. This holds good even for the most powerful among the terms of Muslim religious life such as, for instance, *tawhid*, 'recognition of the oneness of God', and *adDin*, 'the true religion', and many others that are used constantly and emphatically. None of them equals *ilm* in depth of meaning and wide incidence of use. There is no branch of Muslim intellectual life, of Muslim religious and political life, and of the daily life of the average Muslim that remained untouched by the all-pervasive attitude toward 'knowledge' as something of supreme value for Muslim being. *Ilm* is Islam, even if the theologians have been hesitant to accept the technical correctness of this equation. The very fact of their passionate discussion of the concept attests to its fundamental importance for Islam.[4]

But the concept was not left simply as a concept. It was a practical concern, which flowed directly into the splendid and exhilarating Muslim renaissance which took place in the first five centuries after Muhammad. It was a literal renaissance, a literal rebirth, of Greek science and learning, which was then extended vastly in many different directions. Traces of the Arab renaissance have left their mark in the English language, not least in the fact that we refer to 'arabic numerals', but also in words which begin with the arabic article 'al' (the Arabic word for 'the'), such as algebra, alkali, almanac, alHambra, alembic, algorithm, alchemy, and in many names of stars, as can be seen, coincidentally, in A. P. Herbert's 'Ode on the Names of Stars':

> Let us rename the stars. The ancient names
> Are not sufficient for the cosmic flames.
> The Arab steered his course across the sand
> Keeping *Achernar* on his starboard hand.
>   He held his camel's head
>   On *Skat* or *Tarazed*.

He fed his camel and lay down to rest
   When *Alpheratz* was bearing North by West.
When *Nath* no more was seen
He knew the corn was green:
When *Nath* was seen again
He cut the golden grain.
   He knew *Mizar*
He knew *Alshain*,
And *Sadalsund*, the lucky star,
   That brought soft rain.
He knew *Mirzam* and *Alnilam*,
   The pearly string,
He knew *Menkalinan*
Aldebaran,
And *Sheratan*,
   The star of Spring.
But what is *Alchiba* to you and me,
Diphda the Frog, or *Deneb Algedi*?
I cannot summon interest in *Skat*,
In *Phact*, or *Saiph*, or *Chaph*, or *Sulaphat*.
In vain *Alphacca* twinkles up and down,
'The brightest pearl in Ariadne's crown'.
I do not know her. I should not complain
If *Alchiba* was never seen again.[5]

The point of referring to the Arab renaissance is to emphasize that when alGhazali was recognized as a great master in the world of learning, he was recognized as being so at a time of massive intellectual achievement. He did not repudiate the worth of that achievement *in toto*. It follows that the reasons for his attack on the philosophers and his withdrawal into Sufi contemplation (during which period he wrote his major philosophical and theological work) are far more complicated than Russell and Nicholson imply. For one thing, they are complicated by the political circumstances in which he lived. Indeed, in 1095, when alGhazali withdrew from Baghdad, it is clear that he had supported the losing side in a struggle for the supremely powerful position of *wazir* (vizier). It may, therefore, be more accurate to say, not that he withdrew but that he fled. Consequently, there are those who would interpret alGhazali as a rather cheap political time-server, whose ideas consequently are not of much worth or substance. But that interpretation is to make the mistake of supposing that if one can specify

political constraints which control a person's work into one outcome or another, the worth of that work has been emptied of value;
but that certainly does not follow as a necessary conclusion. Franz
Boas fled from Nazi Germany and then devoted much of his
anthropological expertise to the refutation of Nazi racist theories;
but the political constraint over his life and work does not *ipso
facto* reduce the worth of that work. AlGhazali similarly devoted
time and energy to refuting the ideologies of religious groups, like
the Batinites, who achieved political power, but that fact in itself
does not make alGhazali's work unworthy of attention.

In fact, alGhazali remains a far more intriguing figure than
popular accounts might lead one to suppose. He was one of the
earliest in the western tradition to understand the empiricist
challenge to theology, and one of the few who, far from attempting
to evade the challenge, explored the possibility of realigning theology with an empiricist theory of knowledge. In what way, and to
what effect, did he do so? In answering that question I have illustrated his arguments from parts of the modern philosophical scene.
It is, of course, a dangerous procedure: it may suggest that alGaz-
ali and twentieth-century philosophers are being regarded as inter-
changeable, or that alGhazali is being treated as though he had
twentieth-century problems in mind. Emphatically that is not the
case, nor is any such impression intended. The point of making
some comparisons with modern arguments is simply to draw out
more sharply the edge of alGhazali's own argument, in terms which
are more familiar at the present time. The fact remains that alGhazali's thought is of interest in its own right. But while important
parts of it still remain untranslated into English, it is possible that
those who are unfamiliar with his extensive writings may find some
pointers from the present-day scene helpful in discerning the
underlying concerns of his thought.

2. THE OCEAN OF KNOWLEDGE

FROM his earliest years, alGhazali threw himself without reserve or compromise into what he called 'the vast ocean of knowledge'. It is a description which he used on several occasions, as in this autobiographical account in *Munqid min adDalal* (*The Deliverance from Error*):

I never ceased, from my first youth, from the time before I was twenty until now (and I am now more than fifty), to throw myself into the depth of the ocean. I plunged into the gulf without hesitation, not at all like a man timid or afraid. I sunk into the depths of obscure questions; I threw myself into problems; I let myself dive headlong into the abyss; I scrutinized the beliefs of every sect; I searched out the doctrinal idiosyncracies of every religious group (i).

The *Munqid min adDalal* is alGhazali's own account of how he came to form his philosophical and religious opinions. Although it is highly schematized, it nevertheless gives us important insight into the formation of his opinions and his reasons for them. It certainly emphasizes his enthusiasm. But like others before and after him who have glimpsed the possibility of knowing all that is worth knowing, alGhazali rapidly discovered how little a single life can achieve, as he reflected in the *Ihya*:

To make an effort even to the limit of one's capacity falls far short of what would be necessary, for what there is to be known [of God] is an ocean. It is impossible to sound its depth, and men can only explore its shores, and near limits in so far as that is able to be done . . . (i. 3. 3; cf. i. 5).

What limit even the limited inquiries which are possible are the confusion and conflict among those who lay claim to knowledge. 'The schemes for the world's regeneration', as Thomas Love Peacock put it, 'evaporate in a tumult of voices'.[1] In this chaos of conflicting opinion, alGhazali discerned four ways in which his contemporaries claimed to be able to approach genuine or worthwhile knowledge, through *alm el kalam* (academic theology), through Batinism (which in alGhazali's understanding means accepting the inspired and infallible authority of an Imam or specially inspired leader), through Philosophy (philosophers being those who establish knowledge through logic and proof), and through Sufism (through ways of life and exercise which seek to attain direct experience of the presence and vision of God).

What alGhazali discovered was that although he could impose this fairly simple scheme of types of epistemology, such a scheme does not diminish the conflicts and confusion which occur within it. Among the Batinites, or among the Shia, for example, there are many claimed Imams; among the philosophers there are many rival schools and theories. AlGhazali (not unlike Josephus a thousand years before) claimed to have tried out a number of the possibilities for himself (*Munqid*, iii. 1). Just as Josephus had himself baptized and joined an Essene community (according to himself)[2] so alGhazali did his best to sympathize even with the commitment of the *zindiq*, the materialist who detaches the effect of God from the world, and is thus an 'atheist' in a practical sense.

In the midst of so many rival possibilities, alGhazali's goal remained constant: it was, in his own words, a quest to understand the nature of things *bihaqaiq*, beyond equivocation, in terms which are absolutely truthful to the underlying reality. The word *haqq* is usually translated as 'truth' but it implies the absolutely solid, unequivocal foundation, which cannot be moved. And since that was alGhazali's goal, it is not surprising that he was led very rapidly to a radical empiricism, to sense-perception at the foundation of knowledge. He put it in this way in the *Munqid* (i): 'Let me emphasize again: my aim was always to know the underlying reality of all things: it was nothing less than an attempt to grasp what all things really are in themselves. So it seemed to me that the only absolute certain and reliable knowledge (*ilm ulyaqini*) is that which offers itself as an object to sense perception, in a way not open to doubt.'

But is not sense-perception often deceived? Or to put it another way, radical empiricism of this sort still has to account for certitude: how do the objects of sense-perception establish themselves as being what they are, particularly when many of our assured judgements are inferred from sense-perception? They are not directly perceived, and in any case might be mistaken. In the *Munqid* (ii) alGhazali took two examples of the way in which what is directly perceived actually yields a misleading account, the movement of a shadow which according to direct perception cannot be seen to move, and the size of a star which according to direct perception seems to be the size of a pinhead. In the *Tahafut* (Q2) he took a more extensive example, the argument adduced by philosophers and derived from Galen to demonstrate that the world or universe has not had a beginning in time. Galen's argument, according to alGhazali, was this:

If the sun were liable to cessation, indications of decay would be observable in the process of time. But the observations of astronomers show that its size has remained constant for thousands of years. If, in this long period, it has not decayed, it follows that it is indestructible (and not liable to cessation).

One of the great exercises of Arab philosophy was to take Aristotle's preoccupation with syllogistic argument and refine the types and applications of syllogism to the furthest possible degree. AlGhazali was well versed in the exercise. One of his writings, *alQistas alMustaqim*, is an exercise of this kind: it is an attempt to construct syllogisms out of Quranic material. So in this case alGhazali quoted the syllogistic form into which the philosophers had cast Galen's argument: if the sun is liable to cessation, it must decay; but the apodosis is not possible (because sense-perception eliminates it); therefore the protasis is not possible either.

AlGhazali advanced against that argument two perfectly correct empiricist arguments: first, the conditional sentence depends on perfect induction. In order to establish it, we would have to have a knowledge of all instances, of how, for example, cessation occurs; but we do not have a knowledge of all instances; therefore we cannot deny the possibility that cessation might occur in other ways. But second (and here one can transfer the argument into even more Humean language), let it be accepted, for the sake of argument, that there is in this case a sufficient constancy of conjunction in our observation of the natural order to establish that decay accompanies or precedes cessation (ceasing to be in a previously observable form); even so, to quote alGhazali directly:

How did Galen know that the sun is not undergoing decay? . . . If the sun, which is thought to be one hundred and seventy times larger than the earth . . . loses as much as a line of hills, that loss will not be apparent to the senses . . . We are told that gold and sapphire are composed of elements liable to decay. But if a sapphire is kept a hundred years, sense perception will not discern the loss it has suffered. Equally with the sun: what it has lost during all the time it has been observed astronomically is comparable to what a sapphire loses over a hundred years: in neither case can sense perception observe it.

So alGhazali did not deny that such propositions are conceivably either true or false. Nor did he deny that one can envisage the circumstance in which they might be verified—some very distant future date at which this cluster of sense impressions presenting itself to me as a sapphire no longer presents itself to some future observer. But what alGhazali called certain and reliable knowledge (*ilm ulyaqini*) depends on the conditions of verifiabilitiy at least being specified, if not actually produced.

In this way, alGhazali was driven (according to his own account) to cut down the foundations of knowledge even further. It seemed to be the case that truth (absolute truth, truth beyond doubt) is either analytic or logical or verifiable in specifiable circumstances. Of an analytic truth, alGhazali took the example that $3 + 7 = 10$ (thus accepting mathematical truths as analytic), and from that analytic proposition we can infer that 10 must always be greater than 3 (*Munqid*, i.). Of a logical truth, alGhazali took the example that there cannot be simultaneously p and not-p, in the sense that there cannot be an entity which is both existent and non-existent at the same point in space and time (*Tahafut*, Q17). AlGhazali understood 'verifiable in specifiable circumstances' (though he did not, of course, use that phrase, but simply described worthwhile knowledge as having to meet that condition) as meaning that all propositions are ultimately parasitic on sense-experience, and true propositions are those for which one can envisage the circumstances in which they would be perceived to be true or false.

Here alGhazali believed that he had reached the bedrock foundations of knowledge. But here also there would seem to be no room for theology or for metaphysics, since by definition if a metaphysical proposition could meet those conditions it would become physics. AlGhazali was even clear enough in his empiricism to resist one of the arguments which in a later age seemed for a while to offer a line of defence against Humean and post-Humean scepticism, the appeal to miracles. In the *Munqid*, alGhazali argued that there can be putative propositions supported by impressive miracles, but if they fail to meet his criterion of being either analytic or extensively verifiable, such propositions are neither true nor false. They are interesting and curious but 'literally senseless', in relation to what counts as genuine knowledge:

It is clear to me that genuine knowledge [*ilm ulyaqini*] is that in which whatever is to be known presents itself in such a way that no doubt accompanies it, that no possibility of falsification or illusion accompanies it, and that the subject [i.e. that to which the object presents itself] cannot envisage even the possibility of such illusion or falsification. So, genuine knowledge must be free from error to such a degree that even if the attempt is made by someone who changes stones into gold or a staff into a serpent, it does not engender the slightest doubt or denial. For example, I know that 10 is greater than 3: even if someone says to me, 'No: 3 is greater than 10, and in demonstration I will change this staff into a serpent'—and let us accept that he accomplishes it and that I observe him doing it: there is no consequence to me except in so far as I wonder how he did it. So far as doubt about knowledge is concerned, *fala* [none at all].[3]

So, as alGhazali wrestled as a young man with the problems of knowledge ('how do we know what we know?' 'how can we be sure of what we know?' and the like), he felt himself driven to a very strong principle of verification to serve as a guarantee of genuine propositions. The above passage concludes: 'After all this I knew that whatever I do not establish as knowledge in this way, and whatever I do not establish as genuine in this manner of being genuine [*yaqin*], is not trustworthy and cannot count as true; and knowledge which cannot count as true cannot be genuine.'

What, then, in summary, did alGhazali try to establish as a reliable foundation of knowledge? This summary may help to make it clear:

[He] divided all genuine [*yaqin*] propositions into two classes: those which, in later terminology, concern 'relations of ideas', and those which concern 'matters of fact'. The former class comprises the *a priori* propositions of logic and pure mathematics, and these [he] allowed to be necessary and certain only because they are analytic . . . Propositions concerning empirical matters of fact, on the other hand, [he] held to be hypotheses, which can be probable but never certain [such as the sun decaying]. And in giving an account of the method of their validation [he] could hope to have explained the nature of truth.

But that summary, which does not seriously distort or misrepresent alGhazali (as the examples quoted should make clear) was not written about his work at all. It is part of the opening paragraph (with the pronouns changed) of the first edition of A. J. Ayer's *Language, Truth and Logic*. This is a point of very real interest, because it indicates the seriousness and the thorough-going radical honesty with which alGhazali attacked the problem of knowledge in his youth. However, although he did not in any way repudiate the analytic and empirical foundations of knowledge, he began to realize that what had seemed straightforward in the enthusiasm of youth, did not seem anything like so simple later on; and here again the connection with Ayer is not remote. When Ayer looked back on that edition of *Language, Truth and Logic*, he wrote: 'Being in every sense a young man's book, I have come to see that the questions with which it deals are not in all respects so simple as it makes them appear; but I still believe that the point of view which it expresses is substantially correct.'[4]

That is exactly what also happened to alGhazali. There were two main reasons which made alGhazali change his mind and come to believe that his earlier classification of genuinely mean- ingful propositions had been too narrow. The first is directly com- parable to one of the points on which Ayer had to acknowledge that his original proposal was not satisfactory—his attempt to dis- tinguish between a 'strong' and a 'weak' sense of the term verifi- able. Originally he had argued that ' "a proposition is said to be verifiable in the strong sense of the term, if and only if its truth could be conclusively established in experience", but that "it is verifiable, in the weak sense, if it is possible for experience to render it probable" '.[5] But subsequently he came to see that the strong sense of verification can never occur, because 'however strong the evidence in its favour, there would never be a point at which it was impossible for further experience to go against it'. That is very similar to alGhazali's realization that we can never, in the relative situation of time (as he puts it in the *Tahafut*), attain a condition of perfect induction.

But Ayer rapidly went on to observe that there *does* seem to be

a class of empirical propositions of which it is permissible to say that they can be verified conclusively. It is characteristic of these proposi- tions, which I have elsewhere called 'basic propositions', that they refer solely to the content of a single experience, and what may be said to verify them conclusively is the occurrence of the experience to which they uniquely refer. Furthermore, I should now agree with those who say that propositions of this kind are 'incorrigible', assuming that what is meant by their being incorrigible is that it is impossible to be mistaken about them except in a verbal sense.[6]

That is exactly the position reached by alGhazali when he came to discuss the meaning of *yaqin* at the opening of the *Ihya*. *Yaqin* is actually a more complicated word than has appeared in the discussion so far, because it is also the word used in Sufi mysticism to describe the knowledge of the otherwise unseen which invades a person in a state of god-relatedness; and alGhazali undoubtedly used the term in that sense of self-authenticating knowledge—conviction granted in experience through, for example, direct intuition which for the person involved is unequivocal and beyond doubt. This complicates, and indeed threatens, alGhazali's empiricism from a modern point of view, because of the familiar problems of moving from private conviction to public verification. However, to some extent alGhazali was aware of the problem, because in the *Ihya* he discussed two major contexts in which *yaqin* (subjective certainty) arises: one is in Sufism (the intuitive certainty of the mystic that God is); the other is the use of the term by philosophers and academic theologians for whom the term *yaqin* implies *taqlid*, acceptance on the basis of authority. Certainty arises from aquiescence to authority, so that *yaqini* knowledge is that which constrains assent beyond doubt, because a context figure of legitimate authority (i.e. legitimate within the system itself) has required it.

It is obvious that alGhazali's observations are psychologically correct: people *do* form unshakeable convictions in the ways described, and that is part of the reason (as he stated in the *Munqid*, i) why Christian children grow up as Christians, Zoroastrian children as Zoroastrians, and Jewish children as Jews. But those observations, however correct they may be, have little to do with an empiricist theory of knowledge. Such a theory must necessarily ask whether subjective certainty and authoritative statement are well grounded, and if so where, in a publicly verifiable way. Consequently, alGhazali argued that *both* those extremes of arriving at conviction are defective in isolation; or to put it another way, *yaqin* in the Sufi sense of subjective certainty is suspect unless it can be related to *yaqin* in the philosopher's sense: since one may be subjectively certain of doubtful or false propositions, *yaqin* in the Sufi sense cannot confer truth on content; it can only become publicly available if it can be related to truth of content independently

established. But conversely *yaqin* in the authoritative sense is barren unless it is related to *yaqin* in the Sufi sense. Knowledge
offered on the basis of *taqlid*, authority, may be true, but unless it
can (at least in principle) be checked out and the conditions of its
verification known when it is appropriated, or made informative,
in human lives, it remains as neutral to us as one stone is neutral
to another in a field. *Taqlid* does not confer truth on content in
any abstract sense: it remains to be appropriated in experience,
which is the *locus* of verification. To whom, to put it briefly, is an
incorrigible proposition incorrigible?

Because alGhazali was principally concerned with religious propositions about putative matters of fact, much of his discussion
about *yaqin* concentrates more on the subjective side, as, for
example, at the opening of *Mustasfa*, where he asks how conviction
and certainty arise, and only then how they are justified. In addition he remained committed to the defence of the value of religious
faith and of the truth of Islam. It is this which creates the impression of a fideistic theologian, whose mind is made up before the
inquiry begins. But even if that is so, there is not the slightest
doubt that one can disentangle from alGhazali's writing a concern
for the conditions of knowledge which is as serious as that of any
empiricists of more recent times. AlGhazali was perfectly clear
that *yaqin* refers to a psychological condition in which all doubt has
been removed, and that consequently it can be paraphrased as
'certainty'; and he knew equally well that human beings arrive at
'certainty' in different ways and without necessarily being justified
in doing so. Therefore when he discussed *yaqin* in the *Ihya* he was
concerned to map the ways in which doubt or the possibility of
of doubt is removed: psychologically it is removed by argument,
by authoritative statement (which occurs, in alGhazali's opinion only
among the simple and the credulous), and through syllogistic reasoning (*alburhan*). In addition, doubt is removed through intuitive
certainty, as among the Sufis: intuitive conviction may be falsified,
but that does not alter the psychological observation that it eliminates doubt while it lasts: 'It may be reported that a certain
person does not believe in death, but in fact there is no real doubt
about it. Or another person may be intuitively certain that the means
of sustenance for his life will turn up, though it is entirely possible
that they never will' (*Ihya*, i. 6). To all these conditions the term
yaqin can be applied because they are conditions in which doubt

has been removed, though in the two examples it is, or may be, unjustified.

Consequently, alGhazali set before all these the condition of *yaqin* where doubt is justifiably removed, and drew attention to the nature of the justification—sense experience. Meaningful propositions, or what alGhazali called *marifa alhaqiqiya* (incorrigible or basic propositions which can be accepted as true), are those which arise from evidence which leaves no room for doubt or any possibility of doubt: 'To give an example of this condition: if a wise person is asked, "Is there in existence [*fi'lwujud*, literally, in that which has been or can be found] anything eternal?", he will not be able to respond, because the eternal is outside direct observation (*gair mahasus*), unlike, for example, the sun and moon which are directly perceived' (*Ihya*, i. 6).

It is obvious (or at least it was to alGhazali) that not all such propositions can be verified or falsified by the individual concerned. Consequently, they may depend on a report, such as the proposition 'Mecca is a town in Arabia', even though we have not been there ourselves; or they may depend on experiment, such as the proposition, cooked *saqamuniya* (the Greek *skammonia*, *Convolvulus scammonia*, well known to Aristotle) acts as a laxative; or they may depend on some form of *dalil*, demonstration. The term *dalil* is also complicated. Basically, *dalla* means 'he displayed', 'he showed', 'he exhibited', 'he indicated'. But *dalil* gained a much more technical sense of 'guide' on the way to the hereafter, as in the Introduction to *Ihya*: 'The attempt to travel on the way to the hereafter is onerous with neither *dalil* nor companion'. In addition, it came to mean 'demonstration', particularly through syllogistic proof, *burhan*; and that particular sense is sometimes contrasted with knowledge based on sense-perception, so that it is virtually an analytic truth in contrast to a synthetic truth verified in the necessary ways, as in *AlIqtisad fi'lItiqad*: '*Dalil* is what is known by logic and not by sense-observation.' Yet there is in fact a connection between the two. An adequate demonstration can be established in two ways: first, through literal demonstration, i.e. verification through sense-experience; second, through logical argument.

Where the grounding of demonstration in sense-experience is concerned, it is hard to know how in Arabic one could reproduce more accurately the opening pages of *Language, Truth and Logic*. Beyond any doubt, alGhazali recognized that it is impossible for

every individual to verify every proposition individually, because
in that case historical propositions (for example) and many geographical propositions would not be meaningful. According to
alGhazali, it is simply necessary to specify the conditions in which
the claimed object of knowledge presented itself for observation to
some observers, or could do so. So he argued specifically (*Ihya*,
i. 6):

You can easily understand that there is a difference in your acceptance
that Mecca exists and that Fadak exists [a village north of Medina], or
in your acceptance that Moses existed and that Joshua existed [the
point being that Joshua is not mentioned by name in the Quran]. Yet
they are equal in fact (as propositions), because they are equally based
on reports that have come to us. The only reason why one seems
stronger and clearer in your own mind than another is because the
evidence is stronger in the one case since more historians have mentioned
it.

The propositions are comparable as propositions because one can
specify the conditions in which they could be verified—that at a
singular point of space and time a bundle of sense-perceptions
presented itself to an observer, that bundle of sense-perceptions
being named *Yusha*, Joshua, and reported as such under that
name. Had we been there, the same bundle of sense-impressions
would have presented itself to us. Similarly, if we travelled in
Arabia, propositions about the existence of Mecca and Fadak could
be verified.

But what possible status can this leave to the propositions of
theology? How can they meet the condition of verification as
alGhazali described it? The Quran, for example, affirms that God
sits on a throne: does this mean that a throne with God on it will
one day present itself to observation? If it does, the fatal Muslim
offence of *tashbih* (of anthropomorphism, of reducing God to the
order of his creation) is surely entailed. If it does not so present
itself, then how can we be sure that any propositions about God are
factual? This and the related problem of attributes had been a
battleground in the history of Muslim theology. Some Muslim
theologians had tried to hold the ground by affirming the attributes
bila kaif, without knowing how. But that agnosticism did not
satisfy alGhazali: it came too close to *taqlid* to accepting things
on the basis of authority.

AlGhazali knew perfectly well that many people have to proceed on that basis, because they do not have the time (or perhaps even the mental capacity) to sort out all propositions for themselves. But in that case, as we have already seen, it is all the more important for theologians and philosophers to test and verify propositions, not simply for their own satisfaction, but on behalf of others who cannot, or will not, do it for themselves. It is ironic that this rigorously conceived understanding of the social function of the philosopher and the theologian was completely misunderstood in Christendom and was distorted into the view that Muslims held a notion of 'double truth'—one for the credulous, the other for the intelligentsia—a notion which Aquinas (sharing the general ignorance of Islam) not surprisingly attacked. In fact, truth is uniform, but alGhazali did not believe that it is a necessary condition of salvation that all believers must be academic theologians. On the other hand, there must be *some* people who are concerned with the issue of truth in theological propositions. Such propositions, particularly where they involve existence claims (e.g. about God, or the Garden, or the Fire) cannot escape the challenge of truth (and therefore of verification) which is addressed to other existence claims (e.g. about Joshua or Fadak). But in that case, how can theological propositions survive as meaningful or genuine? It was to that question that alGhazali turned his mind.

3. EMPIRICISM AND THEOLOGY

IT has been pointed out so far that alGhazali was well aware of the diverse ways in which a sense of God arises in human consciousness—as a consequence of the social contexts in which we are born, through a fideistic acceptance of what we are told, through rational argument, and above all through direct intuition, as the Sufis claimed (though the experience was not confined to them). Toward the end of the *Ihya*, alGhazali made the point that we can experience the universe in many different modes and make use of it for many different purposes. This creates a kind of hierarchy of experiencing, in which we transcend the layers of perception which first occur to us, and through which we are led into an increasingly rich and profound understanding of all that the universe can yield us—until in the end, in alGhazali's view, we suddenly break through to see it as a language of God's expression: 'Green things and running water may be loved for their own sake, not simply for the sake of eating what is good for the body and of drinking water. So too with the fragrant blossom and the flowers and the birds . . . The very sight itself is able to yield delight in the mind, and delight encourages a deep thanksgiving.'[1]

Out of such experience one is led to consider the nature and worth of the consciousness which apprehends and of the universe which supplies the material of apprehension, and it is that which yields to us what alGhazali called 'spiritual vision', a particular way of seeing the universe and ourselves within it as derived from God and related to him.[2] Such a way of seeing is necessarily incomplete, but alGhazali had no doubt as a matter of observation that it is a straightforward possibility of being human: it is, in other words, a potential capacity of human experiencing which is engaged by some but not by all.

Even so, the outstanding question of ontology remains, which can best be expressed in the phenomenological terms through which alGhazali himself approached it: what is it necessary to infer as the existent sufficient ground for the experiences in consciousness (mediated through cues arising in the universe) which occur and which are suggestive of God-relatedness? Is it, for example, necessary to infer anything more than the universe itself, which is simply being read or interpreted in a particular way? If it is felt necessary to infer an existent reality, not wholly contained within the universe as that presents itself to immediate observation, which is then characterized theistically, how could such an existence claim be established as true or false? It was to those questions that alGhazali directed his attention.

It is obvious that he was in some immediate difficulty: since he had come to the conclusion that true propositions must be either analytic or verifiable in specifiable circumstances, at least in principle, to some observer, how could that be reconciled with propositions about God who does not present himself for observation as an object among objects? In attempting to answer that question, alGhazali did not abandon his hard-won theory of knowledge. That theory *was* hard-won, because at one stage it reduced him to almost total scepticism, for exactly the same reasons (according to his own account) as those described in Ayer's *The Problem of Knowledge* (pp. 36 f.):

There was a time when people believed that examining the entrails of birds was a way of discovering whether a certain course of action would be propitious, whether, for example, the occasion was favourable for joining battle. Then any sceptic who doubted the value of such a method of divination would have been questioning an accepted canon of evidence. And it is now agreed that he would in fact have been right. But the justification for his doubt would have been not philosophical but scientific . . . The peculiarity of the philosopher's doubts is that they are not in this way connected with experience . . . His contention is that any inference from past to future is illegitimate. Similarly, he will maintain not merely that there are circumstances in which a man's senses are liable to deceive him, as when he is suffering from some physiological disorder, but rather that it is to be doubted whether the exercise of sense-perception can in any circumstances whatever afford proof of the existence of physical objects.

The young alGhazali went to the limits of scepticism along both those routes, the scientific and the philosophical. As an example of the first kind of scepticism (the scientific), he challenged the pretensions of astrology to be counted as genuine knowledge, and he did so, exactly as Ayer describes, on grounds of evidence. It was by no means an easy argument to conduct or win, because astrology was widely practised at the time. It was as much a commonplace then as it is now for those who look at their stars in a daily paper. It is not difficult for Ayer to look back on divination and point out, to use his own words, that 'it might have been the case that these so-called omens were systematically connected with the events which they were supposed to presage, but experience shows otherwise' (p. 36). As Burke put it, it is not difficult to be a Whig on the events of a hundred years ago.[3] It is much harder to be so before the accumulation of experience has given one the advantage of hindsight—particularly in a case like astrology where it is widely practised, and where its predictions are sufficiently general; for in that case, it is probable that it will be confirmed on many occasions, and that consequently it will maintain sufficient plausibility. For this reason astrology is actually very difficult to falsify (or to put it more accurately, it may not be difficult to falsify, but it is difficult to persuade people who believe in it that it has been falsified). There was a sad but good example of this in the *T. V. Times* in 1973. During the week February 3–9 of that year, its editing and writing were handed over to women—'It's the week the girls take over.' The column on the stars was taken over by Eve Cuming from the regular astrologist, Maurice Woodruff, and she made him the subject of her star forecast:

He will have a mixed year and should pay attention to his health. Before getting involved in legal proceedings he should be cautious: faulty advice may be given, causing disastrous results. He shouldn't make changes or he might lose close and cherished friends, and his warm, generous nature could attract the wrong kind of people. If encouraged they could change the whole pattern of his life and affect his emotional stability as well as his career, resulting in anxiety (p. 44).

However, Maurice Woodruff died during that very week. The following week the *T.V. Times* commented.

There was a strange coincidence in the fact that Maurice Woodruff's column did not appear in *T.V. Times* last week for the first time in 10 years. The reason was that he handed over to guest astrologer Eve Cuming . . . Eve chose to make Maurice the subject of the week's personality forecast and wrote: He will have a mixed year and should pay attention to his health . . .'.

Well, he did have a mixed year—mixed between living and dying. But that example shows how impossible it is to falsify astrology for people who believe in it. The part quoted in the subsequent comment was the *only* part which could be distorted into an impression that Woodruff's otherwise totally unforeseen death was somehow foreseen in the stars: no mention was made of the other parts of the prediction at all.

In alGhazali's time astrology was even more usual: it was an important part of the resources on which very many people drew to help them in their construction of a life-way from birth to death. It is therefore all the more impressive that alGhazali argued against the propositions which occur in astrology as having any status in genuine (*yaqin*) knowledge. Some of his arguments were derived from specifically Muslim considerations: there is a mismatch between astrology and what is counted as fundamentally resourceful in the construction of appropriate Muslim utterance. But his main argument is that the *whole* evidence does not establish sufficient constancy of conjunction, between the disposition of the stars as cause and events on earth as effect, to establish astrology as genuine knowledge. That *some* predictions are confirmed does not affect this somewhat Humean point—indeed, it simply *makes* the point. This is summarized by alGhazali in the *Ihya* (i. 1. 3) in this way: 'A reason why astrology is blameworthy is that it is simply guessing, and common sense knows that its predictions are not established with certainty, nor even with probability . . . The few instances where an astrologer happens to be right are coincidental.'

AlGhazali accepted that an astrologer's guesses may be informed guesses, and may indeed be sensitive to what is genuinely causative, but even at that level we have no access to certainty:

His prediction is like the guess of a man who sees clouds forming on the mountains and predicts that rain will fall that day. Rain may indeed fall, but equally it is possible that a strong sun will disperse the clouds. It is not sufficient for there to be clouds in the sky to predict with certainty that rain will fall. There may be other conditions of occurrence which cannot be determined. In the same way, the sailor guesses that his voyage will be safe because he relies on the way in which he knows that the winds usually behave. But there are unknown factors which constrain the movements of winds, and these the sailor cannot possibly know. As a result, he may indeed guess correctly on some occasions, but on others he will be wrong . . . So astrology is blameworthy because it is absolutely useless . . . It is a waste and dissipation of that which is man's most precious possession, time and his life.

AlGhazali did not deny that astrology or indeed magic can be accompanied by startling events, and that apparently, as he put it in the *Tahafut* (Q17), the use of a talisman does produce effects: 'So they draw up a horoscope and produce mysterious and amazing results in the world. For example, they are able to banish snakes or scorpions or things of that sort through their knowledge of magic.' But alGhazali insisted that those actions may simply be coincidental to a much greater complexity of causation, and the fact that they cannot always repeat the effect in relation to their own claimed cause (the magic or the horoscope) suggests that coincidence is a more likely account of what is happening.

AlGhazali's discussion of astrology was offered as an example of the way in which he pursued Ayer's first type of scepticism (p. 213), scepticism on empirical or scientific grounds. But he also pursued the second and more fundamental scepticism as well. AlGhazali's own account has already been quoted (p. 203) of the way in which he became doubtful about the reliability of knowledge grounded in sense-experience even though he was entirely sure that it could not be grounded anywhere else; and it is clear that alGhazali was exercised by exactly the same two examples which occur in the passage on scepticism in *The Problem of Knowledge* already quoted (pp. 202 ff.), that any inference from past to future is illegitimate, and that it is to be doubted whether the exercise of sense-perception can in any circumstances whatever afford proof of the existence of physical objects.

On the first of them, we have already seen that alGhazali was undoubtedly sensitive to the contention that 'any (absolutely certain) inference from past to future is illegitimate' though he was prepared to accept degrees of probability. 'Similarly,' as Ayer put it,

he will maintain not merely that there are circumstances in which a man's senses are liable to deceive him [and that is exactly the position reached by alGhazali (see pp. 202 f.) over the movement of a shadow, or the size of a star], but rather that it is to be doubted whether the exercise of sense-perception can in any circumstances whatever afford proof of the existence of physical objects.

That is exactly the line along which, as a young man, alGhazali was drawn. According to the *Munqid* (ii), alGhazali came to believe that perhaps the whole of experience is a kind of dream. Just as presentations in a dream seem to be real until one wakes up, so perhaps what presents itself as 'real' in waking experience would seem equally insubstantial from another perspective. AlGhazali therefore asked whether that was what Muhammad had meant when he said,

Men are dreaming: when they die, they wake up . . . So maybe the life of this world is a dream in relation to the world hereafter; so that when a man dies, things seem entirely different from their present appearance; and in that connection he says to him; 'We have taken away from you your covering, and your sight today is acute' (s. 1. 21).

Those considerations reduced alGhazali to despairing scepticism:

Such arguments require to be refuted by demonstration [dalil]; but since nothing can be demonstrated unless one admits a foundation of certain knowledge, and since such a foundation is exactly what is being denied, it follows that the demonstration cannot possibly be established. This vitiating disease lasted almost two months during which I became a sceptic [safsatah] in actual fact, though in theory and in what I spoke with my mouth I was not . . . (Munqid, ii).

Although alGhazali moved away from that extreme scepticism, and began to reconstruct a theory of knowledge in the way explored in the last chapter, this undoubtedly remained a constant input in the devastating critique which alGhazali now proceeded to launch against metaphysics and theology. We have just seen that al-Ghazali focused his unease about certitude on the problem of induction: previous experience of weather enables probability of judgement, but not certainty. But the greater the constancy of conjunction there is, the greater the degree of certainty which obtains. In the *Tahafut*, alGhazali concentrated on what was also the precise central problem for Hume, the observation of cause and effect: surely the fact that we observe effect following cause requires that there is a necessary relation between the two. If that is so, then there cannot be any problem of induction, because we can certainly extend that necessity from observed to unobserved instances. But (familiar objection) we do *not* observe cause and effect as a direct and invariable part of our perception; we build up observations, not only of contiguity and succession, but also of constancy in particular conjunctions. In that way we attain in certain areas high degrees of confidence, but never absolute certainty of consequence.

That is exactly alGhazali's argument. What he undertook to

criticize was the proposition of the metaphysical philosophers that (to quote the *Tahafut*, Q 16), 'the connection observed to obtain between causes and effects is a necessary connection, and that consequently it is impossible to think of a cause without its associated effect, any more than one can produce an effect in independence from its cause'. AlGhazali did not deny the latter point as a matter of evidence, but he resisted the conclusion, as Hume did also, that a necessary connection is actually observed in the relation. So he argued (Q 17):

In our opinion the connection between what is taken to be the cause and the effect is not necessary (*daruriyya*) . . . Take, for example, any two things, such as drinking and the cessation of thirst; eating and the cessation of hunger; touching fire and being burnt; the sun rising and the light increasing; cutting the head off a body and death; the use of medicine and the restoration of health; the use of a purgative and the loosening of the bowels; or any other set of events which are observed in medicine, astronomy, natural science or mechanics: . . . the conection between them cannot be established as necessary and indissoluble.

AlGhazali then included in his statement: 'The relation is simply a consequence of their being brought to be in that way by the decree of God.' That last phrase—'by the decree of God'—obviously looks like a theological platitude, innocent in the mouth of a preacher, but fatal in the argument of alGhazali. If we cannot observe a necessary relation in the proximity of two events, how much less, surely, can we observe the decree of God? But that is exactly the point which alGhazali is actually making. The function of that phrase in alGhazali is to make the point that even if all that we observe is a consequence of the creative word of God (as the Quran puts it), it is still not arbitrary, nor can it ever be so. God's *qadir*, his 'power over all things', is logically restricted, and for that reason is not arbitrary in the universe, as alGhazali argued (Q 17):

No one has power over the impossible. What is meant by the impossible is the assertion of p and not-p; or the assertion of the particular and the denial of the inclusive; or the assertion of two and the denial of one. Propositions of this kind constitute the impossible; but what is not impossible is within *qadir*.

AlGhazali then went on in the *Tahafut* to derive from Aristotle the example which Quinton also derived from Aristotle, in *The Nature of Things*, in his discussion of the first of his four problems of substance, individuation:

Another kind of necessarily individuating property is position in space and time ... What proves this is the familiar but highly important metaphysical truth that no two things can be at the same place at the same time ... Individuals are, to use an old world, *impenetrable* ... A complete, that is to say spatial *and* temporal, position is either monogamous or virginal, ontologically speaking. So to state the position of a thing is to predicate a conjunction of properties of it and is necessarily to individuate it ... A concrete individual or Aristotelian substance is a set of qualities manifested at a position, and of such things the Aristotelian principle of inherence is correct. Both *form*, that is to say shareable properties, and *matter*, that is to say position in space and time, are essential logical parts of an individual. Position and qualities alone are abstract. We do not encounter them alone in perception, but only in the conjunction with each other that constitutes a concrete individual.[4]

AlGhazali in the same way accepted that it is a logical necessity of individuation that no two things can be at the same place at the same time, nor can one person be in two places at the same time, and he accepted also that substance, to be intelligible, requires the co-inherence of form (shareable properties) and matter (position in space and time). That is the only way in which perceptions could present themselves as evidential. But that simply means, to go back to the phrase 'by the decree of God', that the conditions of individuation were recognized by alGhazali as a *logical* constraint over the possibilities in a created order.

So when alGhazali argued that the observed relation between two sets of events, touching fire and being burnt, is not a necessary relation, nor can we be sure from the observation of many instances that the relation will obtain in all instances (i.e. the relation is not, in alGhazali's term, 'indissoluble'), and when he then said that they are as they are by the decree of God, he was simply affirming two things: first, that nothing in a created order (supposing there is one) can possibly escape being in the condition of createdness; but second, that nevertheless things are brought to be as they are, not arbitrarily, but within the constraints of what is logically possible. The reason why the *qadir* of God cannot be observed directly in sense-perception in the relations of events or of properties (any more than cause-and-effect can be observed directly in sense-perception) is because in this case all examples are examples of the same case, namely either of being in a created order, or of *not* being in a created order: either they all are, or they all are not; and where there cannot be discrimination there cannot be genuine knowledge. To put it in the more modern terms of Gilbert Ryle, 'there can be false coins only where there are coins made of the proper materials by the proper authorities'.[5] But in this case, since all coins are either false or genuine, it is quite impossible to know whether any coin is false or genuine. It might then be argued that in that case we might just as well live as if they are all genuine (as if the world is the creation of God) and get on with the commerce and business of life. That 'as if' attitude to coins is life-enabling for the businessman, and that 'as if' attitude to creation is life-enabling for the religious man. But those attitudes do not, and cannot, confer truth on content, except in a provisional sense that we acquiesce in a convention. This leads to the familiar Islamic form of occasionalism; but this theory of knowledge also suggests that if no sense-experience can possibly be relevant to the determination of the truth or falsehood of the proposition that all things are a consequence of the decree of God (since all sense-experience is equal in that respect), and if that putative proposition is not a tautology, then we must 'hold that it is metaphysical, and that, being metaphysical, it is neither true nor false, but literally senseless'?[6]

Yes, answered alGhazali, that is exactly what we must hold, that the attempt of metaphysical argument to establish certainty in relation to propositions of that sort is certain to fail. The fundamental weakness of metaphysics *in practice* (i.e. as practised in alGhazali's time), and the reason why, in alGhazali's opinion, it is so misleadingly useless, lies in the fact that philosophers, having observed the certainty with which reason arrives at judgements of truth in logic and in mathematics, then assume that by the exercise of reason they will be able to attain comparable certainty in other areas of human inquiry.

In other words, they had reached a position like that of Descartes, on that famous occasion in the stove-heated room on his way back to the army from the Emperor's coronation, thinking his own thoughts for a whole day and coming to the belief that a bridge could be built by reason from the known and established to the unknown and unperceived:

Those long chains of perfectly simple and easy reasonings by means of which geometers are accustomed to carry out their most difficult demonstrations had led me to fancy that everything that can fall under human knowledge forms a similar sequence; and that so long as we avoid accepting as true what is not so, and always preserve the right order of deduction of one thing from another, there can be nothing too remote to be reached in the end, or too well hidden to be discovered.[7]

It was exactly that kind of metaphysical bridge from the known to the unknown which the philosophers of alGhazali's time had tried to build, and alGhazali had done much for a time to help build it. Now he jumped about on it, to see how much weight it would carry, and found that it would carry none.

For what is clearly observable is that metaphysical arguments are not like mathematics and cannot be established as certain in that way. As alGhazali put it (*Tahafut*, Introd.):

There is nothing stable or constant in the propositions advanced by philosophers . . . They try to infer the truth of their metaphysical propositions from the certainty of mathematics and logic . . . But if their metaphysical propositions had been as conclusive and necessary as their mathematical knowledge, they could not have differed among themselves over metaphysical questions, because they do not in fact differ over mathematics.

But if metaphysical arguments cannot be derived from analytic truths, they certainly cannot be derived from the only other resource of genuine (*yaqin*) knowledge, sense-perception. As al-Ghazali had argued, it is not possible to establish as necessary or indissoluble even so obvious a relation in appearance as cause-and-effect, as when contact with fire results in burning:

There is no argument [in favour of the fire being the agent and thus the relation being one of necessity, that this is what fire always does] except from the observation of burning at the time of contact with fire. But observation strictly shows that the one accompanies the other [literally, is with the other], not that it is by the other, with no cause other than it . . . Existence [alwujud] *with* a thing does not establish a necessity of being *by* it (*Tahafut*, Q17).

How then are the propositions of natural science established? By sufficient constancy of conjunction: that is as much alGhazali's answer as Hume's: 'When something possible is repeated one time after another it impresses itself on our memory, and thus its constant repetition in a consistent pattern impresses itself beyond doubt' (*Tahafut*, Q 17).

But where is the sufficient constancy of conjunction at the foundation of moral or of religious judgement, or indeed at the foundation of the majority of metaphysical propositions? Al-Ghazali was acutely aware (quite as much as Voltaire or anybody else in the eighteenth century) of the reality of cultural relativity (the variety, that is, which obtains in the religious scene, and the accidents of birth and upbringing, which constrain individuals into one belief rather than another). As Pascal put it, what is true on one side of the Pyrenees is not necessarily true on the other.

So where is the sufficient constancy of conjunction which might justify metaphysical propositions? Nowhere, answered alGhazali. For, if such constancy of conjunction could be found, there could not be antinomies of metaphysical reason; and yet there are. In the *Tahafut*, alGhazali took twenty examples of metaphysical propositions which cannot be established with certainty, and through some of them he illustrated that the use of reason is divided, in the sense that both the thesis and the antithesis can be proved to equal satisfaction.

Of Kant's four instances, alGhazali has the first and the last two, but not the second. The first, 'the world is, as to space and time, infinite', occurs as alGhazali's first and second Problems; the third, 'there are in the world causes through freedom: there is no liberty but all is nature', occurs as Problem 17. The fourth, 'in the series of world-causes there is some necessary being: there is nothing necessary in the world, but in this series all is incidental', occurs as Problem 10. AlGhazali's other examples are almost entirely theological, though some are drawn from traditional Greek instances which were still very much alive—for example, are the heavens a living being whose movements are voluntary? On that particular question (Problem 14), alGhazali stated that the metaphysical thesis (that the heavens are living and that they obey God in their motion) is incapable of excluding the antithesis that the movement of the planets is related to the movement of a stone when it falls, and that it is determined in the same way without consciousness in the subject. AlGhazali concluded: 'It is clear that the metaphysical proposition (that the heavens are living), even if we accept that it is more probable than any other hypothesis, cannot exclude the other hypothesis. It follows that the proposition is inconclusive and that it cannot be grounded.'

It was on this fundamental ground of the inability of reason to

establish certainty in metaphysical issues, summarized in the antinomies of reason, that alGhazali challenged the belief of the
philosophers and theologians that their arguments were capable
of yielding genuine (*yaqin*) knowledge. He knew perfectly well
that systematic theologians might respond to the challenge 'So
what?' They might well be inclined to reply that the task of theology is to respond to what is accepted as the self-givenness of God
(the revelation of God), not to subordinate theology to the world
in order to justify the ways of God to men. AlGhazali had sympathy with that argument and summarized it in the Introduction
to the *Tahafut*:

Provided the beginning of the world in time is proved, it is all the
same whether it is a round body or a simple thing, or an octagonal or
hexagonal figure . . . Investigation into these facts is no more relevant
to theology than an investigation into the number of the layers of an
onion, or the number of the seeds of a pomegranate, would be. What we
are interested in is whether the world is the product of God's creative
action, whatever the manner of that action may be.

It may seem as though alGhazali was tempted to move in a similarly fideistic direction, because in the *Tahafut* he ultimately
condemned metaphysical philosophy for casting doubt on two
fundamental propositions without which belief is impossible:
that God is, and that there will be a final day of judgement, 'the
two indispensable principles, the two constantly recurring themes
in the teaching of all the prophets'.

That clearly seems to sell the pass. But in fact there was a different and technical reason which made alGhazali join those two
propositions together as the necessary condition of faith, as will
be seen at the end of this chapter. In the first instance, alGhazali
was simply concerned to point out that philosophers create doubt
about those metaphysical propositions, *not* because they can refute
them, but because they cannot establish *certainty* about them. Nor
is that inability a consequence of a temporary failure to find the
right arguments. It is a consequence of the limits of reason at the
bounds of sense, and no amount of casting about for bigger and
better arguments will ever change the situation, despite what the
philosophers themselves believe. Faced with a difficulty they argue:
'There must be a solution somewhere in the disciplines developed
by the masters of old; perhaps we have failed because we have not

adequately applied logic and mathematics to this question' (*Taha-fut*, Introd.).
But alGhazali commented:

There is nothing in these facts [of sense-observation or analytic truth] which proves or disproves metaphysical propositions. To hold that there is, would be like saying: 'To know whether this house was produced by a conscious, willing, able, and living builder, one must first discover whether it has six or eight sides, and how many beams and bricks it has.' Such a statement would be completely absurd. It would be like saying: 'The temporal character of an onion cannot be known, unless the number of its layers is counted'; or 'The temporal character of a pomegranate cannot be known, unless the number of its seeds is counted.'

But in that case, what, if anything, can be meaningfully said about the existence of God? At this point, alGhazali was much assisted by the fact that he wrote in Arabic. Philosophical writers in Arabic had the advantage of having two resources of vocabulary (at least)[8] on which to draw. First, they had the Greek philosophical vocabulary which had been transposed into Arabic, and second, they had their own native tongue. When they came to discuss questions of existence and essence they could do so in terms designed to be equivalent to the Greek vocabulary—such terms as *anniyya* (existence), or *mahiyya* and *huwiyya* (essence). But the force of the underlying Arabic, which had not been applied to philosophical discussion before the advent of Islam, yielded in some instances a very different kind of argument. In the case of *wujud*, in particular, it enabled alGhazali to discuss existence-propositions in a way which was highly congenial to his empiricist theory of knowledge. *Wujud* undoubtedly represented (or was intended to represent) Greek words for 'being', such as *to einai* and *to on* (of which Afnan, *Lexicon*, gives examples). Yet as Afnan (*Terminology*, p. 29) points out, 'the Translators had chosen the use of the verb *wajada* knowing full well that that denotes existence and not being'. In other words, it has an underlying *Arabic* sense which persisted in and through at least some uses of the word.

The term *wujud* occurs in the passage already quoted about the existence (*wujud*) of eternal objects (p. 209), and it occurs also in the passage quoted about the existence of Mecca (p. 210): 'There is a difference in your acceptance that Mecca exists . . .'. In fact alGhazali simply wrote, '. . . in your acceptance *biwujud Makka*'. *Wujud* comes from the verb *wajada*, he found. It might, therefore, literally be translated, 'in your acceptance of the having been foundness of Mecca'. However, translation has to make some compromise with the language into which the translation is being made —though preferably not *too* much, as Cornford observed of Jowett's version of Plato's *Republic*: 'One who opened Jowett's version at random and lighted on the statement that the best guardian for a man's "virtue" is "philosophy tempered with music" might run away with the idea that in order to avoid irregular relations with women, he had better play the violin in the intervals of studying metaphysics.'[9]

In the case of *wujud*, it is clear that 'findability' is involved in its reference to possible existence. To believe in the existence of Mecca is therefore to believe in the findability of Mecca, or to believe that Mecca is findable; to believe in the existence of Moses is to believe in the findability of Moses, that Moses was available to be found at a moment in space and time. *Wujud* is thus a word which lent itself admirably to a radically empiricist theory of knowledge: propositions entailing existence can only be meaningful provided that their findability can be specified—the circumstances in which they are, were, or will be findable, in the sense that sense-impressions offer themselves to observation.

The use of *wujud* as an existence term enabled alGhazali to maintain an empiricist theory of knowledge even when dealing with such elusive propositions as those dealing with historical events or the putative existence of unseen objects. The advantage of *wujud* was that it allowed for the possibility that genuine propositions yielding *yaqin* (certainty) could be established by either verification or falsification or both. The combination of the two is highly important, because verification on its own cannot, even in principle, establish conclusively the truth (and thus meaningfulness) of the proposition 'All sheep are white', nor can falsification on its own establish the falsity (and thus meaningfulness) of the proposition, 'there exists one unicorn'. For this reason, when Hempel advanced that criticism against the Verification principle and the Falsification principle, Rynin responded by adopting what he called 'the simple, natural and obviously correct expedient'[10] of putting the two together: 'A sentence is c-meaningful (cognitively meaningful) if and only if it is either verifiable or falsifiable,

i.e. is governed by truth rules specifying either necessary or sufficient truth-conditions.' In this way 'all sheep are white' may not
be verifiable, but it is certainly falsifiable in principle—we might
find a black sheep; similarly, 'there exists one unicorn' may not
be falsifiable, but it is certainly verifiable in principle—we might
find one.

But now the question arises, what of the claimed existence of
God? How can theological propositions entailing existence-claims
meet the conditions of this radically empiricist theory of knowledge? An Arab philosopher could not demand greater stringency
here than in any other case. Or to put it another way round, an
Arab philosopher would feel himself required, not to produce God
as an immediate object among objects for his existence to be meaningfully affirmed, but to specify the circumstances in which what
is descriptively affirmed in the term Allah, God, is *wujud*, findable.
There are two levels on which the *wujud* of God can be claimed.
The first is on the level of report, the second is eschatological.
There are great problems in the notion of eschatological verification, but leaving the actual problems on one side for the moment,
it is clear that propositions about God's actions after death (e.g.
God rewards his faithful servants) are only verifiable or falsifiable
in principle in that condition. There is also a present level of *wujud*
in relation to God, in which some human beings report the *wujud*
of God (the findability or foundness of God) in their own experience. On that level (the level of report) the *wujud* (the findability) of God is affirmed by those who report a knowledge
by acquaintance, and where alGhazali was concerned there were
two main extensive categories involved: prophets, who (on this
view) are constrained into that outcome by God relating himself
to the world through that mode of communication; and Sufis,
those who through contemplation or asceticism or some deliberated practices in life attain, or are given, what they claim to be
direct apprehensions of the *wujud* (findability) of God. It is precisely for this reason that not only does the term *yaqin* occur in the
Sufi vocabulary (subjective certainty); so also does the term *wajd*,
from the same root as *wujud*. *Wajd* became an almost technical
term among the Sufis for representing the enraptured state of
mind, or soul, of one who intentionally endeavours to align his
life with the life and word of God. The state described is not one
which human beings create: it is one which they sometimes dis-

cover quite surprisingly and unexpectedly—one in which they are overwhelmed. Nevertheless there are conditions and practices which lead toward it: thus *wajd* describes the state which can arise in the straightforward recitation of Quran, but which arises far more frequently in the religious chant. In the *Ihya*, alGhazali described what happened to a young man (in fact, what almost happened to Muhammad) in conversing with God: he threw himself from the top of a mountain and killed himself: 'He was deeply seized (*taraba*) thereby, and realized the state of *wajd*, and threw himself down because of that state of *wajd*.'[11] So the term *wajd* was used to describe a state in which it seems to be the case that one is seized by a direct apprehension of God, and in which the *wujud* (the findability) of God is, for the one who experiences it, beyond denial.

But may not these reports be mistaken? Yes, answers alGhazali, certainly. Therefore, even at this preliminary level (and certainly at the eschatological level) it may be necessary, so to speak, to go to Mecca, in order to verify whether the conditions of the *wujud* (the findability) of Mecca are satisfied. It may be necessary to test for oneself the specified conditions in which it is claimed that the *wujud* of God is discernible—i.e. offers itself evidentially, to go back to the language of the *Ihya*. We cannot do this eschatologically without dying; but we can do it at the preliminary level wherever it is claimed that the *wujud* of God is accessible to us.

And *that* is what suddenly paralysed alGhazali into silence in front of his university class. He saw, with increasingly inescapable clarity, what his own astringently empiricist argument required of him in relation to the *wujud* of God. It required, not that he abandon the rigour of his theory of knowledge, but that he take that rigour equally seriously in this case. The *wujud* of God is as inaccessible to metaphysical argument and to philosophy as the observation of cause-and-effect is to sense-perception. But it does not follow that theology is thereby constrained into either fideism or oblivion. It means that from the human end one must apply to the claimed *wujud* of God the same conditions and procedures that one would apply to the claimed *wujud* (findability) of anything else. One must attempt to specify the conditions in which the *wujud* of God would be met. Anyone who wishes to be personally certain must enter those conditions himself.

In those circumstances, there was no alternative but to resign his university lectureship and withdraw into a degree of isolation in order to practise Sufi meditation and exercise. Political change may have been the trigger, but the logic of the argument drove him to that particular response. Sufis claimed a direct knowledge of God, even in at least one case a relatedness which came close to identity. AlHallaj had claimed *an' alHaqq* (I am alHaqq) and had been executed for so doing. AlGhazali certainly rejected that overstatement, but he could accept that it was a mistaken description of an unmistakable experience:

If you place coloured liquid in a clear bottle, the bottle takes on the colour of what is inside it, and the unprepared onlooker confuses the bottle and the contents. It was in this way that when [the will of] God manifested itself in the body of Jesus, people made this kind of mistake and began calling Jesus God. It was the fatal mistake of identifying the bottle with its contents. They went wrong in calling him God.[12]

Even in his period of withdrawal, when he explored Sufi experience for himself, alGhazali did not lose his rational wits, and he argued within the *Ihya* itself (written during this period) against the widespread abuse of Sufi experience in, for example, extravagant personal claims which are parasitic on that experience, or in speaking with tongues (a phenomenon which, in alGhazali's view, is 'impressive but useless').

Nevertheless, he recognized (because he verified it in his own experience) that the acceptance of Sufi practice into the construction of one's own life, leads to a direct intuition of God's *wujud*, findability—indeed, foundness. Accordingly he could go some of the way to meet Ayer's point about experience in his debate with Copleston:

I [do not] wish to restrict experience to sense-experience; I should not at all mind counting what might be called introspectible experiences, or feelings, mystical experiences if you like. It would be true, then, that people who haven't had certain experiences won't understand propositions which refer to them; but that I don't mind either. I can quite well believe that you have experiences different from mine . . . I should be in the position of the blind man, and then I should admit that statements which are unintelligible to me might be meaningful to you. But I should then go on to say that the factual content of your statements *was* determined by the experiences which counted as their verifiers or falsifiers.[13]

According to alGhazali the claim to the *wujud* (the findability) of God by direct acquaintance can be verified or falsified within the specific Sufi practices which lead to it—and that is why al-Ghazali spent so much time in, for example, evaluating and describing the relation of the musical context to the Sufi experience.

The second major category of those who affirm the *wujud* of God on the level of report is that of the prophet, and here obviously alGhazali was thinking primarily of Muhammad, although he accepted (and appealed to the fact) that there have been many prophets in different religions, who have been designated as such by their transmission of words and actions derived (as they believed) from a resource external to themselves—i.e. from externality theistically characterized. The appeal is by no means so naïve as it appears to the modern mind, although (as will be seen) there are insuperable problems about it, if it is the only court of appeal. But it is here that the silence of alGhazali before his university class is linked directly to the silence of Muhammad on Mount Hira when he was overwhelmed by the sense of God requiring him to be a prophet. The record makes it clear that Muhammad, on that occasion, was not in any sense seeking to be a *prophet*, but that at the time he was simply seeking conviction and insight into the possible nature of theistic reality in the midst of the many confusing and conflicting claims among his contemporaries to an authentic knowledge of God.

It is not possible to review in detail the circumstances of Muhammad's early life before he believed that he was called to be a prophet, and in any case the problem of authenticating details in that period is very great. Nevertheless, one fact emerges with great clarity in general terms: Muhammad had been exposed to the diversity of religious and theistic claims from an early age, and this came increasingly to puzzle and exercise him. In the Hejaz (the part of Arabia surrounding his home of Mecca) there were rival gods and goddesses among the polytheists, and in addition there were Jewish and Christian tribes who claimed to be worshipping *one* God and who yet denounced each other's. That seemed particularly absurd, since if they were all worshipping the one theistic reality that exists, they must be worshipping the same God; *ergo*, they ought not to be denouncing each other. But Muhammad became aware of even greater diversity: he went on at least two trading expeditions to Syria, and he was well aware that the rivalries endemic there between different Christian parties (such as Chalcedonians, Nestorians and Monophysites, though Muhammad was not aware of the details) had been translated into political terms: he knew from report that the Monophysites from Abyssinia had established themselves in the south of Arabia and had tried to extend Christian rule to the north, even to the extent of mounting an expedition against Mecca which had only been defeated by an outbreak of disease in the invading army.

The year of the Abyssinian attack on Mecca was the year (at least traditionally) of Muhammad's birth, and it is clear from his subsequent life and reported sayings, and from the Quran, that the religious and political conflicts which it epitomized seemed to him to be a deep and fundamental problem. How *could* those who claim to worship the only theistic reality disagree with each other? In fact, Muhammad was not the first or the only one of those who recognized the costly folly of religious and political divisions. There were others in the Meccan situation who were attempting to recover the unity implicit in devotion to one God alone. There were, for example, some people known (in the anglicized form of plural) as *hanifs* who are reported as having attempted to recover the religion of Ibrahim (Abraham), the ancestor of the Arabs, who had himself turned away from the worship of many gods to the worship of God alone.

This movement, although eccentric and small in numbers, may well have been a decisive input into Muhammad's consciousness. Ibrahim as a *hanif* is much celebrated in the Quran, and the reason is not surprising. Quite apart from biblical tradition that up to, but not beyond, the time of Abraham, the ancestors of the Jews had 'worshipped other Gods' (Josh. 24:2), many stories were told of how Abraham had derided and destroyed the idols of the Chaldaeans, and how he had exposed the futile impotence of idolatry and polytheism. The stories were widely told and known (some are repeated in the Quran) and Abraham thus became the type of those who reject polytheism and adhere to God alone. But Abraham was the father of Ishmael, and Ishmael, as Genesis itself affirms, was the father of the Arabs. So any Arab who gave his allegiance to the one God could legitimately regard himself as following the religion of Abraham, without necessarily becoming a Jew or a Christian.

There are some traces that this was happening before the time of Muhammad. Ibn Qutaybah records six who did this, and Ibn Ishaq records four. Of these, some subsequently became Jews or Christians, but it was not absolutely necessary to do so. Zayd b. Amr, for example, did not, although he tested both religions:

Zayd b. Amr stayed as he was: he accepted neither Judaism nor Christianity. He abandoned the religion [*din*] of his people and abstained from idols, animals that had died, blood, and things offered to idols [cf. Acts 15:29]. He forbade the killing of infant daughters, saying that he worshipped the God of Abraham, and he publicly rebuked his people for their practices.[14]

Although the passage is in some respects suspect (the word for 'abandoned', for example is *itazala*, which underlies the name of an early movement in Islam, the Mutazilites, and may therefore have been introduced here under the influence of that later use), the reference to the Acts' settlement is of interest, because it suggests a possible background of this non-Jewish 'religion of Abraham': the Acts' settlement is much disputed, but in general terms, it seems to have been an attempt to hold together in the early Christian Church those who believed that Christians should still be bound by Torah (as the word of God which had not been repudiated), and those who believed that Gentile converts in particular had been set free from the obligations of Torah. The Acts' settlement represents a minimal obligation which would make life in common with Gentiles possible, for those whose roots were still planted, at least in part, in Jewish soil. Jewish Christian sects increasingly lost ground: some took refuge in Persia, as Nestorians were to do later, and it seems likely that others took refuge in Arabia—the other area close to the Roman world which the Romans seemed incapable of conquering. If that is so, this *milla* (life-way) of Abraham is not a later invention of Islam read back into earlier history, as some have suggested, but a genuine expression of an Arab sense of their own history.

A man who followed this life-way was known as *hanif*. This word has presented further problems. In the languages related to Arabic it has a bad sense, meaning 'apostate', 'unbeliever', but in Arabic it has a good sense, referring to one who follows Abraham in rejecting idols and polytheism. It is possible, therefore, that in Arabic the word originally meant something similar to 'apostate' but since in the Quran it is particularly used of Abraham who apostasized from idolatry, it meant 'protestant' against *evil* beliefs. In the Quran it is in fact possible to translate the word as 'protestant' in that sense; and since it refers to the entirely proper protest of Abraham against the prevailing (polytheistic) religion of his time, it comes in Arabic (under the influence of the Quran) to have an invariably good sense. This suggestion has not won much favour, but it does at least make sense of the conflicting evidence.

It is not known how many *hanifs* there were. The Quran comments favourably on them, but it does not seem that Muhammad, in his bewilderment at the diversities of men and their beliefs, was drawn to join them (unless, as has been suggested, the verb 'he practised *tahannuth*' in the accounts of his vision (see the passage from alBukhari below) should be read 'he practised as a *hanif*' changing the *th* into *f*). But, in fact, the *hanifs* in any case could only have seemed to represent one more possibility (albeit the right one) among many—one more sect. So Muhammad was driven into increasing isolation in his quest for greater certainty in the conflict of religious beliefs—his quest, indeed, for the reality behind the gods of human devotion. He began to take himself to a cave on the mountain of Hira, close to Mecca, partly to fulfil the Qurayshi rituals in every detail, but partly to put a kind of pressure on God, and to enter into a kind of struggle with God alone. Here, at least, there is a possible contact with the *hanifs*, because it was at the same place, on the mountainside of Hira, that the *hanif* Zayd b. Amr took refuge when he was expelled from Mecca for denouncing the idols and the rites associated with them. It was on one of Muhammad's visits to Hira that the blinding, overwhelming moment of vision occurred: he suddenly saw the direct and obvious truth of God, breaking through the conflicting beliefs and rituals of men, and establishing with Muhammad the direct sense of his reality beyond the speculations of men.

Muhammad later told Aisha that he had already, before this single moment, received visions of great brightness and splendour in his sleep, and that these had driven him into his increasingly solitary struggle with God: according to Aisha's later account, he had seen 'true visions, resembling the brightness of daybreak, which were shown to him in his sleep; and Allah made him love solitude so that he liked nothing better than to be alone'. The great moment of vision is recorded in many sources. AlBukhari (whose collection of *hadith*, or traditions, about Muhammad became one of the most authoritative in Islam) recorded this account:

Aisha said: The first part of revelation was granted to the apostle of God in a true dream during sleep, so that he never dreamed a dream without there coming the likeness of the light of dawn. Then solitude became dear to him, and he used to isolate himself in the cave of Hira, where he devoted himself to God [literally, practised *tahannuth*]; and he remained there several nights before coming back to his family and taking refreshment for that purpose. Thus he used to return to Khadija and take refreshment for a similar period until alHaqq [the Truth] came while he was in the cave of Hira. And the angel came and said, 'Recite [or 'read'].' He answered, 'I am not one of those who recite [or 'read']. He said: 'Then he took me and pressed upon me until it was unbearable; then he let me go and said: "Recite." I said, "I am not one of those who recite." So he took me and pressed upon me a second time until it was unbearable; then he let me go and said: "Recite." I said, "I am not one of those who recite." So he took me and pressed upon me a third time; then he let me go and said: "Recite in the name of your Lord who created—created man from a drop. Recite! and your Lord is most generous (s. xcv. 1–3)." '

Then the apostle of God returned with it, with his heart trembling, and went into Khadija and said, 'Hide [or 'wrap'] me, hide me!' So she hid him until the awe [*arRaw*] left him. Then he said to Khadija (telling her what had happened): 'I am terrified for my life.' Khadija answered: 'No, by God! God will not bring you to disgrace, for you bind together the ties of relationship, you carry the burdens of the weak, you earn what you earn to give to the destitute, you welcome the guest and you help where there is genuine distress.'

The sense of fear and of 'cosmic shock' did not diminish when the impression of the vision receded. At first, according to at-Tabari's account, Muhammad thought that he had gone mad (*majnun*, possessed by jinn), or at least that he had become one of the other possessed creatures who were not uncommon in Arabia, a *kahin*, a *sahir*, or a *shair*. People who give the impression (by going into a trance or into an ecstatic state) of being possessed by an outside spirit or god are extremely common in all traditions: in origin, as has been seen (pp. 77–84), the Israelite prophets emerged from that background. Such people are then highly valued because they seem to be a link between men and God; but often they are also greatly feared because they are out of the ordinary, and bring the extraordinary into the midst of human life. In Arabia, the *kahin* was one who, in a possessed state, uttered sharp and often enigmatic sayings, and claimed to foretell the future; the *sahir* was a controller of magic, and the *shair* was a more elaborate rhythmic poet. Muhammad was later accused of being all four (i.e. those three plus *majnun*)—or perhaps, more accurately, his claims for a unique status for the Quran (the utterances which came through him) were dismissed as being nothing more than the utterances of one of those figures: see, for examples, lxix. 41 f. (*kahin* and *shair*), xxxviii. 3 (*sahir*, where his 'magic' is mocked as being nothing more remarkable than turning all the gods into one God!), and lxviii. 2 (*majnun*).

Immediately after the vision, Muhammad was terrified that he had become one of those creatures, and he decided on suicide rather than that. Yet on his way to a cliff edge on the mountain, he again had an overwhelming impression of Jibril (Gabriel) restraining him. Eventually Khadija sent out a search party which found him still standing at the same spot, transfixed. When he came back to Khadija, he told her that he was sure he had seen something on the mountain, but that he feared that he was now possessed. With great steadiness and common sense Khadija advised him to wait and see what transpired—'After all,' she added, 'perhaps you did see something'. 'Yes,' he answered, 'I really did.'

Khadija then consulted Waraqa b. Nawfal (one of the four *hanifs* recorded by Ibn Ishaq) who had 'attached himself to Christianity and studied its scriptures until he had thoroughly mastered them'. He at once offered reassurance: to him, Muhammad's experience sounded like the experience of Moses when *namus* (i.e. *nomos*, or Law) was given to him on Sinai. However, he warned Muhammad that he would be treated with hostility and expelled from Mecca: 'No man ever brought what you bring without being treated as an enemy.'

There can be no doubt of the disturbing and compelling nature of Muhammad's experience, or of its consequence. From this point on, he knew, with an overwhelming simplicity, that for God to *be* God, he must be *God*. Put like that, it perhaps sounds complicated, but the truth which came upon Muhammad like the sudden light of dawn was actually very simple: there cannot be *less* than God if there is God at all: there cannot be other gods, or divisions of one god from another. There can only be *one* theistic reality, one source of all creation, the unproduced producer of all that is. It follows that the whole creation is a single unity when seen in relation to God, and that anything which disrupts that unity, whether in wars or in conflicting beliefs, is a rebellion against the order which God desired and intended in creation.

> Say: He is God, alone [literally, 'one'],
> God the absolute.
> He does not beget, he is not begotten,
> And there is none in any way equal to him (cxii).

It is hard to convey in words the blindingly dramatic simplicity of this realization that if God *is*, then he must be God: he cannot be less than that: either God, or—nothing; there cannot be anything in between. In a sense, Muhammad's life and message become a working out of the consequences of that basic vision: all life, every aspect of life, is derived from the fundamental unity of God: consequently, every aspect of life—the creation of every thought and action—must be recognized as being derived from God and must 'bear witness that there is no God but God'.

The most immediate consequence was *not* that Muhammad suddenly 'became a prophet'. Indeed, although his conviction of the absolute reality of God was now total, it is clear that initially he had no idea how to handle or understand the extraordinary experience in the cave. If, as was discussed in *The Sense of God* (pp. 144 ff.), the labels we attach to our emotions and experiences are vital in enabling us to handle them—or indeed live with them—successfully, then it is all the more remarkable that Muhammad could find no labels in his experience up to that point with which to identify what was happening. It was only later that he came to think that the figure confronting him must have been Jibril (a label derived from the Jewish/Christian tradition). In other words, the experience which overwhelmed Muhammad did *not* fall within any of the extensive categories available to him, but was literally *sui generis*. As a result, he did not immediately become a prophet or proclaimer of God's word in public. In fact, even the original sense which he had (of words occurring within him which did not seem to come from his own initiative or control) suddenly dried up, in the period of the so-called *fatra*, the withdrawal or cessation of the words which Muhammad felt he had been receiving from God. The conflict in the accounts makes it impossible to reconstruct the exact sequence of events. According to atTabari (on the basis of azZuhri's traditions), the first parts of the Quran to be uttered (after xcvi. 1–5, which came within the vision) were lxviii. 1–5, lxxiv. 1 f., and xciii. 1 f. There then occurred the *fatra*, which threw Muhammad into deep despair: it is at this point that azZuhri locates the urge to suicide. The revelations were then restored with lxxiv. 1–4 (despite the fact that lxxiv. 1 f. has already been placed in the earlier period). According to Ibn Ishaq, some unspecified revelations occurred, then the *fatra*, which was broken by sura xciii. In addition, he (and others) makes it clear that the period in which there was no public ministry lasted for three years.

But even if the details are uncertain, the main point is clear: Muhammad was uncertain where the vision would lead him, or what its implications were: in this period he stayed within his family. Yet early on he felt the same impression of words within him struggling to get out—words which seemed to him to be not of his own creation, but to arise within him as though they had been brought to him from outside, or, as he believed, from God: but their restoration gave him a new confidence and a new realization that he must share these words with others:

> You who are wrapped in the cloak,
> Arise and give warning! (lxxiv. 1 f.)

So began his proclamation of the words which now form the Quran. In the simplest sense, the Quran represents the consequences of the command *iqra* ('read' or 'recite') in the opening vision. The Quran in its present form is a collection of the utterances given to Muhammad, as opposed to the ordinary human words which he spoke in the course of his life, many of which are collected in *hadith* (the traditions which record details of Muhammad's life, and which constitute an example for Muslims in their own lives). The distinction between the words spoken by Muhammad as a prophet (as mediator or communicator of words coming from God), and the words spoken by him as a man among men, was unmistakable, both to himself and to others. The distinction was unmistakable in a superficial sense because there was sometimes a visible difference in appearance when Muhammad was uttering the Quran. There are several records in *hadith* of this change in appearance, of which these are some examples, taken from the collections of Muslim and alBukhari:

Over the apostle of God was a garment [cf. lxxiv. 1 p. 236], with which he was covered; then Safwan b. Yala put his hand under, and saw that the apostle of God was red in the face, and that he was snoring. Then it was removed from him.

Ubadah b. asSamit said: 'When the revelation came down on him, the prophet was like one overwhelmed with grief and his face changed. According to one report he hung down his head and his companions did the same . . .'

A tradition from Aisha: Harith b. Hisham asked the apostle of God: How does revelation come to you? He answered: 'Sometimes it comes to me like a clanging [*salsala*] of a bell, and that is heaviest upon me; then it leaves me and I remember from what he has said; and sometimes the angel comes to me resembling a man and speaks to me and I remember what he says.'

Aisha said: 'I saw him when revelation came down on him, when the day was extremely cold, then it left him, and his forehead was dripping with sweat.'

Zaid ibn Thabit said: 'God sent down [revelation] on his apostle, when his leg was resting on mine, and the weight was so great on me, I feared my leg would be crushed.'

But more important than the visible change in appearance was the fact that the utterances sounded unlike ordinary speech, and in their total effect they were unlike anything that had been heard before in Arabic style. They were not *wholly* unlike previous forms of utterances: they were sufficiently reminiscent of the styles of the *kahin* and of the *shair* for Muhammad's enemies to dismiss the Quran as being nothing more remarkable than that; and we have seen that Muhammad himself thought initially (even if only momentarily) that he must have become one of those figures. Yet at the same time, the total construction and effect of the Quranic passages is entirely different. The poems of a *shair* were constructed with rhythm, rhyme, and metre; the Quran is certainly rhythmical, and its verses are usually tied by rhyme, but it has broken free from metre, and it is expressed far more directly and expansively. The utterances of a *kahin* were shorter and more enigmatic, as in this example recorded by alMasudi:

> By the light
> By the twilight
> By the dusk
> By the darkness of night,
> What awaits you is coming upon you.

There are certainly passages in the Quran which are expressed
in that style, but they become the foundation of a far more general
message: see, for example, suras lxxxix, xci, xcii, xciii, xcv. The
connection with the other styles is unmistakable, and yet the result
in the Quran is wholly different. Since Muhammad was familiar
with the styles of *kahin* and *shair*, it is not surprising to find reminiscences of those styles in the way in which the pressure of words
within him flowed forth. The nearest analogy lies, perhaps, in the
way in which someone who is deeply saturated in the language of
a particular style—for example, the Prayer Book—is capable of
developing a similar style in speech, as in the gathering momentum
of a preacher, or as George Eliot described in the case of Caleb
Garth: referring to Peter Featherstone's hatred of Bulstrode, Mrs.
Garth asks her husband:

'What reason could the miserable creature have for hating a man whom
he had nothing to do with?' 'Pooh! where's the use of asking for such
fellows' reasons? The soul of man', said Caleb, with the deep tone and
grave shake of the head which always came when he used this phrase—
'the soul of man when it gets fairly rotten, will bear you all sorts of
poisonous toadstools, and no eye can see whence came the seed thereof.'
It was one of Caleb's quaintnesses, that in his difficulty of finding
speech for his thought, he caught, as it were, snatches of diction which
he associated with various points of view or states of mind, and whenever he had a feeling of awe, he was haunted by a sense of Biblical
phraseology, though he could hardly have given a strict quotation.[15]

To suggest that the style of the Quran may be a consequence of
a comparable reminiscence of the styles of *kahin* and *shair* utterance, which were then transformed into something completely
unlike them (particularly in content) would be unacceptable (not
to say abhorrent) to a Muslim: to him the distinctiveness of the
Quran—the complete absence of anything else even remotely like
it—is one of the signs that its origin must indeed be with God, and
that it was 'given' to Muhammad or 'sent down' upon him (the
usual words in the Quran for what might otherwise be termed
revelation) in such a way that he was simply the mouthpiece of
what are in fact the words of God: Muhammad did not modify
them or create them himself; and this view is supported for Muslims by the verses in the Quran which refer to 'the mother of the
book' in heaven: 'With God is the mother of the book' (xiii. 39).
In the classic theological formulation of alMaturidi, derived from

Abu Hanifah (*Wasiyat*, § 9): 'The Quran is the speech of God, written in the copies, preserved in the memories, recited by the tongues, revealed to the prophet. Our pronouncing, writing, and reciting the Quran are created, but the Quran itself is uncreated.' The same point was expressed by Ibn Kullab in a single sentence: 'The matter inheres in God, the reciting is created, acquired by man.'

What at least must be accepted is that the Quran is completely unlike any other utterance of that or any other time, and that Muhammad recognized the different nature of Quranic utterance when it pressed forward in his speech. The Quran itself warns Muhammad not to try to hasten or control the process, but to allow it to occur as it will within him:

> Do not move your tongue with it to hasten it.
> Surely it is for us to assemble it and to recite it.
> So when we recite it, follow its recital.
> Then surely, it is for us to explain it. (lxxv. 16–19)

Much later, when Muhammad was a successful leader, there were some attempts to produce alternative Qurans, probably on the part of those who wished to succeed Muhammad when he died:

Musaylima gave himself out as a prophet, and played the liar. He said: 'I am a partner with him in the affair.' . . . Then he began to utter rhymes in the *saj* metre and speak in imitation of the style of the Quran:

> God has been gracious to the pregnant woman:
> He has brought forth from her a living being that can move
> From her very midst.

He permitted them to drink wine and fornicate, and let them dispense with prayer, yet he was acknowledging the apostle as a prophet.[16]

But these attempts were so obviously an imitation that they simply threw into relief the uniqueness of the Quran—a point which the Quran itself makes, when it challenges those who disbelieve it to produce something like it if they can:

> If you are in doubt concerning what we have sent down on our servant, then produce a sura [section] like it, and summon your witnesses beside God if you are true.
> But if you cannot—and certainly you cannot—then fear the fire whose fuel is men and rocks, prepared for those who refuse belief. (ii. 22)

It is to the phenomenon of the Quran as mediated through a prophet that alGhazali appealed as the second area in which claims to the *wujud* of God are justified on the level of report, though prophet and Sufi are obviously related. AlGhazali had been reduced to paralysed silence in front of his university class because his long struggle with the problem of knowledge had led him to believe that metaphysical theology is incapable of yielding certainty, and that to ask how a statement is known to be true is to ask what grounds there are for accepting it. In the period of his withdrawal and partial isolation, he had verified in his own experience the claims of the Sufis that God is *wujud*, findable, and that there are specifiable procedures and conditions in which the ultimate, eschatological findability of God is sufficiently anticipated for us to know that the final beatific vision is possible. Consequently there are grounds for accepting the truth of the proposition, 'God rewards his faithful servants'. But the Sufi experience is derivative from the *wujud* (the foundness) of God which occurred in the transformation of Muhammad's life and in the consequence of the Quran. Sufi and prophet together specify the conditions in which the *wujud* (the findability) of God can be discerned in the transformation of our own lives.

But are there not other explanations of that experience? Yes, certainly; that must in principle be the case. There is no way to cross what Schmidt called the phantom bridge between experience and the claimed cause of that experience[17] except by crossing it. The prophet and the Sufi point to the conditions and procedures through which the *wujud* of God may be discerned. Perhaps we are cognitively mistaken in what we believe we apprehend, or in what we believe apprehends us. But empirically, in terms of what happens in experience (in, for example, the recitation of the Quran), alGhazali's argument was that the prophet and the Sufi together are sufficient grounds for accepting the experiment into ourselves.

> O make but trial of his love,
> Experience will decide
> How blest they are, and only they,
> Who in his truth confide.

AlGhazali had no hesitation in accepting that faith to be cognitively meaningful and publicly intelligible (in other words, to be a serious option for others) must be experimental, and he did not evade the challenge of specifying the data which form the basis of such an experiment. Whether he succeeded in establishing 'our right to make what appears to be a special sort of advance beyond our data' may obviously be open to question, since the thorough-going sceptic can question *any* such advance—'from sense-experiences to physical objects, from the world of common sense to the entities of science, from the overt behaviour of other people to their inner thoughts and feelings, from present to past'.[18] But alGhazali was at least consistent in recognizing that there must be data: the prophet and the Sufi together offer the informational cues which, if they are accepted into the construction of our lives, transform the experience of that liveliness.

Yet still the question remains: even if we enter into the Sufi conditions of ascertaining the *wujud* of God by direct intuition, have we in fact succeeded in crossing the phantom bridge? Claims to dramatic experience in brain behaviour (and no one doubts the dramatic nature of many such experiences) cannot in themselves confer truth on the claimed cause of such experiences; the most they allow is an inference to what must be the sufficient ground for the appearances in consciousness to occur which do occur in the condition of serious attentiveness to the possibility of God. AlGhazali was well aware of that objection. And *that* is why he insisted (p. 223) on belief in God and in the last day (of judge-ment) as indispensable. In doing so, he was claiming that the only condition in which claims to the findability of God can be finally verified is eschatological. Any philosopher who tries to establish by argument that the last day is an impossibility is not only doomed to failure (because of the inability of metaphysics to establish certainty in such propositions by argument), he must also be strongly resisted and condemned for failing to see that that is the only circumstance in which theological propositions entailing existence-claims can meet the conditions of worthwhile and gen-uine knowledge. AlGhazali denounces the philosophers in the *Tahafut* (conclusion) in forthright and religious language:

To brand the philosophers with infidelity is inevitable, so far as three problems are concerned—namely:
  (i) the problem of the eternity of the world, where they maintained that all the substances are eternal;
  (ii) their assertion that Divine Knowledge does not encompass individual objects;

(iii) their denial of the resurrection of the body.

All these theories are in violent opposition to Islam. To believe in them is to accuse the prophets of falsehood, and to consider their teachings as a hypocritical misrepresentation designed to appeal to the masses. And this is blatant blasphemy to which no Muslim sect would subscribe.

But the reason for the denunciation of the philosophers on these three points remains that if the religious attitude on those questions lapses, then there are no circumstances in which the *wujud* of God could be conclusively verified or falsified. So although alGhazali expressed the point in a way which entangled it in religious polemic, the underlying argument is more important—and more impressive—than the surface way in which it was expressed. AlGhazali did not abandon the rigour of his empiricist theory of knowledge. He therefore faced the challenge of specifying at least some circumstances in which the effect of God can be discerned, and he pointed to the prophet and the Sufi. But he knew that even the experience of the latter (which he tested for himself) cannot confer truth on the content of the propositions derived from it concerning the unobservable cause of it. He therefore concluded that theological propositions are nevertheless meaningful and can yield *yaqin*, genuine certainty, because one can specify the condition in which verification can, in principle, occur, namely, the last day; and for that reason he insisted on that and on a resurrection body (i.e. a conscious continuity of identity in a form which will be capable of making that verification) as a way of drawing attention to that condition as one which satisfies the demands of an empiricist theory of knowledge: 'The fact of God's existence is apprehended by men's reason, but he can only be seen as he is (*binafsihi*) by that gift of spiritual vision, which is given to the righteous in eternity.'

There are undoubtedly considerable problems involved in the notion of eschatological verification, some of which will be discussed in IV.3 and in the final section. But that does not alter the impressive way in which alGhazali developed his argument. Perhaps 'developed' is too systematic a word, since the argument has to be disentangled from the diffuse and often much more specifically religious concerns of alGhazali's writing. In the end it may be said that alGhazali did nothing more than follow the advice of his teacher, alJuwayni, 'Keep to the religion of the old women'.

But alGhazali's great achievement was to show why and how the old women may well be justified in their devotion. The prevailing characterizations of God may be defective, as Muhammad had found. But from Muhammad's crisis on Mount Hira and from alGhazali's in Baghdad was produced an imagination of the possibility of God which issues in Islam, total allegiance. Yet for others, crises of such profundity in the prevailing senses of God lead in a very different direction, not to the possibility but to the impossibility of God as the final and only point of worthwhile reference. Such an outcome does not occur in recent times alone: we have seen it already occurring to some in Greece; it occurred also, with even more extensive consequences, to the Buddha.

IV

BUDDHISM

1. THE SENSE OF GOD IN BUDDHISM

WHEN Marx wrote the foreword to the published version of his doctoral thesis, he referred to the effort of Gassendi to rehabilitate Epicurus after the many centuries during which Epicurus had been banned by the Church. He described it as an attempt on the part of Gassendi 'to conciliate his Catholic conscience with his heathen knowledge, and Epicurus with the Church—an obviously futile effort. It is like throwing the habit of a Christian nun over the exuberant body of the Greek laïs.'[1]

It must surely seem an equally futile effort to throw the habit of a western theism over the passive body of a Buddhist monk. Of all religions, Buddhism is the one which seems at first sight to be most explicitly and necessarily indifferent to theism—an indifference which has been described as non-theistic or atheistic. Is it, indeed, a religion at all? There have been denials—sometimes angry denials—that it is, on the ground that if religion is taken to imply the dependence of human lives on supernatural beings, such as a creator god, then Buddhism cannot be a religion.

A classic summary of this argument occurs in Schmidt's *The Origin and Growth of Religion*. Having defined religion as 'the knowledge and consciousness of dependence upon one or more transcendental, personal Powers to which man stands in a reciprocal relation' (p. 2), he then expanded the point in a way which led to the exclusion of Buddhism as a religion:

And the words 'personal Powers' call for explanation. It is of course possible to feel oneself dependent upon impersonal powers, but it is not possible to enter into reciprocal relations with them, since they cannot answer from their side. Consequently, it makes no difference whether it is a material force, as for example the vast and mighty universe, or some inexorable law thereof. Both are dumb and unresponsive to the human personality. Hence also primitive Buddhism, inasmuch as it recognises no personal gods, cannot be considered as a religion, but only as a philosophy. Later Buddhism indeed, and Buddhism everywhere that it has become a popular religion, has included in its wide-reaching system innumerable personal deities, brought in by a thousand backdoors (p. 2).

On such grounds, it has seemed possible (at least to some) to set a question mark against the very word 'religion', and to describe Buddhism in its essential character as a way of life or as an analytic philosophy—that is to say, as a rigorous attempt to analyse the appearances of the universe and of all life within it, without inferring substance (*substantia*) from appearance. How, then, can it be possible to examine 'the sense of God' in Buddhism? It can be done, at least initially, by landing on the shores of Ceylon with seventeenth and eighteenth-century travellers and by observing with them what they saw. Their observations were summarized by William Hurd in what he called *A Complete and Impartial View of all the Religions in the Various Nations of the Universe*. It is one of the earliest attempts to make a survey of religions, and although one should by no means believe all travellers' tales, nevertheless the impression which Hurd recorded is very clear:

The inhabitants of Ceylon are all Pagans, for although some of them acknowledge there is one supreme God, yet they allow of many subordinate ones to act under him; and this was the idolatry of the antient [*sic*] Greeks and Romans. Thus they have gods for agriculture, some for navigation, for sickness, and for almost every thing. All their idols are represented by the most fantastic and monstrous images. One of these is formed like a giant, and by them called *Buddu*, who lived a very holy and penitent life.[2]

In that passage is summarized the apparent paradox of Buddhism, a paradox which can be observed as much in the twentieth as in the seventeenth century, as indeed it could have been observed at *any* time in the two and a half thousand years of Buddhist history. It is the paradox that theoretically Buddhism is not generated by theistic belief, and its goal in enlightenment and nirvana is certainly not characterized theistically. Yet in practice the lives of the vast majority of Buddhists are theocentric: they are directed toward God or gods and they derive support from theistic resources.

So on the one hand, interpreters of Buddhism to the west, since the nineteenth century, have usually made much of the non-theistic character of Buddhism; on the other, observers of life in Buddhist countries have consistently reported that the reality does not correspond to that description. Therefore on the one side, T. H. Huxley could take Buddhism as an example of an ethical religion of reason (the very point which became so important in the apologetic of the World Buddhist Fellowship: 'Buddhism is the only religion acceptable to the scientific mind, as has been said by Einstein. Buddhism is the religion for the present age of science and reason'[3]):

A system which knows no God in the Western sense; which denies a soul to man; which counts the belief in immortality a blunder and the hope of it a sin; which refuses any efficacy to prayer and sacrifice; which bids men look to nothing but their own efforts for salvation; which in its original purity, knew nothing of vows of obedience, abhorred intolerance, and never sought the aid of the secular arm; yet spread over a considerable moiety of the Old World with marvellous rapidity, and is still, with whatever base admixture of foreign superstitions, the dominant creed of a large fraction of mankind.[4]

Similarly, when Quilter wrote in 1902 his *Guide for Today to Life as It Is and Things as They Are*, he could conclude: 'The primitive form of Buddhism is atheistic, it denies the existence of gods, and of the soul, declaring that all is subject to change, decay, and rebirth.'[5]

Yet against this, in the other side of the paradox, stands the succinct statement of de la Vallée-Poussin: 'Faire du Bouddhisme un rationalisme, c'est s'interdire d'y rien comprendre.'[6] The force of that statement rests partly on a closer attention to what Buddhist texts actually contain, and also on the observation of the way in which the majority of Buddhists actually construct their lives. There has been no shortage of observers of the practice of Buddhism in recent times, all of whom have drawn attention to the devotional, ritualistic, and theistic character of Buddhist life—for example, Bechert in the lands of Theravada Buddhism, Gombrich in Sri Lanka, King and Spiro in Burma, Bunnag and Tambiah in Thailand, to take only the most familiar examples.

It was this gap between theory and practice which led Spiro to describe Burmese Buddhism as a religion of proximate salvation. What he meant by that phrase was that although the canonical teaching of the Buddha points to the eventual goal, not of salvation in any usual sense of that word, but of nirvana (a state even beyond salvation), Buddhists in practice have as their goal in rebirth states of being in much closer proximity to their existing situation, including rebirth in heaven as a blissful spiritual being, as a *deva*, or as a god:

Typically, instead of renouncing desire (and the world) Buddhists rather aspire to a future worldly existence in which their desires may find satisfaction. Contrary to nibbanic Buddhism, which teaches that frustration is an inevitable characteristic of samsaric existence, they view their suffering as a temporary state, the result of their present position in *samsara*. But there are, and they aspire to achieve, other forms of samsaric existence which yield great pleasure. These range from the earthly existence of a wealthy human being to the heavenly existence of a blissful *deva*.[7]

But the situation is even more ambiguous than that. Spiro was writing of proximate *ultimate* salvation, but the same applies to proximate *immediate* salvation. Buddhists in practice utilize resources for the construction of a way through particular limitations which are drawn from outside the Buddhist universe. For example, Jane Bunnag commented on Thai Buddhism:

It is interesting to see that Buddhist beliefs and those which are commonly labelled 'Hindu' or 'Animistic' to some extent fulfil complementary functions. The *Khammic* theory does for example provide only a very generalized explanation of the individual's social condition, an explanation which is psychologically inadequate in a situation of crisis. In such circumstances Hindu techniques of astrology can be used to isolate the immediate source of the trouble, and in the case of illness, a cure, also regarded as being *khong sasana phram* (part of the religion of the Brahmins), can be applied.[8]

There is, then, an apparent paradox, one which is neatly summarized in the English and German titles of a book by von Glasenapp. In English, the title is, *Buddhism—a Non-Theistic Religion* (and he insists that it *is* a religion, despite the absence of an absolute deity, since many of the functions which other religions supply in the construction of human lives are certainly found in Buddhism). But in German, the title, far from including the words *atheismus* or *nicht theistisch*, is *Buddhismus und Gottesidee*. The German title is more appropriate, because the book is in part a survey of the way in which gods *do* occur in Buddhism.

How is this conflict to be resolved—the conflict between what
is claimed to be the canonical teaching of the Buddha and the way
in which that teaching has been implemented in life? Not surprisingly, many different answers have been given, and here again
there is a polarity in the answers suggested. That in itself is an
indication of the reality of the paradox of theism in Buddhism.

At one extreme, there are those who maintain that the elimina-
tion of God as a resource and a goal in the construction of human
lives has proved to be impossible, because the informational
significance of God (i.e. of informative externality theistically
characterized) is unequivocal, at least to some of those human
beings who attend with sufficient seriousness to that possibility.
Admittedly, the point is not usually expressed in that somewhat
jargonistic way. Colloquially it is more often expressed by talking
of (for example) the god-shaped blank at the heart of human lives,
which in some way or another demands to be filled. The point is
reinforced by observing that in Mahayana Buddhism (in Sri Lanka
and Burma the Buddhism is Theravada which is more conservative
in relation to the Pali Canon), the Boddhisattvas (the enlightened
ones who turn back just as they are about to attain nirvana and
come back once more to the world in order to help suffering
humanity) are frequently treated almost as gods, or even as gods.
This became particularly obvious with the development of the
Trikaya (Three Body, or Three Agent) understanding of the
Buddha: The Body of Ultimate Foundation, or Reality (*Dhar-
makaya*), the Body of Enjoyment or Bliss (*Sambhogakaya*) which
is the form of the celestial Buddhas, and the Body of Transformation (*Nirmanakaya*) through which he was able to be present
on earth. *Bhakti* or devotion to the form of the celestial Buddhas
will obviously be appropriate.

This is probably most familiar in the case of Amitabha Buddhism, which is in practice a devotional cult: Dharmakara, a
bhikkhu, set his intention to become a Buddha, but vowed also to
restrain himself from the attainment of final enlightenment until
he could rule in a blissful land from which all evil had been banished. Eventually he established the 'western paradise', Sukhavati,
and receives into that paradise those who have set their own intention toward him and to the attainment of that particular goal,
and who call on him at the time of their death. Mahayana and
Tantric Buddhism eventually developed vast pantheons—enor-

mous assemblies of gods and goddesses—in relation to whom cults and rituals of great formality and complexity were devised. The opening of the Lotus Sutra (a basic Mahayana text) describes the crowds which met to hear the Buddha's teaching which the Lotus Sutra contains, and Boddhisattvas and gods are present in great numbers:

Such bodhisattvamahasattvas as these, eighty thousand in all. At that time there was Sakra Devendra with his following of twenty thousand divine sons; there were also the Divine Son Excellent Moon, the Divine Son Universal Fragrance, the Divine Son Precious Light, and the four great heavenly kings with ten thousand divine sons in their train; the god Sovereign and the god Great Sovereign followed by thirty thousand divine sons; Brahma Heavenly King, the lord of the saha-world, Great Brahma Sikhin and Great Brahma Light, and others, with their following of twelve thousand divine sons. Then in the congregation bhikshus, bhikshunis, upasakas, upasikas, gods, dragons, yakshas, gandharvas, asuras, garudas, kimnaras, mahoragas, human and nonhuman beings, as well as minor kings and the holy wheel-rolling kings: all of this assembly, obtaining that which had never been before, with joy and folded hands and with one mind looked up to the Buddha.[9]

A more systematic theology gradually emerged in Tantric Buddhism, focused on the five Dhyani Buddhas and their families, who in turn were emanations from the meditation of a single theistic figure, known in Nepal and Tibet as Svayambhu and Adi-Buddha, and in other texts as Vajrasattva, Heruka, and Hevajra. To find monotheism of that kind as the focus of Buddhist life is usually held to be either the syncretistic destruction of authentic Buddhism, as Conze maintained ('It is at this point that Buddhism at last deviates completely from its original teachings, and prepares the way for its own extinction'[10]), or the practical demonstration of the human capacity to apprehend and receive input from theistic reality which is simply a matter of fact in human experience, as the 'g.b.h.' argument maintains—not the 'grievous bodily harm' argument, but the 'god-shaped blank at the heart' argument.

That explanation of the paradox of theism in Buddhism was summarized by Farquhar in 1925 in this way:

Now Buddhism was an atheism; but the worship of a god or gods was clearly essential for the laity. How was this to be provided in an atheistic religion? They took the very man who denied the existence of God,

Gautama the Buddha, and exalted him to the position of the Supreme, *Devatideva*, 'The god above the gods', while his chief companions and certain mythical personages became the ordinary gods of the Buddhist pantheon. The worship was simply Hindu image-worship applied to Buddhist persons. Thus does Buddhist history provide an absolute demonstration of the futility of atheism.[11]

That particular wording of this explanation is unlikely to be put forward in exactly that way by a Buddhist. But the same explanation does appear in a Buddhist form. For example, Bh. Sangharakshita, wrote on one occasion of *saddha*, a word which he suggested can best be translated as 'faith':

But this English word has a number of meanings and shades of meaning. Which of them, if any, coincides with the emotion to which Buddhists appropriate the term *saddha*? According to *Webster's New International Dictionary* faith is primarily the 'act or state of acknowledging unquestioningly the existence, power, etc., of a supreme being and the reality of a divine order.' Buddhists, however, deny the existence of a supreme being. If faith is to be adopted as the equivalent of *saddha* the dictionary definition must obviously be amended. For God we shall have to substitute the Buddha, not because of any similarity in their nature and functions, but because of the equipollency of their respective positions.[12]

If we then turn to the dictionary again, in order to find out what is meant by 'equipollent' we find the following: '1. Equal in force, power or validity . . . 2. The same in effect or signification (implying that money could be dispensed with if something equipollent were provided). / Something that is equipollent (as in signification)'[13]

So the implication is clear: the Buddha is not a supreme being in a theistic sense; nevertheless, as the one who is fully enlightened and whose teaching offers the means of our enlightenment and of our directing the flow of appearance toward nirvana, he attracts to himself attitudes of gratitude and awe which in theistic religions would be directed to God.

Expressed in the traditional Buddhist terminology this is the great asseveration . . . which echoes from one end of the Tipitaka to the other, and which is today repeated by millions of Buddhists as part of their daily worship: 'He is the Lord, the Arahat, the All-Enlightened, the Endowed with Knowledge and Conduct, the Happy One, Knower of the World, Supreme Charioteer of Men to be Tamed, Teacher of Gods and Men, Buddha, the Lord.'[14]

In fact, in the strictest sense, it is uncertain whether the Buddha is in a position to be addressed in that way, because one of the famous *avyakatani* (questions which the Buddha refused to answer or even discuss: see further pp. 296–8) was the question of the Tathagatha's state (the Perfected One's state) after dying: 'the Tathagatha is after dying; the Tathagatha is not after dying; the Tathagatha neither is nor is not after dying'. Which of those is correct? The Buddha refused to comment. Nevertheless, the argument, whether expressed by Buddhists or non-Buddhists, is correct in pointing out that many Buddhists *do* address the Buddha or *a* Buddha as though he is in a position to hear them and to help them in the process of their life-construction.[15]

All this represents a particular set of explanations of the paradox of theism in Buddhism at one extreme: the sense of God, the imagining that God is, with all the consequences of that speculative image, seems to be a constitutional necessity of the human frame: 'Fecisti nos ad te et inquietum est cor nostrum, donec requiescat in te.'[16] Or as Coomaraswamy, an Indian commentator on Buddhism, put it: 'The necessities of *bhakti* [devotion] determined the appearance of all deities in visible forms'[17]—literally so in this case, because he was arguing that the existing Yaksa figures were translated into the cult images of the Buddha and of the gods.

At the opposite extreme in the explanation of theistic beliefs in Buddhism stand the answers which affirm quite simply that popular or theistic Buddhism is a defective Buddhism which the Buddha tolerated (because he knew that many people would not be able to enter immediately into the dharma, the true and appropriate way) but which he knew was far removed from final enlightenment; and this argument, at the opposite pole of explanation, may be summarized as the 'backdoor corruption' argument (the 'thousand backdoors' of Schmidt, p. 245). The Buddha realized that men cling desperately to anything which they believe might deliver them from the wreck of time, decay, and death. They cling to the gods as though the gods will persist when all else disintegrates. But the insight of the Buddha was that there is nothing but the process of change and decay and again-becoming which carries all with it. There is nothing apart from the process and nothing within the process which can endure.

There is not even an enduring self or soul within the rapidly changing sequence of human appearance. There is nothing but the process:

I knew as it really is: this is *dukkha* [suffering]; this is the arising of *dukkha*; this is the cessation of *dukkha*; this is the course leading to the cessation of *dukkha*. I knew as it really is . . . [To me] freed, came knowledge through the freedom: I knew: destroyed is rebirth, lived is the Brahma-life, done is what was to be done, there is no beyond for this state of things. This was, brahmin, the third knowledge attained by me in the third watch of that night. Ignorance was dispelled, knowledge arose, darkness was dispelled, light arose, even as I abided zealous, ardent, with a self that has striven (Vin. P. i. 1. 7).

That is the famous and brief description of Gautama's break-through to enlightenment. The true nature of reality is change, in-volving decay and death. The attempt to rescue something (such as a soul) from the process, or to find some resting place (such as a god) immune from the process is to create *dukkha*, a fight against the inevitable which must be lost. But how could he possibly share that insight with others? There is no immediately obvious good news in such a gospel. If the transitory, dissolute nature of all apparent reality, including the appearance of one's self, leaves nothing to be salvaged from the wreck of time, then there are no immediate consolations in *this* enlightenment.

> As stone to dust
> No hidden self expels
> But yields its elemental nature to the storm,
> No soul, no substance, penetrates the form
> Of this apparent flesh: and change foretells
> The soul is iron propagating rust.

So men and women in the Buddha's view are like children building sand-castles on the edge of the sea as the tide comes in: they dig moats and channels to divert the invading waves, they heave dry sand to the first breach in the wall, and for some time they may even create an island in the tide as it creeps, indifferent to all this effort, up the beach. But in the end it is to no purpose, and the sea eventually erases all trace of the castle and reduces it to the level of the submerged sand. There is no defence against the process of change, decay, and death, nor is there any substan-tial reality to be discovered and rescued within the wreck: there

is nothing substantial, nothing standing underneath, no underlying or persisting reality. There is nothing but the process of
change and reappearance itself.

The enlightenment exposed the *dukkha* of *dukkha* (the truly
agonizing reality of suffering) as being the attempt to find something which is immune from dissolution and decay, when in reality
there is no such 'thing'. But 'human kind cannot bear very much
reality'; and it was profound sympathy and yet despair which
reduced the Buddha immediately after his enlightenment to
silence—the fourth of the quadrant points of silence of this book:

Then to Vipassi the Exalted One, Arahant, Buddha Supreme, this
occurred: 'What if I were now to teach the Dhamma [the true and
appropriate way]?' Then to him this occurred: 'I have penetrated this
Dhamma, deep, hard to perceive, hard to understand, calm, sublime,
not to be grasped by logic alone, elusive, intelligible only to the wise.
But here we have the human race, attaching itself to the things to which
it clings, holding on to them, taking delight in them. And for such a
a race, attaching itself to the things to which it clings, holding on to
them, taking delight in them, it is far too hard for them to realise
that one thing is conditioned by another, and that everything which
happens is constrained into its outcome by preceding cause. Far too
hard, also, is the bringing to rest of the activities of life, the renouncing
of all that flows into rebirth, the destruction of craving and the extinction of passion, the perfect cessation, nirvana. And if I were to teach the
Dhamma, and those who heard did not respond to it with assent, that
would be a heavy weariness to me and a deep hurt.'

And then to Vipassi the Exalted One, Arahant, Buddha Supreme,
were revealed all at once these lines never heard before:

> All this which I have gained through arduous toil,
> Why should I try to make it further known?
> How can this Dhamma be, by men, absorbed,
> Who in their lives are seized by lust and hate?
> It is too difficult, too subtle, too profound,
> Too much against the grain of common sense.
> By those in bondage to desire, in shrouding mists of ignorance,
> It cannot be discerned.

Thinking about it, with these words in mind, Vipassi turned away from
making any effort, and away from declaring Dhamma openly. (Dig. N.
ii. 35 f.).

The great moment of breakthrough for the Buddha came when
he saw that there is no self or soul or persisting entity within the

human form of appearance which continues through all experience
and which might pass through death. The human form is not a
vehicle which a soul (a driver) gets into, drives through life, and
gets out of at the other end. The human form is an aggregate, a
flowing together and brief coalescence of all the constituent elements which are in a constant process of change, one moment of
tate giving rise immediately to the next. But those who heard this
view of the true nature of reality would be likely (so the Buddha
thought) to regard it as involving their own oblivion and annihilation. If there is no soul or continuing self, then death is the end
of *me*; and the Buddha recognized that that is a frightening prospect, when realized for the first time. In fact, the Buddha was *not*
preaching oblivion and annihilation, and he strongly opposed any
who thought in that way. But he knew how his insight would be
regarded if he started to proclaim it publicly, and he had no wish
to be ridiculed—or for that matter to engage in pointless activity.
He therefore lapsed into silence: what point could there be in
trying to persuade men who cling to their world, to their souls,
to their gods as though they are substantial, that they are in fact
totally, destructively, and unequivocally wrong?

So far, then, it must seem supremely clear that the opposition
between the prevailing senses of God and the insight of the Buddha
into the true nature of reality was absolute; and that his silence
came from his realization that the plausibility of God as characterized in myth and ritual in the Indian context of his time had
totally collapsed. On this basis it would seem that the paradox of
theism in Buddhism must be resolved by Schmidt's 'backdoor
corruption argument' (p. 245), of theism swamping the pure original message; in that case, it might be held that the later excesses
of popular Buddhism should not be allowed to obscure the
rational non-theistic insight of the Buddha.

The argument that the advent of the gods in Buddhism is a
contradiction of the Buddha's fundamental insight and represents
a later corruption of his teaching gains obvious support from the
fact (already referred to) that Buddhism in its later history did
assimilate many gods. But the issue is not whether that happened,
but whether such assimilation is appropriate or inappropriate
when tested against the resources which are regarded as indispensable for the construction of authentic or inauthentic utterance
in the early Buddhist case—in this case the Pali Canon (not that the

theistic assimilation cults would necessarily *themselves* regard the canon as constituting that authoritative resource; it remains simply a standard of judgement on the issue of whether the paradox of theism is or is not a later corruption of an earlier and purer Buddhism).

On this basis, there is no doubt that the 'backdoor corruption argument' cannot be accepted in its simple form, for two connected reasons. The first lies in the question, How late is later? Wherever one can cut into earlier sections of the progress of Buddhism through time, there is a surprising correspondence between behaviour then and now. This is a point very much emphasized by Gombrich—indeed, it is a point of departure for his whole book: 'Let me state at the outset a general conclusion. I found the Buddhism which I observed in Kandyan villages surprisingly orthodox' (p. 40). By 'orthodox' he meant 'that the doctrines of the villagers would have been approved by Buddhaghosa and that most of their religious practices would have been familiar to him and his contemporaries' (p. 45). He then commented (pp. 45 f.):

But I also said that I found this orthodoxy surprising. Why so? I suppose it is unusual for the religion of a society to change so little over 1,500 years; certainly it is unusual for societies of which we have the records. But my surprise was caused rather by the frequency with which I had been told, by books and by people, that Sinhalese village Buddhism was corrupt. 'Corrupt' was the word generally used by laymen; in academic circles this word sounds too pejorative to be respectable, and is replaced by 'syncretistic' or some periphrasis . . . Sinhalese villagers have been judged corrupt Buddhists because they say and do things which the judges think are incompatible with what is said in the Pali Canon. In particular most Sinhalese believe gods and demons to exist and make offerings to them under various circumstances.

But are 'the judges' to whom Gombrich refers even correct in stating that Sinhalese beliefs in the existence of gods and demons are incompatible with what is said in the Pali Canon? That question leads to the second reason why the 'backdoor corruption argument' has to be resisted. Whatever the status of God or the gods may be in the Canon, there is no doubt at all that they have *some* status. Canonical Buddhism is *not* non-theistic or atheistic in the sense that the existence of God or gods is denied. Exactly the reverse, their existence is affirmed, however much the notion of existence is amended in a Buddhist direction, and however much, therefore, traditional characterizations of God have to be amended also. It may then be a question whether the consequent Buddhist characterization of theistic reality is itself plausible, or whether it is of sufficient character for a believer in another tradition to recognize it as being *adequately* theistic. There could be many such questions about the Buddhist characterization of the gods. But that theistic realities in *some* characterization exist is not denied in the Pali Canon; indeed, it is undoubtedly affirmed, as will be seen.

Can one therefore say that the beliefs are peripheral, in the sense that the gods are held to exist, not as *super*natural beings introducing effects into the lives of men from the outside, but as natural —as being simply a part of the way things happen to be? The Buddha in that case would have had no particular interest in denying a cosmological perspective which supposes that the gods exist, although many of the claims about the nature of that existence are mistaken from his point of view. What he *did* deny to to the gods was an ontological status which would have removed them from the process of *dukkha* (i.e. of dissolution and impermanence). The gods simply belong to the process of change and decay as much as anything else, a point very accurately picked up by Huxley:

Accepting the prevalent Brahminical doctrine that the whole cosmos, celestial, terrestrial, and infernal, with its population of gods and other celestial beings, of sentient animals, and Mara and his devils, is incessantly shifting through recurring cycles of production and destruction, in each of which every human being has his transmigratory representative, Gautama proceeded to eliminate substance altogether; and to reduce the cosmos to a mere flow of sensations, emotions, volitions and thoughts, devoid of any substratum.[18]

On this argument the gods *are* peripheral, because they are brought firmly within the natural, and if the twentieth-century scan of nature has subsequently found no trace of them, that is not disturbing to Buddhism because it has never seriously supposed that the gods make any abiding difference to the reality in which our own lives are set—the reality that we too are impermanent, and that there is no self, no substantial 'I', which persists through the wreck of time. The 'gods' can then be regarded as having been in origin primitive and pictorial representations of psychological and mental states, and they can accordingly be de-mythologized and deprived of even the limited ontological status which they have in the Pali Canon—an interpretation which is exemplified in this passage from Govinda:

The only world of which the Buddhist speaks is the conscious universe which can be experienced in the microcosmos of the human mind and which is represented by the various stages of life and realized by in-numerable kinds of living beings. If we speak of the 'human world', the 'animal world', the 'plant world', etc., we do not think of different places, different material worlds, and yet we know that we speak of something which is real or even more real than any material object which we can see and touch. Likewise the Buddhist universe deals with facts, the reality of which does not depend on their materiality (which may or may not exist) but on their psychological truth, the possibility of their experience. All the heavens and hells are within ourselves, as possibilities of our consciousness . . . [footnote]: The translation of the term *deva* with 'god' may be justified from the etymological point of view, but it misses the real meaning. The idea of god or of gods suggests the faculties of a world-creator or at least supernatural powers of creation, controlling the destinies of men. Gods are expected to be immortal, to be masters over life and death, and to receive the worship and the prayers of their devotees. The Buddhist 'devas', however, are neither worshipped nor regarded to be eternal, they are mortal like all other living beings and subject to the laws of causation. Though existing under more fortunate circumstances and endowed with a higher form of consciousness, they have no power over man and are bound to their own karma which may lead them again to the human plane. For this reason the devas cannot even be compared to the angels of Christianity.[19]

There is in that argument an important truth, and what that truth is will shortly become apparent. But the argument as it stands still has to be modified by the Canon at one critical point: according to the Canon it is *not* the case that the gods have no significant effect in the process of human or world appearance. Furthermore, there is no doubt that those effects are derived from a resource external to the human subject, and that they make an important difference to human lives. The gods, according to the Canon, *can* be causative in the flow of appearance which humans identify as their life. It follows that if they can be causative it is by no means inappropriate (using the Canon as an isomorphic map against which the appropriateness of projected utterance can be tested—a use of the Canon which the Buddha is himself reported to have encouraged) to relate the construction of one's life-way to those resources through such means as prayer and sacrifice.[20] Contrary to Govinda's opinion, gods in at least some forms of theistic appearance do receive worship and prayer, and they do have power to change and affect the lives of men—i.e. to go back to Govinda's phrase, they undoubtedly 'have power over man', and consequently (contrary to his opinion) gods *are* worshipped by many Buddhists.

It remains the case that those practices do not, and cannot, establish a 'self' or 'soul' which the gods can bring into a heaven abstracted from change and decay. But if the gods which in some sense undeniably exist can be causative in the flow of appearance which can be identified as the life of Gautama on this earth, then to that extent at least they can be causative in the flow and appearance which we identify as our own life. It is this which restores the paradox of theism to Buddhism, because the paradox is visible in the Buddha's own life (as that life has been recorded). Theistic reality does create real and differentiating consequence in the Buddha's life.

The point can be seen in miniature and in concentration in the Buddha's enlightenment, and in the way in which the introverted silence after the enlightenment (see p. 253) was broken. It was not broken because the Buddha had a sudden change of heart, arising from his own initiative, or because he had a great feeling of sympathy and compassion for his afflicted fellow-men. It was broken by God—according to the Buddhist record. The details of this will be discussed in the next chapter. In the meantime, it is important not to underestimate the fact of the paradox of theism in Buddhism, and certainly not to attempt to explain it away by driving a wedge between the popular practice and the analytic psychology, as though one *or* the other must be the true and essential reality of the Buddha's intention. That dominant mode of explanation was effectively summarized by Thomas in earlier days:

It is still disputed whether original Buddhism was 'nothing but vulgar magic and thaumaturgy coupled with hypnotic practices', or whether Buddha was a follower of some philosophic system in the genre of Patanjali's . . . and then with the Mahayana movement a transformation [took place] through a new theory of reality and a conception of the Enlightened One which made him indistinguishable from the highest conceptions of Hindu deity.[21]

But the reality of the theistic paradox is *not* created by academic observation. Its reality can be seen in the tension which it sometimes produces in individual Buddhist lives. At one time, Theravada Buddhism in Ceylon had seemed to Lama Govinda to be the ultimate and perfect condition for progress in Dharma: 'To me Ceylon had seemed the fulfilment of all my dreams; and in the certainty of living there to the end of my days I had built myself a hermitage in the heart of the island.'[22] But then he received an invitation to take part in a conference in Darjeeling, and after some hesitation he decided to go in order to refute what he believed to be the corruptions of Buddhism outside the Theravada tradition. 'Here was an opportunity to uphold the purity of the Buddha's teaching, as preserved in Ceylon, and to spread its message in a country where the Buddha-Dharma had degenerated into a system of demon-worship and weird beliefs.'

But then, when he found himself 'in the middle of this weird world of Lamaism, neither knowing the language of the country nor the meaning of those countless images or symbols which surrounded me in the frescoes and statues of the temple, except when they represented the universally known figures of Buddhas and Bodhisattvas', he found also that he could not return to Ceylon. The richness of the new life which opened up for him was a critique of what he now believed to be the barren poverty of his previous commitment. It is as though Edmund Gosse, instead of writing *Father and Son*, had suddenly been converted to Continental Catholicism. Govinda described the contrast between the intellectual and the ritualistic Buddhism, with particular reference to the role of music in Tibet and its absence in Ceylon:

All this moved me all the more as during the last years in Ceylon I had been starved of all musical inspiration, which is entirely absent in Southern Buddhism (*Theravada*) on account of the mistaken view that music is merely a form of sense-pleasure. In consequence of this the religious life had taken on a dry, intellectual form of expression, in which together with the lower also the higher emotions were suppressed and all negative virtues were fostered to the extent that no great personality could arise—i.e. rise above the level of the accepted norm. Book-knowledge had become more important than experience, the latter more important than the spirit. No wonder, therefore, that it was believed that no *Arahans* (realised saints) could arise after the first millennium of the Buddhist era, in other words, that for the last

1,500 years the Buddhadharma in Ceylon had existed only in theory, or at the best as a belief, since (according to the Sinhalese themselves) Ceylon had not produced a single saint during this long period and it was no more possible to enter into the higher states of *dhyana* or direct spiritual insight. It was, therefore, impossible even to discuss deeper experiences of meditation, as it was regarded preposterous to assume that anybody could actually realise any of the higher states of consciousness of which the sacred texts speak so often. Thus Buddhism had become a matter of the past, a creed or a distant ideal towards which one could strive by leading a moral life and committing to heart as many sacred texts as possible.[23]

The tension between ritualistic theistic Buddhism and text-based Buddhism is not imposed academically from the outside: it can be experienced on the inside. It is a fundamental mistake to attempt to 'explain away' theism in Buddhism as though it is peripheral to the Buddha's insight or intention. There is no doubt that the existence of theistic realities is understood as a Buddhist kind of existence (and what that means will be seen in more detail in the next chapter). But the phenomenological fact remains, that *some* existential inference is demanded by the appearances in consciousness which actually occur. Whether the Buddha drew the correct inferences, remains the theistic issue in—and with—Buddhism.

2. THE REJECTION OF GOD IN BUDDHISM

WHEN the Buddha first saw with an almost blinding lurch of realization the true nature of all existence, he felt initially that he could not share that insight with others. A verse came flooding into his mind (p. 253):

> It is too difficult, too subtle, too profound,
> Too much against the grain of common-sense.

He withdrew into silence, existing simply in the enlightenment of his own awareness. The silence was broken, not because of a change of heart on the part of the Buddha, but because of the initiative of God. There was indeed a particular reason implied in the record for that initiative, as will be seen. But according to the record, there would be no Buddhism (i.e. the Buddha would not have broken his silence) if there had not occurred to him an impression of an input derived from a resource external to himself which was characterized theistically as Brahma. It was that input which moved him from silence to public preaching. Put in more poetic language, it was God, Maha Brahma, the great Brahma (Brahma Sahampati according to the Vinaya version and in the Majjhima Nikaya), who appeared and challenged the Buddha to the compassion which is characteristic of the god's own nature:

Thinking about it, with these words in mind, Vipassi turned away from making any effort, and away from declaring Dhamma openly. Then one of the great Brahma gods became aware in his own mind of what Vipassi was thinking, and it occurred to him: 'Alas, the world will perish, perish altogether if Vipassi the exalted one, Arahant, Buddha Supreme, turns away from making any effort, and away from declaring Dhamma openly. Then the great Brahma, with as little effort as a strong man bending or stretching his arm, vanished from the Brahmaloka [the Brahma world] and appeared before Vipassi. Then he threw his outer robe over one shoulder, bent his knee to the ground, saluted Vipassi with joined hands, and said: 'Master, may the Exalted One proclaim the Dhamma openly: may the One to be welcomed proclaim the Dhamma openly. There are people whose eyes are not altogether obscured, who are perishing, because they have not heard the Dhamma. They will acknowledge and accept it.'

According to the story the Buddha then repeated his refusal and the reason for it. Three times Maha Brahma had to repeat the request. But then the Buddha,

attending to Brahma's entreaty, surveyed the world, because of his compassion to all beings, with a Buddha's eye. And as he looked, he saw some whose eyes were scarcely obscured at all, others whose eyes were much obscured; some with acute minds, others not so; some disposed to good, others to evil; some alert, others indolent, some very much aware of the dangers in rebirth and of again-becoming in other worlds as a consequence of evil-doing. As in a pool of different coloured lotus-plants, some of the plants rooted in the water, growing in the water, never emerge above the surface, but live as best they may submerged; others rooted in the water, growing in the water, float on the surface; others, rooted in the water, growing in the water, reach up above the surface in full splendour; so in the same way the Buddha surveyed the world, with a Buddha's eye, and saw people in different conditions . . . Then Maha Brahma spoke these lines to Vipassi:

> As on a mountain top a man might stand
> And watch the multitude beneath the height,
> Look now yourself, as from the heights of truth,
> With wisdom and with insight now possessed,
> From grief set free, behold the grief-afflicted world,
> Captive in suffering from birth to death.
> Come now, and conquer, leader of seeking men,
> Traverse the world, Exalted One, and teach,
> Teach men the Way, and some will understand.

Then Vipassi, the Exalted One, Arahant, Buddha Supreme, replied:

> The way which leads to this is opened wide,
> Let those who hear at once send forth their faith . . .

Then Maha Brahma reflected: 'It is by me that a way has opened up for the proclaiming of Dhamma by Vipassi . . .' And with that thought, he bowed down before Vipassi, and passing by him on the left side departed. (Dig. N. ii. 36 ff.)

Here, then, in the Buddhist record itself appears to be a causal initiative taken by theistic reality which moved the Buddha from silence to eloquence. What account is to be given of this? There is an obvious and a very common explanation of this theophany. Taking its clue from the way in which Maha Brahma arranged his robe on one shoulder and saluted the Buddha with joined hands, it points out that this is an attitude of subservience. It is the manner in which a disciple comes to a superior teacher, in order to seek instruction. So the point of the legend might then be seen as a way of stating from the outset that the gods are less than the Buddha and that they themselves have to bow down and seek instruction from him. That is exactly the explanation offered by A. K. Warder, in *Indian Buddhism* (p. 50):

It appears strange that the God of Brahmanism should be brought in to guide the Buddha. The intention must have been to place the Buddha above Brahma by making the latter appear in the role of suppliant. As in other texts, where Brahma appears, the aim may have been satirical, making the supposed creator and master of the world afraid that his creation would perish unless the Buddha saved it.

On this argument, the record is claiming that what the gods cannot do in terms of salvation, the Buddha can; what is more, Maha Brahma recognizes that the Buddha's salvation (the attainment of nirvana) is the true goal, and that the salvation usually associated with the gods (of a soul enjoying eternal union with, or contemplation of, God) does not feature at all. So the point of the story would thus be to emphasize that the gods (or at least the great Brahma) recognized the Buddha at the very moment when he broke through to enlightenment, and they accepted that what they cannot do, he can.

That explanation is by no means implausible. It is reinforced by the fact that there are in the Canon many descriptions of the gods in that relation of subservience to the Buddha, as will be seen. But the argument that the story was therefore meant ironically and was introduced simply to exhibit the diminished status of the gods in relation to the Enlightened One is an entirely different matter. It is certainly not what the texts say, as they have come down to us. No doubt one can amend the texts, and eliminate the episode of Maha Brahma altogether, although there is no justification for this. Mrs. Rhys Davids was once accused of having done exactly that (of having excised the incident as coming from an earlier part of Gautama's life, when he was exploring the possibilities of theism before he finally abandoned them). In fact, in her book, *What Was the Original Gospel in Buddhism?*, she wrote something far more sensitive and accurate (pp. 20 f.):

There is yet this to say: In that he [Gautama] needed urging by That Who sees where he at the time saw not, the Helper is shown as not self-sufficient. He gave, I said, a call, but to him first a call came. Either the episode was told by him—no witnesses are mentioned—or it is pure fiction . . . And we read, that he was psychically gifted and in frequent communion with the unseen, finding 'pure happiness' in this. Adherents look upon him as attaining enlightenment alone, as just the automatic fruition of his own resolves and efforts in countless past 'lives'. Yet there has been left, in this moving record, of the Hesitation, the inspiring message, giving the lie to the ideas that the messenger was all-wise, all-knowing, a self-dependent orphan in the universe. Like other great Helpers, he was instrument, medium of a more than himself; wise he was but not all-wise.

But even supposing it *was* a later interpretation, even then one would have to insist that whoever included this story, at whatever date, did not include it in a form which can be regarded as ironic: the function of Brahma is causally decisive in setting the wheel of Dhamma in motion. 'It is by *me* that a way has opened up for the teaching of Dhamma.' Even if Maha Brahma is conceding to the Buddha primacy in the role of proclaiming and of thereby opening the eyes of men to their true condition, the fact remains that God and the Buddha are partners, according to this story, in a common enterprise, and that the god was required causatively to bring the Buddha into an active role. One cannot even read or recite the sentences with an ironic inflection, as one can, for example, pick up Pausanias' comment on the Athenian Altar of Pity and read it with an ironic intention:

The Athenians are the only Greeks who pay honours to this very important god in human life and human reverses. It is not only that love of the human race is in their institutions, but they worship gods more than other people; they have altars of Shame and Rumour and Impulse; obviously, people who have more religion than others get their share of good luck in proportion.[1]

The Greek may be strictly neutral, but the background surveyed briefly in I.5, of the death of God in the Greek world, makes it clear that a Greek might well have given to the Greek words of Pausanias a very ironic inflection. But it would be difficult to do so with the Pali sentences. They cannot easily be read in that way, nor can the story as a whole be taken in that way.

The point is even clearer in the later version in the Mahavastu

(iii. 314 ff.). In that version, the point about silence is even more emphatic, since it adds other traditions about the Buddha's determination to remain silent. Twice the Buddha reflects on the impossibility of opening the eyes of men to their true condition, and twice he states his decision, 'Let me then abide in silence on a mountain in the wilderness . . . Let me then abide in silence all alone in a tract of wilderness.' Then not only Maha Brahma, but also Sakra, lord of the *devas*, appear in order to appeal to the Buddha. Sakra makes his appeal first.

But the Exalted One kept silent and would not give his consent that he should set rolling the wheel of dharma. Then Great Brahma said to Sakra, lord of the devas: 'Friend Kosika, not so are Exalted Ones, Arhans, perfect Buddhas entreated to set rolling the wheel of dharma. Tathagatas, Arhans, and perfect Buddhas, when so entreated will not set rolling the wheel of dharma.' When this had been said, Sakra, lord of the devas, replied to Great Brahma: 'Friend Great Brahma, you knew the perfect Buddhas of old, and so do you yourself implore the Exalted One to set rolling the wheel of dharma.' And so Great Brahma, arranging his robe over one shoulder, held out his joined hands to the Exalted One and addressed him in a verse:

> Arise, you who have triumphed in the struggle,
> Full of insight, on-going through the world free of fault.
> Teach dharma, O Sugata, and those who learn will grow.

But the Exalted One kept silent. Then Great Brahma, Sakra, lord of the devas, the devas Suyama, Santusita, Nirmita, Vasavartin, the Four Great Kings, the many hundreds of Yaksas and the many hundreds of the Yaksas' retinue, perceiving the Exalted One's unwillingness to set rolling the wheel of dharma, were pained and grieved. They bowed their heads at his feet, saluted him from the right, and forthwith disappeared.

It is only after those abortive appeals that the Mahavastu moves on to the same account as the one in the Digha Nikaya and the other versions. The silence of the Buddha is profound and cannot be moved even by appeals to consider the unhappy plight of others. It is the silence of one for whom the plausibility of available god-concepts has collapsed—indeed, has become irrelevant. There is no way in which theistic resources (accepting that they are available) can do what needs to be done—construct in the sequence of a human existence a substantial continuity which might escape the transience and impermanence of all things. The death of God is, at that moment, absolute.

There have been few more massively intellectual moments in human history. In the scan of the limitations impeding the construction of a life-way, Gautama had become aware, as do all men, of the intransigence of time and of the inevitability of change, but he accepted the intransigence of those limitations as the basic and fundamental characteristic of all apparent existence. The point is obvious in the familiar story (Dig. N. ii. 21 ff.) of the way in which Gautama became aware of that fact in his youth. According to the story, Gautama was originally a prince whose father attempted to protect him from all awareness of the evils of the world and of life. He had three palaces built for him 'and he had them fitted with every kind of gratification for the five senses'. While he was young Gautama never stirred from them. But then one day he ordered a chariot-driver to drive him through the park. As they went along, 'he saw an aged man as bent as a roof gable, decrepit, leaning on a staff, tottering as he walked, afflicted and long past his prime'. He therefore asked the driver:

'What has that man done, that his hair is not like that of other men, nor his body?' 'He is what is called an aged man, my lord.' 'But why is he called aged?' 'Because he has not much longer to live.' 'But then am I too subject to old age, one who has not got past old age?' 'You, my lord, and we too, we all are of a kind to grow old, we have not got past old age.'

At once, Gautama ordered him to drive back to the palace, where his father surrounded him by even more sensuous pleasures. But eventually Gautama ordered the driver to take him out once more, and this time he saw a sick man, and he realized that he cannot escape sickness. A third time he went out, and this time saw a crowd of people building a funeral pyre. He asked the driver what they were doing. 'It is because someone, my lord, has ended his days.' . . . 'What is "ending one's days"?' 'It means, my lord, that neither mother, nor father, nor other kinsfolk will see him any more, nor will he ever again see them.'

Gautama immediately realized that he too must die. What can be set against age, sickness, and death? On his fourth excursion Gautama saw a possible answer: He saw 'a shaven-headed man, a Wanderer, wearing the yellow robe'. In other words, he saw an

attempt to project a way through the limitations—a life-construction which involves, as the driver explains, 'being thorough
in the religious life, thorough in the peaceful life, thorough in good
actions, thorough in meritorious conduct, thorough in harmless-
ness, thorough in kindness to all creatures'. The speculation
therefore arose that perhaps by withdrawal from the world and by
a corresponding commitment to dhamma (to appropriate action)
it will be possible to liberate one's abiding self from suffering and
death, and to project one's actual self like an arrow into the heart
of God.

To Gautama, this had sufficient plausibility to make him follow
the same life-way, first in a community, then in solitary isolation.
It was there that he struggled with the intransigence of all those
limitations on the construction of an enduring life-way:

Now there arose, brethren, in the mind of Vipassi the Bodhisat, when
he had gone to his place, and was meditating in seclusion, the following
consideration: 'Verily this world has fallen upon trouble; one is born,
and grows old, and dies, and falls from one state, and springs up in
another. And from this suffering, moreover, no one knows of any way
of escape, even from decay and death. O when shall a way of escape
from this suffering be made known, from decay and from death?
(Dig. N. ii. 30 f.).

It was then that the great realization occurred that there is no
self to be rescued: the impression of self occurs through the causal
sequence which starts from birth itself: for 'where birth is, there
is decay and dying' (Dig. N. ii. 31). But birth necessarily involves
becoming; and becoming depends on laying hold of the means of
becoming; and laying hold of the means of becoming depends on
desiring; and desiring cannot occur without feeling; and feeling
depends on relation to otherness; and relation depends on the
senses; and the senses have to label otherness with name-and-
form; and name-and-form cannot occur without cognition.

But then it follows that cognition cannot occur without name-
and-form, and there is nothing beyond. There is, therefore,
nothing but the sequence: 'Only in this way can one be born or
grow old or die or fall from one condition to be reborn in another'
(ii. 32). There is no other way in which 'this entire body of ill'
can come to be: ' "Coming to be, coming to be!"—at that thought
there arose to Vipassi the Bodhisat a vision into things not called

before to mind, and knowledge arose, reason arose, wisdom arose, light arose.' But then, of course, the sequence can be unravelled: for if birth ceases so does becoming; and so also, at the end of the sequence, name-and-form cease to be. In this way, and in this way only, suffering genuinely ceases to be. ' "Ceasing to be, ceasing to be!"—at that thought there arose to Vipassi the Bodhisat a vision into things not called before to mind, and knowledge arose, reason arose, wisdom arose, light arose' (ii. 35).

By realizing how suffering arises, the way to the cessation of suffering becomes obvious: moreover, the price which has to be paid for this way to cessation has only to be paid in *false* currency, which one is well rid of! All that has to be given up is the *false* projection, that there is a soul to be rescued, and that there are gods or a god who will assist in that redemption. In fact, the appearance of a soul or of a god belongs as much to the conditioned sequence of genesis as any other appearance. But this, although it was the sudden breakthrough to enlightenment, was nevertheless exactly what reduced the Buddha to silence. Men are deeply and profoundly attached to their projected life-ways—to their false currency. Like the British Government clinging to the sinking pound and the social contract, they cling to the appearance of substance, of some 'thing', a soul and a god, which will survive the wreck. Like George Eliot in the Fellows' Garden at Trinity[2], the Buddha removed the two great scrolls (the two great supports) of human life, God and immortality, and he left the world, not quite with George Eliot's Duty, but with something very like it, dhamma, appropriate action which will direct the flow and the chain of conditioned genesis toward the final cessation, the equilibrium of nirvana.

It would seem, therefore, that to attribute the initiative to God in the breaking of the Buddha's silence is an impertinent absurdity. Indeed, later tradition might well have found the whole report embarrassing, at a stage when the Buddha was believed to have a perfect knowledge of all worlds, including heavens and hells, and was believed to see with the eye of Brahma, and to be a teacher of gods and men:

One who has won the truth, an Arahat . . . a Buddha, he, by himself, thoroughly knows and sees, as it were, face to face this universe—including the worlds above of the gods, the Brahmas, and the Maras, and the world below with its recluses and Brahmans, its princes and peoples—and having known it, he makes his knowledge known to others.[3]

How then, could it be possible for God to intrude causatively in the life of the Buddha and contribute to the construction of that life an external effect? But in fact there is no attempt to eliminate the tradition in the later accounts. To the contrary, the Mahavastu (as has just been seen) actually elaborates the tradition. What, then, are we to make of the status of Brahma who effects so dramatic a change in the life-construction of the Buddha?

The first and most obvious point is to reiterate the subservient status of Brahma in relation to the Buddha. He and other gods are consistently portrayed as figures who approach the Buddha in a humble and suppliant attitude. That was the purpose of the description of Brahma 'throwing his outer robe over one shoulder, stooping his right knee to the ground, and raising his joined hands' in salutation. The inference is obvious: the gods are able to survey the world of men and animals, and they have great compassion when they see the suffering which occurs, but they are impotent to effect salvation from this situation, and they therefore approach the Buddha through Brahma as their representative, to do for the world what the gods cannot do, namely, to convey into the consciousness of men a true insight *de rerum natura*. Nevertheless, the second and equally important point remains that the *existence* of the gods is *not* disputed. This is so obvious and uncontroversial that it does not need particular elaboration. However, it can at least be emphasized that those who thought that the Buddha's teaching involved the non-existence of gods or heavenly beings were contradicted by him. This is specific in Maj. N. ii. 209 f., where the question of the existence of the devas is raised, and it is answered unequivocally in the affirmative. The passage in question actually occurs in the Buddha's own account of his progress toward enlightenment and of the status of *brahmacariya* (Brahma-intended life) in that exploration, until he reached the third meditation. At that point, exactly corresponding (structurally) to Brahma's entreaty in the *narrative* version, Sangarava raises the question:

'Do the devas exist [*atthi deva ti*]?' 'Certainly, Bharadvaja, it is known to me that there are devas.' 'But why do you, good Gautama, on being asked if there are devas say that it is certainly known to you that there are devas? Even if this is so, Gautama, is it not a vain falsehood?' 'If on being asked, Bharadvaja, "Are there devas?" one should say: "There are devas," and should say: "Certainly they are known to me," then the conclusion to be reached by an intelligent person is indubitable, namely, that there are devas.' 'But why did not the revered Gautama explain this to me at the beginning?' 'The world is loud in its agreement, Bharadvaja, that there are devas [*Ucce (uccena) sammatam kho etain, Bharadvaja, lokasmini yadidain atthi deva ti*] .

The existence of the gods is equally taken for granted in Maj. N. ii. 130 f. in a dialogue in which the son of King Pasenadi asks:
' "Do the devas exist?"
"Why ask such a question?"
"Are devas reborn on earth or not?"
"The malevolent ones are, those who are not malevolent are not." '
At that point in the dialogue the son of King Pasenadi asks whether the malevolent devas are capable of dislodging the good devas from their on-going condition. Ananda intervenes with an example:

'As far as the realm of King Pasenadi (extends), and there where King Pasenadi holds dominion and sway, is King Pasenadi able to drive away or banish from that place a recluse or a brahman [*samanam va brahmanam*] whether he is meritorious or not meritorious, whether he is *brahmacariya* or not?'
'Yes, he has that power.'
'Has he that power outside his own dominions?'
'No.'
'Have you ever heard of the devas of Thirty-three?'
'Yes, and so has the king.'
'Tell me: can the king Pasenadi of Kosala expel or banish them from their abodes?'
'He cannot even see them, much less expel or banish them.'
'In the same way the malevolent devas who are again-becoming cannot even see the devas who are not malevolent and on-going, so how could they expel or banish them from their abodes?'

It is clear, therefore, that the Buddha accepted contemporary cosmology as factually correct—the layers of hells beneath, of the world, and of the heavens above—and he accepted all of them as peopled by the forms of appearance which are appropriate to them —for example, Maras and asuras in the hells below, devas and brahmas in the heavens above. So the assemblies of the thirty-three Vedic gods, of the Maras and of the Brahmas are accepted in Dig. N. ii. 109 as being as factual as the assemblies of nobles, brahmans, householders, and wanderers. Consequently, it is possible for vast numbers of gods and spirits to assemble on such occasions as the death-bed of the Buddha: 'In great numbers, Ananda, are the gods of the ten world-systems assembled together to behold the Tathagatha [perfected one]. For twelve leagues . . . there is no spot in size even as the pricking of the point of the tip of a hair which is not pervaded by powerful spirits.'[4] Similarly in the Canon elsewhere, vast numbers of gods or other-than-this-worldly forms of appearance are described as being as real as any other forms of appearance. The different gods in the Canon have been listed and described by Masson, and there is no need to repeat the exercise here.

For this reason it is not surprising to find that theistic issues are not seriously engaged in the Dialogues, because at least so far as existence claims are concerned there is nothing at issue. In the many arguments or controversies which the Buddha had, it is rare to find anyone *defending* theistic beliefs *against* the Buddha, as though they are a central or important issue (though there are, as we shall see, some arguments directed by the Buddha against prevailing ideas about God, or against prevailing characterizations of God). But if we take as an example the Payasi Sutta—the only dialogue set in a period *after* the Buddha's death—the opposition to Buddhist ideas expressed by Payasi is certainly not a defence of *theism* as though that is a major issue or objection from the theist's point of view to the Buddha: 'Now at that time there came over Payasi an evil view of things to this effect: Neither is there any other world, nor are there beings reborn otherwise than from parents, nor is there fruit or result of deeds well done or ill done' (Dig. N. ii. 316).

Those are the views opposed to the Buddha's claims. Theistic belief (at least in existence terms) is non-controversial, and in the argument between Kassapa and Payasi it is actually Kassapa the Buddhist who defends theistic propositions against the scepticism of Payasi, who doubts, for example, the belief that there can be rebirth in the form of gods. In other words, not only is theism in a general sense non-controversial, it is actually the case that Buddhists can appear as defenders of the proposition that theistic reality exists against pure materialism.

What *are* disputed are the conclusions drawn about the nature of the gods, and above all, any kind of conclusion which exempts the gods from being a part of the process of change and of rebirth. That is the crucial issue. It has been pointed out already that the Buddha accepted an entirely straightforward naturalistic cosmology, in which the whole world-system passes through a cycle of growth and decline, until eventually it passes away. At that stage, some continuities of existence have been reborn in heavenly worlds; but as their merit is exhausted they sink into lower levels of existence until a new world-system evolves. In Dig. N. iii. 84 ff. that cosmology is described in naturalistic, non-theistic terms. There is no external creator god who is in control of this operation. The gods are within the process; they are not independent of it.

How, then, does the impression of independence arise—the impression of the independence of God and the independence of a soul, or *atman*, which, by relating itself to God, becomes that part of a man (according to post-Vedic belief) which escapes eventually from rebirth? In Dig. N. i. 17 ff, the Buddha takes the same naturalistic cosmology as in Dig. N. iii. 84 (as being the factually correct account) and he shows how, within that process, the Brahmins and the recluses draw mistaken conclusions from the evidence. They maintain the continuous existence of some aspects of *atman* and the world and the cessation of other aspects. How does their mistake arise? It arises because when the world-system comes to an end, many aeons away, beings have been reborn in a transcendent state. But when the world system begins to reappear, then, naturally, the palace of Brahma (god) appears in its due place in that order. The moment then arrives when a being, 'because his span of years has passed or his merit is exhausted, falls from the transcendent state and comes to life in the palace of Brahma'. When other beings subsequently fall as well, they think that the prior and unique appearance of the one before them in the palace must be Brahma, the Great Brahma, the Supreme, the Mighty, the All-seeing, the Ruler, the Lord of all, the Maker, the Creator, the Chief of all appointing to each his place, the Ancient of days, the Father of all that are and are to be. And we must have been created by him. And why? Because, as we see, it was he who was here first, and we came after (Dig. N. i. 17 ff.).

Here (as also in the Patika Sutta, Dig. N. iii. 28 ff.) there is a naturalistic explanation of how people arrive at the sense of God (and in the Patika Sutta, at the sense that the world was created by a creator God). That naturalistic explanation accepts and depends on what would appear to be a *super*-natural frame of reference—a heaven or heavens literally 'above' the natural world. But it is only supernatural in a trivial sense, since the Buddhist simply extends the category of the natural to include the heavens (and the hells) within what naturally occurs in the multiplicity of again-becoming. So the Buddha accepted the reality of other-than-this-worldly appearances in the continuous flow of change and reappearance, all governed by a constant law of appropriate consequence in relation to what has gone before. But he rejected any conclusion which suggested that some of those appearances can extract themselves from the process to which everything is subject.

In exactly the same way he accepted the reality of the devas in a heavenly world, who have a reminiscence of their previous forms of appearance; and precisely because he accepted that as *factual*, he could use the fact to explain how there comes into being the sense of a soul which endures and passes from birth to birth: because the devas can remember previous modes of being in the continuity of again-becoming, they conclude (wrongly) that there must be some eternal substance which is continuous, whereas in fact there is nothing but the succession of states with one giving rise to the next:

There are devas whose span of life is not to be reckoned either by counting or by computation, and yet with whatever individuality they have previously existed, whether as corporeal or incorporeal, whether as percipient, non-percipient, or neither, there is reminiscence of former dwelling-place both as to the manner thereof and in detail (Dig. N. iii. 111).

So although the reality of the gods and spiritual beings was not disputed, what were disputed were the false opinions which theistic believers (for example, brahmins and recluses) held about the status of those beings, particularly if an independence for those beings from the flow of change and decay was inferred, and above all if a supreme creator god was inferred who is not only independent of creation but able to initiate creation and secure redemption from it.

Belief in a supreme creator god was held to be destructive, because it leads to fatalism or to inertia: if such a god is ultimately responsible, what is the point of initiative in one's own case? That is the argument in Ang. N. i. 173 ff. against 'the recluses and brahmins who teach thus, who hold this view: Whatsoever weal or woe or neutral feeling is experienced, all that is due to the creation of a Supreme Deity [*issara-nimmana-hetu*].' Furthermore, as the Buddha pointed out, belief in a creator god makes that god responsible (at least indirectly) for 'murderers, thieves, the unchaste, liars, slanderers, the abusive, babblers, the covetous, the malicious, and those who hold perverse views', and once again moral responsibility is reduced. In short, it makes God responsible for evil.

There are, therefore, arguments in the Canon against false opinions about the gods, but not arguments against the gods as such. But the *status* of the gods is drastically altered and reduced. Consequently it must seem so far that, although the gods do have a status in Buddhism, they are almost irrelevant to the construction of a life-way leading toward nirvana, since the gods themselves are *in via*, and are presumably hoping to attain nirvana as well. It would seem to follow that the gods are necessarily ineffective in relation to man's salvation, precisely because there is no salvation *from*, or out of, the process of change. Indeed, the contrast between the Buddha and the gods is at this point absolute, because the only possible 'salvation', if one can use that word, arises from the enlightenment which the Buddha shares with his fellow-beings, and from the construction of a life-way with that insight as its resource and constraint.

This contrast is summarized in the Kevaddha Sutta, where Kevaddha begs the Buddha three times to perform some wonder or superhuman act (*iddhi*) of the kind that were believed to be possible for particularly holy men—of going into more than one form, of becoming invisible, of going through a wall or a mountain, of walking on water, of travelling cross-legged through the sky with the ease of a bird on the wing, of touching the moon and the sun, of reaching, even in the body, up to the heaven of Brahma (Dig. N. i. 212). Each time the Buddha refuses, saying that the purpose of following his instruction and of joining the Sangha is not to develop powers of that sort (even though, according to Dig. N. iii. 1 ff., the Buddha *did* perform *iddhi-patihariya* (wonders beyond the power of man) in order to convince a sceptic).[5] Those powers say nothing of the status of the person, since it is always possible to maintain that they have been achieved by some magic device, which is quite independent of the person employing it. The power which the Buddha makes manifest is the power of understanding and insight, which transforms the person.

Then follows, in the Kevaddha Sutta, the famous illustration of the man who wants to know where the four great elements, earth, fire, water, and wind pass away to, leaving no trace behind. The man uses his power of ecstasy to go up to the world of the gods, and the gods pass him on from one to another, completely unable to answer his question. Eventually he arrives at the great Brahma himself, and he asks of Brahma the same question. Brahma answers: 'I am the great Brahma, the Supreme, the Mighty, the All-seeing, the Ruler, the Lord of all, the Controller, the Creator, the Chief of all, appointing to each his place, the Ancient of days, the Father of all that are and are to be!'

The man replies: 'I didn't ask you whether you are what you say you are. I simply ask you where the four great elements— earth, fire, water, wind—go to leaving no trace behind?' Again the same response comes from Brahma, so a third time the man has to ask the question. Then Brahma takes the man by the arm and leads him away into a quiet corner, where no one can overhear them; 'These gods', he says, 'the retinue of Brahma, hold me to be such that there is nothing I cannot see, nothing I have not understood, nothing I have not realized. Therefore I gave no answer in their presence. The truth is, I do not know where those four elements cease leaving no trace behind.' Then Brahma tells the man that he has done wrong in neglecting the Buddha who alone can answer that question. So the man returns to the Buddha who answers the question for him (Dig. N. i. 221 ff.).

The contrast between the Buddha and the gods is constantly reiterated along the same lines, emphasizing the impotence and inefficacy of the gods in comparison with the Buddha. So the gods, for example, are completely unable to banish fear (Sam. N. i. 288 f.) but the eightfold path can cast out *any* fear (Ang. N. i. 180). Their ultimate impotence is summarized in Ang. N. ii. 172 (cf. Ang. N. iii. 54 ff.):

No recluse, or brahmin, no Deva, no Mara, no Brahma can be surety against four things. What four? That what is of a nature to decay may not decay; that what is of a nature to be diseased may not be diseased; that what is of a nature to die may not die; that the fruit of those evil deeds that defile and lead to again-becoming . . . may not come to pass.

Not surprisingly the gods are portrayed (as has already been illustrated) coming to the Buddha for instruction and advice, so that they may advance in the process of again-becoming toward the attainment of nirvana. This is a main theme, for example, in the Sakka Suttas in Sam. N. i. 216 ff., where Sakka and the gods worship the Buddha, and as a clinching irony Sakka has to be taught how to do it properly.

The point is indeed taken so far in its emphasis that enlightened Buddhist teachers actually manifest themselves in heaven, in order to correct or to encourage the gods—so that one can say that whereas in Christianity there is a harrowing of hell, in Buddhism there is a harrowing of heaven, as, for example, when Mogallana the great (Maha Mogallano) goes to the heaven of the thirty-three gods, and in a profoundly formal way, with three repetitions on earth and in heaven, Sakka acknowledges the worth of the Buddha, the Dhamma, and the Sangha (Sam. N. iv. 269 ff.).[6]

From all this, it can be seen that there is a recurrent implicit argument against attributing to the gods any status outside the whole process of change and again-becoming, of which, according to the Buddha, they are a part. But at times explicit arguments are also advanced against particular theistic propositions or assertions. Perhaps the best known of these is the long argument recorded in the Tevijja Sutta. It opens with a dispute between two young Brahmans about which two Brahmanical teachers is to be relied on as making manifest 'the straight path, the direct way which makes for salvation, and leads him, who acts according to it, into a state of union with Brahma'. The first response of the Buddha was to clarify the theoretical point, that it is not a case of simply two alternative teachings among the Brahmans: there are *many* different teachings. However, the two young Brahmans argue: 'Just as near a village or a town there are many and various paths, yet they all meet together in the village—just in that way are all the various paths taught by various Brahmans.' And when the Buddha asks them if all the Brahmanical paths *do* lead to the same destination, union with Brahma, the young Brahmans reply, yes.

That is identically the argument put forward repeatedly by Radhakrishnan: 'We may climb the mountain by different paths but the view from the summit is identical for all.'[7] Here the issue is exactly comparable to the issue between the pagan Symmachus and the Christian Ambrose in the late fourth century A.D., as Prudentius recorded it:

> He [Symmachus] says: The mighty secret of mysterious truth
> By many ways and different paths is sought.
> A hundred roads and varied ways must trace
> That course which searches out the hidden God.[8]

Ambrose firmly replies:

> The truth is far from that: the following
> Of many paths holds only wandering doubts
> And straying more confused. Only the single way
> Avoids such error: no turning of the steps
> Into diverted ways, no hesitation
> Before a multitude of different paths.

The Buddha comes very close to articulating an 'Ambrosean' argument, that since by definition we have not yet arrived at the goal, how *can* we be sure that all paths are leading there? Presumably some may turn out to have been leading in the *wrong* direction all the time. So the Buddha says that since no Brahman has at any time seen God face to face, how can they be so sure that their teaching will lead to union with that which they have not seen and in fact know nothing about?

It is like a string of blind men, clinging to one another: the first cannot see, nor the middle, not the last. Just so is the talk of the Brahmans versed in the three Vedas nothing but blind talk: the first cannot see, nor the middle, nor the last. The talk then of these Brahmans versed in the three Vedas turns out to be ridiculous, mere words, a vain and empty thing![9]

Very well; but the answer can then be made that there are at least indications of God in the world or in the universe, cues of theistic presence which justify the projection of a life-way which will lead to a fuller vision of him in the end; and that is why, from the Brahminical point of view, it is legitimate to worship the moon and sun. In that case, argues the Buddha, are you maintaining that the worship of the moon and sun leads to union of the soul (*atman*) *with* the moon or the sun? The young Brahmans reply, 'Certainly not, Gautama!' But then how is the bridge to be constructed from the worship of the tangible and visible to the invisible which no one has ever seen? Indeed, on what grounds can we suppose that there is anything, so to speak, to construct the bridge toward?

Well: perhaps it is that the manifest and tangible enable us to envisage the ideal reality of which these objects of worship are inadequate approximations. They are the steps of a ladder by which we can rise until we no longer have need of it. In that case, suggests the Buddha, it is like the ideal of the most perfect and most beautiful woman. What in fact would her characteristics be? By what scale of values could one ensure that one person's sense of the ideal corresponds to that of his neighbour? Perhaps the reason why the ideal has never been realized lies in the fact that it is literally unrealizable. It turns out to be a mental construct, with no correspondence in reality.[10] So the first line of argument against traditional claims about God is the 'Have you seen Small anywhere about' argument, of *The House at Pooh Corner*:

'Have you seen Small anywhere about?' 'I don't think so,' said Pooh. And then, after thinking a little more, he said: 'Who is Small?' 'One of my friends-and-relations,' said Rabbit carelessly. This didn't help Pooh much, because Rabbit had so many friends-and-relations, and of such different sorts and sizes, that he didn't know whether he ought to be looking for Small at the top of an oak tree or in the petal of a butter-cup . . . 'So I want you, Pooh, to search by the Six Pine Trees first, and then work your way towards Owl's house, and look out for me there. Do you see?' 'No,' said Pooh.[11]

And 'No' said the Buddha; and that is the first line of argument developed in the Sutta against Brahmanical theism. The second is a literal *argumentum ad homines*. Even if the Brahmans could overcome the theoretical problems of being certain that their teaching will lead men to a union with that of which one cannot be certain, they themselves do not give any impression of having set out in that direction, let alone of having attained it. In other words, if they exemplified detachment from this world and attachment, even in a preliminary sense, to another—to A. N. Other—that at least would be some encouragement. But, says the Buddha, they are as a man standing on the bank of a river, who wants to get to the other side. He goes down on his knees and begs the other bank of the river to come over to him—without, needless to say, much success.

In just the same way do the Brahmans versed in the three Vedas—omitting the practice of those qualities which really make a man a Brahman, and adopting the practice of those qualities which really make men non-Brahmans—say thus: 'Indra we call upon, Soma we call upon, Varuna we call upon, Isana we call upon, Pajapati we call upon, Brahma we call upon, we call upon, we call upon.' . . . That these Brahmans, by reason of their invoking and praying and hoping and praising, should after death and when the body is dissolved, become united with Brahma—never can such a condition of things come to be!

And why not? Because they are the same man on the river bank, but this time his arms are bound behind him with a chain. What is the chain which binds the Brahmans? It is their attachment to this world through their senses. And they are the same man again, but this time he lies down on the bank, covers up his head and goes to sleep, and hopes that somehow he will wake up on the other side. So the Brahmans cover their heads in the entanglements of worldly concern and hope somehow to wake up somewhere else.

Those are two important lines of argument advanced against Brahmanical theism which is repudiated emphatically, not to say derisively—though, as will be seen at the opening of the next chapter, it is not repudiated absolutely. But in general terms, it follows that the whole Vedic, or post-Vedic, apparatus through which men have attempted to relate themselves to the gods, and through which also they have attempted to relate the gods beneficially to the construction of their own life-way, is fundamentally mistaken; and it is here, obviously, that the Buddha appears as part of the very extensive protestant dissent from Brahmanical religion which emerged also in such movements as the Jains. It is the inefficacy of the gods which is the focus of the Buddha's protest: since sacrifices do not produce consistent consequences, the gods cannot be relied on to protect those who are devoted to them. The protest is made frequently and in many different forms. It is made anecdotally in the Jataka stories, as in this example:

Once on a time, when Brahmadatta was reigning in Benares, the Bodhisattva was born a brahmin in the north country, and on the day of his birth his parents lit a birth-fire.

In his sixteenth year they addressed him thus, 'Son, on the day of your birth we lit a birth-fire for you. Now therefore choose. If you wish to lead a family life, learn the Three Vedas; but if you wish to attain to the Brahma Realm, take your fire with you into the forest and there tend it, so as to win Maha-Brahma's favour, and hereafter to enter into the Brahma Realm.'

Telling his parents that a family life had no charms for him, he went into the forest and dwelt in a hermitage tending his fire. An ox was given him as a fee one day in a border village, and when he had driven it home to his hermitage, the thought came to him to sacrifice a cow to the Lord of Fire. But finding that he had no salt, and feeling that the Lord of Fire could not eat his meat-offering without it, he resolved to go back and bring a supply from the village for the purpose. So he tied up the ox and set off again to the village. While he was gone, a band of hunters came up and, seeing the ox, killed it and cooked themselves a dinner. And what they did not eat they carried off, leaving only the tail and hide and the shanks. Finding only these sorry remains on his return, the brahmin exclaimed, 'As this Lord of Fire cannot so much as look after his own, how shall he look after me? It is a waste of time to serve him, bringing neither good nor profit.' Having thus lost all desire to worship Fire, he said—'My Lord of Fire, if you cannot manage to protect yourself, how shall you protect me? The meat being gone, you must make shift to fare on this offal.' So saying, he threw on the fire the tail and the rest of the robbers' leavings and uttered this stanza:

> Vile Jataveda, here's the tail for you;
> And think yourself in luck to get so much!
> The prime meat's gone; put up with tail today.

So saying the Great Being put the fire out with water and departed to become a recluse. And he won the Knowledges and Attainments, and secured his rebirth in the Brahma Realm.

Equally, the protest is made in argument and observation; and the main drive of the argument, in addition to the emphasis on the inefficacy of sacrifice, is to insist that sacrifices and the god-relatedness which they imply or claim are irrelevant to the issue of salvation. Quite apart from the empirical observation that the correlation between sacrifice and event is insecure, sacrifice and god-relatedness are a literal side-track: they are beside the point, a diversion from the main issue, which is nirvana. There is thus no denial of the possibility of god-relatedness, any more than there is a denial that the gods exist; but since god-relatedness is not the final goal, it is far better to leave the apparatus of sacrifice and cult on one side. If people do feel the need to sacrifice, then they should re-interpret sacrifice and god-relatedness in Buddhist terms. Consequently, there is, in the Canon, a very considerable exercise in de-mythologization, in which the sacrifices of Brahminical theism are re-interpreted in Buddhist terms.

A good example of this occurs in the Brahma Suttas (Sam. N. i. 136 ff.). The opening of this is the *Ayacanam*, the Entreaty of

Brahma at the time of the Buddha's hesitation; but then follow
episodes in which various Brahma gods encounter the Buddha.
In the first of them, Brahma Sahampati actually appears as a
Buddhist teacher, encouraging a widow whose son has become a
follower of the Buddha to cease offering her habitual sacrifice to
Brahma and to give it instead to the follower of the Buddha—to
become in other words, a 'giver', the basic structural bond of
Buddhist society which relates the lay person to the community
Buddhist. In the second episode, Baka the Brahma god is represented as holding views diametrically opposed to Buddhism:
'This [Brahma-life] is permanent and stable; this is eternal, this
is absolute, this is unchanging in its essence; here there is no birth,
nor decay, nor death; no falling from, nor rising up to; and beyond
this there is no further salvation.' In response to this, maintaining
the perfect symmetry of opposition, the Buddha does what the
Brahma gods usually do: he appears in the world as effortlessly
as a healthy man can stretch or bend his arm—only of course the
Buddha materializes in the Brahma world, a device or technique
which frequently occurs in descriptions of the Buddha's authority
and power. Brahma Baka welcomes the Buddha, and the Buddha
tells him that he and the other gods have won their rebirth into
this state, not, as they suppose, because of the sacrifices which
they offered, but because of acts of compassion which are the true
'rituals and good works' winning enlightenment. In the same way,
in a discourse at Savatthi, the Buddha is able to state how it was
that Sakka, the ruler of the gods, achieved rebirth in that state:

> In the days when Sakka, ruler of the gods, was a man,
> he undertook and carried out seven rules of conduct [*vatapadani*]
> whereby he attained his celestial sovereignty. What were they?
> As long as I live, may I maintain my parents.
> As long as I live, may I revere the head of the family.
> As long as I live, may I use gentle language.
> As long as I live, may I utter no slander.
> As long as I live, with a mind rid of stain and selfishness,
> may I conduct myself in the home with generosity,
> with clean hands, delighting in renunciation,
> amenable to petitions, delighting in sharing gifts.
> As long as I live may I speak the truth,
> As long as I live may I not give way to anger; if anger
> should arise may I swiftly repress it (Sam. N. i. 228).

The Buddha then argues that what is good enough for the gods is good enough for men; or, putting it more positively, he encourages his followers to translate sacrifice into generous action toward their fellow-beings, particularly their family and immediate associates. This can be seen in Dig. N. iii. 180 ff., where the Buddha de-mythologizes and makes prosaic the worship of the young Sigala:

Thus have I heard: The Exalted One was once staying near Rajagaha in the Bamboo Wood at the Squirrel's Feeding-ground. Now at this time young Sigala, a householder's son, rising betimes, went forth from Rajagaha, and with wet hair and wet garments and clasped hands uplifted, paid worship to the several quarters of earth and sky: to the east, south, west, and north, to the nadir and the zenith.

And the Exalted One early that morning dressed himself, took bowl and robe and entered Rajagaha seeking alms. Now he saw young Sigala worshipping and spoke to him thus:

'Why, young householder, do you, rising betimes and leaving Rajagaha, with wet hair and raiment, worship the several quarters of earth and sky?'

'Sir, my father, when he was dying, said to me: Dear son, you should worship the quarters of earth and sky. So I, sir, honouring my father's word, reverencing, revering, holding it sacred, rise betimes and, leaving Rajagaha, worship on this wise.'

'But in the religion of an Ariyan, young householder, the six quarters should not be worshipped thus.'

'How then, sir, in the religion of an Ariyan, should the six quarters be worshipped? It would be an excellent thing, sir, if the Exalted One would so teach me the doctrine according to which, in the religion of an Ariyan, the six quarters should be worshipped.'

The Buddha does as he is asked, and having told Sigala how he should behave, he says: 'So how, young householder, does the Ariyan disciple protect the six quarters? The following should be looked on as the six quarters; parents as the east, teachers as the south, wife and children as the west, friends and companions as the north, servants and work people as the nadir, religious teachers and brahmans as the zenith.'

De-mythologization was by no means limited to the sacrificial system. It can occur with reference to the gods themselves. Thus in Ang. N. i. 132, parents are claimed to be Brahma in relation to their children; consequently it is appropriate to relate to them as theistic believers relate to Brahma:

Monks, those families where mother and father are worshipped in the home are reckoned *sabrahmakari*. Those families where mother and father are worshipped in the home are ranked with the teachers of old. Worthy of offerings, monks, are those families where mother and father are worshipped in the home. 'Brahma', monks, is a term for mother and father [*Brahma ti bhikkhave matapitunnam etam adhivacanam*]. 'Teachers of old [*pubbacariya*]', monks, is a term for mother and father. 'Worthy of offerings [*ahuneyya*]', monks, is a term for mother and father. Why so? Because mother and father do much for children, they bring them up, nourish and introduce them to the world.

In this way, even the great goals of Brahmanical religion, the Brahma-intended life (*brahmacariya*) and Brahma-attained (*brahmabhuta*), were re-mythologized:

Bhikkhus, this *brahmacariya* is not lived to cheat or cajole people. It is not concerned with getting gain, profit, or notoriety. It is not concerned with a flood of gossip nor with the idea of 'let folk know one as so-and-so'. No, bhikkhus, this *brahmacariya* is lived for the sake of self-restraint, for the sake of abandoning, for the sake of detachment to passions, for the sake of making to cease.

> For self restraint and for abandoning,
> Heedless of what men say of it, this *brahmacariya*
> Did that Exalted One proclaim as going
> Unto the plunge into Nibbana's stream (Ang. N. ii. 26).

Is it then the case that *all* instances of such terms as *brahmacariya*, *brahmabhuta*, *brahmapatta*, have been de-mythologized so that 'brahma' has become an adjective, 'pure' or 'best-intended'? It is an almost unanimous opinion that that is the case. So, for example, Murti, refuting (rightly) an argument for an original Buddhism which included the concept of a self, stated: 'Much cannot be built on the use of such terms ... for they connote purity, serenity, and "blessed state"; they have lost all implications of a Brahma- or atma-metaphysics.'[12] However, that widespread opinion depends on a correspondingly widespread misunderstanding of the sense of God in Buddhism, as will be seen. But even if not all instances of brahma compounds are adjectivally de-mythologized, certainly a great many of them are, so that the terms, which outside Buddhism describe a god-intended and perhaps also god-united life, come to mean life in a Buddhist character.

From all that has been said in this chapter, it must seem obvious that the Brahmanical goal of union with Brahma has been excised as being irrelevant. It is not denied that union with Brahma is possible, but it can only be temporary, because Brahma is himself involved in the process of *dukkha* (of change and impermanence). So far, then, it would seem that the sense of God in Buddhism can only be positive in a trivial sense, but negative in any sense that a theistic believer would regard as important; and that in turn would suggest that the interpretation of the paradox of theism in Buddhism, which regards it as an accommodation of popular cosmology which is of no quintessential significance in Buddhism, is correct.

That conclusion might seem at first sight to be supported by the fact that theistic issues are not prominent in the history of Buddhist philosophy. They are not *absent* from (for example) Abhidhamma texts. Thus the Kathavatthu certainly records discussion of the status of the gods or of the worlds of the gods, in terms which are not (as one would expect) entirely complimentary. Alan Bennett once remarked, 'God, whatever else He is, and of course He is everything else, is not a fool.'[13] But the Abhidhamma discussion sometimes seems to suggest not only that he *is* a fool, but that like Epaminondas, he hasn't even got the sense he was born with. However, it is important not to make too much of the absence of extensive theological discussion. The paucity of discussion is linked partly to the fact that the existence of theistic reality is *not* controversial, and partly also to the fact that when the Buddha was probed by questioners on issues of status of that sort, he refused to be drawn or to make any clear response—the second great silence of the Buddha's life (pp. 296 ff.).

Nevertheless, the impression undoubtedly remains that theistic belief is tolerated, but that a predominantly negative judgement is passed on it. But in fact there is another side to the picture, a more positive side, the implications of which have considerable phenomenological importance in understanding the human sense of God.

3. THE REALIZATION OF GOD IN BUDDHISM

IN the last chapter, attention was drawn to the Tevijja Sutta, in which two main lines of argument were advanced against Brahminical theism (pp. 276-9). The arguments exemplify the negative judgement which the Buddha passed on such beliefs. However, it was pointed out that the judgement was not *entirely* negative. In the second line of argument (the *argumentum ad homines*), the Buddha took as an illustration the man on one bank of a river who wishes to reach the other bank, and he used the illustration in several ways to illustrate different defects among the Brahmans. But in the first use of the illustration (pp. 278 f.), the condemnation is not absolute: a distinction is drawn between the usual Brahman who intermingles various corrupting qualities of life with his God-directed intention, and the Brahman who is authentically such. The distinction is developed in the last part of the Sutta, where one of the young Brahmans goes on to ask the Buddha whether he can show them the way that leads to the realization of the state of union with Brahma and can thus save the Brahman race. The Buddha, far from repudiating the request, does exactly as he is asked: he summarizes the way whereby 'the Bhikkhu who is free from anger, free from malice, pure in mind and master of himself will, after death, when the body is dissolved, become united with Brahma' (Tev. S. 81).

The goal of realization of union with God is not dismissed as unimportant or as undesirable. Indeed, far from it: it is encouraged as a proper and worthwhile goal in the process of again-becoming. Thus whereas the summaries of the Buddhist way in other Suttas lead to the condition of being *arhant*, of being in the state of freedom from all attachments, and of peace of mind through insight, in this Sutta the way leads to union with Brahma. It is not even said that it is mistaken or misguided to seek that union: it is, maybe, an interim attainment, but it is, even so, an interim goal which the Buddha does not oppose.

The Sutta actually makes no mention of the goal of arhant at all. The very point of the argument is to maintain that there is a way in which a condition of rebirth in the Brahma world can come to be. So the comment of T. W. Rhys Davids on this Sutta is entirely misleading (though it is illuminating, because it illustrates how much the western interpretation of Buddhism has attempted to eliminate theistic reality from Buddhism, in order—one may guess —to make it more congenial to the modern mind): 'It should be recollected that the argument here is only an *argumentum ad hominem*. If you want union with Brahma—which you had much better not want—this is the way to attain it.'[1] But the parenthesis is entirely Rhys Davids's invention. It is not actually stated in the Sutta that 'you had much better not want it'. That is the intellectualizing comment of one who would clearly have preferred it if no myths and no concession to theism had occured in the Canon at all.[2]

But such comments do occur; and they occur sometimes *not* as *argumenta ad homines*, but in contexts of real and positive approval. The goals of union with God, of rebirth in the heavenly worlds, and indeed of rebirth *as* a god, are all held out in the Canon as legitimate and desirable. It was pointed out in the last chapter that the possibility of union with Brahma could indeed be re-expressed in terms of Buddhist norms, and that terms like *brahmacariya* and *brahmabhuta* are frequently de-mythologized. But that does not eliminate the possiblity of actual union with God, or of rebirth in heaven, as an outcome in the process of change and of again-becoming. That is, indeed, claimed to have been the Buddha's own experience. One example has already been given in the Jataka story which was designed to demonstrate the futility of sacrifice (pp. 279 f.). Despite the futility, the story nevertheless ended by saying that the ascetic *did* attain union with Brahma, and the ascetic was, of course, the Buddha in a previous birth. In other Jataka stories, the Buddha actually was Maha Brahma (99, 134, 135), or he actually was Sakka (300, 393). But the possibility is in any case not controversial in the Canon, as in this example from Dig. N. iii. 145:

Whereas in whatsoever former birth, former state of becoming, former sojourning, the Tathagatha, then being human, took on mighty enterprise . . . by the doing and by the accumulating of that Karma, by the mass and the abundance thereof, he when the body perished was after death reborn in a bright and blessed world. There he was endowed with a larger measure than other devas in ten matters, to wit in celestial years, beauty, happiness, glory, dominion, sights, sounds, odours, tastes, and touches. Deceasing thence and attaining life as you know it, he acquires this mark of the superman, to wit: feet with level tread, evenly placing his foot upon earth, evenly drawing it up, evenly touching earth with the entire surface of the foot.

Consequently, as it was possible for the Buddha, so also for other men is it possible to attain rebirth in heaven, or rebirth as a deva or as any other 'other-than-human' reality. For this reason the gods frequently rejoice at the Buddha's activity, because his teaching creates (through its effect on the process of again-becoming in many instances) a large number of new appearances among the gods. There is an example of this in Dig. N. ii. 200 ff. The spirit Jana-Vasabha reports to the Buddha that the assembly of the gods has been filled with great joy, because there have been new births among the gods, and the new gods, 'because they have lived the higher life under the Exalted One, outshined the other gods in appearance and glory'. The gratitude of the gods to the Buddha for so increasing their number is expressed in a hymn of praise recited by Sakka, the ruler of the gods:

The Thirty-Three, both gods and Lord, rejoice,
Tathagatha they honour and the cosmic law sublime,
For now they see the gods new-risen, beautiful and bright,
Who recently have lived a holy life,
The mighty Sage's hearers, who had won to higher truths,
Come hither, and in glory all the other gods outshine.
This they behold right gladly, both Lord and Thirty-Three,
Tathagatha they honour and the cosmic law sublime. (Dig. N. ii. 208.)

In the light of this, it is obviously not surprising to find that attentiveness to theistic reality has serious and differentiating consequences in the construction of life. It is, for example, through identification with the devas that the soiled mind can be cleansed. This is stated in Ang. N. i. 210 f., in a passage summarizing various means through which this can be achieved. Of these, one is meditation on the happy state of the gods, and the realization that the same faith which directed the process of rebirth to that state in *their* case is equally possible in one's own: 'This Ariyan disciple is said to keep the deva-watch: he dwells with the Devas: it is owing to the Devas that his mind is calmed, that delight arises, that the uncleanness of his mind is abandoned.' For this reason, keeping one's mind constantly attentive to the gods is included in the six objects of necessary and desirable attention, in Ang. N. iii. 284: '*Bikkhus*, there are these six states of attentive intentionality [*anussati*]. What six? Intentionality towards the Buddha, towards Dhamma, towards Sangha, towards virtue, towards generosity, towards devas.'

It follows that rebirth according to intention, including rebirth in the form of gods, is possible. In the sequence of again-becoming, it is repeatedly emphasized that one attains what one fixes one's mind and intention on (provided obviously it is accompanied with appropriate behaviour, and is not vitiated by inappropriate behaviour).[3] So natural and obvious is this possibility that it is in fact a common outcome in the Jataka stories. If the outcomes of again-becoming in the main Jataka stories are quantified, we find that in the 232 stories in which an outcome in terms of rebirth is actually specified, the following is the result:

> rebirth according to *Karma* (according to what is deserved), 76;
> rebirth in the *Brahmaloka*, 91;
> rebirth in the *devaloka*, 16;
> rebirth in heaven, 37;
> rebirth in hell, 8;
> attainment of nirvana, 4.

So, of the specified instances, just over 65 per cent have a theistic outcome, and there is no sense whatsoever that that outcome is a failure. The figure may, of course, be even higher, because 'rebirth according to karma' may itself lead to union with God, if that outcome is (as it may be) 'what is deserved'.

It follows, obviously, that if rebirth as a god or as a deva is part of the long sequence of change and again-becoming, it may be possible to fall from that status and to be reborn as a human, or even in some lower form of appearance. An example of this has already been seen (p. 272) in the Buddha's explanation of how human beings arrived at the false impression that there is a supreme creator god; but even in general terms it is a common theme (see, e.g., Dig. N. i. 18). In Ang. N. v. 59 f. it is put in these terms:

Bhikkhus, as far as the moon and sun move in their course and light up all quarters with their radiance, so far extends the thousand-world system. Therein are a thousand moons, a thousand suns . . . a thousand heavens of the Thirty-Three, one thousand Yama-worlds, one thousand heavens of the Devas of Delight, one thousand heavens of the Devas who delight in creation, one thousand of those Devas who delight in the creations of others, and one thousand Brahma-worlds. As far as the thousandfold world-system extends, therein the Great Brahma is reckoned supreme. Yet even for him there is change and reverse. So seeing, the Ariyan disciple with insight feels revulsion: in him, so feeling revulsion, interest in the highest of the high fades, not to speak of the lowest of the low. There comes a time, bhikkhus, when this world runs down [*samvattati* as opposed to *vivattati*, evolving]. As it does so, beings are generally reborn as Shining Devas . . . For a long, long time they stand fast. Bhikkhus, when the world runs down, it is the Shining Devas who are reckoned chief. Yet for the Shining Devas there is change and reverse.

However, it is also the case that having been reborn as a God or in a heavenly world, it is possible *not* to reverse and fall, but to go on further, as in Ang. N. iv. 62 f. In another passage (ii. 183 ff.) different levels of attainment, *devapatta, brahmapatta, nejja-patta, ariyapatta*, are described, which may clearly be the basis of on-going and of not again-becoming in a lower form of appearance.

But what both those two (moving down or moving up) have in common is that rebirth in union with God or in the form of a god is not a permanent condition. It is an interim stage (though one which may endure for a *koti* of *kalpas*) in the long sequence which one may hope may eventually issue in nirvana. That is the funda-mental and necessary point in the Buddhist sense of God. It means ultimately that rebirth in connection with theistic reality is undesirable (because it is still only a half-way house), even though it is more desirable than rebirth on this earth, and *far* more desirable than rebirth in the lower layers of hell (consequently, there is no paradox, nor anything particularly surprising, in lay Buddhists setting their sights on heaven, as described in IV.1, pp. 246 f.).

The basic and necessary point of the last paragraph appears in innumerable examples, of which the best-known is perhaps the image of the log floating in the Ganges (Sam. N. iv. 179 f.), through which the Buddha exemplified the hazards of 'floating' to nirvana: 'If you do not ground on this shore or that shore, if you do not sink in midstream, if you do not stick fast on a shoal, if you do not fall into hands human or non-human, if you are not caught

in a whirlpool, if you do not rot inwardly, then, brothers, you will
float to Nirvana.'

All these are then exemplified: 'And what is "being caught by
non-humans?" . . . A certain person lives the Brahma-intended
life (*brahmacariya*) with the wish to be reborn in the company of
some class of devas, with the thought: May I, by virtue or practice
or by some austerity or by righteous living, become a deva or one
of the devas—this is being caught by non-humans.' From that it
is clear that to be reborn as a deva is an unhappy distraction
on the way to nirvana. The same appears in the advice on how to
conduct a pastoral visit to a sick man (Sam. N. v. 409 f.):

Suppose the sick man says, 'My thoughts are removed from human
pleasures of sense and fixed upon the four deva kings', then let the
other say: 'More excellent than the Yama Devas, the Devas of Delight,
the creative Devas, the Devas who rejoice in the work of other Devas,
so it would be better for you to fix your thoughts on the Brahma-world
[*brahmaloka*].' Then if the sick man's thoughts are so fixed, let the
other say, 'My friend, even the Brahma-world is impermanent, not
lasting, tied to the appearance of a person. Well for you, friend, if you
raise your mind above the Brahma-world and fix it on cessation from
the person-appearance.'[4]

But although the attainment of union with God and the realization of theistic reality may be nothing more than interim stages,
there is not the slightest question in Buddhism (not simply in
canonical Buddhism) that such attainment and realization are
possible and indeed likely. That is why it is necesary to be extremely
cautious before accepting the prevalent argument (referred to
on p. 283) that the central and crucial phases, *brahmacariya* and
brahmavihara, have always been secularized in Buddhism and
emptied of theistic content, by being de-mythologized into ad-
jectives meaning 'pure' or 'best-intended'. There is no dispute
that *brahmacariya* has in some instances been transacted into a
novel and specifically Buddhist outcome. That was necessary
because the term, which has deep roots in the Brahmanic tradition, has a strong and different theistic content in that other
tradition. For example, in the Atharva-Veda, the *brahmacarin*
virtually becomes in this life an incarnation and mediation of
Brahma: 'A *brahmacarin* in the full glory of his holy functions and
monastic habits is treated as an incarnation of Brahma; from him

the Brahma springs, and in his holy life (*brahmanam*) the Brahma is glorified' (trans. Bloomfield, p. 89).

In the Upanishads it has become much more a stage in the process of rebirth, a particular style of life (increasingly defined) which leads toward union with Brahma. According to Chandogya Up. 8.4.3, only those who arive at the Brahma-world through the stage of *brahmacariya* come into an enduring possession of the Brahma-world: 'Only they find that Brahma-world who practise the life of *brahmacariya*: only they possess that Brahma-world.'

So the definition of *brahmacariya* became increasingly socio-logical: it came to refer to a particular stage and style of life in the process toward the realization of *atman* and the relation of *atman* to Brahman. For Shankara, *brahmacariya* has become the stage through which every authentic brahman must pass, in which he is celibate and has renounced all desire for women, and in which he lives with a teacher who instructs him.

It is a comparably functional and structural interpretation of the phrase which sometimes occurs in the Buddhist use of it, and it can still have a straightforward theistic reference. In general terms, it is used of any Brahma-intended life, so that it becomes a word for a seriously practised religious and moral life. Thus it is used of the Jatilas, who lived at the same time as the Buddha, and it is used of the life of Sariputta and Mogallana among the Paribbajakas before they became Buddhists. The Buddha himself says that he lived a life of *brahmacariya* in a previous birth, and the life-style of *brahmacariya* is described as one of extreme austerity and asceticism.

To some extent, those uses are comparable to the plural uses of *elohim* in Scripture (see pp. 47 f.), which refer straightforwardly to the actual historical situation in which people believed in many gods. But as the word *brahmacariya* was transacted into a Buddhist outcome, it retained the same structural and functional type of reference, but the content was transformed by Buddhist controls. It continued, therefore, to refer to the ideal life-style, which leads to the goal, but obviously the goal and the life which leads to it are redefined in Buddhist terms. *Brahmacariya* becomes the life-style which leads to cessation of *dukkha* and to the attainment of nirvana. The Buddha summarized his own mission as, 'One thing only do I teach, *dukkha* and the deliverance from *dukkha*'; consequently, it is not surprising to find *brahmacariya* attached to that goal, as in the appeal of the Buddha: 'Come, *bhikkhu*, live the life of *brahmacariya* in order that you may make an end of *dukkha*.'

So in general, because the Buddhist goal of nirvana has been substituted for the theistic goal of union with Brahma (or with Brahman theistically characterized), *brahmacariya* in many instances no longer bears any direct relation to Brahma. There is, therefore, no doubt that the term has frequently been secularized and emptied of theistic content. The same is also true of the term *brahmavihara*. They are the four godlike attitudes or four divine states of disposition, of *metta* (faithful love), *karuna* (compassion), *mudita* (usually translated as 'sympathetic joy'), and *upekkha* (balance or equanimity). It is in those four states of mind that the *bhikkhu* must contemplate the world and must do so with deliberation: 'He must let his mind, infused with *metta*, pervade one quarter of the world, then the second, then the third, then the fourth; and so the whole world, above, below, around, everywhere, with mind freed from anger and malice.'

Once again, there is no doubt that the *brahmaviharas*, which were cultivated outside Buddhism (for example, by the Paribbajakas, those who detach themselves from home and family and become wanderers in the world, of other religious affiliations), have been transacted into a Buddhist outcome. This can be seen most specifically in Sam. N. v. 115 ff., where the Buddha is asked whether he teaches the *brahmavihara* in the same way as the Paribbajaka do. The Buddha in his reply attaches to the four divine states of mind an additional term, *cetovimutti*, an addition which qualifies the divine states and which is found in other passages as well. The effect of the addition is to transfer the reality of these 'states of mind' to a condition beyond the simple attainment of union with Brahma. *Cetovimutti* means 'freedom of mind', detachment from the conditions of 'again-becoming' through the four states of mind. As a result, Buddhaghosa (the great commentator on the Pali Canon) simply included *brahmavihara* among the basic methods of Buddhist meditation: in the Vissudimagga (pp. 244–70), Buddhaghosa anthologized from the Canon forty foundations or supports of concentration or meditation and in the *kammatthana* he included the *brahmavihara*.

It follows that the case is strong for maintaining that theistic reference has been excised from the term, despite the appearance of *brahma* in it, and that *brahma* has become an adjective meaning 'highest' or 'best'. But that deduction put in such absolute terms (as, for example, in the statement by Murti, p. 283) is to transfer western preoccupations into the entirely different Indian context in which Gautama was born. It is to make the mistake of supposing that theism can only be conceived in extra-natural terms. The Buddha did indeed oppose that interpretation of theism. It has been seen already how emphatically he brought the gods within the natural and regarded them as a part of the one reality in which human appearances are also set. There is nothing outside that reality which can afford to the gods a refuge from the same process of change and impermanence which is the characteristic of all appearance. So the gods can be supernatural but not extra-natural. Yet, as we have also seen, the Buddha did not deny the real existence of the gods, in his sense of existence. It follows, therefore, that there was no need for the Buddha to excise theistic reference from those terms in all cases. There is nothing in the least embarrassing to Buddhism (except to some forms of its western and Californian interpretations) to suppose that the flow of appearance can be directed toward God and that union with God is possible. Because the gods fall within the range of the natural (of what happens to be possible in the many forms of appearance), there is no dichotomy between attainment of Brahma and attainment of nirvana, although the point repeatedly emphasized remains, that attainment of Brahma is only an interim stage on the way to nirvana. It is possible to have a godlike state of mind because that state of mind *is* the one which the gods possess. In other words, as rebirth in the form of a god is possible, so also it is possible to see as the gods see, and there is consequently no need to construe *brahmavihara* metaphorically in all instances. It is transacted into a Buddhist outcome in some instances, but at the same time, without strain or distortion, it can retain a theistic reference. And that is why, in the Jataka stories, there are thirteen instances where the cultivation of *brahmavihara* is described as leading to the attainment of the Brahma-world, and it is clear that nothing metaphorical is intended, or is indeed possible. In the same way, there is no embarrassment or discrepancy in allowing that non-Buddhists cultivate those states of mind and attain the appropriate theistic goal. For example, according to Dig. N. iii. 111, a recluse or brahman by right concentration can develop a mental state of such a kind that he can see 'with pure deva-eye, surpassing the sight of men, beings as they decease and are reborn . . .'. In other words, attainment of Brahma outside Buddhism is not impossible, and in that sense we are entitled to talk of 'anonymous Buddhists', as Rahner and others have talked of anonymous Christians.

So what is at issue is not *whether* union with Brahma or the attainment of the Brahmaloka (Brahma-world) is possible. It is simply a matter of fact that they are possibilities in the flow of rebirth and continuing appearance. The deliberate endeavour to cultivate divine states of mind (*brahmavihara*) may lead exactly where it ought to lead, to rebirth in the Brahmaloka—with no excision of theistic reference, as, for example, in the case of the two kings, Makhadeva and Sudassana, who cultivated *brahmavihara* and were reborn in the Brahma-world.[5] What was at issue for the Buddha is whether other paths in other religions which are claimed to lead to the condition of *brahmabhuta* (Brahma-attained) do in fact lead there. It is accepted in the Canon that they *can* lead there, and there is nothing paradoxical about that acceptance, because, since the gods exist, there is no problem for the Buddhist in accepting that men may become god-related. What the Buddha criticized was the *practice* of other religions, of which an example has already been given (p. 278). What people do (particularly when they are hypocritical about it) is often entirely mistaken as a way to attain a goal (God-relatedness) which the Buddha does not deny is possible. Equally, the conceptual mistake of theism is that although it correctly (correctly from the Buddhist point of view as much as from the theistic point of view) identifies the fact that the causes of these, and other, experiences must be external to ourselves, it then infers that that externality demands independence from the total process of change and again-becoming. And since consequently theistic systems attribute to the gods an entirely erroneous ontological status outside the natural, it follows that what they say about the ways which may lead to god-relatedness will be equally fraught with error. Thus the Majjhima Nikaya frequently refers to *brahmabhuta* and the path leading to it, but in i. 341 ff. the contrast is drawn between the extreme ascetic, who endeavours to reach that condition through his asceticism but who is in fact nothing but a torturer of himself and a plague to others, and the middle way between licence and ascetic absurdity, the Buddhist way which actually leads to the condition (*brahmabhuta*).[6]

Similarly in Majj. N. iii. 116 f., the Buddha does not deny the sincerity of those who set out to attain Brahma through extreme detachment and asceticism, but he points out that the very conditions which that asceticism demands contain the seeds of its defeat. The ascetic goes off into a remote place, but the greater his reputation for holiness becomes, the more pilgrims and curious people flock to see him, thereby destroying his solitude and encouraging spiritual pride:

And how, Ananda, is there affliction for the Brahma-intended? As to this, Ananda, a Tathagatha arises in the world, a perfected one . . . teacher of devas and men, an Awakened One, a Lord. He chooses a secluded lodging in a forest, at the root of a tree, on a mountain slope, in a wilderness, a hill-cave, a cemetery, a forest-haunt, in the open air, or on a heap of straw. While he is living remote like this, brahman householders crowd in on him and townsfolk as well as country folk. When they do so, he does not become infatuated, he does not fall in love, he does not become envious, he does not revert to abundance. But a disciple of this Teacher, applying himself to this Teacher's aloofness, cultivating it, chooses a remote lodging in a forest . . . While he is living remote like this, they crowd in on him and he does become infatuated, falls in love, becomes envious, and reverts to abundance. This, Ananda, is called the afflicted Brahma-intended . . . This affliction is more ill in result, more terrible in result than either the affliction of teachers or the affliction of pupils; and moreover it conduces to downfall.

Although, therefore, the Buddha rejected many of the traditional ways through which men had endeavoured to attain union with Brahma, he did not reject the possibility of that union. On the contrary, he brought that possibility within the range of what is naturally possible in the continuing process of change and reappearance. So it is not the case that the word *brahma* has undergone a verbal transaction through which it has invariably been transformed from a noun into an adjective; what has happened is that it has become adjectival in some instances, but only because its meaning is guaranteed by the substantive—by the noun which continues to have ontological reference, so far as ontology is an appropriate word in a Buddhist context.

So when the Pali dictionary defines *brahmapatta* (the realization

of brahma) as 'arrived at the highest state, above the devas, a
state like the Brahma gods', the definition is possible only because
it can be known what it is like to be a Brahma god, or to be in a
state of union with such a god; and since Upali the Jain, in his
confession of Buddhist faith, refers to the Buddha as Brahma-
patassa, it is conceivably the case that this union can be realized
even before death.

So it begins to emerge that there is *no* paradox of theism in
Buddhism: Buddhism is irredeemably theistic. God and the gods
are simply a part of 'what there is'—they are a part, that is, of
the total process of change and again-becoming. To a theistic
believer of the time, that no doubt seemed a very inadequate
characterization of theism. What was fundamentally characteristic of the theism which the Buddha encountered (as it is of most
theistic systems) was the placing of God in situations of at least
some independence from the process of change and rebirth, since
it is in relation to what is independent that a soul or self may
hope to achieve a related independence or salvation. It might,
therefore, have been possible for a contemporary theistic believer
to have challenged the Buddha on metaphysical grounds and to
have asked him to clarify his understanding of the ontological
status of such appearances as gods, or indeed of the world itself,
of the continuing life-principle in the human body, or even of the
Tathagatha, the perfected one, after he had died.

But on such metaphysical issues the Buddha refused to be
drawn. There is no doubt that the Buddha encountered metaphysical arguments of great sophistication and variety. But like
Hume, when he sought ground on which to stand in the middle
of the quagmire of metaphysics he was met, so it is reported, by
equivocation, by the wriggling of worms:

When a question on this or that is put to him [the metaphysician] he
resorts to equivocation, to wriggling like a worm: 'If you ask me whether
there is another world—well, if I thought there were I would say so.
But I don't say so. And I don't think it is thus or thus. And I don't
think it is otherwise. And I don't deny it. And I don't say there neither
is, nor is not, another world.

It all sounds remarkably like a contemporary politician on television or at a press conference. There was indeed a very remarkable example of political worm wriggling in 1975, when Mr.

Prior asked a question in a Commons' standing committee about the possible closed shop in journalism:

Mr. Albert Booth, Minister of State for Employment, said the Government was seeking neither to deter nor encourage forms of closed shops, to outlaw them or to require them. He did not take the view that it was right to have a closed shop in journalism or that it was wrong. It was not correct for him to make that judgement. He was not qualified to do so.[7]

On some issues the Buddha *was* prepared to enter into argument, and some examples of his refutation of traditional theistic claims have already been given (pp. 277 ff.). But on the famous *avyakatani* ('the (speculative) views that are not explained, (being) set aside and ignored by the Lord (Bhagavata)')[8] he refused to be drawn into commitment or argument, because even if answers were forthcoming they would be irrelevant, in a Husserlian sense of irrelevance, to the main issue—the issue of 'what must we do?'

The speculative questions, according to the Pali Canon, are: 'The world is eternal, the world is not eternal; the world is an ending thing (finite), the world is not an ending thing (not finite), the life-principal (*jiva*) is identical with the body, the *jiva* is one thing, the body another; the Tathagatha is after dying, the Tathagatha is not after dying, the Tathagatha neither is nor is not after dying.' In the Buddhist Sanskrit texts the questions are extended to fourteen. There are a number of different explanations of the Buddha's silence on these issues, summarized both in Murti and Jayatilleke. But Jayatilleke is undoubtedly right to point out that whatever additional motives the Buddha may have had, 'the Buddha had a Pragmatist reason . . . for rejecting these questions' (p. 473). In other words, they were like Huxley's questions of lunar politics:

If a man asks me what the politics of the inhabitants of the moon are, and I reply that I do not know; that neither I, nor anyone else, have any means of knowing; and that, under these circumstances, I decline to trouble myself about the subject at all, I do not think he has any right to call me a sceptic . . . So Hume's strong and subtle intellect takes up a great many problems about which we are naturally curious, and shows us that they are essentially questions of lunar politics, in their essence incapable of being answered, and therefore not worth the attention of men who have work to do in the world.[9]

So when the Buddha responded to those questions by not responding—by remaining silent—he explained why, through the famous parable of the man wounded by an arrow: before the man will allow anyone to attend to him, he demands to know what sort of arrow it is, who fired it, and where it came from. In the same way, when Malunkyaputta asked the Buddha about those issues, he replied by asking him a question: 'When you set out toward *brahmacariya* under my direction, did you say, "I will set out in that direction only if you will answer these questions?" ' Malunkyaputta answers no, he made no condition of that sort. Therefore, he is left to infer that it is possible to proceed toward enlightenment and to the cessation of again-becoming without having first solved those issues. There are more important things to do than answer such questions first.

It follows that there will be no serious theological discussion in Buddhism, *not* because Buddhism is atheistic and has eliminated theistic reality from its world-view (since that estimate of Buddhism is false), but because the Buddha refused to interest himself in questions of that sort—for example, questions of whether the reduced ontological status which he attributed to theistic reality is sufficient to account for the appearances in consciousness which he did not deny and which occured in his own case. To waste time on such issues would be like saying to a man on his way to Victoria on the underground, that many people travel to Victoria by bus, and that they meet such wonderful people on buses that really he, the traveller, ought not to arrive at Victoria until he has sorted out whether the claims to bus-experiences are true or false. By the time the appeal has been made to his intellectual curiosity the train has come to rest in a station whose descriptive labels unmistakably say Victoria. What would be the point of such a conversation about bus-experiences to a man who is just arriving at Victoria anyway? And what would be the point of such a conversation about theistic experiences to a man who is just arriving at enlightenment?

But here alGhazali is a better guide than Huxley and the Buddha. Men and women may 'have work to do' (Huxley was characteristically Victorian in assuming, even if subconsciously, that only *men* have work to do in the world) not only in this world but in a continuity beyond this particular life—and with that the Buddha would have agreed. But alGhazali was surely right to see that that assertion will as a matter of fact lose its claim on human attention if it is never prepared to discuss the possibility that it *is* comparable to questions about lunar politics. These are propositions about *putative* matters of fact, and although alGhazali was sufficiently empiricist to agree with the Buddha that the proof of the pudding is in the eating, and that consequently it is more important to lay hold of one's spoon and fork than to go on studying the menu, the theistic pudding is very differently described on the Muslim and the Buddhist menus.

> Which shall the soul-hungry choose?
> The palaces and cool thighs of paradise
> Continuous in eloquent expression, or else lose
> Himself as soul in endless seas of time?

Questions of lunar politics lose their claim on human attention, not as a matter of *principle*, but because it can be sufficiently shown that they are questions about claimed realities which turn out to be non-existent: Huxley and his contemporaries could advance the proposition that there are no inhabitants on the moon, and they could specify the conditions in which the proposition could be verified or falsified (e.g. of someone going to the moon and taking a look, even though they could not undertake the journey themselves); and in due course it is verified that questions about the politics of the inhabitants of the moon are vacuous, because there are no inhabitants to be political.

But questions about theistic reality are nothing like so simple to handle, because Buddhism is in complete agreement with other theistic traditions that there *are* appearances or occurrences in consciousness of God-relatedness which *seem* to require a resource external to the subject for them to occur in consciousness in the way in which they do occur. The phenomenological reinforcement which Buddhism offers is all the more impressive because of the dominant tendency in Buddhism to say that theistic effect may be factual, but it is trivial in comparison with the more important goal of nirvana, and is better left on one side. That may or may not be right (a point to which we will return) but the phenomenological experience is extremely clear, as in such passages as Ang. N. iv. 302:

Bhikkhus, before my awakening, while I was not yet completely awakened . . . I perceived auras [*obhasam sanjanami*] but I saw no forms [*rupa*]. Bhikkhus, to me there came the thought: 'If I were both to perceive auras and to see forms [i.e. the ground of them], knowledge and vision within me would thus be purified.' Bhikkhus, later on, living zealous, earnest, resolute, I both perceived the auras and saw the forms, but I did not stand with, talk to, or engage in conversation with any of those devas.

But then he *is* drawn into engagement with the devas, constantly refining the ontological status of those appearances in consciousness which originally were just vague experiences, but which he came to know must be grounded in the reality of devas, 'in the world of devas, with its Maras and its Brahmas'.

The Buddha, therefore, did not deny the correctness of the phenomenological report that there are experiences of effect in the construction of a life-way which are derived from externality which in some instances is characterized appropriately as theistic. Nor did he attempt to explain them away as being a misreading of experience. So, for example, in the Mahali Sutta he is reported to have maintained that such experiences are entirely real and worth while, and that they can be cultivated by appropriate methods of concentration. Equally he maintaned that they are at a very low and trivial level compared with enlightenment which lies at the end of the eightfold path. But still the fact remains that the validity of the experiences and the externality of their cause was accepted by the Buddha in a perfectly straightforward manner. Mahali reports a pastoral question put to him by Sunakkhatta:

'It is only three years, Mahali, since I first came under the Blessed One and I can see heavenly forms, pleasant to behold, fitted to satisfy all one's desires, exciting longing in one's heart. But I cannot hear heavenly sounds like that.' Now [Mahali asks the Buddha], are there such heavenly sounds, which he could not hear, or have they no existence?

And the Buddha replies:

'They are real, those heavenly sounds, pleasant, fitted to satisfy one's desires, exciting longing in one's heart, which he could not hear. They are not things of nought.' (Dig. N. i. 152.)

So the reality of effects derived from externality theistically characterized is not denied. For example, in Dig. N. iii. 103 f. one of the four ways of revealing what is in the mind of another is by listening to 'a sound uttered by humans or non-humans or devata, and one says, "You are thinking thus . . . " ' Consequently, it is not surprising that when the Buddha tells his followers about the previous manifestations of the Enlightened Ones, and they ask whether it is by the discernment of the Tathagatha that he remembers all about the Buddhas of the past, or whether the gods have revealed it to him, he replies that it is both (Dig. N. ii. 8 ff.).

So the Buddha had no difficulty in recognizing and specifying the differentiating effects of theistic reality. He strongly contested what he believed were mistaken conclusions drawn about the *nature* of that reality, and he held that many people were profoundly mistaken in their beliefs about God. But they were mistaken about *something*: that is the crucial point. There is an example of this in Sam. N. v. 232, where Brahma Sahampati, 'reading with his mind the mental reflection of the Exalted One', appears (with the usual formula) to confirm the Buddha's reflection that 'there are five controlling faculties which, cultivated and made much of, plunge into the Deathless, have their end and goal in the Deathless. What five? The controlling faculty of faith, energy, mindfulness, concentration, and insight.'

Here, as usual, Brahma Sahampati appears in the attitude of respect (the attitude of the disciple before his teacher) and confirms the truth of the Buddha's reflection, and this exemplifies the common theme (pp. 268, 276) that the Buddha is the teacher of gods as well as men. But the continuation of the episode exemplifies another theme as well, the contribution of effect which theistic reality feeds into the Buddha's life:

Once upon a time, sir, when Kassapa was the supremely Enlightened One, I was practising the holy life. Men knew me then as Sahaka the monk. Then it was, sir, that by cultivating and making much of these five controlling faculties, and by restraining sensual lust in things of sense, on the breaking up of body, I was reborn in the Happy World after death, in the Brahma-World. Thereafter men knew me as Brahma Sahampati, Brahma Sahampati!

So it is, Exalted One! So it is, O Happy One! I know it! I see it, that these five controlling faculties, if cultivated and made much of, do plunge into the Deathless, do end and have their goal in the Deathless.'

That is clearly confirmation of the Buddha's teaching of a very high order. It is indeed an empirical verification, depending for its validity on the fact that a bundle of sense impressions correctly labelled as Sahaka the monk behaved in the way described

and experienced the consequences described. It makes no sense
to suppose that the Buddha or the first narrator of the story did
not accept the putative truth-propositions which the story contains; for if the story was composed simply as a story (for the
purposes, say, of anti-theistic polemic), then the 'naturalistic'
explanation of how and when people began to label a real continuity of appearance as Brahma Sahampati collapses. It cannot
serve as a description, still less as an explanation, unless, after
the dissolution of the body, the particular continuity of again-
becoming which had presented the appearance of Sahaka the monk,
was reborn in the Brahmaloka in such a way as to justify the label,
Brahma Sahampati, Brahma Sahampati. The Buddha may well
be maintaining that people were entirely mistaken to characterize
Brahma Sahampati as having escaped from the flow of change
and again-becoming or of on-going toward Nirvana. Even if,
for the sake of argument, Brahma Sahampati has made his U.D.I.,
his unilateral declaration of metaphysical independence, he has
not achieved the reality, nor can he ever do so. So popular beliefs
about theistic reality are mistaken; but they are mistaken about
something.

Or *are* they mistaken? What clearly remains at issue for those
who defend theistic claims is whether the Buddha's undoubted
and continuing sense of God was adequately or correctly characterized by him. For the orthodox Buddhist it was necessarily so,
because of the Buddha's traditional attribute of omniscience, as a
result of which it would seem that he could not have been mistaken
in what he said about the gods being a part of the process, and not
exempt from it. However, omniscience, as opposed into inerrancy,
does not entail always being right in what one says, though one
would presumably know that one was mistaken. Be that as it
may, the Buddha's drastic re-characterization of the sense of God,
following the collapse in plausibility for Gautama of the prevailing senses of God, does not in fact eliminate the ontological
issue between theistic believers and Buddhism, because both
sides are making claims about putative matters of fact; and since
the propositions are mutually exclusive (theistic reality is involved
in the process of change to such an extent that it is a part of the
process and will eventually disappear: theistic reality is contingently related to the process of change in a way that does not
entail its eventual disappearance), it is clear that while both

sides may be wrong, they cannot both be right. How, if at all, can the issue be decided between them?

The theist maintains, on the basis of the same and (so far as the Buddhist is concerned) undisputed phenomenological experience, that although the ground or cause of that experience is known in and through the natural, he (she, it, or they) is not contained wholly *within* the natural, but is independent, at least to the extent of being the unproduced producer of all that is—and is consequently that which has always been the case. It would, therefore, be perfectly acceptable to follow the Buddha in re-defining the natural to include this relatedness to the other, and there would be considerable advantage in so doing, because it would remove much contemporary argument about theism from its Victorian frame of reference: it would be a way of extending our understanding of what is naturally possible, and it would help to break down the obstinate narrow-mindedness of twentieth-century western man. But the fundamental ontological issue still remains, whether the ground or cause of those experiences of relatedness to externality theistically characterized (which con-tributes unmistakable effect to the construction of human lives) is wholly contained within the continuity of universal process, or whether it is sufficiently apart from that process to make stable and continuous the experience of relatedness beyond the ravages of time. There is only one way in which one could verify whether either of those propositions is true, and if so, which one, and that is by attaining (or failing to attain) the proposed condition.

In more technical language, this is known as 'eschatological verification'; the Buddha would obviously excise the word 'eschatological' and substitute something like 'intermediate but *post hoc* verification', but the general point remains the same. The problems of eschatological verification are considerable and have frequently been rehearsed. For example, if such phrases as 'God-relatedness' or 'beatific vision' imply that God is verified in some way which is continuous with our verification of 'objects among objects' in our present experience, then how can traditional claims that God is not, and cannot ever be, an object among objects survive; and can the notion of God remain consistent if he does become verifiable in that sort of way? Or again, a second example, the question has to be asked what the continuity of the experiencing subject is who now sees through a glass darkly but

then (it is claimed) will see face to face. If there is no continuity of
the subject, then how can the godness of God be verified to *me*?
And if not to me, or to some subject in continuity with present
experience, then how can this kind of verification have any status
in the community of human knowing? The issue was put succinctly
by L. A. Tollemache in the nineteenth century, long before the
debate was formulated in its present terms: 'What are the conditions of the "future life", and what sort of *Ego* is to survive?
One clergyman represents heaven, as consisting

> "Of sexless souls, ideal choirs,
> Unuttered voices, wordless strains." '10

In that case, one is bound to wonder what sort of continuity is
being affirmed.

A third problem might be called 'the smoke without fire'
problem: if we claim that certain of our experiences arise from
an invisible reality, God, we can only infer that they arise from
God if we already know something about that invisible reality,
since otherwise, for example, we may simply be describing a
further part of our experience with a particular language; and
to appeal to revelation as giving us that 'something of knowledge'
is simply to postpone the problem by one stage. The problem is a
very familiar one in the Christian tradition, usually expressed in
terms of the question of how a special revelation could be recognized unless there were a background of general revelation
against which to assess it. But in more general terms, to say 'there
is no smoke without fire' relies on some experience of observing
the connection between fire and smoke. However, in this case
there is an intermediate state: supposing we had never observed
fire, and had only ever observed smoke. Supposing we lived in a
valley, and in the next valley lived a tribe of bonfire enthusiasts,
but we had never seen a bonfire, and had never seen into the
other valley directly. We would nevertheless observe the glow at
night as well as the smoke by day: would it in fact be impossible
to infer some invisible reality as being necessary to produce the
observed effect? We might very well infer the wrong putative
reality, but equally we might infer something approximating to
the true condition of cause. Phlogiston was inferred as necessary
to produce combustion; unknown quantity rays, or x-rays, were
inferred as necessary to produce the glow on the photographic

plate in proximity to the cathode ray tube which was being used in a quite different and unconnected experiment. The decision can go either way: the inference may be unnecessary and wrong; but it may equally be right and be confirmed by its coherence in further experiments.

The inference of God seems historically to have been established in a very comparable way. By the fact of birth we are born into information nets of varying degrees of formality and complexity. Among them are the systems of information process which transmit theistic symbols as potentially resourceful for the appropriate construction of life. They may do much more than that, but a system of theistic information process will do *at least* that. It will maintain the possibility that God is the goal (the object of worship) and the resource (the unproduced producer of all that is) of life; and it will suggest the means through which we can be established as participant members in that network of information. All this remains neutral to us if we are not born in such an information context, or if we never encounter such an information context, or if we do not allow those cues of information to become informative in the construction of our own lives—that is to say, in the processes of storage and retrieval in brain-behaviour. If we do, then there is no doubt that those items will act as constraints over the outcomes in life, and it is possible that they will yield to us a direct sense of the reality of God, possibly of very great intensity indeed. The putative theistic reality which has been inferred to account for experience and the transformation of life has been described in a multiplicity of ways, many of which may well be more on the side of phlogiston than they are of x-rays. In other words, it becomes clear that certain theistic descriptions are incoherent or improbable in relation to the claimed differentiation in experience, and they go, as Mencken observed, to extinction. But how do we sort out which is which? How can we even know that the senses of God, on which the multiplicity of often bizarre descriptions are parasitic, are actually senses of *God*? Are we correct to infer the reality of the invisible other who yet seems within the experience to be correspondent with us?

Those are the questions at which alGhazali arrived, and in relation to which he insisted that belief in the resurrection and in a day of confrontation with God was indispensable for meaningful theological propositions. The language is pictorial, derived from the Quran, but in more general terms it is simply expressing the view that there must be specifiable circumstances in which the propositions of theology can be seen to be true or false. To suggest that this might be after death is not to be committed to explaining *how* that might occur, it is simply to specify what would have to be the case in general terms for verification to occur. It may seem highly improbable that there will be any continuity of conscious identity through death (though actually the advances in recent years in the understanding of information process and energy flow in the universe make that outcome after death an entirely possible one, and indeed, in the present developments of insight and understanding, it may even be a probable one). But that is beside the *theoretical* point being made here: all that is required for a conventionally theistic characterization of God to falsify the Buddhist characterization of God is for the information flow, which both accept as already occurring between God and man, to become stable—that is, for the self-giving of God in informative terms, which is already received as input (and Buddhists do not dispute that) and is expressed in the response of worship and prayer (as equally in the construction of life), to become a permanent condition of information. In that way it is conceivable that 'I' (the self constituted in this information flow) could continue to live and move and have that degree of responsive being within the information net which is characterized as God, and which is already in being for us to enter into.

Some issues undoubtedly remain. The Buddhist (if he pays any attention to what the Buddha is reported to have said and done) would fully accept that to continue in an information net after death, far from being inconceivable, is actually very likely. The flow of appearance and of again-becoming makes that possible. But the Buddhist would surely maintain that continuity in this condition does not imply stability: no matter how many aeons one may be in the Brahmaloka, one day the condition will dissolve and rebirth will occur. So the theistic case is falsifiable from the Buddhist point of view if rebirth always occurs—but not verifiable, because eternity cannot be exhausted. But while that absolute condition of information obtains—and that is what traditional descriptions of the beatific vision have attempted to articulate—the Buddhist may as a matter of fact be wrong.

What remains in any case important in the Buddhist sense

of God is the testimony it bears to the basic phenomenological fact, that a sense of God appears historically to have been created in human consciousness, not as a matter of intellectual speculation, but as a consequence of a direct apprehension of theistic effect in the construction of life-ways. It may well be the case that many believers in theistic traditions accept this at second-hand and do nothing much about it in their own case. Equally, it will certainly be the case that many characterizations of the ground or resource of theistic effect will turn out to be absurd or mistaken in the condition of final verification, supposing it ever occurs. But the survey undertaken in this book and in *The Sense of God* suggests that those possibilities occur only because they are parasitic on genuine and extensive apprehensions of a resource of effect external to ourselves, concerning whose nature we are able to be mistaken, but on occasion are perhaps able also to be approximately correct in the inferences drawn.

V

THE RELIGIOUS IMAGINATION
AND THE SENSE OF GOD

In the Fitzwilliam Museum in Cambridge there hangs a large picture by Paolo Caliari, better known from his place of origin as Veronese. It is not a picture which is likely to produce on its own any great admiration for the artist. It gives an impression, not of imaginative daring and excitement, but of prosaic competence and conformity. The painting is large and almost entirely conventional. It is a picture of a somewhat obscure classical subject, the story of Hermes and the two sisters Herse and Aglauros. Hermes, messenger of the gods, has fallen in love with Herse. This is made known to Aglauros, who is consumed with envy and tries to prevent Hermes coming to see her sister Herse. As a result, Hermes touches her with his wand, and she is turned into a statue, and that is the moment represented in the picture.

The story was included by Ovid as one of his Metamorphoses, and although he touched on it quite briefly the subject did at least evoke from him some quite dramatic writing—as, for example, when he described the bitter envy of Aglauros for her sister: it was, he says, 'like the burning of weeds which do not burst into flame, but are none the less consumed by smouldering fire.'[1] But from Veronese the subject seems to have evoked very little. The two heroines appear quite undisturbed by the appearance in their midst of a man with winged feet wearing little else but a helmet. Plump and elegantly disposed, they play their appointed parts in the drama with what Robert Louis Stevenson once described as 'a heavy placable nonchalance like a performing cow'. It is typical, conventional and dull. If it is a representative example of Veronese's work, one might well be justified in accepting the verdict that he was a deserving but undisturbing artist, following without question the conventions of his time. Yet *this* was the man, who, in July 1573, appeared in Venice before the Inquisition; and he appeared before the Inquisition precisely because his paintings *were* disturbing and because they *did* go against the conventions of his time; or perhaps one should say, not 'paintings' in the plural, but in the singular, because it was one painting in particular which was called in question by the Inquisition. It was a picture of the Last Supper commissioned by the Prior of San Giovanni to go into the refectory of his monastery.

The immediate cause of complaint was very simple: in the foreground of the picture there appears, very prominently, a large dog. The Inquisition thought the picture would be more dignified if Mary Magdalene were substituted for the dog. But this was really only an excuse to bring Veronese before the Court, because in fact there were far more serious issues at stake. Veronese seems to have been aware that this was so, because when he was asked by the Inquisition what the picture was intended to represent, he replied, either with extreme stupidity or with extreme astuteness, 'It is a picture of the Last Supper, taken by Jesus with his Apostles in the house of Simon.'

The reply is either very able or very ignorant, for there was, according to the Gospels, no such thing. We know, obviously, of the Last Supper, and we know also of a feast at the home of Simon the leper, where the woman anointed him with precious ointment. But there is no possible way at all in which the two occasions might be connected. If this was not a plain mistake, it suggests that Veronese may well have been aware that the storm was about to break, and that he was already, literally, beginning to shift his ground. For what *was* at issue? It was not simply the substitution of Mary Magdalene in the place of a well-bred beagle; it was the whole character of the picture. Some of its details are entirely conventional: the Supper has been transferred to a classical Renaissance setting with formal Italian palaces and churches in the background; but that was usual. The figure of Christ is in the centre with a halo encircling his head; and that also was usual. What gave offence was the *rest* of the picture.

It is a sort of M.G.M. wide-screen production, painted on a very wide canvas with the Supper taking place across its whole width. There was some necessity for it to be a wide picture, because it had to fit the space in the refectory. This meant that if the picture was to fill the whole canvas, many more than the usual thirteen people (Jesus and his twelve disciples) would have to be included. It was the added figures which caused offence, because the picture is indeed 'filled up' with a great many highly unlikely characters. There are present at this Last Supper, for example, two German soldiers in armour, a clown with a parrot on his arm, two dwarfs, a man with a nose-bleed, and even Veronese himself in an eloquent self-portrait. At a rough count there are forty-nine people present at this Last Supper, or fifty counting the dog. Not surprisingly, therefore, the Inquisition asked Veronese: 'Who, then, do you believe was really at that Supper?'

He replied: 'I believe that Christ was there, with his Apostles; but if any space remains in the picture, I adorn it with other figures, of my own invention . . . I saw this was a large one and and could hold many figures.'

'But then,' they went on, 'does it appear fitting to you, that at the Last Supper of our Lord there should be introduced jesters, drunkards, Germans, dwarfs, and such-like scurrility?'

He replied, 'No.'

There was no suggestion on the part of the Inquisition that the imaginative activity was wrong in itself, or that there was no value in relating the events of Christ's life to the contemporary scene. What was at issue was the actual way in which Veronese had done it. In a particularly significant exchange, the Inquisition asked him,

'What is meant by the armed man, clothed after the German fashion, with a halberd in his hand?'

'Of that,' said Veronese, 'I should need to speak at more length.'

'Speak.'

'We painters,' he said, 'allow ourselves the same liberties as do poets and madmen; therefore I made these halberdiers, one of them drinking and the other eating, at the foot of the stairway, yet both ready to do their service. For it seemed to me to be fitting that the master of the house . . . should have such servants.'

'And the fellow dressed like a clown, with a parrot perched on his fist—to what end did you portray him?'

'As an ornament,' said Veronese, 'according to custom.'[2]

That anecdote has been recorded at some length because it summarizes the tension which occurs in the characterization of the human sense of God. In *The Sense of God* and in the present work an attempt has been made to listen to the accounts being

given in certain behavioural sciences and in certain theistic traditions of the ways in which a sense of God occurs in human
consciousness. The behavioural and the theistic-tradition accounts
both make it entirely clear that the symbolic representation of
claimed theistic reality is transmitted in increasingly formalized
systems of information process, in which procedures of transmission and control are developed to ensure that process. At the
same time, both accounts are in agreement that the continuity of
any tradition gains its vitality from the individual appropriation
of informative symbols, in ways which may be highly dramatic and
creative, but which may also create great strain in a system if they
become too idiosyncratic or individual (unless, of course, they
remain private).

Both aspects (of systematic transmission and individual appropriation) are exemplified in the incident of Veronese before the
Inquisition. The Inquisition represents a mechanism of transmission and control, scanning the utterance (the picture) and testing
it by the procedure of match and mismatch against the basic
informational resources of the Christian tradition; and Veronese
represents the individual appropriation of the basic informational
resources through which they are transacted into a novel and
unique outcome. The liberty of the poet and the madman does
not necessarily disrupt or threaten the system (clearly not,
because the Christian, and many other strongly bounded religious
systems can be—and have been—creative and inspiring), but it
can disrupt the system if the idiosyncrasy of the utterance makes
a connection between resource and expression impossible or
difficult to discern; and from the point of view of the system,
that is serious, because the system is designed to be life-giving
(i.e. to transmit inputs from resource to new realization) to more
lives than one. However, since the aim *is* to be life-giving (so that
the individual in that perspective is infinitely more important
than the system), the tension is inevitable. But in this example
of individual and system, of artist and inquisition, the fact remains
that in *neither* case do we need to infer theistic reality to account
for what is going on. From the perspective of information process,
we are simply observing the systematic and the individual aspects
of the history of symbols in a particular tradition. Nothing within
the incident demands an ontological ground for the symbols in
order to account for what is happening.

But the behavioural and the theistic-tradition accounts both suggest that that is not the whole of the story. In both cases we have seen, first, that there is space within the system and within the mechanism of individual appropriation for direct input to be received from externality which is not necessarily derived from the system itself (although it may be mediated through it); and second, that the phenomenological account of the experience of such input is sufficiently coherent and widely attested to suggest that an inference to a sufficient ground for the experience external to the subject is justified. In this way, crises of plausibility in prevailing characterizations of the nature of theistic reality do not always lead to extinction; nor, for that matter, do they always lead to the success of control within the system in maintaining the *status quo*. They may lead to a new characterization of the possibility of theistic effect in the construction of human life precisely because the signal strength from that putative reality continues despite the collapse of its existing characterization.

This leads to a further and even stranger point. It emerges from these studies of behavioural and theistic accounts of the human sense of God that the claimed reality of theistic reference seems itself to occur in consciousness in informational terms, as though the nature of that apparent reality shares the characteristics of an information system or net. All types and shadows have their ending, and any characterization of theistic reality is necessarily inadequate, since it is derivative, not from an immediate vision but from a direct intuition. The strong insistence on the *via negativa*, on the *bila kaif*, on the *neti, neti*, not this, not this, of all developed theistic traditions makes the same point. Yet tentative approximations *are* possible, because the inputs from the claimed reality are not themselves without character. They impress themselves on the human subject, according to the phenomenological account, as though they are signals transmitted either directly in the mode of contemplation or meditation, or through the channels of occurrence in the natural order, through, for example, observing the external world in a particular way, or through an encounter with another person, or through reading, or through the rituals and symbols of particular religious contexts.

The inference to be drawn from this is that the reality external to ourselves must, if it exists and if the accounts of experiencing relation to it are not all false, resemble something like a stable condition of information, an information net into which we can be specifically linked and from which we can receive signal inputs. Prayer and worship then become a natural means through which we lock into an information net which already pre-exists us, and which was there already, long before we entered into it; and intercession becomes one of the many human languages of love (one of the many different ways in which human beings express their love for each other and actually do something about it), whereby we connect others to the same information net; in which case, intercession is not a question of trying to 'bend the will of God', it is simply a practice in one particular mode (by no means the only one) of relating others to the resource of theistic effect without dictating the consequence (much as the four men carried the palsied invalid into the presence of Jesus and left him in that presence).

That account, bizarre though it may seem, appears to do justice to the way in which phenomenologically the sense of God manifests itself and makes itself felt, and to the way in which human beings respond in worship, prayer, and intercession. But it does not make much comment of the *nature* of a field or stable condition of information of that sort, or on how one can conceive its existence in relation to the universe which we observe more directly. In other words, it does not comment on the aseity of God (on what God is in himself) except, perhaps, to observe that if such a field of information existed of the kind which seems to signal inputs to us as it does, it would have to contain reciprocity and a channel of communication. In other (less jargonistic) words, if the Trinity did not exist, it would be necessary to invent it. In a similar way it is possible, from the perspective of information process, to conceive that we may be able to enter into an information net which already exists and which could obtain as much after as before death; and for that reason the phrase from the creed *communio sanctorum* has gained a new and profound importance.

So even if it were accepted that the ultimate verification of the claimed other term in the sense of God-relatedness is immediately unimaginable, it does not follow that it is necessarily unintelligible. What would have to occur would be a continuity of the information flow which initially establishes the sense of God-relatedness, although now in a new condition of information, not unlike the transfer of memory-core into a new and different realization. The *wujud*, the findability, of God (that God is findable) presses in upon us—or can do so—when we allow the cues of God-related-ness to become resourceful and informative in the construction of our lives:

> . . . I within did flow
> With Seas of Life, like Wine;
> I nothing in the world did know,
> But 'twas Divine.[3]

We may even do this, not for the sake of verification, nor even (dare we say it?) for the sake of cognitive meaningfulness, but because of the amazing wonder of this possibility which is able to occur within our strange architecture of matter; and this is a common theme to those on the inside of experience: 'He has become a drop in the ocean, a mote in the rays of the sun, a part of the whole. In this state, he is raised above death and the fear of punishment, above any regard for Paradise or dread of Hell.' Or again: 'If you were to offer to sell me Paradise for a moment of my present time with you . . . I would not buy it. If you were to place before me hell-fire, with all it contains of torment, I would think it mild compared with my state when you are hidden from me . . . Do with me as you will.'

Not for the sake of heaven, not for the sake of reward, not for the sake of anything but itself do we respond (if we do) with adoration and hope, as though what we sense already, here and now, to *be*, in the correction and the inspiration of our lives, will continue to be the resource of what we are.

The points of departure are necessarily the cues which arise in the universe and in the theistic traditions. If they become informative in the construction of our lives, they work in and through the material accumulation of what we have so far become, but they may well transform or transfigure that material into a new outcome. It is very much as Henry Moore described the problem of carving a Madonna and Child for St. Matthew's Church in Northampton:

When I was first asked to carve a Madonna and Child for St. Matthew's although I was very interested I wasn't sure whether I could do it, or whether I even wanted to do it. One knows that religion has been the inspiration of most of Europe's greatest painting and sculpture, and that the Church in the past has encouraged and employed the greatest artists; but the great tradition of religious art seems to have got lost completely in the present day, and the general level of church art has fallen very low . . . Therefore I felt it was not a commission straight-away and light-heartedly to agree to undertake, and I could only promise to make notebook drawings from which I would do small clay models, and only then should I be able to say whether I could produce some-thing which would be satisfactory as sculpture and also satisfy my idea of the 'Madonna and Child' theme as well . . . I began thinking of the 'Madonna and Child' for St. Matthew's considering in what ways a Madonna and Child differs from a carving of just a Mother and Child—that is, by considering how in my opinion art differs from secular art. It's not easy to describe in words what this difference is, except by saying in general terms that the 'Madonna and Child' should have an austerity and a nobility, and some touch of grandeur (even hieratic aloofness) which is missing in the everyday 'Mother and Child' idea. Of the sketches and models I have done, the one chosen has I think a quiet dignity and gentleness. I have tried to give a sense of complete easiness and repose, as though the Madonna could stay in that position for ever (as being in stone she will have to do).[4]

Here it is the artist who is undertaking the work of translation on behalf of others, so far as he can. But the informational point remains the same, that the continuity of a religious tradition depends on the appropriation of what has up to that point been fundamentally resourceful, and on the translation of those re-sources into the construction of utterance in life. And that essen-tially is the work of prayer: prayer is to realize and lock into the information net, which already exists long before we do anything about it; and it is to allow those informational cues (which we have no doubt inherited in a particular cultural situation and which Freud may be entirely right in saying that we approach for all sorts of base and abject motives) so to rest and move and live within the disposition and intention of our brain-behaviour, that we—the very subject of that behaviour—are moved beyond the inherited point of our departure into a new and volunteered dependence—until, indeed, we realize in ourselves the meaning of Augustine's otherwise quite unverifiable assertion, 'God is the only reality, and we are only real in so far as we are in his order, and he in us.' The material of our selves is thereby shaped and formed into that condition of relatedness as though we could stay in that position for ever, which being dead we will have to do.

None of us can draw a line and start again. None of us can trade in what we have inherited genetically and acquired culturally so far, and start again in a brand-new model. To that extent, we are all casualties of birth. But what we make of ourselves and what is made of us depends in part on what we allow, or refuse to allow, to be resourceful in the continuing work of construction. This does not in any way deny that initiatives may come from God—indeed, an informational understanding of the sense of God-relatedness in the human condition suggests that such initiatives would not be particularly surprising: an Asharite or Barthian emphasis in theology is wholly intelligible in information terms. But in the end it is the sense of God-relatedness which is the *sui generis* reality on which theological inference about the nature of the other term in the relationship is parasitic (and we have seen in the case of Israel that the sense of God-relatedness was so unequivocally real that they accepted it for what it was, in its own right, without even drawing the inference that it would continue after death—the exact reverse of Marxist and Freudian interpretations of the origin and power of religion). That is why the sense of God does not depend, as Rahner puts it, on 'running through the theological statements about God's attributes (his life, his truth, his justice, his eternity, his knowledge, his power, his love)', except 'in order to understand that we do not grasp him *with* these statements no matter how legitimate they are, and that we must take everything away from God that has been thought about him, so that we can give ourselves to him, to his being in itself, to his inexhaustible life. "Deus semper maior".'

But in that case how can we say anything about God at all? Does not that reduce us, in turn, to silence? Yes it does. But the four quadrant points of silence explored in this book may perhaps remind us that there is more to this argument about the sense of God than argument. We have looked with some care at people overwhelmed by the impossibility of prevailing characterizations of God, who yet, reduced to the desperation of their own silence, heard the word made flesh within them speak once more.

> It is the shut, the curfew sent
> From there where all surrenders come
> Which only makes you eloquent.

'Elected silence'; not evasive of argument, but attending to the resource of our most hopeful, yet perhaps most foolish, eloquence.

The sense of God does not confer truth on content; nor does it necessarily answer questions, though it does for some people. But it does invade our lives, or it can do, if we are attentive to the resources from which it becomes possible.

Here, then, we come full circle, and return to the question posed in *The Sense of God* (p. 40):

What are the capabilities of this particular organization and assembly of matter which makes us what we are? We know that we are capable of walking, eating, talking, drinking; we know that we are capable of experiencing feelings which we label (culturally) as beauty, truth, love. Is it also possible that we are capable of God—capable of experiencing feelings and effects which we label theistically [i.e., label appropriately as God-derived or God-related]?

But here no one can go further on another person's behalf. Each of us at this point has to take up his pen and write his own answer —but write it in the language of life. If one goes back to the picture by Veronese and looks closely at the painting of a step in the bottom right-hand corner, one will see depicted on the step as though it is an inscription, 'Paulus Caliari Veroneseus fecit'; Paul Caliari of Verona made it: I, Paul, and no other, this is what *I* have done. In the same way, we, eventually, have to add our own signature to whatever work of translation of resource into utterance we have made in our own life: I, and no other, did this: this is mine, this is what I did with all that God offered me informatively of himself to be translated into life. As Chrysostom put it long ago: 'Let us then draw him to ourselves, and invite him to aid us in the attempt, and let us contribute our share—goodwill, I mean, and energy. For he will not require anything further, but if he can meet with this only, he will confer all that is his part.'

> The illusion does not need reiteration,
> The abject need, the infantile deceit:
> See how I am written in the same letters of pain,
> Construed and parsed by an equal grammar.
> The heavens proclaim a varied population
> Of man's imagined devilries and gods.
> No doubt. But the unguarded, the unwanted, the
>   rough seizing moment:
> Not by command or by constraint
> The surface of the pool trembles:
> It is the terror of a possible truth.

It was excellent as a dream,
As a guilt, as a compensation.
Then I could cultivate God as a garden,
Lay down paths and weed the theology.
But what if the dream outlines the shape,
Creates what was there before the creation,
Imagines what was there to be imagined?
The earthquake in the soul
Splits the security of explanation.
My other self, my self, my other,
And love between, the correspondent fire;
The image made beyond outside the self,
The print of otherness
With unexpected action of its own
And all initiative:
So rapt the feeling, some will feel it so,
I come like passionate lover to the soul
And rape the mystic on his bed of pain.

REFERENCES

INTRODUCTION

[1] Mencken, *Prejudices*, pp. 232 ff. In *Treatise on the Gods*. Mencken gave a marginally higher value to religion because of its connection with poetry: 'If theology ever goes to the boneyard, then poetry will probably go with it. The two, after all, are much alike; both are based on the theory that it is better to believe what is false than to suffer what is true' (p. 349). Cf. his comment on Christian Science: 'It is certainly not a science . . . and no Christian theologian would venture to call it Christianity. It is simply a kind of poetry—an organised belief in the palpably not true' (pp. 349 f.).

[2] Nietzsche, pp. 163, 164.

[3] MacGregor, pp. 14 f.

[4] 'I believe that there is *life* everywhere—not material only, not merely what is palpable to our senses—but immaterial and invisible as well. We believe in our own immaterial essence—call it "soul" or "spirit" or what you will. Why should not other similar essences exist around us, *not* linked on to a visible and *material* body? Did not God make this swarm of happy insects, to dance in this sunbeam for one hour of bliss, for no other object, that we can imagine, than to swell the sum of conscious happiness? And where shall we dare to draw the line, and say, "He has made all these and no more?" ' (p. 690).

[5] Astor, p. 4.

[6] Wordsworth, p. 187.

[7] Byron, p. 92.

[8] *The Tempest*, i. 2. 355.

[9] Eliot, p. 160.

[10] Quotation from Newsom, p. 10.

[11] See, e.g. Aldrich, pp. 279 ff., Brown, pp. 317 ff.

[12] See Bibl. under Lindsay.

[13] *The Sense of God*, p. 54.

[14] Young, p. 524.

[15] Richards, p. 200.

[16] Blake, p. 198.

[17] Webb, ii, p. 422.

[18] Lear in Chisholm, q.v., p. 77.

[19] Quoted from Auden, p. 126.

[20] 1 Kgs. 22:6.

[21] General Confession from the Book of Common Prayer, 1662.

[22] Rom. 7:19.

[23] See the discussion of this in *The Sense of God*, p. 88. The quotation is from Ashby, p. 130.

[24] Blake, p. 144.

[25] See *The Sense of God*, p. 108.

[26] Reade, pp. 188 f.

[27] So, e.g. Welch, p. 180: 'Yama, who in Vedic times had presided over the happy realm of the fathers, was transformed by the Buddhists into the Lord of hell and the superintendent of punishment there. Pretas, who had

previously been persons in the intermediate state between rebirths, were now considered to be in a separate path, only one level higher than hell. The sufferings of anyone reborn as a preta were appropriate to his evil deeds: the former slanderer was reborn with an ulcerated mouth exuding a foul smell. The former backbiter was doomed to keep eating the flesh of his own back. . . . Most pretas also suffered the tortures of Tantalus. When they were thirsty and went to the river, it turned to blood. When they sought refuge from the heat in a shady place, it became like a furnace. The variety of their deformities and frustration is painted with alarming detail in the Petavatthu, an early Buddhist collection of preta stories.'

[28] Pittendrigh (see Bibliography) has suggested that 'teleonomy' is a better term for describing goal-directed behaviour than 'teleology' because of the latter's Aristotelian associations with final causes.

[29] Reade, p. 437.

[30] Mic. 6:8.

[31] George, p. 75; but see also the further discussion in this book on pp. 189 f.

[32] For a fuller discussion of these points, see *The Sense of God*, pp. 131 ff.

[33] Jones, ii. 211.

[34] See, e.g. Fleming, pp. 14 ff.

I.1

[1] Harnack, p. 5.

[2] Singer, p. 49.

[3] Jung, p. 4.

[4] Schechter, pp. 1 f.

[5] For a summary, see Bowker, *Jesus and the Pharisees* pp. 9–11.

[6] Laquer, p. 84.

[7] Herzl, *Jewish State*, p. 30. Herzl, *Diaries*, p. 367, makes it clear that he also considered Uganda seriously. The proposed site was an area in what is now Kenya, near Nairobi. See also Rabinowicz, for the British exploration of this proposal.

[8] But cf. Weizmann's recollection of the occasion, in *Trial and Error*, p. 88.

[9] See *Jesus and the Pharisees*, pp. 15 ff.

[10] Op. cit., p. 16.

[11] Pirqe Aboth, i. 1.

[12] Deut. 6:4-9; 11:13-21; Num. 15:37-41.

[13] For a summary of, and references to, attitudes to Jews in the Roman world, see Hart, pp. 5 ff.

[14] According to Nehemiah Emsouni, who spent twenty-two years with Aqiba as a pupil, Aqiba taught him that the minutiae of Torah, even apparently inconsequential particles like *gam*, *raq*, and *eth* (what one might almost regard as 'the jot and tittle of the law') are full of meaning in each instance of their use: see J.Ber. ix. 5 (7); B.Men. 29b.

[15] J.Ber. ix. 5 (7).

[16] Finkelstein, p. 277.

[17] Livneh, p. 163. The 'festival of trees' is *rosh haShannah la-ilanoth*, more usually referred to by its date (15th Shevat) as Tu (15) BeShevat (though in the early rabbinic period the date was one of the issues between Bet Shammai and Bet Hillel: see, e.g. M.R.H. i. 1; B. Erub. 7a). It was originally a spring festival, connected with the computation of the annual tithes of fruit, but it came subsequently to express the close ties which bind Israel to the soil of the promised land.

[18] Neh. 13:1–3.

[19] Neh. 2:11–7:3.

[20] Neh. 13:23–9.

[21] Rosenzweig, p. 56.

[21] Maimonides, *Mishneh Torah*, *Sefer haMadda*, 'Study of Torah', i. 6.

I.2

[1] The Ugaritic texts are notoriously difficult to interpret but this is certainly one possible interpretation: so, e.g. Driver, p. 21: 'As thus interpreted, the poem [Baal] depicts the introduction of the youthful Baal as a god of fertility into the Ugaritic pantheon and the establishment of his supremacy, under El's suzerainty, over all the other gods, exercising power over earth as god of rain.' Cf. also Kapelrud, pp. 73 f., 92: 'His (EL/IL's) position in the Ugaritic pantheon is therefore taken by the young, strong and very active Baal, who ascended to the throne after a complete victory over his enemies.'

[2] On these, see Bright, p. 96.

[3] For a fuller discussion of this, see Eichrodt, 1. 184–7.

[4] Cf. also Judg. 18:24.

[5] See also 1 Sam. 6:5, 17:43; 1 Chr. 10:10, 14:12; Ezra 1:7. Note also the speech of Naomi in Ruth 1:15, though that may be singular. There is one example of non-Jewish plural usage which attributes, not significance, but *non*-significance, to the *elohim*, the usage which occurs in the words attributed to the envoy of Sennacherib, King of Assyria, telling the people to surrender Jerusalem: 'Beware lest Hezekiah mislead you by telling you that Yahweh will save you. Did the *elohim* of any of these nations save his land from the King of Assyria? Where are the *elohim* of Hamath and Arpad? Where are the *elohim* of Sepharvaim? Where are the *elohim* of Samaria? Did they save Samaria from me? Among all the *elohim* of these nations is there one who saved his land from me? So how is Yahweh to save Jerusalem?' Is. 36:18–20; Cf. ibid. 37:12 and the parallels in 2 Kgs. and 2 Chr.

[6] Koehler, p. 53; cf. also Ahlstrom, *Syncretism*, pp. 46 ff.

[7] But for prohibitions specifying *elilim*, see Lev. 19:4 (N.B. context in v. 2), 26:1–13.

[8] Blake, 'To Nobodaddy', *Writings*, p. 161; see also 'Let the Brothels of Paris be opened' and 'When Klopstock England defied', op. cit., pp. 185 f., 186 f. Cf. Hab. 2:18 f.

[9] Cf. Josh. 22:22; Ps. 82:1, 6; 95:3; 96:4 f.; 97:8; 135:5; 136:2; Zeph. 2:11; 2 Chr. 2:5.

[10] Astruc argued that Moses used, and combined in writing Genesis, four different memoirs, A, B, C, and D. Memoir C recorded 'all the facts concerning the family of the patriarchs' (*Conjectures*, p. 433), and Memoir D 'tous les faits, qui estoient étrangers à l'histoire des Hebreux'.

[11] 'Cet ouvrage estoit composé depuis quelque tems, mais j'hésitois à le publier, dans la crainte que les pretendus Esprits-forts, qui cherchent à s'étaier de tout, ne pussent en abuser pour diminuer l'autorité du Pentateuque.' (*Conjectures*, opening words of the Preface.)

[12] Gen. 17:5, 15.

[13] For details, see Bowker, *Targums*, pp. 140 f.

[14] Bowker, *Correlation*, p. 102.

[15] For illustrations, see Bowker, *Targums*, pp. 118 f. and further refs. ad loc.

[16] On the importance of the family and of education of a son, see e.g. Belkin, pp. 162, 167 ff., Waxman, pp. 362–9.

[17] The phrase is Ringgren's: 'Von den vielen Theorien über den Ursprung des Jahweglaubens ist die Keniterhypothese die einzige, die eine gewisse Wahrscheinlichkeit für sich hat' (*Israelitische Religion*, p. 30). The Kenite hypothesis suggests that Moses adopted a Kenite god and led the people out of Egypt in the name of that god. Because of the success of the Exodus, the god was adopted as the tribal god, and his name was 'read back' into the earlier traditions. This argument picks up the statement that Moses, after he fled from Egypt, took refuge among the Midianites, or Kenites (Judg. 4:11), and married into this tribal group (Exod. 2:16–22). It was Cain, according to Gen. 4:15, who received the mark of Yahweh on his forehead; cf. also Exod. 18.

[18] For a summary of this argument see Weippert, pp. 5–46.

[19] Erith, p. 175.

[20] For a summary, see Weippert, pp. 55–62.

[21] Judg. 5:16 f., 23.

[22] Jehonadab ben Rechab emerged in Jehu's pro-Yahweh purge and assisted in the destruction of the worshippers of Baal (2 Kgs. 10:15). According to Jeremiah, the Rechabites do not drink wine, 'because our ancestor Jonadab son of Rechab gave us this order: "You must never drink wine, neither you nor your sons; nor must you build houses, sow seed, plant vineyards, or own property; but you must live in tents all your lives, so that you may live long on the soil to which you are alien" ' (Jer. 35:6 f.).

[23] Allister, p. 18.

[24] Eliot, p. 469.

[25] Op. cit., pp. 475, 487.

[26] Op. cit., p. 485.

I.3

[1] Colenso, p. 33.

[2] Ibid., p. 128.

[3] 'While translating the story of the Flood, I have had a simple-minded, but intelligent native,—one with the docility of a child, but the reasoning powers of mature age,—look up and ask, "Is all that true? Do you really believe that all this happened thus,—that all the beasts, and birds, and creeping things, upon the earth, large and small, from hot countries and cold, came thus by pairs, and entered into the Ark with Noah? And did Noah gather food for them *all*, for the beasts and birds of prey, as well as the rest?" My heart answered in the words of the Prophet, "Shall a man speak lies in the Name of the Lord?" (Zech. xiii. 3). I dared not do so' (Colenso, p. vii). The defence of literal inerrancy was nevertheless maintained. Thus 'A Lancashire Lad' responded to Colenso that what was possible in the case of the steamship, *The Great Eastern*, in two years was certainly possible in the case of the Ark in 120—a misunderstanding of Gen. 6:3, though a mistake which curiously approximates to a rabbinic interpretation of that verse (see Bowker, *Targums*, pp. 156 f.): 'This Ark, from its dimensions given, must have been greater than "The Great Eastern" steamship. And pray how was she built, launched, and fitted out in a couple of years, and can be now laden or unladen in a few weeks? We ask: What would 3,000 pairs of wild beasts, birds and creeping things, with 3,000 tons of provisions, be to her? Just a fair ballast to keep her steady at sea for "twelve months". Yet Noah who, like Abraham, no doubt had hundreds of servants born in his own house, took 120 years to build, fit up, and gather food for all' (Lancashire Lad, p. 5).

[4] 'Die Sinaiüberlieferung ist also sichtlich sekundär in eine schon vorhandene

überlieferung von der Wüstenwanderrung eingelegt worden . . . Offenbar ist dieser überlieferungskomplex erst verhältnismassig spät in die kanonische Darstelling der Heilsgeschichte eingefügt worden' (von Rad, p. 189).

[5] Beyerlin, pp. 169 f.

[6] For this, see Baltzer, Appendix; Pritchard, pp. 203–5.

[7] See, e.g. Harvey, Hillers, and Wright, and for the possible dramatic enactment of the curses, see Fohrer.

[8] Clements, p. 16.

[9] Another cautionary note is sounded by Albrektson, p. 122, to the effect that Israel was not unique in using a covenant understanding to express its sense of its relatedness to God. But that observation does not affect the argument developed here that the covenant form was a powerful mechanism of information transmission and control. See also Labuschagne, pp. 135 ff., and for comparably cautious remarks, see McCarthy, pp. 12 f.

[10] e.g. Judg. 2:11–13, 3:7, 8:33, 10:6–14, Hos. 2.

[11] e.g. 1 Kgs. 11:7–10, 33.

[12] This may be the meaning of Anathyahu at Elephantine: see Cowley 44.3, and the discussion in Kraeling, pp. 87 f.

[13] For the general issues surrounding this, see Bronner.

[14] See Ahlstrom, *Syncretism*, esp. p. 13.

I.4

[1] Eissfeldt, p. 684.

[2] See the summary in Ahlstrom, *Joel*, p. 136.

[3] e.g. Humbert, 'Le Problème', pp. 1, 13 f.; *Problèmes*, p. 293.

[4] e.g. Jer. 23:30–2: 'So, then, I have a quarrel with the prophets—it is Yahweh who speaks—that steal my words from one another. I have a quarrel with the prophets—it is Yahweh who speaks—who have only to move their tongues to utter oracles. I have a quarrel with the prophets who make prophecies out of lying dreams—it is Yahweh who speaks—who recount them, and lead my people astray with their lies and their pretensions. I certainly never sent them or commissioned them, and they serve no good purpose for this people—it is Yahweh who speaks.' Cf. Mic. 3:5, Ezek. 13.

[5] The prophetic action, or *oth*, is an enacted representation, in symbolic form, of a future eventuality. It releases the event in miniature in such a way that nothing can avert it—in a sense, it has happened already. Thus, when Jeremiah put a wooden yoke on his shoulders to release into the present the necessity of subjection to Babylon, another prophet, Hananiah, disagreed with Jeremiah. But it was not sufficient to argue against Jeremiah, or to pronounce a contradictory oracle: neither of those procedures would have dislodged Jeremiah's *oth*. Instead, 'the prophet Hananiah took the yoke off the neck of the prophet Jeremiah and broke it. In front of all the people Hananiah then said, "Yahweh says this, This is how, two years hence, I will break the yoke of Nebuchadnezzar" ' (Jer. 28:11). Hananiah could not avert the released event, but he could enact the next sequence in the future. Jeremiah's response was to report an instruction from Yahweh that he should now make an iron yoke, to indicate that there will be a second campaign and captivity. For a summary of the prophetic *oth* and for the possibility that this lies behind the action of Jesus at the Last Supper, see Bowker, 'Prophetic Action', and pp. 133 f. of this book.

[6] See Jer. 6:16, Isa. 21:6, Hos. 8:1.

[7] So, e.g. Nowack, p. 359. For an entirely different analysis of these two

chapters as forming a unity (though compiled from independent items) see Lescow, who suggests that the composition was made after the Samaritan schism.

[8] Ps. 19:1–4.

[9] De Caussade, p. 19.

[10] See Ringgren, 'Esther', pp. 5 ff.

[11] Macholz has argued that kingship did not displace local jurisdiction, but simply continued the extra-ordinary functions of the judges in a new locus; but the ideational point would still remain the same. On the importance of the cult-gods encountered in Jerusalem, see Stolz.

[12] For a summary of the arguments connecting the kings with the Psalms, see Eaton.

[13] For details of this and refs. see Bowker, *Jesus and the Pharisees*, pp. 66 f.

[14] On this verse, see Porter, pp. 51–3.

I.5

[1] Pirqe Aboth i. 4.

[2] See, e.g., B.Sukk. 28a, B.B.B. 134a.

[3] B.Ber. 48a.

[4] The word 'immanence' is not used in its full technical sense, but simply to draw the contrast with 'transcendence' in locating the issue of effect.

[5] Wesley, pp. 475 f.

[6] *The Times*, 15 May 1969, p. 8.

[7] Gibbon, pp. 331 f.

[8] '. . . I may therefore venture to say that the air of reality (solidity of specification) seems to me to be the supreme virtue of a novel' (p. 355).

[9] Trans. McGregor.

[10] For examples of these stories, see Bowker, *Targums*, pp. 187 f.

[11] Diels (Xenophanes fr. 11), 11. B. 11.

[12] Segal, p. 27.

[13] Diels (Anaximander fr. 1.). 12. B. 1.

[14] *De Nat. Deorum*, i. 53.

[15] Knox, p. 5.

[16] Krieger, pp. 12 f.

[17] Thucydides, *History*, iii. 58: 'In the name of the gods who witnessed our alliance in the past and for the sake of our good service to Hellas, we beg you to relent.'

[18] 'I have given proper and due regard to the gods, and to men just and irreproachable actions. Consequently, I have confident hope for the future, and the present disasters do not fill me with fear as they might. They may even be coming to an end, for sufficient good fortune [*eutuchia*] has attended our enemies, and if one of the gods was angry when we set out on our campaign, by now we have been punished more than enough' (vii. 77).

[19] Longinus, *On the Sublime*, iv.

[20] i. 78. Cf. i. 84, iii. 49 (it is *kata tuchen* that no wind opposes the second trireme), iv. 64, v. 102 (the Melians argue that *tuchai* can counter an imbalance in the numbers of opposing forces), vi. 23, 78, vii. 61.

[21] There is a similar use in i. 65 and vii. 71, where in both cases hope is abandoned unless something paralogical occurs. The sense of 'outside one's calculation' occurs in iii. 16, vii. 28 (the Athenian endurance is paralogical, because no one thought they could maintain the war for more than three years at the outside after an invasion of Attica). In ii. 85 the Spartan defeat at sea is to themselves *paralogos*, but the force of *paralogos* in this instance is *not*

because they cannot explain it at all—in fact, they attribute the defeat to cowardice; it is, rather, that they cannot arrive at a correct explanation, because of their inexperience in sea battles. Cf. also ii. 61, viii. 24 (where Thucydides tersely comments, that if the Chians made a mistake as a result of the paralogical nature of human life, they at least had some grounds for proceeding as they did).

22 Merlan, pp. 485 f.

23 'Aristotle found it necessary to complete his metaphysics by the introduction of a Prime Mover-God . . . The Greek gods who surrounded Aristotle were subordinate metaphysical entities, well within nature. Accordingly on the subject of his Prime Mover, he would have no motive, except to follow his metaphysical train of thought whithersoever it led him. It did not lead him very far towards the production of a God available for religious purposes. It may be doubted whether any properly general metaphysics can ever, without the illicit introduction of other considerations, get much further than Aristotle. But his conclusion does represent a first step without which no evidence on a narrower experiential basis can be of much avail in shaping the conception. For nothing, within any limited type of experience, can give intelligence to shape our ideas of any entity at the base of all actual things, unless the general character of things requires that there be such an entity' (Whitehead, pp. 215 f).

24 Dodds, p. 244.

25 e.g., *Ant.* ii. 60, 349 (note the issue in 348). The final incident of *The Jewish War*, the death of Catullus, is also claimed by Josephus as a demonstration, no less remarkable than others, of the *pronoia* of God (*War* vii. 453).

26 For Josephus' claim to *aletheia*, see, e.g., *War* vii. 455; cf. *Ant.* ii. 4.

27 *War* v. 362.

28 Diels (Demokritos), 55. B. 267. Note also the summary of this in de Sainte-Croix, pp. 16 f., who stresses the distinction 'between, on the one hand, the relations of *individuals inside the State*, where there are laws, enforced by sanctions, which may enable the weak to stand up to the strong . . . and on the other, the relations *between States*, where it is the strong who decide how they will treat the weak, and moral judgements are virtually inapplicable' (p. 16).

29 *War* vii. 259–74.

30 Diels (Demokritos), 55. B. 30.

II.1

1 For an account of these, see Bowker, *Targums*, App. II.

2 For a summary of the change in attitude to the holy spirit, see Bowker, *Targums*, pp. 44 f.

3 For a summary of *merkabah* visions, and for the argument that they are the background of Saul's vision on the road to Damascus, see Bowker, 'Merkabah Visions'.

4 But see Vermes, *Jesus*, pp. 21 f. on this word.

5 e.g. 1:21, 3:1, 6:2; 1:44; 2:23 ff.; 10:2 ff; 11:11, 17; 14:12.

6 4:38, 9:38, 13:1, 14:14.

7 5:35, 10:17, 20, 12:14, 19, 32.

8 For the emphasis on the teaching of Jesus, see 1:21 f., 27, 29, 2:2 ff., 3:14, 6:34, 11:18.

9 For a summary, connecting Jesus with this background, see Vermes, *Jesus*, pp. 42 ff.

[10] For Judah b. Durtai, see Bowker, *Jesus and the Pharisees*, p. 131.

[11] For a summary of the material on Honi, see Vermes, *Jesus*, p. 69–72.

[12] The strong emphasis that Jesus insisted on the journey to Jerusalem appears in all the Gospels: e.g. Mt. 16:21, 20:17 f., Mk. 10:32 f., Lk. 9:51 ff., 13:33 f., 18:31, Jn. 7:1–13.

[13] On the verse from Isaiah, see Bowker, 'Mystery'.

[14] Mk. 14:27. Note also the preceding action in Mk. 14:8, where the curious Greek suggests that the anointing has been interpreted as being attached to an event which is certain to happen, and in a sense already has happened.

[15] For a fuller discussion see Bowker, 'Prophetic Action'.

[16] *Jesus and the Pharisees*, p. 50.

[17] See op. cit., p. 23.

[18] The absence of 'signs' remains a Jewish objection to Jesus as a claimed messiah: see, e.g., Sandmel, pp. 32 f.

[19] 'Demnach betrachte ich als den eigentlichen Gegenstand der Untersuchung die messianische Selbstverhüllung Jesu in nachsten und engsten Sinne des Wortes' (Wrede, p. 211). For an extensive survey of subsequent discussion, see Clark.

II.2

[1] Some of the material in the first part of this chapter has appeared in more detailed form in my article, 'The Son of Man', in *The Journal of Theological Studies*, April 1977. My thanks are due to the Editors for allowing me to reprint parts of the article.

[2] Higgins, p. 87: 'It may well be that agreement will never be reached, even if the correct solution is found in the future or, for all we know, already exists among the widely divergent ones familiar to workers in this field.'

[3] Hoskyns and Davey, p. 153.

[4] Op. cit., p. 155.

[5] It was first published in 1921, and translated into English in 1934.

[6] See Bibl. ad loc.

[7] Conzelmann, *An Outline*, pp. 136 f.

[8] Conzelmann, *Grundriss*, p. 156.

[9] Hahn, p. 21.

[10] For examples of those who adopt those positions, see Bowker 'Son of Man'.

[11] Horne, ii. 420.

[12] For details see Bowker, 'Son of Man', pp. 24 f.

[13] Lindars, p. 59. In contrast, Hindley has argued in any case for a date 'during or soon after the Parthian campaign of Trajan' (p. 564).

[14] Lindars, op. cit., p. 52.

[15] Leivestad, p. 267.

[16] Lindars, op. cit., p. 54.

[17] e.g. by Borsch: see Bibl. ad nom.

[18] See Bibl. ad nom.

[19] Bultmann, i. 30.

[20] Vermes, *Jesus*, p. 186.

[21] Op. cit., p. 165.

[22] Trans. Vermes.

[23] Meg. Taan. records that on Tammuz 14, the *sepher gezeroth* of the Sadducees was abrogated (Lichtenstein, *Megillath Taanith, H.U.C.A.*, viii (1931), p. 331). It also records three issues in which the decisions of the Sadducees differed from those of the Hakamim, of which one is the interpretation of 'an eye for

an eye'. However, the issue is not recorded elsewhere as a dispute between them before A.D. 66. On the other hand, it was certainly a matter of dispute as early as the Mekilta whether redemption or compensation was possible in the case of a human death, or whether the *lex talionis* must be applied. For a summary of the issues, see *B.B.Q.* 83b.

24 For details, see Bowker, *Jesus*, pp. 7 f.
25 For details, see Bowker, ibid., pp. 24 ff.

II.3

1 Though some categories were, in general terms, close. Thus Votaw has argued that the Gospels correspond to the biographies of Greek and Roman celebrities which were designed to exhibit their teaching.
2 For a summary, see, e.g., Furnish.
3 For details, see Bowker, 'Merkabah Visions'.
4 For a strong statement of the improbability of that proposal, see Hengel.
5 Anselm, *Cur Deus Homo?*, i. 4.
6 Chalcedonian Definition 4.
7 Sterne, p. 77.
8 D. Jones, p. 79.
9 Sanday, p. 159. The phrase 'a tentative modern Christology' is the title of ch. vii.
10 Quoted from Fuchs, pp. 323 f.

III.1

1 Valentine, p. 63.
2 Carlyle, p. 247.
3 De Caussade, i. 1. 54.
4 Rosenthal, p. 2.
5 Herbert, p. 56.

III.2

1 Peacock, p. 85.
2 Josephus, *Life*, 10–12 (2).
3 *Munqid*, i; but note that alGhazali did not deny the possibility of miracles. In fact, he affirmed their possibility within certain conditions against metaphysical attempts to *prove* their impossibility (see, e.g., *Tahafut*, Q17). He also defended the authenticity of Muhammad's miracles (*Ihya*, ii. 20).
4 Preface to the revised edn., p. 5.
5 Op. cit., p. 9.
6 Op. cit., p. 10.

III.3

1 Much of *Ihya*, iv. 39 is concerned with meditation on the wonder of creation.
2 'By the visible world [*alam almulk*], known also as *alam ashshahada* [the realities which offer themselves evidentially], I mean the world perceived by the senses. By the unseen world [*alam almalakut*], known also as *alam alghaib* [the realities which are hidden from immediate perception and have to be inferred], I mean the world perceived by spiritual vision [lit., the light of direct intelligence]' (*Ihya*, i. 2. 4).

3 'Few are the partisans of departed tyranny; and to be a Whig on the business of an hundred years ago, is very consistent with every advantage of present servility,' Burke, p. 7.
4 Quinton, pp. 17, 28.
5 Ryle, p. 94.
6 Ayer, *Language*, p. 31.
7 Descartes, *Discourse on Method*, § 2.
8 i.e. some (notably Ibn Sina/Avicenna) had the considerable advantage of writing in Persian as well, a language of greater subtlety than Arabic for philosophical purposes: for discussion of Arabic and Persian key terms in ibn Sina, see Morewedge, pp. 173–7. For the problems involved in translating Greek terms into Arabic, see Afnan, *Terminology*, pp. 29–34 (a section entitled appropriately, 'The Limitations').
9 Cornford, pp. v f.
10 Rynin, p. 113.
11 The nature and conditions of *wajd* are discussed by alGhazali in *Ihya*, ii. 18.
12 For alGhazali's attack on the formula *an'al-Haqq*, see *Ihya*, ii. 18. 2.
13 Ayer and Copleston, 'Logical Postivism', p. 743.
14 Ibn Ishaq, *Life* (Wüstenfeld), p. 144.
15 Eliot, *Middlemarch*, p. 441.
16 Ibn Ishaq, *Life*, p. 946.
17 See especially P. F. Schmidt, p. 135, for discussion of the phantom bridge which some try to cross from acquaintance experience to knowledge by description.
18 Ayer, *Problem*, p. 78.

IV.1

1 Marx, p. 13.
2 Hurd, p. 94.
3 'The Buddha Dhamma Alone Can Save the World', *International Buddhist News Forum*, i, 1961, p. 2. The argument connecting Buddhism and modern science is common: for an extended example, see Luang Suriyabongse.
4 Huxley, *Evolution*, p. 13.
5 Quilter, p. 294.
6 De la Vallée-Poussin, p. xvi.
7 Spiro, p. 67.
8 Bunnag, p. 21. Complementarity of rituals derived from fundamentally different informational resources is emphasized also by Ebihara with reference to Buddhism and folk religion in Cambodia (p. 190).
9 Trans. B. Kato, Y. Tamura, K. Miyasaka.
10 Conze, p. 190.
11 Farquhar, p. 268.
12 Sangharakshita, p. 302.
13 *Webster's Third New International Dictionary* . . . , Springfield, 1961, ad loc.
14 Sangharakshita, p. 302.
15 Buddhists have, of course, faced this issue. For example, Obeyesekere comments on the application of the Singhalese concept of *varan* (delegated authority) to 'the Buddhist pantheon in Ceylon': 'How could any supernatural being obtain varan if the Buddha no longer exists? This difficulty is overcome by positing two types of varan, direct and indirect. Direct varan is that obtained directly from the Buddha when he was alive by certain supernatural beings, e.g., Sakra and Kataragama. Later on, after the Buddha was no

more, these beings in turn gave varan to others, thus redistributing power
and authority initially obtained from the Buddha. But all varan, direct or
indirect, ultimately devolves from the Buddha' (p. 13).

[16] Augustine, *Confessions*, i. 1.
[17] Coomaraswamy, i. 29.
[18] Huxley, p. 19.
[19] Govinda, *Psychological Attitude*, p. 175.
[20] Consequently, it is entirely appropriate that the Atanatiya Sutta (Dig. N. iii.
194 ff.) should be devoted to the correct forms of protective prayer.
[21] Thomas, p. 57.
[22] Govinda, *The Way*, p. 13.
[23] Ibid., p. 31.

IV.2

[1] *Guide to Greece* (trans. P. Levi), i, xvii. 1.
[2] See Bowker, *The Sense of God*, p. 70.
[3] Among many examples, see Dig. N. i. 49, 87, 111, 150, 224; ii. 76; Sam. N.
ii. 170; iii. 28; Majj. N. i. 179, 401; ii. 133 f.; Vin. iii. 1.
[4] Dig. N. ii. 139; cf. Ang. N. i. 65. It is on this verse that Buddhaghosa later
elaborated an 'angels on the point of a pin' comment, since twenty to sixty
devas can stand on a point pricked by a gimlet without jostling one another.
[5] Cf. also Dig. N. i. 106; iii. 6, 77; Sam. N. v. 282 f.; Majj. N. iii. 11, 97 f.;
Ang. N. iii. 17.
[6] There is also a Buddhist harrowing of hell, anticipated in the fact that when
the Bodhisattva is born, the radiance which shines in heaven shines also in
the lowest worlds of blackness. See, e.g., Majj. N. iii. 120.
[7] Radhakrishnan, p. 75.
[8] Prudentius, *Contra orationem Symmachi*, ll. 847–50.
[9] Cf. Majj. N. ii. 170 for the same illustration.
[10] Cf. the different application of this argument in Majj. N. ii. 33.
[11] Milne, pp. 37 f.
[12] Murti, p. 24.
[13] Bennett, p. 61.

IV.3

[1] Rhys Davids, T. W., i. 299.
[2] Cf. also the comments on Patika Sutta (*Dialogues*, iii. 1) and Lakkhana Sutta
(ibid., 136).
[3] The proviso is an obvious, but necessary, safeguard, since intention alone
is not sufficient—indeed, intention filled with expectation or imagination of
the goal is actually self-defeating: see, e.g., Majj. N. iii. 140, Ang. N. iv. 54 ff.,
v. 18, Dig. N. iii. 239 ff.
[4] The same sequence to the same effect (that to be reborn in the Brahmaloka
still leaves something more to be done) occurs in Sariputta's advice to
Dhanarjani in Majj. N. ii. 194 ff.; cf. also the questions of the brahman Dona
in Ang. N. ii. 37 ff.
[5] Majj. N. ii. 76, Dig. N. ii. 196.
[6] See also Majj. N. i. 412 f., ii. 160.
[7] *The Times*, 17 Jan. 1975, p. 4.
[8] Majj. N. i. 426.
[9] Huxley, *Lay Sermons*, pp. 144 f.
[10] Tollemache, p. 210.

V

[1] *Metamorphoses*, ii. 809–11.
[2] Friedenthal, pp. 113–18.
[3] Traherne, 'Wonder', ll. 21–4.
[4] Quoted from Read, pp. 154 f.

BIBLIOGRAPHY

AFNAN, S. M., *Philosophical Terminology in Arabic and Persian*, Leiden, 1964.
—— *A Philosophical Lexicon in Persian and Arabic*, Beirut, 1969.
AHLSTROM, G. W., *Aspects of Syncretism in Israelite Religion*, Horae Soderblomianae, v, 1963.
—— *Joel and the Temple Cult of Jerusalem*, Suppl. to Vetus Testamentum, xxi, Leiden, 1971.
ALBREKTSON, B., *History and the Gods: An Essay on the Idea of Historical Events as Divine Manifestations in the Ancient Near East and in Israel*, Coniectanea Biblica i, 1967.
ALDRICH, H., 'Organizational Boundaries and Interorganizational Conflict', *Human Relations*, xxiv, 1971, pp. 279 ff.
ALLISTER, W., *A Handful of Rice*, London, 1961.
ASHBY, W. R., *An Introduction to Cybernetics*, London, 1964.
ASTOR, M., *Tribal Feeling*, London, 1964.
ASTRUC, J., *Conjectures sur les Memoires originaux, dont il paroit que Moyse s'est servi pour composer le livre de la Genèse*, Brussels, 1753.
AUDEN, W. H., *A Certain World*, London, 1971.
AYER, A. J., *Language, Truth and Logic*, London, 1956.
—— *The Problem of Knowledge*, London, 1957.
AYER, A. J., and COPLESTON, F. C., 'Logical Positivism—a Debate', in Edwards, P., and Pap, A., eds., *A Modern Introduction to Philosophy*, New York, 1965, pp. 726–56.
BALTZER, K., *Das Bundesformular*, Neukirchen-Vluyn, 1964.
BECHERT, H., *Buddhismus, Staat und Gesellschaft in den Ländern des Theravada-Buddhismus*, Schriften des Instituts für Asienkünde in Hamburg, xvii, 1–3, 1966–73.
BELKIN, S., *In His Image: The Jewish Philosophy of Man as Expressed In Rabbinic Tradition*, London, n.d.
BENNETT, A., *Forty Years On*, London, 1969.
BEYERLIN, W., *Origins and History of the Oldest Sinaitic Tradition*, Oxford, 1965.
BLAKE, W., *The Poetical Works*, London, 1914.
—— *Complete Writings*, Oxford, 1972.
BORSCH, F. H., *The Son of Man in Myth and History*, London, 1967.
—— *The Christian and the Gnostic Son of Man*, London, 1970.

BOWKER, J. W., *The Targums and Rabbinic Literature*, Cambridge, 1969.
—— *Problems of Suffering in Religions of the World*, Cambridge, 1970.
—— *Jesus and the Pharisees*, Cambridge, 1973.
—— *The Sense of God: Sociological, Anthropological and Psychological Approaches to the Origin of the Sense of God*, Oxford, 1973.
—— 'Prophetic Action and Sacramental Form', *Studia Evangelica*, iii, 1964.
—— 'The Correlation of Theological and Empirical Meaning', App. II in *Marriage, Divorce and the Church*, London, 1971.
—— 'Merkabah Visions and the Visions of Paul', *Journ. of Sem. Stud.*, xvi, 1971.
—— 'Mystery and Parable: Mark iv. 1–20', *J.T.S.*, xxv, 1974, pp. 300–17.
—— 'Assimimilation où rejet? Théologie chrétienne et compréhension de la souffrance dans les religions orientales', *Concilium*, 1976, pp. 111–21.
—— 'The Son of Man', *J.T.S.*, xxviii, 1977, pp. 1–30.
BRIGHT, J., *A History of Israel*, revised edn., London, 1972.
BRONNER, L., *The Stories of Elijah and Elishah as Polemics against Baal Worship*, Leiden, 1968.
BROWN, W. B., 'Systems, Boundaries and Information Flow', in *Academy of Management Journal*, ix, 1966, pp. 317 ff.
BULTMANN, R., *Theology of the New Testament*, London, 1952.
BUNNAG, J., *Buddhist Monk, Buddhist Layman: A Study of Urban Monastic Organisation in Central Thailand*, Cambridge, 1963.
BURKE, E., *Thoughts on the Cause of the Present Discontents*, London, 1951.
BYRON, G. G., *The Poetical Works*, Oxford, 1964.
CARLYLE, T., 'Biography', in *Critical and Miscellaneous Essays*, London, 1887, ii, pp. 217–60.
CARROLL, L., *The Complete Works*, London (Nonesuch), n.d.
CHISHOLM, L., *The Golden Staircase*, London, 1928.
CLARK, J. L., *A Reexamination of the Problem of the Messianic Secret in Mark in its Relationship to the Synoptic Son of Man Sayings* (Yale Univ. Ph.D., 1962), Univ. Microfilms, Michigan, 1966.
CLEMENTS, R. E., *Prophecy and Covenant*, London, 1965.
COHEN, I. (ed.), *The Rebirth of Israel: A Memorial Tribute to Paul Goodman*, London, 1952.
COLENSO, J. W., *The Pentateuch and Book of Joshua Critically Examined*, i, London, 1862.
CONZE, E., *Buddhism, Its Essence and Development*, Oxford, 1960.
CONZELMANN, H., *Grundriss der Theologie des Neuen Testaments*, Munich, 1967.

—— (Trans. J. Bowden), *An Outline of the Theology of the New Testament*, London, 1969.

COOMARASWAMY, A. K., *Yaksas*, Washington, 1928, 1931.

CORNFORD, F. M., *The Republic of Plato*, Oxford, 1955.

COWLEY, A. E., *Aramaic Papyri of the Fifth Century B.C.*, Oxford, 1923.

DE CAUSSADE, J. P., *Self-Abandonment to Divine Providence*, London, 1959.

DE LA VALLÉE-POUSSIN, L., *Bouddhisme, opinions sur l'histoire de la dogmatique*, Paris, 1925.

DE SAINTE-CROIX, C. E. M., *The Origins of the Peloponnesian War*, London, 1972.

DE SAINT-PIERRE, J.-H.-B., *Studies of Nature*, iv, London, 1809.

DIELS, H., *Die Fragmente der Vorsokratiker*, Berlin, 1922.

DODDS, E. R., *The Greeks and the Irrational*, California, 1971.

DRIVER, G. R., *Canaanite Myths and Legends*, Edinburgh, 1956.

EATON, J. H., *Kingship and the Psalms*, London, 1976.

EBIHARA, M., 'Interrelations between Buddhism and Social Systems in Cambodian Peasant Culture', in M. Nash, q.v., pp. 175–96.

EICHRODT, W., *Theology of the Old Testament*, London, 1961.

EISSFELDT, O., *Einleitung in das Alte Testament*, Tübingen, 1964.

ELIOT, G., *Middlemarch*, Oxford, 1967.

—— *Daniel Deronda*, London, 1970.

ERITH, L. E. P., 'The History of Israel', in (ed.) C. Gore *et al.*, *A New Commentary on Holy Scripture*, London, 1928.

FARQUHAR, J. N., 'The Christian Outlook on Other Religions', in (eds.) A. S. Peake and R. G. Parsons, *An Outline of Christianity*, v, London, n.d., pp. 263–74.

FINKELSTEIN, L., *Akiba: Scholar, Saint and Martyr*, Cleveland, 1962.

FLEMING, D., 'Galen on the Motions of the Blood in the Heart and Lungs', *Isis*, xlvi, 1955, pp. 14–21.

FOHRER, G., *Die symbolischen Handlungen der Propheten*, A.T.A.N.T., liv, 1968.

FRIEDENTHAL, R. (ed.), *Letters of the Great Artists*, London, 1963.

FUCHS, W. R., *Computers: Information Theory and Cybernetics*, London, 1971.

FURNISH, V. P., *The Love Command in the New Testament*, London, 1973.

GEORGE, A. G., *Makers of Literary Criticism*, ii, London, 1967.

GEORGE, F. H., *The Brain as a Computer*, Oxford, 1973.

GIBBON, E., *The Decline and Fall of the Roman Empire*, i, London, 1956.

GOMBRICH, R., *Precept and Practice: Traditional Buddhism in the Rural Highlands of Ceylon*, Oxford, 1971.

GOVINDA, A., *The Psychological Attitude of Early Buddhist Philosophy*, London, 1961.
—— *The Way of the White Clouds*, London, 1974.
HAHN, F., *The Titles of Jesus in Christology: Their History in Early Christianity*, London, 1969.
HARNACK, A., *Das Wesen des Christentums*, Leipzig, 1900.
HART, H. ST. J., *A Foreword to the Old Testament*, London, 1951.
HARVEY, J., 'Le "*rib*-pattern", réquisitoire prophétique sur la rupture de l'alliance', *Biblica*, xliii, 1962, pp. 172 ff.
HENGEL, M., *The Son of God*, London, 1976.
HERBERT, A. P., *Bring Back the Bells*, London, 1943.
HERZL, T., *The Jewish State*, London, 1930.
—— *The Diaries of Theodor Herzl*, New York, 1956.
HIGGINS, A. J. B., 'Is the Son of Man Problem Insoluble?' in (eds). E. E. Ellis and M. Wilcox, *Neotestamentica et Semitica*, Edinburgh, 1969, pp. 70–87.
HILLERS, D. R., *Treaty Curses and the Old Testament Prophets*, Rome, 1964.
HINDLEY, J. C., 'Towards a Date for the Similitudes of Enoch: an Historical Approach', *N.T.S.*, xiv, 1967, pp. 551–65.
HORNE, T. H., *An Introduction to the Critical Study and Knowledge of the Holy Scriptures*, London, 1828.
HOSKYNS, E., and DAVEY, N., *The Riddle of the New Testament*, London, 1931.
HUMBERT, P., 'Le Problème du livre de Nahoum', *R.H.P.R.*, xii, 1932, pp. 1–15.
—— *Problèmes du livre d'Habacuc*, Neuchatel, 1944.
HURD, W., *A Complete and Impartial View of all the Religions in the Various Nations of the Universe*, London, n.d.
HUXLEY, T. H., *Lay Sermons, Addresses and Reviews*, London, 1871.
—— *Evolution and Ethics*, London, 1893.
JAMES, H., 'The Art of Fiction', in A. G. George, q.v.
JAYATILLEKE, K. N., *The Message of the Buddha*, London, 1975.
JOHNSTON, G., and ROTH, W., *The Church in the Modern World*, Toronto, 1967.
JONES, A. E., 'Psycho-Analysis and Christian Religion', in *Essays in Applied Psycho-Analysis*, 2 vols., London, 1951.
JONES, D., *Anathemata*, London, 1972.
JUNG, L. (ed.), *The Jewish Library: I, Faith*, London, 1968.
KAPELRUD, A. S., *Baal in the Ras Shamra Texts*, Copenhagen, 1952.
KING, W. L., *A Thousand Lives Away: Buddhism in Contemporary Burma*, Oxford, 1964.

KNOX, B. M. W., *The Heroic Temper: Studies in Sophoclean Tragedy*, California, 1964.

KOEHLER, L., and BAUMGARTNER, W., *Lexicon in Veteris Testamenti Libros*, Leiden, 1953.

KOROŠEC, V., *Hethitische Staatsverträge: ein Beitrag zu ihrer juristischen Wertung*, Leipziger Rechtswissenschaftliche Studien, lx, 1931.

KRAELING, E. G., *The Brooklyn Museum Aramaic Papyri*, New Haven, 1953.

KRIEGER, M., *The Tragic Vision*, New York, 1960.

LABUSCHAGNE, C. J., *The Incomparability of Yahweh in the Old Testament*, Leiden, 1966.

LANCASHIRE LAD, A. *The Siege of Rome, and 'Bishop Colenso' Slain with a Sling and a Stone*, Manchester, n.d.

LAQUER, W., *A History of Zionism*, London, 1972.

LEIVESTAD, R., 'Exit the Apocalyptic Son of Man', *N.T.S.*, xviii, 1972.

LESCOW, T., 'Redaktionsgeschichtliche Analyse von Micha 6–7', *Z.A.W.*, lxxxiv, 1972, pp. 182–212.

LICHTENSTEIN, H., *Megillath Taanith*, H.U.C.A., viii, 1931.

LINDARS, B., 'Re-enter the Apocalyptic Son of Man', *N.T.S.*, xxii, 1975.

LINDSAY, P. H., and NORMAN, D. A., *Human Information Processing: An Introduction to Psychology*, New York, 1972.

LIVNEH, E., 'The Test of Israel', in Longworth, P. (ed.)., *Confrontations with Judaism*, London, 1967.

LUANG SURIYABONGSE, *Buddhism in the Light of Modern Scientific Ideas*, Bangkok, 1956.

MCCARTHY, D. J., *Old Testament Covenant: A Survey of Current Opinions*, Oxford, 1972.

MACGREGOR, G., 'No Living with or Without God', in (ed.) Johnston, q.v., pp. 9–21.

MACHOLZ, G. C., 'Die Stellung des Königs in der israelitischen Gerichtsverfassung', *Z.A.W.*, lxxxiv, 1972, pp. 157–82.

MAIMONIDES, M., *Mishneh Torah*, ed. cit., Berlin, 1868.

MARX, K., 'Foreword to his Doctoral Thesis', in *Marx and Engels on Religion*, Moscow, n.d., pp. 13–15.

MASSON, J., *La Religion populaire dans le canon bouddhique pali*, Louvain, 1942.

MENCKEN, H. L., *Prejudices, Third Series*, London, 1923.

—— *Treatise on the Gods*, New York, 1930.

MERLAN, P., 'Aristoteles' und Epikurs müssige Götter', *Zeit. für Phil. Forschung*, xxi, 1967, pp. 485–98.

MILNE, A. A., *The House at Pooh Corner*, London, 1934.

MOREWEDGE, P., *The Metaphysica of Avicenna (ibn Sina)*, Persian Heritage Series xiii, London, 1973.

MURTI, T. R. V., *The Central Philosophy of Buddhism*, London, 1974.
NASH, M. (ed.), *Anthropological Studies in Theravada Buddhism*, Yale, 1966.
NEWSOM, J., *The Education of Girls*, London, 1948.
NICHOLSON, R. A., *A Literary History of the Arabs*, Cambridge, 1956.
NIETZSCHE, F. W., *Die fröhliche Wissenschaft*, in *Nietzsche's Werke*, v, Leipzig, 1899.
NOWACK, W., 'Micah', in (ed.) J. Hastings, *A Dictionary of the Bible*, iii, Edinburgh, 1900.
OBEYESEKERE, G., 'The Buddhist Pantheon in Ceylon and its Extensions', in (ed.) M. Nash, q.v., pp. 1–26.
OSBORN, F., *Advise to a Son*, London, 1689.
PEACOCK, T. L., *Crotchet Castle*, New York, 1967.
PERLITT, L., *Bundestheologie im Alten Testament*, W.M.A.N.T., xxxvi, 1969.
PITTENDRIGH, C. S., 'Adaptation, Natural Selection and Behaviour', in Roe and Simpson, q.v., pp. 390 ff.
PORTER, J. R., 'Psalm xlv.7', *J.T.S.*, xii, 1961, pp. 51–3.
PRITCHARD, J. B., *Ancient Near Eastern Texts Relating to the Old Testament*, Princeton, 1950.
QUILTER, H., *What's What: A Guide for Today to Life as It Is and Things as They Are*, London, 1902.
QUINTON, A., *The Nature of Things*, London, 1973.
RABINOWICZ, O. K., 'New Light on the East Africa Scheme', in Cohen, q.v.
RADHAKRISHNAN, S., *The Bhagavadgita*, London, 1963.
READ, H., *Henry Moore: A Study of His Life and Work*, London, 1965.
READE, W. W., *The Martyrdom of Man*, London, 1968.
RHYS DAVIDS, C. A. F., *What Was the Original Gospel in 'Buddhism'?*, London, 1938.
RHYS DAVIDS, T. W., *The Dialogues of the Buddha*, London, 1956.
RICHARDS, F., *Old Soldier Sahib*, London, 1936.
RINGGREN, H., 'Esther and Purim', *S.E.Å.*, xx, 1955, pp. 5 ff.
—— *Israelitische Religion*, Stuttgart, 1963.
—— 'Israel's Place Among the Religions of the Ancient Near East', in *Studies in the Religion of Ancient Israel*, Suppl. to Vetus Testamentum, xxiii, Leiden, 1972, pp. 1–8.
ROE, A., and SIMPSON, G. G., *Behaviour and Evolution*, New Haven, 1958.
ROSENTHAL, F., *Knowledge Triumphant: The Concept of Knowledge in Medieval Islam*, Leiden, 1970.
ROSENZWEIG, F., *Fragmente aus dem Nachlass*, Berlin, 1938.
RUSSELL, B., *History of Western Philosophy*, London, 1954.

RYLE, G., *Dilemmas*, Cambridge, 1954.

RYNIN, D., 'Cognitive Meaning and Cognitive Use', *Inquiry*, ix, 1960, pp. 109–31.

SANDAY, W., *Christologies Ancient and Modern*, Oxford, 1910.

SANDMEL, S., *We Jews and Jesus*, London, 1965.

SANGHARAKSHITA, BH., *A Survey of Buddhism*, Bangalore, 1966.

SCHECHTER, S., 'The Rabbinical Conception of Holiness', *J.Q.R.*, x, 1898, pp. 1 ff.

SCHMIDT, P. F., *Religious Knowledge*, Glencoe, 1961.

SCHMIDT, W., *The Origin and Growth of Religion: Facts and Theories*, London, 1931.

SEGAL, C. P., 'Nature and the World of Man in Greek Literature', *Arion*, ii, 1963, pp. 19–53.

SINGER, S., trans., *The Authorised Daily Prayer Book of the United Hebrew Congregations of the British Empire*, London, 1957.

SOULIS, E. M., *Xenophon and Thucydides: A Study on the Historical Methods of Xenophon in the* Hellenica *with Special Reference to the Influence of Thucydides*, Athens, 1972.

SPIRA, A., *Untersuchungen zum 'Deus ex Machina' bei Sophokles und Euripides*, Kallmünz, 1960.

SPIRO, M., *Buddhism and Society: A Great Tradition and its Burmese Vicissitudes*, London, 1971.

STERNE, L., *The Life and Opinions of Tristram Shandy*, London, 1948.

STOLZ, F., *Strukturen und Figuren in Kult von Jerusalem*, B.Z.A.W., cxviii, Berlin, 1970.

TAMBIAH, S. J., *Buddhism and Spirit Cults in North-eastern Thailand*, Cambridge, 1970.

THOMAS, E. J., *History of Buddhist Thought*, 1933.

TOLLEMACHE, L. A., *Stones of Stumbling*, London, 1893.

Transactions of the Third International Congress for the History of Religions, Oxford, 2 vols., 1908.

VALENTINE, M., *An Introduction to Psychiatry*, 2nd edn., Edinburgh, 1962.

VERMES, G., *The Dead Sea Scrolls in English*, London, 1962.

—— 'The Use of *bar nash/bar nasha* in Jewish Aramaic', in Black, M., *An Aramaic Approach to the Gospels and Acts*, Appendix E, Oxford, 1967.

—— *Jesus the Jew*, London, 1973.

VIELHAUER, P., 'Gottesreich und Menschensohn in der Verkündigung Jesu', in *Festschrift für Günther Dehn* . . ., Neukirchen, 1957, pp. 51–79.

—— 'Jesus und der Menschensohn: zur Diskussion mit H. E. Tödt und E. Schweizer', *Z.Th. K.*, lx, 1963, pp. 133–77.

VOLKMAR, F., *Israel in der Wüste: Traditionsgeschichtliche Untersuchung der Wustenüberlieferung des Jahwisten*, Marburg, 1970.

VON GLASENAPP, H., *Buddhism—A Non-Theistic Religion*, London, 1970.

VON RAD, G., *Theologie des Alten Testaments*, i, Munich, 1958.

VOTAW, C. W., *The Gospels and Contemporary Biographies in the Greco-Roman World*, Philadelphia, 1970.

WARDER, A. K., *Indian Buddhism*, Delhi, 1970.

WAXMAN, M., *Judaism: Religion and Ethics*, New York, 1958.

WEBB, C. C. J., 'On Some Recent Movements in Philosophy', in *Transactions*, q.v., pp. 416–24.

WEIPPERT, M., *The Settlement of the Israelite Tribes in Palestine*, London, 1971.

WEIZMANN, CH., *Trial and Error: The Autobiography of Chaim Weizmann*, London, 1971.

WELCH, H., *The Practice of Chinese Buddhism*, 1900–1950, Harvard, 1973.

WESLEY, J., *The Journal*, i, London, 1909.

WHITEHEAD, A. J., *Science and the Modern World*, London, 1953.

WILDER, A., 'Art and Theological Meaning', in (ed.) N. Scott, *The New Orpheus*, New York, 1964.

WORDSWORTH, W., *The Poetical Works*, Oxford, 1916.

WREDE, D. W., *Des Messiasgeheimnis in den Evangelien*, Göttingen, 1901.

WRIGHT, G. E., 'The Lawsuit of God: A Form-Critical Study of Deuteronomy 32', in (eds.) B. W. Anderson and W. Harrelson, *Israel's Prophetic Heritage*, London, 1962.

YOUNG, J. Z., *An Introduction to the Study of Man*, Oxford, 1971.

INDEX